A Church of
Passion and Hope

A Church of Passion and Hope

The Formation of an Ecclesial Disposition from Ignatius Loyola to Pope Francis and the New Evangelization

Gill K. Goulding, C.J.

Bloomsbury T&T Clark
An imprint of Bloomsbury Publishing Plc

B L O O M S B U R Y
LONDON • NEW DELHI • NEW YORK • SYDNEY

Bloomsbury T&T Clark

An imprint of Bloomsbury Publishing Plc

Imprint previously known as T&T Clark

50 Bedford Square	1385 Broadway
London	New York
WC1B 3DP	NY 10018
UK	USA

www.bloomsbury.com

BLOOMSBURY, T&T CLARK and the Diana logo are trademarks of Bloomsbury Publishing Plc

First published 2016

British Library Cataloguing-in-Publication Data
Library of Congress Cataloging-in-Publication Data
Goulding, Gill.
A church of passion and hope : the formation of ecclesial disposition from Ignatius Loyola to Pope Francis and the new evangelization / by Gill K. Goulding CJ.
pages cm
Includes bibliographical references and index.
ISBN 978-0-567-66466-2 (hardback : alk. paper)– ISBN 978-0-567-66467-9 (pbk. : alk. paper)
1. Jesuits. 2. Ignatius, of Loyola, Saint, 1491-1556. Exercitia spiritualia. 3. Evangelistic work–
Catholic Church. 4. Catholic Church–Doctrines. I. Title.
BX3702.3.G68 2015
255›.53–dc23
2015017994

ISBN: HB: 978-0-56766-466-2
PB: 978-0-56766-467-9
ePDF: 978-0-56766-469-3
ePub: 978-0-56766-468-6

Library of Congress Cataloging-in-Publication Data
A catalog record for this book is available from the Library of Congress.

Typeset by Fakenham Prepress Solutions, Fakenham, Norfolk NR21 8NN
Printed and bound in India

Ad Majorem Dei Gloriam

And for:
Pope Emeritus Benedict whose simplicity and clarity of
theological expression and humility and courage have
inspired my own theological undertakings;
Pope Francis whose simplicity and humility in apostolic
outreach have challenged my practice;
Two true contemplatives in action for whom I pray with
much gratitude

CONTENTS

CONTENTS

10 The Ecclesial Disposition and the New Evangelization

Conclusion

ACKNOWLEDGMENTS

I am indebted to many individuals and a few significant institutions. The outline for this book was drafted while on Sabbatical for six months in Dublin, Ireland in 2009 where I held the Veale Chair at Milltown Institute of Theology and Philosophy. During this time I visited the Jesuitana collection at Boston College and found much there that was helpful in the early part of this work. The staff also provided digital photography. The work was further developed during a second half Sabbatical at Boston College in 2013 as Visiting Scholar at the Lonergan Research Institute. I am grateful to both institutions and their personnel for the facilities and kindness that enabled me to write without interruption. Additionally I would thank the Association of Theological Schools for the award of a Theological Research Scholarship. I am grateful to my own institution, Regis College, both for granting me the Sabbatical time and for the faculty and students with whom I shared many of the ideas contained herein. In particular I am grateful to a generation of Jesuit Scholastics from Canada, the USA and beyond who enthusiastically engaged with material from this work. The following individuals kindly read the work, made helpful suggestions and as necessary provided reports both for publishers and my provincial: Dr Brian O'Leary, S.J., Dr Finbarr Clancy, S.J., Dr Peter Ryan, S.J., Dr Timothy Gallagher, OMV, Dr Thomas Rosica, CSB, Dr Joseph Schner, S.J., and Archbishop Terrence Prendergast, S.J. Fr. Larry Gillick, S.J., and Fr. Gonzalo Chocano assisted me in remaining sane and growing through the long process of writing. I am also indebted to Beau Holland for archival work and Bloomsbury Press. In particular I thank Anna Turton who persevered in seeing this work through to publication. A final note of thanks must go to my own religious congregation *Congregatio Jesu* who formed me and missioned me as a woman theologian, and the Institute of the Blessed Virgin Mary with whom I live here in Toronto, two branches rooted in Mary Ward.

INTRODUCTION

Dynamic, determinative and durable might well characterize the impact of the *Spiritual Exercises* of Saint Ignatius Loyola from its original formulation in the sixteenth century. This *petit livre* has been of extraordinary significance in the lives of men and women for over 400 years. The impact is dynamic, because the effect on individuals has been a school of discernment and a growth in freedom and spiritual maturity with a concomitant effect upon society. In the sixteenth century such an effect had radical and determinative implications for the development of the Society of Jesus and the renewal of the Roman Catholic Church. The durability of the *Spiritual Exercises* is evident in the way in which they have bestowed life-giving spiritual formation on countless individuals and communities up to the present day.

In the twentieth century the *Spiritual Exercises*—seen after Vatican II as a catalyst assisting the renewal of the Church—also came to have wider influence beyond the Roman Catholic tradition. Other Christian denominations came to value the *Exercises*; and training programs for those who would give the *Spiritual Exercises* were established on an inter-denominational basis.[1] At the turn of the millennium the work of the *Spiritual Exercises* had extended into the area of interfaith dialogue.[2]

Yet amidst all this enthusiasm for the *Spiritual Exercises* and the growth in freedom and grace experienced by many people, one small section of this opus has been consistently overlooked. It is the few pages focused on Rules for Thinking with the Church or Rules for Thinking, Judging, and Feeling with the Church. Why the reticence around this section of the work? Part of the answer lies in the emergence of differing understandings

---

[1] For example at a Jesuit Retreat House in the United Kingdom, St. Beuno's, St Asaph, Denbighshire, Wales, retreatants have for many years been drawn from across all Christian denominations.

[2] It is noteworthy that The Secretariat for the Service of Faith advises Fr. General of the Society of Jesus and his General Council on the main issues that the Society must address in the Service of the Faith. It collaborates with the other Curia Secretariats to animate the service of faith in all apostolic sectors, while also being responsible for coordinating and supporting the work of Jesuits and co-workers in the sector of Pastoral Ministry and Spirituality, with particular attention to the ministry of the *Spiritual Exercises*. The same Secretariat also coordinates the Secretariat for Ecumenical and Inter-religious Relations, and serves as liaison to Groups working in Ecumenism and Inter-religious Dialogue.

of the community that is Church and the relationships existing within this community.

Differing Ecclesiologies

Following the Second Vatican Council[3] and the implementation of the decrees flowing from the Council, there developed an unprecedented theological pluralism and public dissent within the Catholic Church. This was particularly accentuated in North America and especially the USA where religious life went through a period of experimentation and adaptation much earlier and more rapidly than in other parts of the world. This coincided with widespread turmoil within social and political life.[4] There was a climate of protest prevalent within the nation, protests against the "war" in Vietnam and protests for civil rights for persons of color were regular events in major cities throughout the US. Amidst this social upheaval, significant numbers of clergy and religious within the Catholic Church petitioned to be dispensed from their vows and exited religious life.[5] It was a time when many debated about optional celibacy, protested against *Humanae Vitae*[6] and engaged in various liturgical "experiments" all of which involved countless meetings.

Some religious men and women took the lessons that they had learned from involvement in various protest movements and began to apply them to issues within their congregations and within the Church. In this they found encouragement within the developing liberation theology.[7]

---

[3] The Second Vatican Council opened under Pope John XXIII on October 11, 1962 and closed under Pope Paul VI, December 8, 1965. Over 2,000 Conciliar Fathers attended and there were four distinct sessions across Fall 1962, Fall 1963, Fall 1964, and Fall 1965.

[4] On November 22, 1963 President John F Kennedy was assassinated. In 1965 US combat troops were committed to the undeclared war in Vietnam. On April 4, 1968 Martin Luther King Jnr was assassinated, and on June 5, 1968 Robert Kennedy was assassinated.

[5] In 1965 there were 58,000 priests and 180,000 sisters, in 2002 there were 45,000 priests and 75,000 sisters whose average age was sixty-eight; between 1965–2002, the number of seminarians dropped from 49,000 to 4,700. Without any students, seminaries across the country were sold. There were 596 seminaries in 1965 and only 200 in 2002. Kenneth C. Jones, *Index of Leading Catholic Indicators: The Church since Vatican II* (Fort Collins, CO: Oriens, 2003), 8–9.

[6] Pope Paul VI, *Humanae Vitae*, Encyclical Letter of His Holiness Paul VI on the regulation of birth, July 25, 1968.

[7] Liberation theology was a radical movement that grew up in South America as a response to the poverty and ill-treatment of the poorest members of society. The most controversial characteristic was the assertion that the Church should act to bring about social change and ally itself with the working class in order to do so. Some radical priests became involved in politics and trade unions while others aligned themselves with violent revolutionary movements. The most prominent liberation theologians included Gustavo Gutiérez, and Leonardo and Clodovis Boff. It is noteworthy that Pope Francis during his time as the Argentinian Provincial of the Society

Meanwhile, many female religious had become involved with the feminist movement and were prompted to articulate a desire for self-determination with regard to the future of their congregations. This was also a period of experimentation[8] and of great advocacy for lay ministry and encouraged by moves within the Anglican Church some religious became prominent in the movement for women's ordination.[9]

Underlying this external activity were important theological questions particularly concerning the development of doctrine, and the origin, nature and authority of the Church.[10] With an increased emphasis on the importance of justice made notably present within the 1971 Synod of Bishops,[11] there was transference of the language of protesting injustice within society to protesting injustice within the Church. Here, a spectrum of issues (including mandatory celibacy and disciplinary actions against certain theologians), were identified as injustices.[12] From the mid-1970s the restriction of priestly ordination to men was seen as another source of injustice and one, which, according to some commentators, ultimately precluded women from full participation in the Church. In addition, as the twenty-first century approached, the list of injustices lengthened to include the Church's treatment of the divorced and remarried, and of homosexual persons.[13]

---

of Jesus had some severe reservations about Liberation theology, in particular he was opposed to the Marxist analysis and the talk of a class war adopted by some theologians. Yet he embraced the notion of the preferential option for the poor. In addition in the early months of his papacy he met with Gustavo Gutierez, and arising from his concern about environmental issues he contacted Leonardo Boff asking him to send what he had written on eco-theology.

[8] "In 1983, when the revised Code of Canon Law was promulgated and the Holy See proclaimed that the period of 'experimentation' had come to an end, many women and men religious had little or no interest in dialoguing with the bishops on how they measured up to the Essential Elements in the Church's teaching on Religious Life, a document prepared by the Holy See as an assessment tool." Sr. Sara Butler, "Apostolic Religious Life: A Public Ecclesial Vocation," in *Renewing Apostolic Religious Life*, ed. Fr. R Gribble (Washington, DC: Catholic University of America Press, 2011), 54.

[9] On October 7, 1979, Sister Theresa Kane, R.S.M., former president of the LCWR, issued a formal plea during Pope John Paul II's Apostolic visit to the United States at the National Shrine of the Immaculate Conception for "providing the possibility of women as persons being included in all ministries of the church."

[10] This clearly then affected the relationship between religious orders and the hierarchy.

[11] The 1971 Synod of Bishops stated: "While the Church is bound to give witness to justice, she recognizes that anyone who ventures to speak to people about justice must first be just in their eyes; hence, we must undertake an examination of the modes of action, of the possessions, and of the lifestyle found within the Church itself."

[12] "... mandatory celibacy for the clergy; Pope Paul's decision [against the majority opinion] in *Humanae Vitae*; the formal disciplinary measures taken against theologians, like Hans Kung, Leonardo Boff, Charles Curran, and the priests and religious who signed the 'abortion ad' in the *New York Times*; and disciplinary measures against the various men and women religious involved in politics." Sara Butler, op. cit. 55

[13] Here we might note certain Doctrinal Documents of the Congregation for the Doctrine of the Faith: Letter to the Bishops of the Church on the Pastoral Care of Homosexual Persons, October 1, 1986; Some Considerations Concerning the Response to Legislative Proposals on

Further fuel to the fire of protest was added with the revelations from the 1990s onwards concerning clerical sexual abuse and the inadequate measures that had been taken to deal with offenders. This led some members of the Church to demand drastic structural change as they had lost faith in the ability of the hierarchy to lead. In this case the question of ordination had ceased to be the focal area of contention, instead it had been suggested that the Church should be reconfigured to do without a ministerial priesthood and an apostolic hierarchy but should base its governance upon a so-called "discipleship of equals."[14] Since the publication of Elizabeth Schussler Fiorenza's book of the same name in 1993 various feminist theologians have promoted different versions of this agenda.[15]

The differing ecclesiologies, broadly speaking, are based on two opposing positions. This has led to a significant polarization within the US Church but it is a polarization that is mirrored in Europe also. One position has been termed "conservative" and would involve those who accept the hierarchical nature of the Church and adhere to her teaching authority and jurisdiction. Members of this second group are desirous of working with bishops in collaborative endeavors. A different position has been termed "liberal" or "radical."[16] Members of this group make a clear distinction between the church as the "people of God" (which they strongly espouse) and the institutional church (which they clearly disparage). They look for a way forward in the discipleship of equals which, when elaborated, appears as "an unstructured community of believers, devoid of hierarchical authority."[17] Such a model of the Church, however conducive it may appear, does not seem in keeping with Catholic doctrine.

A third position which might helpfully speak to this polarization is that indicated by Pope Benedict XVI in his last meeting with the priests of Rome[18] before his resignation at the end of February 2013. The Holy Father gave his reflections on Vatican II as someone who had been present as a *periti*[19] and he emphasized the joy and enthusiasm with which he went

---

Non-discrimination of Homosexual Persons, July 23, 1992; and Considerations Regarding Proposals to give Legal Recognition to Unions between Homosexual Persons, July 31, 2003. All these documents emphasize the inherent dignity and value of homosexual persons while maintaining the Church's teaching with regard to homosexual relationships.

[14] The term was cited by Elizabeth Schussler Fiorenza in her book *Discipleship of Equals: A Critical Feminist Ekklesia-logy of Liberation* (New York: Crossroad, 1993).

[15] Noteworthy here would be Diana Hayes, *Hagar's Daughters: Womanist Ways of Being in the World* (Mahwah, NJ: Paulist Press, 1995); Margaret Farley, *Just Love: Framework for a Christian Sexual Ethic* (New York: Continuum, 2006).

[16] The term "radical" has also been re-appropriated by some who would hold a "conservative" or "traditionalist" position, in its original meaning of returning to the root of the tradition in the Church.

[17] Sara Butler, op. cit.

[18] The meeting took place February 14, 2013.

[19] Theological expert.

to the Council. He stressed that one clear imperative for the Council was to realize a more complete ecclesiology than had been possible at the first Vatican Council.[20] This Council had focused on the doctrine of the primacy of the Pope, but it was seen that this was just "one element in a broader ecclesiology" already in preparation. What was particularly important to reclaim from Vatican I was the concept of the mystical body of Christ. "The aim was to speak about and understand the Church not as an organization, something structural, legal, institutional, which it also is, but as an organism, a vital reality that enters my soul, so that I myself, with my own soul as a believer, am a constitutive element of the Church as such."[21] Indeed, Pope Benedict emphasized that it was from the encyclical of *Mystici Corporis* that there arose the phrase "'we are the Church, ... we Christians together, we are all the living body of the Church.' And of course this is true in the sense that we, the true 'we' of believers along with the 'I' of Christ, are the Church. Not 'we' a group that claims to be the Church. This 'we are Church' requires my inclusion in the great 'we' of believers of all times and places."[22]

This new emphasis to complete the theological ecclesiology of Vatican I, the Pope explained, then took a natural place alongside the understanding of the unique function of the successor of Peter and the relationship between the Pope and the Bishops. The much-debated term "collegiality"[23] was used to express the nature of this relationship as part of the apostolic succession and in conjunction with the primacy of the Bishop of Rome.[24] Then with regard to the overall nomenclature of the Church, Pope Benedict indicated that there had arisen before Vatican II "a little criticism of the concept of the Body of Christ" and some were concerned that the stress

---

[20] Vatican I: December 1869–October 1870 was interrupted by the Franco-Prussian war.

[21] Pope Benedict XVI meeting with priests of Rome, February 14, 2013. He continued: "In this sense Pius XII wrote the encyclical *Mystici Corporis Christi* as a step towards a completion of the ecclesiology of Vatican I. I would say that the theological discussion of the 30s–40s, even 20s was completed under the sign of the words *Mystici Corporis*." www.news.va/en/news/pope-to-romes-priests-the-second-vatican-council (accessed February 15, 2013).

[22] Ibid.

[23] "The word 'collegiality' was found, which provoked great, intense and even – I would say – exaggerated discussions. But it was the word, it might have been another one." Ibid.

[24] "This was needed to express that the bishops, together, are the continuation of the twelve, the body of the Apostles. We said: only one Bishop, that of Rome, is the successor of one particular apostle – Peter. All others become successors of the apostles entering the body that continues the body of the apostles. And just so the body of bishops, the college, is the continuation of the body of the twelve, so it is necessary, it has its function, its rights and duties." Given the controversy that surrounded the definition of "collegiality" and the implementation of this manner of governance, it is noteworthy that Pope Benedict continued: "It appeared to many as a struggle for power, and maybe someone did think about power, but basically it was not about power, but the complementarity of the factors and the completeness of the body of the Church with the bishops, the successors of the apostles, and each of them is a pillar of the Church together with this great body." Ibid.

on the mystical body might be too exclusive and "risk overshadowing the concept of the people of God." The Conciliar Fathers accepted that the understanding of "people of God" needed to be seen in the context of continuity, a continuity which spanned both the Old and New Testaments and found both its zenith and its fulcrum in Christ and ultimately in a Trinitarian interpretation of ecclesiology.[25]

> The Council rightly accepted this fact, which in the Fathers is considered an expression of the continuity between the Old and New Testaments. We pagans, we are not in and of ourselves the people of God, but we become the children of Abraham and therefore the people of God, by entering into communion with Christ who is the only seed of Abraham. And entering into communion with Him, being one with Him, we too are people of God. That is, the concept of 'people of God' implies continuity of the Testaments, continuity of God's history in the world, with men, but also implies a Christological element. And the Council decided to create a Trinitarian construction of ecclesiology: the people of God-the-Father-Body-of-Christ-Temple-of-the-Holy-Spirit.[26]

There was one more keynote of ecclesiology which became more prominent after the Council, not that it was absent from the Council but it was overshadowed by the other characteristics. This is the element of "the link between the people of God, the Body of Christ, and their communion with Christ, in the Eucharistic union. Here we become the body of Christ, that is, the relationship between the people of God and the Body of Christ creates a new reality, that is, the communion."[27] It is from this point that we may trace the blossoming of a certain Communion Ecclesiology which is seen increasingly as an expression of the Church: "communion in different dimensions, communion with the Triune God, who Himself is communion between the Father, Son and Holy Spirit, sacramental communion, concrete communion in the Episcopate and in the life of the Church."[28]

With the pontificate of Pope Francis, alongside this emphasis on the Church as communion there developed a concentrated focus on the Church of the poor. Like his predecessors he stressed the three-fold call to prayer, conversion and mission. He saw the latter as a clarion call for the Church to move out of her comfort zone and the parameters of the membership to take the good news to the peripheries to the most vulnerable whether it be the poor, the sick, the disabled, children, the elderly, or the despairing

---

[25] This emphasis on the centrality of Christ who leads to a relationship with the Trinity will be revealed as a crucial theme of the book.

[26] Pope Benedict meeting with priests of Rome: February 14, 2013 op cit.

[27] Ibid. He continued: "And the Council led to the concept of communion as a central concept. I would say philologically that it had not yet fully matured in the Council."

[28] Ibid.

intellectual. To all Pope Francis desired that the Church should proclaim the reality of God's mercy and the loving compassion of God's children.[29] The Church was called to be a Church of passion and hope.

In contradistinction to the ecclesiological understanding of Pope Benedict and Pope Francis, the different polarized positions outlined previously led to a public perception that the Church is divided (and that this division exists amongst priests, religious and lay people) by these differing ecclesiologies and the subsequent relationship to the hierarchy that ensues. There are clear consequences of the discipleship of equals ecclesiology that affect religious, not least with regard to the vows that are made at profession, and priests with regard to the promises that are made at ordination.[30] The understanding of the vow of obedience seems crucial here and there appears to be different interpretations. Those who accept the authority of the hierarchy do so because they see their vow of obedience as made to God and that the one who exercises authority does so in God's name and under the influence of the Holy Spirit. It is then in the way of imitation of Christ's obedience that the vow is made. This is also an expression of faith in the Church as the body of Christ endowed with his Spirit that was given to the apostles and their successors for all time.[31] Those who do not accept the authority of the hierarchy have a somewhat different nuanced understanding of obedience, which stresses more an egalitarian interpretation of authority. It is against this contemporary

---

[29] As we shall see in later chapters, Pope Francis was in favor of a hierarchical Church, but did not equate this with the attitude of clericalism to which he was totally opposed. Pope Francis made significant moves that confirmed his continuity with his predecessor.

[30] "With respect to our understanding of the vows as a distinctive element in religious life, it must be said forthrightly that those who reject the God-given authority of the hierarchy, for whatever theological reason, simply cut the ground out from under the vocation to 'religious life' as the Church understands and regulates it. An anti-hierarchical ecclesiology provides absolutely no justification for professing public vows, in particular, for making a vow of obedience. At most, we could promise each other that we will seek God's will, cooperate in carrying out the institute's mission, and take responsibility for participating in community affairs. We have no reason to promise obedience to God unless we believe that the person who exercises authority does so in his name. If we accept the authority of the hierarchy we do have reason to do this because we understand that the authority the religious superior exercises 'proceeds from the Spirit of the Lord' through the hierarchy, that is, because the Bishop or the Holy See 'has granted canonical erection to the institute and authentically approved its specific mission.'" We accept the authority of the hierarchy – its teaching authority and jurisdiction – because we believe that Jesus Christ entrusted his ministry to them. This is part of our faith in the Church as the unique mediator of salvation. This is what justifies our decision to imitate the saving obedience of Jesus by surrendering our wills to another whom we confidently believe mediates God's will to us." Sr Sara Butler, op. cit. 59–60

[31] This is also where there can be a confrontation over justice if some "regard the ministerial office instituted by Christ as itself 'unjust', or if they caution us against collaborating in the pastoral care of the faithful lest we shore up the 'unjust' clerical system; or if they offer theological and pastoral 'alternatives' to Catholics who dissent on matters of faith, morals, or discipline. ... Ideas have consequences and the anti-hierarchical option – which is really 'congregationalism', a Reformation option – continues to be tolerated." Ibid.

contextual background of a difference in interpretation and application of these key elements of obedience and the exercise of authority within the Church that are fundamental for relationships both within the Church and for the Church's mission that we turn to look at Ignatian ecclesiology.

Ignatian Ecclesial Understanding

Ignatius of Loyola is often cited as a passionate defender of the Catholic Church at the time of the Reformation. He and his early companions clearly saw themselves as "men of the Church." The Society of Jesus was formed in order to be at the service of the Church. It did not come into existence for its own progress and development. Rather the Society was focused on "the glory of God and the good of the universal Church."[32] Ignatius was concerned to promote what he called *"sentire cum ecclesia"*[33] with a creative fidelity. From the early deliberations of the first companions in 1539 there was a common understanding that members of the Society were to "fight for God under faithful obedience to His Holiness our Pope and to the Roman Pontiffs who would succeed him."[34]

Jesuit theologians and educators through the centuries have made significant contributions to an understanding of the nature of the Church by its members. In the twentieth century they helped to interpret the developing relationships between the Church and the world espoused by the Conciliar Fathers at Vatican II.[35] The aim of this book is to identify and evaluate characteristics of this Ignatian contribution to the contemporary Church. Utilizing key texts, in particular the Rules for Thinking with the Church, I endeavor firstly to situate Ignatius' sense of Church within his own time. I then ask the question: Is there an Ignatian approach to the Church traceable in later generations of Jesuit theologians? Is there an Ignatian ecclesial disposition that reflects the practice of *sentire cum ecclesia*?

The very term *sentire* is not an easy one to translate literally. It is more than just being favorably disposed towards the Church. It is to be engaged at a deeper level, to think and feel with the whole of one's being, head and heart, with the Church. It is to be willing to grow in communion with the Church. This seemed to involve for St. Ignatius a growth in being at one with

---

[32] *Constitutions* 136. In *The Constitutions of The Society of Jesus and Their Complementary Norms: A Complete English Translation of the Official Latin Texts*, ed. John W. Padberg (St. Louis: Institute of Jesuit Sources 1996).

[33] Thinking with the Church or what the Rules for Thinking, Judging, and Feeling with the Church in the *Spiritual Exercises* call for, is a certain way of thinking, judging and feeling with the Church at a more profound level than mere intellectual adherence to its doctrines.

[34] *Summa* 1539, no. 3, and repeated in *Regimini Militantis* and *Exposcit Debitum*.

[35] Most notably within the conciliar documents *Gaudium et Spes*, and *Lumen Gentium*. Jesuit theological experts (*periti*) included: Karl Rahner and Henri de Lubac.

the Church, not just as a matter of loyalty but also with an effective collaborative communion with the hierarchy of the Church. Such a disposition recognizes not only that every baptized Christian is an equal member of the people of God, but that the differing levels of the hierarchy of the Church are also part of that self-same Church. It involves an attitude that recognizes and embraces all the life-giving forces within that collaborative communion.

The decrees of the 35th General Congregation of the Society of Jesus [GC 35], held in 2008,[36] assist the exploration of these life-giving forces and this communion. For the purposes of this work the sections dealing with the Society's identity and charism; the relationship with the Holy Father; and the decree on obedience[37] are of most significance. Within these particular decrees it is interesting to note the language in which they are couched. Rather than the analytical, precise and action-oriented structure of language which dominate the decrees of the previous three General Congregations, there is a significant inclusion of the language of affect—not merely the emotions but involving the deepest place of the spirit.

These particular decrees of GC 35 call for an engagement of the heart of the reader. They use words such as "fervor" and "zeal" and "fidelity"—words that were prevalent in the vocabulary of Ignatius himself. They call for a contemplative reading, a prayerful pondering and they inspire great consolation. They recall Jesuits and members of the Ignatian family to their roots, just as the Conciliar Fathers at Vatican II requested in the decree *Perfectae Caritatis*[38] on religious life. They have a wider attraction also for any who are drawn to Ignatian Spirituality. They lay stress on an ecclesial experience of being one with Christ at the service of the Church. They indicate that such experience is lived out in an ongoing process of conversion. They emphasize that the spirituality underpinning the Society of Jesus is ecclesial. It involves a "feeling with the Church" as an immediate consequence of love for Christ who continues his promised presence within her. The first companions along with Ignatius felt "at home" in the Church

---

[36] From January 7 to March 6, 2008, the Society of Jesus celebrated their 35th General Congregation in Rome. After the election of Fr. Adolfo Nicolás as the new General Superior, the delegates to the Congregation during the next two months debated different issues relating to the mission, structure and identity of the Society of Jesus.

[37] The complete decrees are: Decree 1. *With Renewed Vigor and Zeal:* The Society of Jesus Responds to the Invitation of the Holy Father; Decree 2. *A Fire That Kindles Other Fires:* Rediscovering our Charism; Decree 3. *Challenges to Our Mission Today:* Sent to the Frontiers; Decree 4. *Obedience in the Life of the Society of Jesus;* Decree 5. *Governance at the Service of Universal Mission;* Decree 6. *Collaboration at the Heart of Mission* (Oxford: Way Books, 2008).

[38] *Perfectae Caritatis:* Decree on the Adaptation and Renewal of Religious Life, proclaimed by His Holiness Pope Paul VI, October 28, 1965. On the fortieth anniversary of *Perfectae Caritatis* the Congregation for Institutes of Consecrated Life and Societies of Apostolic Life organized a symposium held September 26–27, 2005 to reflect on the implementation of *Perfectae Caritatis.*

of their time. Thus, this Ignatian 'feeling' with the Church resonates at the level of affect. It is an integrated response of intellect, affect, and will; and it exemplifies the practice of faith seeking understanding in reciprocity of faith and reason.[39] Ignatius, himself, had a liking for the empirical and a trust in the interplay of intelligence and experience.

Throughout this book I concentrate not simply on Ignatius himself but on what I refer to as a certain ecclesial disposition derived from Ignatius. My concern is to indicate what kinds of themes, emphases and indeed theological positions are consonant with the perspectives or horizon of Ignatius regarding ecclesiology. For my illustrations I rely principally on Jesuit theologians. This is not because I believe that only Jesuits have the Ignatian spirit, nor because I imagine that all Jesuit theologians are authentically Ignatian, but because I would suggest that where we see Jesuits gravitating toward views that in some way correspond to what we identify as Ignatian insights, we might with some legitimacy presume an indebtedness to Ignatius.

The format of this work falls into four sections. The first, I have termed the Ignatian context. It includes three chapters. These focus on: Rules for Thinking with the Church; the Texts Surrounding the Text, and the genesis of the Ignatian ecclesial disposition. Part II directs attention to the sixteenth and seventeenth centuries, and figures who exemplify the ecclesial disposition. There are two chapters taking significant *foci,* and in each there is an exploration of the life and writings of the figure under consideration tracing the ecclesial disposition I outlined in Part I. St. Pierre Favre, S.J. is the subject of Chapter 4. Chapter 5 involves an English figure during the time of great persecution of Catholics in England. This chapter also brings a feminine dimension with a concentration on Mary Ward and the lived female experience of the Ignatian ecclesial disposition.

Part III concentrates attention on two twentieth-century Jesuit theologians whose work is of enormous significance in the twenty-first century. In Chapter 6 we explore the life and work of Henri de Lubac, S.J. Chapter 7 considers the life and work of Cardinal Avery Dulles, S.J. Finally, Part IV explores the Ecclesial Disposition of Ignatius and the Contemporary Papacy. Here, I initially indicate the contextual background of the pontificates of Pope John Paul II, Pope Benedict XVI and the first Jesuit pope, Pope Francis. Chapter 9 then focuses upon the Centrality of Christ, a

---

[39] Cf. John Paul II, *Fides et Ratio,* Encyclical Letter to the Bishops of the Catholic Church on the relationship between faith and reason, September 15, 1998. "Faith and reason are like two wings on which the human spirit rises to the contemplation of truth; and God has placed in the human heart a desire to know the truth—in a word, to know himself—so that, by knowing and loving God, men and women may also come to the fullness of truth about themselves." Introductory paragraph. Pope John Paul asserts that faith and reason are not only compatible, but are essential together. Faith without reason, he argues, leads to superstition. Conversely reason without faith, he argues leads to nihilism and relativism.

fundamental feature of the ecclesial disposition and clearly evident in the lives and writings of all three Popes. The final chapter focuses on a very important theme that has intersected all three papacies namely the New Evangelization. In the Pontificate of Pope Francis there is a clear Ignatian flavor, as he said of himself, "I feel like I'm still a Jesuit[40] in terms of my spirituality, what I have in my heart ... Also I think like a Jesuit."[41] A Jesuit takes perpetual vows at the end of his novitiate, and is thereafter a Jesuit forever unless he formally leaves the Society of Jesus. If a Jesuit is asked to become a Bishop and having received permission from the General Superior accepts to do so, then he is formally "dispensed" from his vows of obedience and poverty. Still the man is traditionally considered a Jesuit. "The best 'proof' of all this may be the official communique from the Jesuit Curia on the election of Pope Francis, in which the Superior General of the Society of Jesus, Father Adolfo Nicolas, referred to him first as 'Cardinal Jorge Mario Bergoglio, S.J.', using the traditional abbreviation for a Jesuit (S.J.) and then called him 'our brother.' Cardinal Bergoglio himself used the 'S.J.' when signing letters addressed to the Archdiocese of Buenos

---

[40] (The three dates listed on a Jesuit's tombstone are: *Natus,* the date of his birth; *Ingressus,* the date he entered the novitiate; and *Obiit,* the date of his death.) Most Jesuits, when they have finished their Jesuit training, or "formation," are invited not only to pronounce the three vows of poverty, chastity and obedience (which they first pronounced at the end of their novitiate), and the special "fourth vow" to the Sovereign Pontiff 'with regards to missions' (that is, an openness and willingness to be sent anywhere in the world, or on any mission by the Pope), but also to make several "promises." Among these is a promise not to "strive or ambition" for any high office or "dignity" in the Society of Jesus or the church. This promise was intended by St. Ignatius to prevent Jesuits from the kind of clerical climbing that he found so distasteful in his time. So Jesuits are supposed to avoid all such offices. But sometimes the Vatican will ask a Jesuit to become a bishop, or an archbishop, often in places where the church has fewer local vocations, or when the Jesuit is considered by the Vatican as an outstanding candidate for the episcopacy. When that happens the Jesuit will ask the permission of the Superior General, and it is almost always granted. (I believe that this is a courtesy; technically, the Vatican can do what it likes and ask whom it likes.) The Jesuit of course can turn down this invitation, as ordination to the episcopacy is a sacrament and cannot be coerced. If the Jesuit accepts the invitation (and he almost always does out of a desire to help the universal church) the Jesuit is then formally "dispensed" from his vows of obedience and poverty. Obedience because he obviously is not taking orders from the Superior General any longer. Poverty, because under canon law a Bishop must own property. (There is a promise that the Jesuit is open to 'taking advice' from the General, if he offers it.) But the man is still considered a Jesuit by tradition—if not canonically." James Martin, S.J., 'Is the Pope Still a Jesuit?', *America,* March 21, 2013. In addition Canon Law states in Canon 705: "A religious raised to the episcopate remains a member of his institute but is subject only to the Roman Pontiff by virtue of the vow of obedience and is not bound by obligations which he himself prudently judges cannot be reconciled with his condition." And usually they themselves consider themselves as member of their orders, even after their ordination to the episcopacy. Often "Jesuit bishops," for example, will stay in the Jesuit residence in a city they are visiting, and they almost always retire in the Jesuit infirmary with their brothers, and are buried in the Jesuit cemetery."

[41] Pope Francis, Interview with Antonio Spadaro, S.J., editor-in-chief, *La Civiltà Cattolica,* September 21, 2013.

Aires."[42] In addition when the Pope met Father General after his election the Pope said that Father Nicolas should treat him "like any other Jesuit." I ask the question is it possible to trace the Ignatian ecclesial disposition in the contemporary papacy culminating in the pontificate of Pope Francis? Finally, in the conclusion, I consolidate the argument laid forth and explore some of the implications of the ecclesial disposition of Ignatius for the Society of Jesus, the Ignatian family, and the Roman Catholic Church, indicating how the Ignatian ecclesial disposition may help us to build a Church of Passion and Hope.

---

[42] Also, Jesuit bishops and archbishops and cardinals are always listed on the first page of the local Jesuit catalog. Avery Cardinal Dulles, S.J., for example, was, after his creation as a cardinal by Pope John Paul II, listed on page 1 of the New York Province catalog until his death. (He is buried in the Jesuit cemetery at Auriesville, New York). James Martin, S.J., 'Is the Pope Still a Jesuit?', *America*, March 21, 2013.

Rules For Thinking, Judging, and Feeling With The Church[1]

352   To have the Genuine Attitude Which We Ought To Maintain In The Church Militant, We Should Observe The Following Rules.

353   *The First Rule.* With all judgment of our own put aside, we ought to keep our minds disposed and ready to be obedient in everything to the true Spouse of Christ our Lord, which is our holy Mother the hierarchical Church.

354   *The Second.* We should praise confession to a priest, reception of the Most Blessed Sacrament once a year, and much more once a month, and still more every week, always with the required and proper conditions.

355   *The Third.* We should praise frequent attendance at Mass; also, chants, psalmody, and long prayers inside and outside the church; and further, the schedules setting the times for the whole Divine Office, for prayers of every kind, and for all the canonical hours.

356   *The Fourth.* We should strongly praise religious institutes, virginity and continence, and marriage too, but not as highly as any of the former.

357   *The Fifth.* We should praise the vows of religion, obedience, poverty, chastity, and vows to perform other works of supererogation which conduce to perfection. We should remember, too, that just as a vow is made in regard to matters which lead towards evangelical perfection, so vows ought not to be made with respect to matters that withdraw one from it, such as to enter business, to get married, and the like.

358   *The Sixth.* We should praise relics of saints, by venerating the relics and praying to the saints. We should extol visits to stational churches, pilgrimages, indulgences for jubilees and crusades, and the lighting of candles in churches.

359   *The Seventh.* We should praise precepts of fast and abstinence, for example, in Lent, on ember days, vigils, Fridays and Saturdays; also penances, not only interior but also exterior.

360   *The Eighth.* We ought to praise church buildings and their decorations;

[1]George E. Ganss, S.J., *The Spiritual Exercises of Saint Ignatius Loyola*, A Translation and Commentary (St. Louis: Loyola University Press, 1992), 133–7.

also statues and paintings, and their veneration according to what they represent.

361   *The Ninth.* Lastly, we should praise all the precepts of the Church, while keeping our mind ready to look for reasons for defending them and not for attacking them in any way.

362   *The Tenth.* We ought to be more inclined to approve and praise the decrees, recommendations, and conduct of our superiors [than to speak against them]. For although in some cases their acts are not or were not praiseworthy, to speak against them either by preaching in public or by conversing among the ordinary people would cause more murmuring and scandal than profit. And through this the people would become angry towards their officials, whether civil or spiritual. However, just as it does harm to speak evil about officials among the ordinary people while they are absent, so it can be profitable to speak of their bad conduct to persons who can bring about a remedy.

363   *The Eleventh.* We ought to praise both positive theology and scholastic theology. For just as it is more characteristic of the positive doctors, such as St. Jerome, St. Augustine, St. Gregory and the rest to stir up our affections towards loving and serving God our Lord in all things, so it is more characteristic of the scholastic teachers, such as St. Thomas, St. Bonaventure, the Master of the Sentences, and so on to define and explain for our times the matters necessary for salvation, and also to refute and expose all the errors and fallacies. For the scholastic teachers, being more modern, can avail themselves of an authentic understanding of Sacred Scripture and the holy positive doctors. Further still they, being enlightened and clarified by divine influence, make profitable use of the councils, canons, and decrees of our Holy Mother Church.

364   *The Twelfth.* We ought to be on our guard against comparing those of us who are still living with the blessed of the past. For no small error is made when one says, for example, "He knows more than St. Augustine," or "He is another St. Francis, or even more," or "He is another St. Paul in goodness, holiness, and the like."

365   *The Thirteenth.* To keep ourselves right in all things, we ought to hold fast to this principle: What seems to me to be white, I will believe to be black if the hierarchical Church thus determines it. For we believe that between Christ our Lord, the Bridegroom, and the Church, his Spouse, there is the one same Spirit who governs and guides us for the salvation of our souls. For it is by the same Spirit and Lord of ours who gave the Ten Commandments that our Holy Mother Church is guided and governed.

366   *The Fourteenth.* It is granted that there is much truth in the statement that no one can be saved without being predestined and without having faith and grace. Nevertheless great caution is necessary in our manner of speaking and teaching about all these matters.

367   *The Fifteenth.* We ought not to fall into a habit of speaking much about predestination. But if somehow the topic is brought up on occasions, it should be treated in such a way that the ordinary people do not fall into an error, as sometimes happens when they say: "Whether I am to be saved or damned is already determined and this cannot now be changed by my doing good or evil." Through this they grow listless and neglect the works which lead to good and to the spiritual advancement of their souls.

368   *The Sixteenth.* In the same way we should take care that we do not, by speaking and insisting strongly about faith without any distinction or explanation, give the people an occasion to grow listless and lazy in their works—either before or after their faith is informed by charity.

369   *The Seventeenth.* Similarly, we ought not to speak so lengthily and emphatically about grace that we generate a poison harmful to freedom of the will. Hence one may speak about faith and grace as much as possible, with God's help, for the greater praise of the Divine Majesty; but not in such ways or manners, especially in times as dangerous as our own, that works and free will are impaired or thought worthless.

370   *The Eighteenth.* It is granted that we should value above everything else the great service which is given to God because of pure love. Nevertheless we should also strongly praise fear of the Divine Majesty. For not only is filial fear something pious and very holy, but so also is servile fear. Even if it brings a person nothing better or more useful, it greatly aids him or her to rise from mortal sin; and once such a one has risen, one easily attains to filial fear, which is wholly acceptable and pleasing to God our Lord, since it is inseparably united with love of him.

PART ONE

PART ONE

The Ignatian Context

1

Rules that Free or Oppress?

The *Spiritual Exercises* began as a collection of memoranda on Ignatius' religious experience at Manresa in 1521. When he left Manresa the *Spiritual Exercises* were largely finished. To this text were added a number of "rules" concerning: Discernment of Spirits; the Distribution of Alms; Scruples; and on Thinking, Judging, and Feeling with the Church.[1] The question arises: Are these rules all integral to the text of the *Spiritual Exercises*? Clearly the rules for discernment of spirits are. With the other rules there is some ambiguity. It is generally agreed by scholars that the Rules for Thinking, Judging, and Feeling with the Church were not composed until later and that they were written by Ignatius partly in Paris, some thirteen or fourteen years after his time in Manresa, and partly in Rome, following his arrival there in 1537.[2]

---

[1] "*Para el sentido verdadero que en la Yglesia militante debemos tener, se guarden las regulas siguientes*" Literally: "For the true sense of things which we should maintain in the Church militant, the following rules are to be observed." Cited in Michael Buckley, S.J., "Ecclesial Mysticism in the *Spiritual Exercises* of Ignatius," *Theological Studies* 56 (1995): 441–63, [449–50].

[2] "Ignatius was constantly re-editing his notebook that contained his Exercises and during his long stay in Paris he added a number of new pieces to it, such as the meditations on the Two Standards, the Three Modes of Humility, and a number of rules. ... It was during this same time that he appended the well-known addition that he called the rules 'For the True Sense Which We Should Have *in* the Church Militant,' as the original Castilian text has it. In the definitive version of 1541, there are eighteen of these rules, but it seems that he added the last five to the original thirteen later on in Italy. Much has been written about these rules, which are considered to be the very quintessence of the Counter-Reformation, and some authors claim that they have traced their literary source to the 1529 Council of Sens. The published *Acta* of this council contain both the decrees of the Council condemning current errors and Clichtove's redaction of orthodox Catholic doctrine, and it has been asserted that either one or both of these two documents is the literary source of Ignatius' *Rules for Thinking with the Church*. Other scholars stress the similarities that appear in these rules with some of the points contained in the unsolicited response of Francis I and the theology faculty of the University of Paris made to Melanchthon on August 30, 1535. However, these scholars do not take into account the fact that Ignatius had left Paris several months earlier and that the text of his *Exercises*, which at the time was in the hands of Favre and that later went into the manuscript called the Cologne Codex, already contained these rules. The fact is that Inigo was more influenced by the atmosphere of Paris than he was by any literary influences." *Ignatius of Loyola*

It is clear that these rules were particularly focused by Ignatius to the circumstances of the sixteenth century Church, beset by the twin poles of Humanism[3] and Protestantism. Thus the directory[4] of Juan Alfonso de Polanco (1573–5) states: "these rules should be especially recommended as an antidote for those who live in places, and deal with persons, suspect of heresy."[5] In the official directory of 1599, mention is made of these rules as being: "helpful for strengthening and encouraging anyone's spiritual life."[6] Alongside this they are to be given to those who live in places where

---

The Pilgrim Saint, J. Ignacio Tellechea Idigoras, trans., ed. with a Preface by Cornelius Michael Buckley, S.J. (Chicago: Loyola University Press, 1994), 331–2.

[3] "Renaissance Humanism, considered formally, was a movement, originating in the towns of Italy and eventually spreading across the Alps that aimed at a major shift within the standard educational curriculum of the later Middle Ages. It proposed to substitute for dialectic, the art fundamental to scholastic discourse, a primary emphasis on grammar, the art of reading and interpreting texts, and, above all, on rhetoric, the art of eloquent and persuasive discourse. ... Promoted on the ground that it was better suited to the needs of the laity and of life in society, humanistic education had profound epistemological and anthropological implications that pointed to an evangelical spirituality significantly different from the more intellectual spirituality of the previous period ... . From the standpoint of the humanists, the lifeless abstractions of scholastic discourse might in some remote sense be 'true' but they were incapable of moving human beings to reform their own lives and devise remedies for the general evils of their age in a situation in which any delay invited catastrophe. But what dialectic could not bring about, they were convinced, rhetoric could, with God's help, accomplish. Their sense of dependence on grace also attracted them to the Bible." William James Bouwsma, "The Spirituality of Renaissance Humanism" in *Christian Spirituality II*, ed. Jill Rait (New York: Crossroad, 1987), 236, 241.

[4] A directory is a form of guidebook for assisting the giving of the *Spiritual Exercises*. The primary directory is the book of the *Spiritual Exercises* itself, where throughout there are instructions for the director on how to accompany the retreatant. This was deemed sufficient during the early years of the Society of Jesus when most of those who gave the *Spiritual Exercises* had themselves been formed by Ignatius and understood the ramifications of the sometimes minimalist instructions contained in the book of the *Exercises*. With the passage of time however it was deemed necessary to provide more detailed instructions to assist retreat directors. Accordingly, supplementary directives were included in a separate book known as a directory. St. Ignatius was aware of this need and made a practice of jotting down a few notes, and had his secretary, Juan de Polanco, bring to him questions that arose about the *Exercises* and then record his answers. After the death of St. Ignatius and with the active support of the fourth Superior General Everard Mercurian (1573–80), Polanco continued working on a substantial directory which had major influence upon the final authorized Official Directory of 1599. For further information see Martin E. Palmer, S.J. (ed.), *On Giving the Spiritual Exercises: The Early Jesuit Manuscript Directories and the Official Directory of 1599* (St. Louis: Institute of Jesuit Sources, 1996).

[5] He continues: "The usefulness of these rules lies not only in helping people to avoid falling into error by thinking differently or so expressing themselves publicly or privately in speech and writing, but also in helping to detect in the statements and writings of others deviations from the Catholic Church's mode of thinking and speaking, and to put other people on their guard against them." Juan Alfonso de Polanco, "Directory of Father Juan Alfonso de Polanco," [112]. Cited in Palmer, S.J. (ed.) *On Giving the Spiritual Exercises*, Document 20, 148.

[6] This underlines the practice of giving the *Spiritual Exercises* not just to those discerning the possibility of priesthood or religious life but to anyone including laity whose spiritual life needed such strengthening and encouragement.

orthodoxy is suspect, and interestingly, there is a special stipulation that they should be given to all those "in ministry."[7] The very thrust of these rules is towards *sentire cum ecclesia*—thinking in communion with the Church. Accordingly, though it is clear that the initial stimulus for the rules was the reality of sixteenth century Church conditions,[8] still today there is a resonance that makes the rules as relevant to the life of the Church of the twenty-first century—the post Vatican II Church—as to the life of the Church of the sixteenth century—the pre- and post-Council of Trent Church.[9] Indeed, I shall argue in the next chapter that the rules are consonant with the entire movement of the *Spiritual Exercises*.

At this point it is time to address the rules directly.[10] It is true that many twenty-first century people turn away from prescriptions of conduct imposed upon them by others and the very format of the first paragraph *To have the genuine attitude which we ought to maintain in the Church Militant,*[11] *we should observe the following rules,*[12] can prove a serious difficulty. Or it may sit with a certain sense of peaceful serenity within the heart of the individual reader. What is proposed is a series of rules to assist a genuine relationship with the Church.

The First Rule—The Essence of the Matter

With all judgment of our own put aside, we ought to keep our minds disposed and ready to be obedient in everything to the true Spouse of Christ our Lord, which is our holy Mother the hierarchical Church.[13] This First Rule gives the essential reason for why Ignatius insists on the importance of a set of Rules for Thinking, Judging and Feeling with the Church. Ignatius loved the Church because he loved Christ. This love for Christ is the intimate

---

[7] "They should be given to all who are in ministry and handle the word of God, since these rules run directly counter to the opinions and statements of the heretics of our time." Chapter 38, [271]. Cited in ibid., 346.

[8] Another way to interpret them from their time is as a set of guidelines for someone nearing the end of the *Spiritual Exercises* who now desires to labor with Christ and spread the reign of God and wants to do this in union with the visible Church.

[9] Clearly Ignatius wrote his Rules before the Council of Trent and therefore had in mind a situation that the Council endeavored to address. At the same time one might reasonably argue that the reforms that the Council of Trent brought into being were assisted by the stimulus for thinking with the Church given by the inclusion of the Rules within the book of the *Spiritual Exercises*.

[10] In my experience, the contemporary response of individuals to these rules runs across an entire spectrum from acceptance and agreement, through a sense of discomfort and being disconcerted, to being thoroughly repelled by the statements made. This, of course, also reflects the sense of commitment to, or alienation from, the institutional Church by each reader.

[11] Church Militant—the Church on Earth, in contrast to the Church Triumphant—the Church in heaven.

[12] Ganss, S.J., *The Spiritual Exercises of Saint Ignatius*, 352.

[13] *Spiritual Exercises* 353.

love that he asks the one making the *Spiritual Exercises* to pray for in the first contemplation of the second week. The Incarnation is one of the most striking meditations in the *Spiritual Exercises* of St. Ignatius Loyola. It encapsulates—as it were—the Ignatian understanding of the universe, the Trinity and Christ himself. It is a microcosm of Ignatius' theological understanding. In this meditation "we" are asked to imagine the Trinity—as it were—in conversation discussing the salvation of the world. The three persons are looking down at the world with all the messy business of life going on. People being born, laughing, crying, hurting, joyful, dying etc. and into this great "guddle" of life God decides to be present and part of human reality. Ignatius "does not sweeten or falsify painful realities. Rather he begins with them, exactly as they are—poverty, forced displacement, violence between people, abandonment, structural injustice, sin."[14] Against this background, Ignatius asks us to consider the great desire in God for human salvation and reconciliation. In Christ God's love becomes present in our midst—Emmanuel—God with us. Ignatius then asks us to shift in our imagination to the annunciation scene with which we are more familiar. Here he calls us to ponder the meeting between Mary and the Angel Gabriel. In Our Lady we see the fullness of a human response to God in her willingness to become the mother of Jesus—the one who saves his people from their sins. In her we see that deep love for God, which issues forth in faith and obedience.

The grace asked for throughout the whole of this meditation and throughout the whole of the second week of the *Spiritual Exercises* is the grace of *"an intimate knowledge of our Lord who has become a human person for me, that I may love him more and follow him more closely."*[15] This *intimate knowledge* is crucial. It is a knowledge that is not merely epistemological, knowledge of the intellect, though it is this also. It is not merely existential, an understanding in our experience, though it includes this too. It is also, and primarily, an ontological knowledge, an apprehension at the level of our very being of God's passionate commitment to each one of us. This is the primordial reality that Ignatius is concerned that we should understand.

It is this most profound apprehension that is the source of any right thinking, that intimate knowledge of God at the source of our being. It is from this intimacy that Ignatius asks us to consider the rules. In so doing, he recalled that Christ had guaranteed that his Spirit would be with the Church until the end of time.

Ignatius uses the term *"spouse"* and *"mother"*[16]—two very intimate terms—to describe the relationship of the individual with the Church. It is a unique intimacy implying communion of being within the Church. The intimate unity: of "Christ with the Church, His spouse, and of us

---

[14] The Society of Jesus, *Decrees and Documents of the 35th General Congregation* (Oxford: The Way Publications, 2008); Decree 2: A fire that kindles other fires, [6].
[15] Ganss, S.J., *The Spiritual Exercises of Saint Ignatius*, [104].
[16] Ibid.

the members of the church with the Church, their mother. Both indicate a unique kind of love: Christ's care for the Church with a love that is nuptial; the Church's care for its members with a love that is maternal."[17] It is to suggest that one and the same Spirit is behind both the hierarchical Church and the most intimate personal experiences.

The metaphor of the Church as spouse clearly derives from scripture and appears in the letters of St Paul[18] and in the book of Revelation.[19] It was a key symbol of the Church in the Middle Ages.[20] In using this metaphor then, Ignatius is consistent with the tradition of medieval use. In addition, St. Bernard uses the term 'spouse' referencing both the individual Christian, all Christians and the unity of the Church. He moves between these three appreciations of the term in his homilies on the Song of Songs [*Sermones super Cantica Canticorum*] which contain the principal texts on the Church as Bride and Mother. The literary genre of the work is an exegesis in the medieval sense. It involves a divine-human drama involving the Bride (both the Church and the individual soul) and the bridegroom Christ.[21] Thus the spousal relationship of Christ and the Church included every individual Christian. "The mysticism of the Church's status was realized in the soul of each of its members and in them all, while each of the members was united with Christ only insofar as the individual person was *intra Ecclesiam*. The individual soul participated in the mystical union between the Church and Christ."[22] Indeed as Bernard outlines the relationship, the individual grows in proportion to his or her becoming the one Church-Bride.[23]

---

[17] Michael Buckley, S.J., "Ecclesial Mysticism in the *Spiritual Exercises* of Ignatius," *Theological Studies* 56 (1995): 441–63, [458].

[18] Eph. 5.32.

[19] Rev. 21.2–3.

[20] A book length study that traces these metaphors throughout the Middle Ages is Megan McLaughlin, *Sex, Gender and Episcopal Authority in an Age of Reform 1000–1122* (Cambridge: Cambridge University Press, 2010).

[21] "*Pour S. Bernard, l'épouse est-elle L'Eglise ou l'âme individuelle aimant Dieu, ou l'ensemble des âmes aimants Dieu? Elle est, pour lui tout cela car cela, pour lui, est la même chose.*" Yves Congar, "L'ecclésiologie de S. Bernard," in *Etudes d'ecclésiologie médiévale* 7: 136–7.

[22] Buckley, S.J., "Ecclesial Mysticism in the *Spiritual Exercises* of Ignatius," 441–63 [455]. Buckley continues: "This tradition of mystical participation in the nuptial union between Christ and his Church is important to bear in mind when one finds this usage in Ignatius's explicit treatment of ecclesiology." In his Letter to Claudius, the Emperor of Abyssinia, for example, Ignatius made a similar ecclesial assertion and substantiated it, as would Bernard with a reference to the Canticle: "The Catholic Church is one throughout the whole world, and it is impossible for one to be attached to the Roman Pontiff and another to the Alexandrian. As Christ the Bridegroom is one, so the Church, His spouse, is only one, of whom Solomon, speaking in the name of Christ our Lord," says in the Canticle, "One is my dove." (Canticle 6:8) [Ignatius of Loyola to Claude, Emperor of Abyssinia (February 23, 1555), *Letters of Ignatius Loyola,* selected and translated by William J. Young (Chicago: Loyola University Press, 1959), [369]. One should notice that the spousal metaphor is critical to Ignatius' argument; "it is not simply a commonplace let fall in an argument whose warrant is other. The church must be one because it is the bride of Christ." Ibid. 456.

[23] "The one Groom has only one 'dove,' one bride, rather than many individual ones. Each

According to Roch Kereszty the theology of the Bride and Mother apparent within Bernard's work "has to be gleaned from meditating on the vicissitudes of the individual soul's developing love relationship with Christ while at the same time realising that the key to the interpretation is the universal drama of salvation history."[24] Michael Buckley suggests that rather than drawing upon Bernard for the image of spouse and mother, it is to Anselm that Ignatius is indebted. The focus for Anselm however was not mystical union but a political dilemma.[25] In this sense "spouse" and "mother" had become "common-place images from which one could argue to freedom and political support."[26]

By contrast, Ignatius's use of these images of "spouse" and "mother" is in line with his desire to cultivate a certain disposition of mind and heart namely: "a spirit open and prompt to obey in all things."[27] This presupposition of spirit becomes an antecedent disposition towards obedience to the Church, because the Church is "the spouse of Christ and our holy mother."[28] Indeed, it is the Spirit of God that gives authentication to the spouse and mother metaphors such that we can understand Christ's care for the Church as a nuptial love and the Church's care for her members as a maternal love. It is the Spirit of God that unites these two realities as Ignatius makes clear in the Thirteenth Rule.[29] Buckley sees this as an

---

soul becomes bride only to the extent that he or she appropriates the loving surrender of the one unique Church-Bride." Roch Kereszty, "Bride" and "Mother" in "*Super Cantica* of St. Bernard: An Ecclesiology for our Time?" *Communio* 20 (1993): 415–36, 423.

[24] Ibid. 418.

[25] "Anselm was struggling with successive English monarchs for the freedom of the Church and the abolition of lay investiture. Because the Church is the spouse of Christ, it must be free. Because it is the mother of the faithful, that through which all were made children of God, Christian princes should not attempt to dominate the Church, but to guard and defend it." Buckley, S.J., "Ecclesial Mysticism in the *Spiritual Exercises* of Ignatius," 457. Buckley includes significant citations from Anselm to illustrate this point.

[26] Ibid. 458.

[27] *Spiritual Exercises* 353. Cf. *Spiritual Exercises* 91 where Ignatius suggests that the grace to be asked for is "the grace not to be deaf to [Christ's] call, but prompt and diligent to accomplish His most holy will."

[28] Buckley, S.J., "Ecclesial Mysticism in the *Spiritual Exercises* of Ignatius," 458.

[29] "'The same Spirit that guides and governs us' gives the key to the nature of this experience of the Spirit within the *Exercises*. For that by which the Church is united with Christ and that by which the Church is generated and governed now realizes itself within the depths of the exercitant: the Spirit of God. This government and guidance lies at the heart of the Ignatian Exercises. It can also be found in critically important moments in the explicit assertions of the *Constitutions*. There, union with the Spirit of the Lord is habitually seen in terms of guidance and governance. [Cf. *Constitutions*, Preamble (134); 2.3 (219); 4.10 (414); 7.2 (624); 8.6 (700, 701). So much does the guidance of the Holy Spirit and discretion come out of charity that Ignatius can say in very difficult cases that "the charity and discretion of the Holy Spirit will indicate the manner that ought to be used" (219). In other places, he unites them through the phrase "discreta caritas." The Holy Spirit guides human persons especially through "writing and imprinting the interior law of charity within them [*Constitutions*, Preamble (134)]. But this same charity or

implicit pneumatology in Ignatius's work. What does Christ give to the Church which constitutes it his spouse? The Holy Spirit. What does the Church instrumentally and sacramentally communicate to its members, the gift which directs their lives and governs them? The Holy Spirit. We shall be returning to this emphasis on the work of the Spirit of God in the later rules and also in our further consideration of the *Exercises* and the *Constitutions*.

Ignatius refers to "the hierarchical Church"[30] in this rule, though this description is rare in his writings. It is important that we do not misinterpret what he means here.[31] Ignatius appreciated the hierarchical Church as a Church of mediation of divine grace both to its members and to the world in which the Church is situated. Such mediation occurs in and through individual believers. For believers, such grace is received in and through the sacraments, primarily the Eucharist and the teaching of the Church, and in the strength of this grace individual believers contribute to the mission of the Church within the world. So as with a body, each part needs to fulfill its proper role. In a similar manner St. Paul speaks of the body of Christ and the importance of each part.[32] "Ignatius looks on the Church as a whole of which nothing can be ignored: neither its ecclesial hierarchy nor the rest of

---

love of friendship is that by which the person is principally united with God [*Constitutions* 10 (813)]. Guidance and union proceed from the same source, the Holy Spirit." Ibid. 459.

[30] Yves Congar maintains that Ignatius was the first person to use the term "hierarchical church," *"Ignace semble bien avoir créé cette expression d' 'Église hiérarchique'" "L'Église de saint Augustine à l'époque moderne,"* 1970, 369 . In a footnote he states *"Sur ces règles et leur contexte historique"* [*se distance d'une spiritualité de tendance individualiste*], cf. J. M. Granero, "Sentir con la Iglesia (Ambientacion hist. De unas famosas reglas)," *Miscel. Comillas* 25 (1956): 203–33. Congar continues within this text to assert: *"C'est cette Église militante qui est la Cité de Dieu, dont le thème es ainsi historicisé et socialisé. Il n'y a pas d'opposition, pas même de décalage entre les structures de droit ou d'autorité et la qualification morale ou spirituelle; il y a identité entre ce que Dieu demande et le service dans cette Église, entre discernment des esprits et jugement de L'Église hiérarchique"* (cf. *Exercises* nos. 170, 352, 365; 13 régle d'orthodoxie; letter du 18.VI. 1536 à Sœur Teresa Rajadella). *Il existe un lien rigoureux, un passage dynamique, entre les termes: Dieu, Église, obéissance, mission.*

[31] *"Es muy frecuente confundir la expresion de 'Iglesia hierarquica' con la expresion 'jerarquia de la Iglesia,' entendiendo ademas esta 'jerarquia' como el conjunto de personas constituidas en autoridad en la Iglesia. Y mas en concreto todavia, de forma casi mecanica, se entiende que hablar de Iglesia hierarquica, o simplemente de Iglesia, es hablar de los obispos y del Vaticano. Esta confusion ha contribudo muy negativamete a la degradacion del concepto, de la imagen y – lo que es peor – de al vivencia de Iglesia, en nuestors tiempos."* Jesus Corella, S.J., *Sentir La Iglesia: Commentario a las reglas Ignacianas para el sentido verdadero de Iglesia* (Bilbao: Ediciones Mensajero. Sal Terrae, 1996). A free translation would be: "We too often confuse the words for hierarchical Church, with the word – 'hierarchy'. Also we understood this hierarchy as consisting of all persons in authority in the Church. And more specifically still, almost mechanically, we can speak of the hierarchical Church or simply the Church, as meaning the bishops and the Vatican. This confusion has contributed very negatively to a degradation of the concept, image and – worse – of the living Church in our times."

[32] 1 Cor. 12.12, 14–27.

its members, neither its charismatic expression nor its canonical discipline, neither its holiness nor its sinfulness."[33]

This First Rule sets the tone for the rest of the rules and looks to evoke a certain love for the Church which is not just intellectual or affective but which encompasses both—even to the most profound depth of a loving soul, and this is an ontological reality. It is a passionate and fervent love. It is to recognize within the Church, by the grace of faith, the source of life which is the presence of Christ. Love of Christ goes with love for the Church and needs to be expressed in concrete acts. This dynamic principle of love, which shows itself more in deeds than in words, is the love Ignatius speaks of in the last contemplation of the *Spiritual Exercises*, 'The Contemplation to Attain the Love of God.'[34] It is this love and confidence in the Spirit of God working within the Church that lies at the heart of Ignatius' disposition towards the Church and guides the formulation of the following rules for thinking with the Church.

The Second Rule—Confession and Communion

The rules that follow all deal more or less directly with speaking about things of the Church in a more or less public manner. Ignatius highly valued communication[35] and realized its power and potential for good and ill. In particular Ignatius asks the reader to *praise, strongly praise or approve* Church practices which were still being attacked by proponents of the Reformation.[36] The sacrament of penance—confession—and the

---

[33] Peter Hans Kolvenbach, S.J., "The Rules for Thinking, Judging, Feeling in The Post-Conciliar Church," *Review of Ignatian Spirituality* 105, XXXV (I/2004): 19–27.

[34] *Spiritual Exercises* 230, "Love ought to manifest itself more by deeds than by words." It is clear that Ignatius considers that for love to be true it must not remain simply within the bounds of affectivity but must have an effective action in terms of deeds. By contrast a lukewarm relationship with the Church where there is little evidence of real commitment is very unattractive. A significant difficulty arises when individuals see themselves apart from the Church and in conversation speak of "the Church" in terms of the institutional structure which does not include themselves. As Kolvenbach, S.J. states, "There must be fervor in our adhesion to the Church, for how can we love the Lord more intensely and distinguish ourselves in total service to him, if we are lukewarm and skeptical towards his spouse?" Ibid.

[35] Ignatius Loyola's prodigious hand-written correspondence accounts for more than 7,000 letters to individuals and communities across the known sixteenth century world. Maintaining frequent communication through letters was an essential feature of Ignatius' understanding of mission, so much so that he enshrined within the Jesuit Constitutions clear instructions for "the exchange of letters between subjects and superiors through which they learn about one another frequently and hear the views and reports which come from the various regions." (*Constitutions* 674). See also *Constitutions* 790, 801, 806.

[36] For an extended study of the conflict over Church practices see Nathan D. Mitchell, "Reforms, Protestant and Catholic," in *The Oxford History of Christian Worship*, eds

Eucharist had been at the forefront of the Reformers criticism. Confession was abolished, and the Reformers denied the sacrificial nature of the mass.[37] Here, Ignatius not only asserts the importance of confession and the reception of the Blessed Sacrament, but goes beyond the ethos of his own time in recommending weekly reception of communion. In this latter recommendation Ignatius is more akin to our contemporary times where weekly and indeed daily communion is possible in countries where priests are available. It is significant also to note a resurgent focus upon the Blessed Sacrament within twenty-first century Church life. In particular, devotion to the Blessed Sacrament expressed in Eucharistic Adoration is more prevalent within the Church and appreciated by growing numbers of young people.[38]

The Third Rule—Church Liturgical Practices

The Church practices that Ignatius asks us to praise in this Third Rule are ones that were again the source of controversy in his time. He begins where he left off in the Second Rule by praising *frequent attendance at Mass*.[39] He then moves to praising the various components of the liturgy, *the whole*

Geoffrey Wainwright and Karen B. Westerfield Tucker (Oxford: Oxford University Press, 2006), 307–50. It gives a more extended discussion of the views of Luther, Calvin, Zwingli and Cranmer on the Eucharist with special mention of the historical context surrounding the frequency of communion in the late Medieval world. Also helpful is Francis Clark, *Eucharistic Sacrifice and the Reformation* (Westminster, MD: The Newman Press, 1960).

[37] In his 1521 treatise *On the misuse of the Mass*, Luther had insisted that "to sacrifice to God and to be consumed by us are not compatible ideas." In short, sacrifice threatens communion. "Eat and drink," Luther comments, "That is all that we are to do with the sacrament. ... But what we eat and drink we do not sacrifice; we keep it for ourselves and consume it." ... [For Luther] ... "The Christian 'offering' is not a sacrifice, but a call to faith and obedience in the Word epitomized by the gospels' command to 'take and eat, take and drink.' ... Calvin's premier Eucharistic preoccupation was the unconditional sovereignty of God, God's absolute freedom, and divinity. Any theory of sacrament that would limit God's sovereignty must therefore be deemed idolatrous." Mitchell, "Reforms Protestant and Catholic," 319–21. Also "Calvin denies the dogma of the Real Presence by insisting that Christ's words of institution, 'This is my body' ... [Mt. 26.26ff.], are to be taken not literally, but figuratively, as metonymy; that is, as a trope that substitutes an associated item for the thing itself." R. V. Young, "The Reformations of the sixteenth and seventeenth Centuries," in *Christian Marriage: A Historical Study*, ed. Glenn W. Olsen (New York: Crossroad, 2004), 273.

[38] There is clear evidence of this appreciation in the numbers of young people attending Adoration of the Blessed Sacrament during World Youth Days and also requesting the possibility of times of Adoration at university chaplaincies and local parishes. In the General Audience November 17, 2010, Pope Benedict XVI referenced this growing appreciation when he stated: "It is consoling to know that many groups of young people have rediscovered the beauty of praying in adoration before the Blessed Sacrament. I think for example of our adoration in Hyde Park London [London, England] during the Papal Visit September 16–19, 2010. I pray that this 'springtime' of the Eucharist will continue to spread in all parishes."

[39] Third Rule, *Spiritual Exercises* 355.

Divine Office,[40] *for prayers of every kind and for all the canonical hours.*[41] Praise here "is more than beautiful chant or well-phrased speech. What is essential is an inner disposition of selflessness. The biblical image of praise is the dance of David before the Ark of the Covenant. David sets aside his regal dignity and vestments. Praise is reverence for God and for godly things in the Church, in a spirit of thanksgiving for grace received."[42]

It is important to bear in mind here that by asking us to praise these things Ignatius is not suggesting that all should adopt them. It is clear that Ignatius provided definite limitations in regard to some of these things in Jesuit life in order to enable the mission of the Society of Jesus.[43] A number of these practices may be more suited to monastic rather than apostolic life, namely the praying of the Divine Office in common. What Ignatius was reacting to in this rule was the tendency of the Reformers to ridicule and denigrate such practices.[44] He was concerned to assert the validity of

---

[40] The Reformers in Europe and England had similar problems to their Catholic contemporaries with regard to the use of the Divine Office. "The [medieval Roman Offices] were too complicated, ... not enough Scripture was read. The difference between the Protestant Reformers and the Catholics were that the former had the sense to realize that the office was for everyone, not just the clergy. So they did not abolish the hours, but put them into the vernacular." Robert Taft, *The Liturgy of the Hours in East and West: The Origins of the Divine Office and Its Meaning for Today,* 2nd edn (Collegeville, MN: The Liturgical Press, 1983), 319. Taft provides a brief overview of the Lutheran and Anglican developments regarding the daily offices. For more in depth study of Luther's views, see the essay by J. Neil Alexander, "Luther's Reform of the Daily Office," *Worship* 57 (1983). For Calvin's criticisms and his reinterpretation of monasticism along the lines of the early Church see *Institutes* IV.13.8–11f. Section 13.10 attacks specific practices in *Calvin: Institutes of The Christian Religion,* Vol. XXI, ed. John T. McNeill, trans. Ford Lewis Battle (Philadelphia: The Westminster Press, 1960).

[41] *Spiritual Exercises* 355.

[42] Kolvenbach, S.J., "The Rules for Thinking, Judging, and Feeling in The Post-Conciliar Church."

[43] "Because the occupations which are undertaken for the aid of souls are of great importance, proper to our Institute, and very frequent; and because, on the other hand, our residence in one place or another is so uncertain, they will not regularly hold choir for the canonical hours or sing Masses and offices. ... our members ought to apply their efforts to the pursuits that are most proper to our vocation, for the glory of God our Lord." Ignatius Loyola, *Constitutions* [586]. As de Guibert states: "In the form of life which his particular vocation has imposed, the Jesuit has had to surrender other paths which might have led him to this familiarity with God just as well if not better, such as prayer in choir with its splendour and strength, the monastic environment with its isolation from the world coupled with its sum total of observances and practices which are so powerful in raising the soul to God. But the Jesuit has a life essentially vowed to an apostolate unhampered by any fetters and requiring him to be ready at any moment, in any place, for any kind of work. In such a life it is mental prayer alone—a contracted and intense mental prayer—which can efficaciously and permanently assure him of what is essential in this indispensable union with God." Joseph de Guibert, S.J., *The Jesuits Their Spiritual Doctrine and Practice: A Historical Study,* trans. William J. Young, S.J. (St. Louis: Institute of Jesuit Sources, 1972), 546.

[44] According to Luther, "Three serious abuses have crept into the service, First, God's Word has been silenced, and only reading and singing remain in the churches. This is the worst abuse. Second, when God's Word had been silenced such a host of un-Christian fables and lies, in

religious life, particularly the monastic way of life and the importance of upholding the prayer of the Church—the Divine Office.

The Fourth Rule—Religious Life and Marriage

The Fourth Rule is integrally linked to the Third Rule. Not only were the Reformers denouncing certain liturgical practices, in particular their scorn was focused upon practices associated with religious life. Accordingly, Ignatius here introduces a confirming adverb for emphasis. He states that we should *strongly praise religious institutes, virginity and continence*.[45] In the measure in which the reality of religious life was under threat from the ridicule of Reformers, so Ignatius saw the need to counter this with a robust defense. In supporting *virginity and continence*[46] also he was upholding the long tradition of consecrated virgins and the value of the state of *virginity*, which had been devalued by the Reformers.

The second part of this rule can cause offence to our contemporary sensibilities. When faced with the clause *and marriage too, but not as highly as any of the former*,[47] it may seem that there was only a grudging praise given to marriage and clearly it was considered inferior to the state of religious life! Certainly it is true that medieval men and women esteemed religious life more highly with regard to holiness.

Again, however, the context is important to bear in mind. In the sixteenth century marriage was always seen as 'a good' and the way of the majority in life. Marriage, at that time, unlike perhaps our own century, did not need to be defended. Catholics and Protestants agreed on the God-given nature of the institution of marriage even when they differed with regard to the sacramentality of marriage.[48] What did need to be defended was the insti-

---

legends, hymns, and sermons were introduced that it is horrible to see. Third, such divine service was performed as a work whereby God's grace and salvation might be won. As a result, faith disappeared and everyone pressed to enter the priesthood, convents, and monasteries, and to build churches and endow them. ... For the time being we can shelve the antiphons responsories, and collects, as well as the legends of the saints and the cross, until they have been purged, for there is a horrible lot of filth in them. All the festivals of the saints are to be discontinued." Martin Luther, "Concerning the Order of Public Worship."

[45] The Fourth Rule, *Spiritual Exercises* 356.

[46] Ignatius' view here is consonant with an ancient and constant tradition of the superiority of virginity/celibacy. A book length discussion of the place of celibacy in the tradition can be found in William E. Phipps, *Clerical Celibacy: The Heritage* (New York: Continuum, 2004).

[47] Fourth Rule, *Spiritual Exercises* 356

[48] See Phipps, *Clerical Celibacy*, where Phipps provides a concise summary of the Protestant views regarding marriage. He includes many citations as he deals with the different views and practices of Luther, Zwingli, Calvin, the Scottish Reformers, Henry VIII, Cranmer, and others. Theological and Scriptural arguments are made, but the language of sacrament seems only

tution of religious life, which had not only suffered attack in a theoretical sense, but had literally been eradicated in some areas.[49]

In this sense then, the greatest need was to praise, indeed *strongly praise,* religious institutes. At the same time Ignatius is also concerned to include marriage and link the two states of life rather than polarize them. In our twenty-first century culture both religious life and marriage have come under considerable pressure and the Church has recognized that both forms of life require support. The way in which Ignatius has linked marriage and religious life finds a similar emphasis in the renewed understanding of the reciprocity of these two states as outlined by Pope John Paul II in his theology of the body[50].

The Fifth Rule—The Importance of Religious Vows

In this rule Ignatius adds more detail to his strong praise of the existence of religious life. Here, he insists on the importance of religious vows. In the

---

to be used when denigrating the Catholic view of celibacy linked to the sacrament of Holy Orders. According to R. V. Young, "the reason for such a denigration of celibacy is due to the explicit denial by the Reformers that marriage was a sacrament," The Reformation coincides with a widespread growth in the perception that marriage was more a personal affair than a social institution. One effect of Protestant doctrine seems certain: to deprive marriage of sacramental status is to secularize it and, in effect, to add momentum to the overall secularization of society, since marriage is the fundamental social institution. Martin Luther himself maintained "There is no Scriptural warrant whatsoever for regarding marriage as a sacrament," and he proceeded to suggest that the nature of marriage is determined by the spirit and conduct of the participants. Calvin's treatment of marriage drew on St. Paul for justification as Young indicates. "When St. Paul calls marriage 'a great mystery' and adds, 'but I speak concerning Christ and the Church'" (Eph. 5.32), he is not calling marriage a sacrament (*sacramentum* in the Vulgate), Calvin maintains, but rather distinguishing between earthly, human marriage and the heavenly mystery of Christ's relation to the Church. Although *mysterion* is the standard Greek term for "sacrament," Calvin derides Catholic interpreters for taking "mystery" literally as the Latin *sacramentum* in the Pauline context, "To treat Scripture thus," he maintains, "is to confound heaven and earth." John Calvin, *Institutes of the Christian Religion* IV.19, 34–6, trans. Henry Beveridge (Grand Rapids, MI: Hendrickson Publisher, 1957), II.646–8. Cited in Young, "The Reformations of the Sixteenth and Seventeenth Centuries," 271, 273.

[49] From 1529 with the beginning of the Dissolution of the Monasteries in England, religious life was systematically destroyed. By the time of Mary Ward's birth in 1585 it was no longer possible to become a member of a religious order within England. As we see in Chapter 5, she had to leave her native land to enter an enclosed convent on the Continent.

[50] The "Theology of the Body" is Pope John Paul II's integrated vision of the human person— body, soul, and spirit. This vision Pope John Paul II shared in 129 Wednesday audiences, which were given between the years 1979 and 1984. His reflections are based on Scripture (especially the Gospels, St. Paul and the Book of Genesis), and contain a vision of the human person. John Paul II discusses who human beings were in the beginning, who they are now (after original sin), and who they will be in the age to come. He then applies this message to the vocations of marriage and celibacy, in preparation for the Kingdom of Heaven.

light of the clear abuses that had been prevalent in religious life in some places,[51] the sixteenth century Reformers had insisted that the vows of religious life had not been lived and could not be lived. This denigration of religious vows has a clear contemporary resonance. Twenty-first century culture not only stresses the impossibility of such vows being lived but also asserts they constitute an unhealthy way of living. In particular the vow of chastity is seen as psychologically and physically repressive; while the vow of obedience is seen to inhibit the true expression of freedom. Indeed, religious life is still considered by some to be wasteful and non-productive. In contrast Ignatius emphasizes the importance of religious vows and the intrinsic value of the gift of a life to God through the making of such vows. Alongside this Ignatius refers to the works of supererogation which are deeds undertaken for others beyond the call of duty. Such deeds may be performed by either married people or religious and are characteristic of the way of life of any individual who values the practice of self-denial.[52]

The vows of obedience, poverty and chastity are vows made to God, which, with divine assistance, may be fulfilled during a lifetime of commitment and service. They are not minor matters to be set aside or withdrawn from in order to enter into another way of life *such as to enter business, to get married and the like.*[53] The religious vows are permanent

---

[51] In 1535 Pope Paul III had appointed a number of expert advisors to consider the serious question of doctrinal and spiritual reform. "In response to the Pope's formal order, this group drafted one of the most extraordinary official documents that we possess concerning the state of the Church on the eve of the Council of Trent (from the end of 1536 to the beginning of 1537), the document is known to historians as 'The Council of the Cardinals and Other Prelates Concerning the Reform to be Implemented in the Church etc.'" [*Consilium delectorum cardinalium et aliorum praelatorum de emendanda Ecclesia, etc.*] edited for the first time in Rome by Blado in 1538. The experts very quickly seized upon what they considered the most baleful abuse: the promotion of ignorant and totally unworthy men to holy orders. From this practice innumerable scandals and suspicion of the ecclesiastic state resulted as well as a certain distrust of any religious sect. ...The *consilium* was particularly severe regarding the regular priests, and the council's criticism explains Ignatius' hesitation, or even repugnance, and that of his companions to form themselves into a religious order. "Many regular priests," declared the experts, "are so corrupt that they really scandalize the laity and gravely hurt the Church by their example." They even proposed that conventual orders be suppressed little by little. We should note, however, that the experts were far from opposing the clerical state itself, and that they recognized implicitly that there still existed religious who remained faithful to their vows." André Ravier, S.J., *Ignatius of Loyola and The Founding of the Society of Jesus*, trans. Maura Daly, Joan Daly and Carson Daly (San Francisco: Ignatius Press, 1987), 38–40.

[52] The practice of self-denial, mortification or self-abnegation is a key discipline evident within the Christian tradition and notably present within the Church during periods of renewal and reform. It is interesting to see that some practice of self-denial is a component of the way of life of many of the new Ecclesial Movements within the Church.

[53] Fifth Rule, *Spiritual Exercise* 357. It is strange that Ignatius should equate getting married [a state of life] with entering business [simply an activity and not a state of life]. The thrust of the rule is to emphasize the importance of religious vows which are permanent commitments, and not to be set aside or withdrawn from.

commitments which orient, and refine, a life and need to be esteemed as such.[54]

The Sixth, Seventh and Eighth Rules— Devotions and Discipline

These three rules refer to a varied set of devotions and disciplines practiced during the time of Ignatius. Many of these are timeless and continue in the same form today such as the practice of *lighting of candles in churches*,[55] noted in the Sixth Rule. Others have seen a development over time as devotions, which of their very nature are designed to assist people through more tangible ways to open their hearts to God. Clearly there were cultural factors at work within the sixteenth century that are no longer operative in the twenty-first century. It is striking, however, to see how many of these practices still remain even if less widespread than in Ignatius' own day.

The *veneration of relics*[56] still exists. The enormous numbers of people who wished to see and venerate the relics of St. Thérèse of Lisieux when they made their way through different parts of the world in 2002 and 2009 testify to this. *Praying to the saints*[57] also remains a popular devotion for many, not least praying to St. Anthony when belongings have gone astray.[58] In addition such a practice underlines the importance of the communion of saints and the oneness of the Church militant (temporal) and triumphant (in heaven). *Visits to Stational Churches*[59] still take place in

---

[54] Within our contemporary context there is a culturally pervasive view which states that young people do not want to make permanent commitments. Contrary evidence indicates that young people do rise to the challenge of permanent commitment. They reject the lukewarm or the mediocre or the apologetic but they embrace with enthusiasm what speaks to their hearts and minds. They can recognize authentic goodness and truth and find it attractive. They seek a deep relationship with God.

[55] Sixth Rule, *Spiritual Exercises* 358.

[56] Ibid.

[57] Ibid.

[58] Many saints are considered to have a special patronage so those with eye problems would pray to St. Lucy, issues to do with the throat would be addressed to St. Blaise etc.

[59] Ibid. In the time of Ignatius certain churches were designated as Stational Churches because they would on occasion be the venue for a stational liturgy. Such a liturgy was "a particular kind of worship service. Its essential elements are four. First, this form of worship always took place under the leadership of the bishop of a city or his representative. Second, this form of liturgy was mobile: it did not always take place at the same church but was celebrated in different sanctuaries or shrines. Third, the choice of church or shrine depended on the feast, fast, or commemoration being celebrated. Fourth, the stational liturgy was *the* urban liturgical celebration of the day." John F. Baldovin, S.J., *The Urban Character of Christian Worship: The Origins, Development, and Meaning of Stational Liturgy*, Orientalia Christiana Analecta, ed. Robert Taft, S.J., no. 228 (Rome: Pont. Institutum Studiorum Orientalium, 1987), 367.

some countries during the season of Lent while *indulgences*[60] *for jubilees*[61] were promulgated by the Church for the Jubilee year of 2000 and for the Year of St. Paul 2008–9. *Indulgences for Crusades*[62] are clearly a thing of the past!

The Seventh Rule takes us into the area of Church discipline. Here, Ignatius emphasizes the importance of an ascetical dimension to life. *We should praise precepts of fast and abstinence, for example in Lent, on ember days,*[63] *vigils, Fridays and Saturdays; also penances, not just interior but also exterior.*[64] In every Christian life the practice of self-denial helps to dislodge our self-centered focus and assist our growth in love for God and other human beings. Periods of fast and abstinence[65] were part of the liturgical year. Lent was the major period for fasting and abstinence, but other days, particularly Friday in commemoration of the death of the Lord, were also observed.

In the twenty-first century the days suggested for fasting and abstinence have been drastically reduced, but the practice is still maintained and even gaining greater prominence. In 2009, Pope Benedict XVI's Pastoral Letter for Lent was focused upon the importance of fasting. "Fasting represents an important ascetical practice, a spiritual arm to do battle against every possible disordered attachment to ourselves. Freely chosen detachment from the pleasure of food and other material goods helps the disciple of

---

[60] Indulgences were based on the conception of the love and mercy of God. An indulgence is an extra-sacramental remission of the temporal punishment due to sin, the guilt of which has been forgiven. This remission is granted by the Church in the exercise of her ministry through the application of the merits of Christ and the saints and for some just or reasonable motive. In the Bull "*Exsurge Domine*" June 15, 1520, Leo X condemned Martin Luther's assertions that "Indulgences are pious frauds of the faithful," and that "Indulgences do not avail those who really gain them for the remission of the penalty due to actual sin in the sight of God" (Enchiridion 75S, 759). The Council of Trent (Session XXV, December 3–4, 1563) declared: "Since the power of granting indulgences has been given to the Church by Christ and since the Church from the earliest times has made use of this Divinely given power, the holy Synod teaches and ordains that the use of indulgences, as most salutary to Christians and as approved by the authority of the councils, shall be retained in the Church; and it further pronounces anathema against those who either declare that indulgences are useless or deny that the Church has the power to grant them." (Enchiridion 989).

[61] Sixth Rule, *Spiritual Exercises* 358.

[62] Ibid.

[63] Ember days (corruption from Lat. *Quatuor Tempora*, four times) are the days at the beginning of the seasons ordered by the Church as days of fast and abstinence. They were definitely arranged and prescribed for the entire Church by Pope Gregory VII (1073–85) for the Wednesday, Friday, and Saturday after 13 December (S. Lucy), after Ash Wednesday, after Whitsunday, and after September 14 (Exaltation of the Cross). The purpose of their introduction, besides the general one intended by all prayer and fasting, was to thank God for the gifts of nature, to teach men to make use of them in moderation, and to assist the needy. Ember days are no longer part of the Church's liturgical life.

[64] Seventh Rule, *Spiritual Exercises* 359.

[65] Abstinence is a practice of not eating any meat on the prescribed day of abstinence.

Christ to control the appetites of nature, weakened by original sin, whose negative effects impact the entire human person."[66]

It is important to note that the practice of fasting has nothing to do with the contemporary passion for "dieting"![67] Rather "Denying material food, which nourishes our body, nurtures an interior disposition to listen to Christ and be fed by His saving word. Through fasting and praying, we allow Him to come and satisfy the deepest hunger that we experience in the depths of our being: the hunger and thirst for God."[68]

The final injunction of this rule—that we should praise *penances not only interior but also exterior*[69]—again focuses on the confrontation with the Reformers. In asserting that we are justified by faith in God alone and not by works, the Reformers had denied the validity of penance, insisting that no action of an individual could in any way affect the relationship between God and human persons. No human action could change the mind or action of God. The practice of penance however, was not, and indeed is not, about trying to "win God over" but rather is about changing the individual. Penance, or self-denial, might perhaps best be seen as a "gesture" indicative of that desire of the heart to follow the leading of the Lord, to be more attuned to the movement of the Spirit, to be open to the love of the Father. It was part of the grounded nature of Ignatius that he praised both interior and exterior penance. Interior penance could be notional or ethereal, exterior penance rooted the desire in concrete reality.

The notion of penance, self-denial, or mortification is deemed narcissistic by contemporary society. It is associated with "cult movies,"[70] in which a warped form of corporal mortification is presented. The reality of penance, as the Church has traditionally understood it, focuses more on the little things of everyday life than on major feats. A form of penance can be as simple as being willing to smile at someone you meet even though you are tired and don't feel in the least like smiling. It may be denying oneself a small item while accompanying the action by a prayer for someone else. In practice it is acting against our human tendency to be self-absorbed and it can assist an opening out to others and, of course, to God. In this way then we: "mortify our egoism and open our heart to love of God and neighbor, the first and greatest Commandment of the new Law and compendium of

---

[66] Benedict XVI, Message of His Holiness Benedict XVI for Lent 2009.
[67] Ibid. "In our own day, fasting seems to have lost something of its spiritual meaning, and has taken on, in a culture characterized by the search for material well-being, a therapeutic value for the care of one's body. Fasting certainly brings benefits to physical well-being, but for believers, it is, in the first place, a 'therapy' to heal all that prevents them from conformity to the will of God."
[68] Ibid.
[69] Seventh Rule, *Spiritual Exercises* 359.
[70] For example *The Da Vinci Code*, a book written by Dan Brown published in 2003 and made into a film in 2006. One of the key characters is Silas, an albino Catholic monk, who is seen to carry out excessive practices using the cilice and the discipline.

the entire Gospel (cf. Mt. 22.34–40)."[71] It is also to become aware that by the graciousness of God any loving act of this nature may be taken up and used in the mystery of God's redeeming work for the life of the world.

The Eighth Rule addresses directly the iconoclastic actions of the Reformers.[72] The latter's assertion was that Church buildings and decorations should be of the most austere to combat the possibility of idolatry. In their zeal for this austerity they had attacked many Church buildings, damaging exterior edifices, 'beheading' statutes, and destroying paintings. By contrast Ignatius asserted that *we ought to praise church buildings and their decorations; also statues and paintings.*[73] At the same time Ignatius took the opportunity to emphasize that it was not these things 'in themselves' that were important to praise and esteem, but *what they represent.*[74]—the action of God in the lives of his saints.

The Reformers saw veneration of such things as idolatry. For example the veneration of a statue of Mary was seen as a form of "Marian worship." This was clearly idolatry since only God should be worshipped. For Ignatius this rule was also a teaching moment. He was able to remind his readers that veneration was the true attitude towards these things, *veneration according to what they represent.*[75] The image of Mary or the statue of a saint in itself as a work of art was not worthy of veneration but the representation of Mary or the statue of the saint could remind the individual believer of the reality of the life of Mary or the particular saint and their relationship with God which caused them to become renowned, and it is this reality that is worthy of veneration. Even in our contemporary twenty-first century Church life this important corrective can be helpful. Such clarity also assists ecumenical relations between the different Christian traditions.

The Ninth Rule—A Positive Attitude to Church Teaching

The Ninth Rule may be seen as a summary of a number of the preceding rules. Again, we see that Ignatius encourages a positive attitude towards the precepts of the Church. This is to be the primary disposition. Thereafter, he

---

[71] Kolvenbach, S.J., op. cit.

[72] An example of Iconoclastic action is the desecration of the Lady Chapel in Ely Cathedral, England. The Lady Chapel is dedicated to the Blessed Virgin Mary, and is the largest of its kind attached to a British cathedral. The chapel once boasted richly carved and painted walls and the finest medieval stained glass windows, with statues adorning every niche, all of which were destroyed or damaged at the Reformation in 1539. The Reformers even went so far as to smash the heads and faces off the tiny statues in the quite detailed medieval wall carvings—only the bodies now remain.

[73] Eighth Rule, *Spiritual Exercises* 360.

[74] Ibid.

[75] Ibid.

suggests an active searching for *reasons for defending*[76] these precepts; and finally reasons for not *attacking them in any way*.[77] Here we have a process clearly outlined: beginning from a positive attitude of reception; moving through a searching for reasons to defend a particular Church teaching; and finally reasons not to attack a particular Church teaching.[78]. The reaction to Church teaching and the action that may flow from this depends to a significant extent upon the attitude towards the authority issuing such teaching. Ignatius puts before us the importance of a positive stance of reception; followed by a search for reasons to defend such teaching; and then reasons not to attack such teaching. In the twenty-first century as in the sixteenth, such a stance is influential upon the way in which Church teaching is received. It is important to reiterate that the attitude of *praise* that Ignatius advocates is in contrast to the tendency to attack and ridicule which he deplores.[79]

The Tenth Rule—A Positive Attitude to Church Authority[80]

The logic of Ignatius' thought moves from emphasizing the importance of our attitude to Church teaching to the importance of our attitude to Church authority. Here the same principle applies as in the Ninth Rule. Our habitual attitude is to be a positive one *more inclined to approve and praise*[81] not only the various teaching and recommendations that superiors might make,

---

[76] Ibid.

[77] Ibid. Clearly what is important here is a basic positive disposition towards Church precepts and teaching as opposed to an attitude of suspicion or cynicism regarding Church precepts and teaching. As Superior General Ignatius was involved with four popes: Paul III (October 1534–November 1549), Julius III (February 1550–March 1555), Marcellus II (April 10–30, 1555), and Paul IV (May 1555–August 1559). "Four popes—and what different temperaments and attitudes they had regarding Ignatius and the Society of Jesus! As far as Ignatius was concerned, these difficulties had little importance for his attitude to the Church." Ravier, S.J., *Ignatius of Loyola and the Founding of The Society of Jesus*, 42.

[78] Perhaps a contentious twentieth century example might illustrate the process; it is one that I have sometimes used with students. I ask them if they think that in 1968 Pope Paul VI deliberately thought how he might make life most difficult for married couples and then issued the Encyclical letter *Humanae Vitae*. Generally students react in astonishment and say of course not. They would identify the Holy Father as a good and holy man. But then when we begin to look at some of the reaction to this encyclical letter they see how some of the attacks made on the document and on the Pope appear to identify with the absurd suggestion that I had put before them.

[79] Cf. Kolvenbach, S.J., op. cit.

[80] George Ganss makes the point that "*Mayores* here means our superiors, as the Vulgate translates it; i.e. the officials or authorities both ecclesiastical and civil." Ganss, S.J., *The Spiritual Exercises of Saint Ignatius*, 199.

[81] *Spiritual Exercises* 362.

but also the very *conduct* of superiors. In this rule Ignatius is not being naïve nor deliberately averting his eyes from the reality of sinful human nature and the consequences of this in human action—even of superiors. He is well aware that, in the Church, there are people in authority whose conduct leaves much to be desired and *in some cases their acts are not or were not praiseworthy.*[82] The sixteenth century and the twenty-first century share a common reality here. His response to this is to indicate that in such a case it is unprofitable to make public denouncements *either by preaching in public or by conversing among the ordinary people.*[83] Our twenty-first century counterparts with regard to publicizing issues would be through utilizing television, newspaper interviews, Facebook, Twitter, and the Internet.

The reason for his reluctance to enter into the public realm Ignatius cites as being the cause of unprofitable public *scandal* and the possibility of a public backlash that would not address any particular situation. Instead of adopting these means Ignatius suggests the way forward is to approach those *who can bring about a remedy* for the bad conduct that has been identified. There is a clear logic here. If something needs to be addressed with regard to a particular superior, it is better to speak about the matter privately with those who would be able to address the matter with that superior and resolve the situation, rather than to arouse a public scandal which can only be detrimental for the Church as a whole and will not necessarily address and resolve the original problem.

This rule brings into focus the question of public accountability that has been a crucial question arising in the twenty-first century Church. An objection that might be raised is that Ignatius' passion for the Church and in particular his support for authority, (exemplified most of all in his attitude towards the Pope where significantly he gives unquestioned support for the Pope), is to ignore situations that have caused discouragement and despair. In the twenty-first century this may be identified with very serious issues of physical or sexual abuse of the vulnerable. Clearly these situations, as Pope Benedict XVI stated, "can never be sufficiently deplored" and indeed "the Church herself suffers as a consequence of infidelity on the part of some of her ministers."[84]

The wisdom of this rule is perhaps to stress that although abuse of authority and bad conduct have occurred on occasion, this does not in itself undermine the legitimate and honorable exercise of authority that does exist within the Church. Also, that in the majority of cases resolving such breaches of conduct is more likely to be successful in private conversations with those who can address the issue than in a public campaign of defamation.

---

[82] Ibid.

[83] Ibid.

[84] Pope Benedict XVI, "Letter of His Holiness Pope Benedict XVI Proclaiming a Year for Priests on the 150th anniversary of the 'Dies Natalis' of the Curé of Ars," June 16, 2009.

Nevertheless, it may be that it is appropriate that a scandalous situation be made public if there is no other way to correct it. The twenty-first century has witnessed such serious issues with regard to the sexual abuse of children by clergy.[85] "Ignatius believed that if our love for Christ, inseparable from love and solidarity for the Church, his Spouse, prompts us, after a prayerful discernment, to speak out, the result will always be [ultimately] constructive."[86] The way Ignatius frames this rule is that such occasions will be exceptional rather than common occurrences. This rule emphasizes that the general attitude to Church authority should be a positive one. When there is clear evidence of unbecoming conduct, the normal manner of dealing with this will be in a private not public manner, with the assistance of others who can deal effectively with the situation. At the heart of this particular rule is the clear belief that the Spirit of Christ continues to be at work within the Church and within those who hold office therein. It is this belief that sustains the vitality of the relationships between individuals and office holders even when the reality of the cross seems most evident within these relationships.

The Eleventh Rule—The Importance of A Comprehensive Theology

In this rule we see Ignatius indirectly owning his indebtedness to his own theological education.[87] Within the context of the sixteenth century many

---

[85] One of the most comprehensive studies of clerical sexual abuse was undertaken in the United States by the John Jay College of Criminal Justice, commissioned by the United States Bishops Review Board and published February 27, 2011 under the title: *The Nature and Scope of the Problem of Sexual Abuse of minors by Catholic Priests and Deacons in the United States*. It indicated that in the period 1950–2002, 4,392 clergy (4 percent of all active clergy) were accused of abuse, of these 929 were priests in religious orders. They were accused of abusing 10,667 minors and 75 percent of all incidents occurred between 1960 and 1984. Of the remaining 96 percent of all active clergy who were not involved in abuse the report makes no mention.

[86] Kolvenbach, S.J., op. cit.

[87] Ignatius received his education after his conversion first in Barcelona in 1524, where a certain Jeroni Ardèvol taught him free of charge; then in 1526 at the university of Alcalá he seems to have been a private student as his name exists on no surviving university list. In Alcalá, after a series of three encounters with the Inquisition after which he was exonerated from any charge of heresy, he made a brief stay in Salamanca and then set out for Paris arriving February 1528. Here he began classes in the humanities (here meaning the study of Latin, where he was repeating some of his study at Barcelona) at Montaigu, which was known as a college of strict discipline (Erasmus and Calvin also studied here). Later Ignatius moved to the College of Ste Barbe for the Arts course which comprised: grammar, dialectics, geometry, cosmology, literature and philosophy."The usual period of study in arts was three and one half years, known as a 'course.' This was almost always followed by an intial trial regency, often in grammar, of one and one half year. The whole five-year sequence was known

Humanists and Reformers were reacting against scholastic theology.[88] Instead they were looking to Scripture, sometimes taken alone with the cry of *sola scriptura* or sometimes in conjunction with the work of the Church Fathers. In this way a polarization had arisen between scholastic and positive theology. Ignatius sought to overcome this polarization, seeing the good in both and the complementary manner in which they aided pastoral effectiveness.

Thus, in this rule Ignatius advocates that *we ought to praise both positive theology and scholastic theology.*[89] He saw that it was important to present doctrine in such a way that it brought people close to *God our Lord in all things*. This is still the pastoral thrust of theology. It is true that Ignatius has more to say about scholastic theology with St. Thomas Aquinas[90] and St. Bonaventure[91] as key exemplars. He saw that by using the discipline of logic these doctors were able to *define and explain for our times the matters necessary for salvation.*[92] This seeming preference for scholastic theology[93]

---

as the *quinquennium* and was the normal period of study and regency required of each student before he assumed direction of another's studies. If the student passed the first examination, the *determination*, he received the baccalaureate in arts. The second examination, conducted either by the chancellor of the University or by the chancellor of the Faculty of Arts, entitled the bachelor to the license (*licentia docendi*). The solemn reception by the Faculty took place in a ceremony called the *inceptio*, an inaugural lecture in which the student officially became a Master of Arts. ... After acquiring the M.A. a man who wished to pursue the doctorate in theology had to undergo thirteen to fifteen additional years of study, teaching, academic disputation, and residence in the Faculty of Theology. [Here] both the Bible and the *Sentences* of Peter Lombard formed the core of this long curriculum." James K Farge, *Orthodoxy and Reform in Early Reformation France: The Faculty of Theology of Paris, 1500–1543* (Leiden: Brill, 1985), 12, 13. This work also gives an interesting insight into cases of heterodoxy during this period and the engagement of the university authorities with the work of both Erasmus and Luther. The proximity of these processes (1523–9) to the time of Ignatius' own studies indicates the likelihood of his awareness of the university's concerns with both the humanism of Erasmus and the Protestantism of Luther. Ibid. 163–208.

[88] Cf. footnote 3.

[89] Eleventh Rule, *Spiritual Exercises* 363.

[90] St. Thomas Aquinas, 1225–74, Doctor of the Church. A prolific Dominican theologian who also taught at the University of Paris. He was perhaps best known for his *Summa Theologia*. Pope Leo XIII in August 1879 in *Aeterni Patris*, On the Restoration of Christian Philosophy stated that Thomas's theology was a definitive exposition of Catholic doctrine. Thus, he directed the clergy to take the teachings of Thomas as the basis of their theological positions. Leo XIII also decreed that all Catholic seminaries and universities must teach Thomas's doctrines, and where Thomas did not speak on a topic, the teachers were "urged to teach conclusions that were reconcilable with his thinking." In 1880, St. Thomas Aquinas was declared patron of all Catholic educational establishments.

[91] St. Bonaventure 1221–74, Doctor of the Church. A prolific Franciscan theologian who taught at the University of Paris. His most notable theological work was his commentary on the *Sentences* of Peter Abelard.

[92] Ibid.

[93] Marjorie O'Rourke Boyle, "Angels Black and White: Loyola's Spiritual Discernment in Historical Perspective," *Theological Studies* 44 (1983): 241–57 argues that "At the Cardoner Ignatius had experienced a great clarity in his understanding and the dynamic of his spirituality tended ever toward discernment and enlightenment."

may have been in part because scholastic theology in the sixteenth century, particularly in Paris, was under siege from attacks by the Reformers.[94] In addition the clarity of thought of the scholastics was very attractive. At the same time it could be argued that the positive doctors exemplified by St. Augustine,[95] St. Jerome[96] and St. Gregory[97] were more akin to Ignatius' position and his concern to activate the affective dimension of persons, alongside intellectual understanding.[98]

The characteristic of positive theology was the ability *to stir up our affections towards loving and serving God our Lord in all things.*[99] This was at the heart of the ministry of the *Spiritual Exercises.* It seems that for Ignatius there was a certain blending together of positive and scholastic theology that covered the interrelationship that our contemporary times would identify as speculative, pastoral and spiritual theology. Such a judicious blend was in order to serve the purpose of making *profitable use of the councils, canons and decrees of our Holy Mother Church.*[100]

---

[94] The primary criticisms of scholastic theology by the reformers were that it was too abstract and not sufficiently biblically based. Clearly the latter charge could not be brought against Aquinas' *Summa Theologia* but his theological method of question and answer was disputed. In addition there was a focus amongst the Reformers upon the accessibility of the scriptures in the vernacular.

[95] St. Augustine 354–430, Doctor of the Church and Bishop. Perhaps his most famous works are the *Confessions* and *The City of God.* He was a great defender of the Church against the heresies prevalent in his time.

[96] St. Jerome c. 340–420. From 386 he led a life of great asceticism and study first in Rome and then in Palestine. He died in Bethlehem in 420. He is perhaps best known for his translation of the Bible and his many commentaries on the different books of the Bible. He also contributed theological and historical works.

[97] St,Gregory the Great, c. 540–604, Doctor of the Church. He was a monk who became Abbot, and from 590–604 was Pope. His canonization by popular acclaim followed at once on his death. He is perhaps best known for his *Dialogues* and for the fact that his theological writings in their synthesis of the work of the Fathers became the textbook of the Middle Ages.

[98] There was a link here to the "humanist understanding of human nature, of what knowledge should be. Instead of localizing knowledge in the intellect, the humanist understood it as a total experience involving the feelings, penetrating the heart, shaping the will, and stimulating the whole person to some active response. Knowledge in this conception, had to be subjectively appropriated in order to constitute, as we might say 'really' knowing. ... A further consequence of this view of knowledge was a disposition among humanists to accept contradiction and paradox as a source of insight." Bouwsma, "The Spirituality of Renaissance Humanism." 238. In more recent times, the intellectual search for truth illumined by Gospel contemplation and integrating the mystery of faith and reason was the focus of attention both for Pope Benedict XVI and also for his predecessor Pope John Paul II who wrote: "Faith and reason are like two wings on which the human spirit rises to the contemplation of truth; and God has placed in the human heart a desire to know the truth—in a word, to know himself—so that, by knowing and loving God, men and women may also come to the fullness of truth about themselves." Pope John Paul II, *Fides et Ratio, Encyclical Letter to the Bishops of the Catholic Church on the Relationship between Faith and Reason,* September 14, 1998, 1.

[99] Eleventh Rule, ibid.

[100] Ibid.

The Twelfth Rule—Comparisons Are Odious

In this rule Ignatius warns against the danger of making comparisons. All comparison is detrimental to someone, at the very least because each person is absolutely unique. It follows that each person has a unique relationship with God. To suggest that we ourselves, or others, are greater than one of the saints – for example more knowledgeable than St. Augustine or excelling St. Paul in goodness and holiness—is *no small error*.[101] It may be wishful thinking but it is also clearly unprofitable! The focus of attention with regard to the saints is to desire to benefit from their intercession and to be encouraged by their example of holiness rather than to seek to surpass them.[102]

The Thirteenth Rule–A Controversial Principle

Of all the Rules for Thinking with the Church, this Thirteenth Rule is probably the one most well known. Over many generations scholars have cited this particular rule either in praise of Ignatius or with contempt. It certainly expresses one of Ignatius' deepest convictions and, as I will indicate, it would have been a conventional belief of the sixteenth century. Ignatius states, *to keep ourselves right in all things, we ought to hold fast to this principle*.[103] He is clearly indicating that what follows is a core principle that he believes will assist authentic living. *What "seems" to me to be white, I will believe to be black if the hierarchical Church thus determines it.*[104] This startling statement comes as a severe affront to the twenty-first century mindset. It seems to fly in the face of all reason and science.

If we look more closely at the context of the sixteenth century we can plumb the depths of this statement more clearly. The wording of this principle may seem emphatic but the doctrinal implications would have

---

[101] Twelfh Rule, *Spiritual Exercises* 364.

[102] This has a direct relation to Ignatius' own life. In his autobiography, regarding his early days of practicing a rudimentary form of discernment he states: "In reading the Life of our Lord and the Lives of the Saints, he paused to think and reason with himself. 'Suppose that I should do what St. Francis did, what St. Dominic did?'" He thus let his thoughts run over many things that seemed good to him, always putting before himself things that were difficult and important which seemed to him easy to accomplish when he proposed them. But all his thought was to tell himself, "St. Dominic did this, therefore, I must do it. St. Francis did this; therefore, I must do it." "Autobiography of St. Ignatius Loyola," [46] in *Saint Ignatius of Loyola: Personal Writings*, trans. with intro. and notes by Joseph Munitiz, S.J. and Philip Endean, S.J. (London: Penguin Classics, 1996), 15, [7].

[103] Thirteenth Rule, *Spiritual Exercises* 365.

[104] Ibid.

been those commonly accepted in the sixteenth century. Indeed, the rule did not come under attack in Ignatius' own time but only in later generations.[105] Definitions of the Church were conceded by all to contradict, in certain cases, the evidence of the senses. The most significant example is when the real body and blood of Christ are defined as present in the Eucharist in what appears to be bread and wine. Indeed, when we celebrate the Eucharist in our contemporary times, this same principle is operative. We acknowledge the Eucharist as the greatest sign of God's love. In this sacrament we see the bread and wine but we believe with the Church that it is the body and blood of Christ. In this way we have already entered into the disposition of this Thirteenth Rule.

Ignatius was convinced that every good impulse, whether personal or ecclesial, derived from the same undivided Spirit of truth.[106] Ignatius is aware of the *seeming* opposition between the freedom of the Spirit at work within the individual and the obedience appropriate in the Church but he

---

[105] The wording is similar to a statement made by the humanist Erasmus who said that white would not be black, even though the Pope were to decide so. He added that of course he realized that the Pope would never do so. Scholars have dissected these comments and have noted that while Erasmus speaks of the substance of black and white, Ignatius speaks of the color of something, which for philosophers of that time was only an "accident" and not about the "substance" of the object. Ignatius was very careful. The fact is that, although the terms of the statements are very similar and somewhat traditional in philosophical and theological discussions, the points the two authors were making are diametrically opposed. Erasmus states that something that is in fact black does not become white, even if, [per impossible] the Pope should so declare it; he is certain that the Pope would not make such a mistake. Ignatius looks not so much to the correctness of the statement which he assumes, but to the disposition of soul. Cf. Robert Blackley Drummond, *Erasmus: His Life and Character As Shown in His Correspondence and Works,* Vol. 2 (London: Smith, Elder & Co., 1873), 242. However, the main defence of the Ignatian statement is made by stressing the verb "seems."

[106] We have already referenced this conviction of Ignatius when exploring the first of these rules. In addition Michael Buckley states: "Categorically, to bring into play a Rahnerian distinction, the Spirit governs through the hierarchical authorities, the prophets, preachers, confessors, and teachers in the Church, through commandments and precepts, through sacraments and Scripture and Tradition, through all of those external means which build up the Body of Christ. Transcendentally, the Spirit guides and governs by the change in human subjectivity, especially through the charity or love of friendship that draws and transforms into unity all human affectivity. The love which moves me and makes me choose such a thing should come down from above (*de arriba*), from the love of God in such a fashion that the one who chooses should feel (*sienta*) first in himself that love which he has, greater or less, for the thing which he chooses, is solely for the sake of His Creator and Lord" [*Exercises* 184]. "It is in this way that the 'Divine Majesty puts order in her desires and so changes her first affection that the reason for desiring and holding one or the other of these things shall be solely the service, honor, and glory of His Divine Majesty.' This experience of love transforms human affectivity and gives human choice/election its direction. It is the greater love that puts order into the lesser loves. And this is itself the effect of the Spirit of God within the human person." Buckley, S.J., "Ecclesial Mysticism in the *Spiritual Exercises* of Ignatius," [459–60].

does not see them as irreconcilable, rather he underlines the one spirit[107] by whom both are informed. *For it is by the same Spirit and Lord of ours who gave the Ten Commandments that our Holy Mother Church is guided and governed.*[108]

Here we might note the bringing together once more of reference to the hierarchical Church at the beginning of the rule, with the image of the Church as "mother" and "spouse" echoing the intimate union we considered in the First Rule. Ignatius' intention is also similar to that of the First Rule to underline the importance of the disposition of soul. A good Catholic, according to Ignatius, will accept a clear definition of the Church even if he or she would be inclined on his or her own, to a different opinion. Such a "good Catholic" would do so as they trusted that the Spirit of Christ continued to work within the Church guiding and governing in truth.

Ignatius formulated this rule in an uncompromising form, but it is also important to note that the rule is short on specifics. This rule is more an indication of a disposition of soul than a practical instrument for theological discourse. Rather it is an appeal to an interior disposition that is able to recognize that "Our holy Mother the Church is the source of life." Accordingly "our attitude toward it is that of faith which enables us to see beyond the immediate with a heart-centered sensitivity to what is true and light."[109] It is this interior disposition and this sensitivity that will be the guiding light in all practical and specific circumstances. Again this is the work of the Holy Spirit, which unites the person with God; gives guidance through the interior law of charity and discernment; and unites the individual with the exercise of governance.[110]

---

[107] Michael Buckley states: "'The same Spirit that guides and governs us' gives the key to the nature of this experience of the Spirit within the *Exercises*. For that by which the Church is united with Christ and that by which the Church is generated and governed now realizes itself within the depths of the exercitant: the Spirit of God. This government and guidance lies at the heart of the Ignatian Exercises. It can also be found in critically important moments in the explicit assertions of the Constitutions. There, union with the Spirit of the Lord is habitually seen in terms of guidance and governance. [Cf. *Constitutions*, Preamble (134); 2.3 (219); 4.10 (414); 7.2 (624); 8.6 (700, 701). So much does the guidance of the Holy Spirit and discretion come out of charity that Ignatius can say in very difficult cases that 'the charity and discretion of the Holy Spirit will indicate the manner that ought to be used.' (219). In other places, he unites them through the phrase '*discreta caritas*']." Buckley, S.J., "Ecclesial Mysticism in the *Spiritual Exercises* of Ignatius," [459].

[108] Thirteenth Rule, *Spiritual Exercises* 365.

[109] Kolvenbach, S.J., op. cit.

[110] The Holy Spirit guides human beings especially through "writing and imprinting the interior law of charity" within them. [*Constitutions*, Preamble (134)], but this same charity or love of friendship is that by which the person is principally united with God [*Constitutions* 10 (813)]. Guidance and union proceed from the same source, the Holy Spirit." Buckley, S.J., "Ecclesial Mysticism in the *Spiritual Exercises* of Ignatius," [459].

The Fourteenth Rule—The Importance of Caution and Clarity

The next four rules focus on the way in which we should talk about faith and doctrine and here Ignatius encourages the use of discrete prudence. Indeed, he suggests we should be reserved in the manner in which we promulgate certain delicate points of teaching. In particular the Fourteenth Rule focuses on the question of predestination. First Ignatius makes a positive statement affirming the reality of predestination and the importance of faith and grace.[111] The question of predestination was one that much exercised the Reformers along with the understanding that faith and not works justify us and that divine grace is the only reality of salvation.[112] There were significant issues contained in these statements which Ignatius takes up in the following rule. Ignatius advises in the Fourteenth Rule that we acknowledge the truth and importance of these doctrines. He follows

---

[111] It is here that the Council of Trent offered a way forward by acknowledging the reality of predestination but not seeing this as an obstacle to the working of grace and the gift of faith. For a detailed consideration of Trent see John O'Malley, S.J., *Trent and All That: Renaming Catholicism in the Early Modern Era* (Cambridge, MA: Harvard University Press, 2000).

[112] Of central importance at the time of the Reformation was the distinction between *fides informis* and *fides formata*. Unformed faith was faith not formed by love and able to coexist with mortal sin. Formed faith was faith formed by and active in love (*fides caritate formata*). The concepts of formed and unformed faith came under direct attack in the Reformation. Rom. 4.9 was interpreted in conjunction with 1 Cor. 3.12–15 and 1 Cor. 13.13 in order to prove that the faith that saved was a faith active in works of love. The distinction between formed and unformed faith rested on a crucial distinction, made by medieval theologians, between the justice of Christ and the justice of God. The justice of Christ was granted in baptism and renewed in the sacrament of penance. This grace both pardoned sin and gradually transformed sinners so that they might be pleasing to God. The Christian was a *viator* ('pilgrim') traveling from the justice of Christ to the final justice of God. Only by cooperating with grace could the Christian do the meritorious works that enabled him to stand before God. To meet the demands of God's final justice, the justice of Christ had to be completed by the righteousness of the believer. ... Only faith formed by love could justify the sinner. In his study of Romans 1.17 Luther discovered the "righteousness of God" was not the righteousness by which God punished sinners but that by which he made the sinner righteous. This exegetical discovery led Luther to believe that the justice of Christ and the justice of God were granted simultaneously. Most importantly, the sinner was justified by faith alone as the life of Abraham and Paul's letters to the Romans and the Galatians made abundantly clear. The doctrine of justification by faith alone required Luther and his fellow reformers to define the nature of this justifying faith and to distinguish it from the scholastic formulations. Throughout the many sixteenth-century polemics, Catholic theologians challenged this conception of faith. Tridentine theologians both rejected justification by faith alone and condemned any notion that faith included the absolute or final certainty of salvation. The decrees of the sixth session of the Council of Trent (1547) made clear that justification included both the remission of sins and the sanctification or inner renewal of the human being. "[It] also explained that only the faith that works through love could justify the sinner. Therefore, faith cooperating with grace in good works increases the justice received through Christ." Susan E. Schreiner, *The Oxford Encyclopedia of the Reformation*, Vol. II, article on "faith" (Oxford: University Press, 1996).

such affirmation immediately with a prudent note that *nevertheless great caution is necessary in our manner of speaking and teaching about all these matters.*[113]

The delicacy that Ignatius advocates is because certain doctrines may easily be misinterpreted by those with little knowledge of theology, and significant anxiety might be aroused in good people. The twenty-first century merits a similar safeguard. Though the level of education is significantly far more advanced, the level of knowledge of faith and doctrine is not of a comparable standard. Ignatius in effect is reminding the reader of the rules that it is important to take the measure of those to whom one speaks, and to be careful in what one says and teaches. The admonition is timeless.

The Fifteenth Rule—Prudent Clarification When Necessary

In this rule Ignatius amplifies his concern with regard to the particular doctrine of predestination. He indicates that *we ought not to fall into a habit of speaking much about predestination.*[114] Nevertheless, if the topic comes up it needs to be dealt with in a way that does not lead people into *error.* In simple form, predestination focuses on the relationship between God and creation. The Reformers' doctrine of predestination, taken from John Calvin, stressed that before creation God determined the fate of the universe throughout all time and space. At the same time Calvin applied this also to salvation. This resulted in the belief that God appointed the eternal destiny of some to salvation by grace, while others were to receive eternal damnation for all their sins. Uncertainty surrounded who might be in which category.[115]

Clearly such a doctrine could produce a variety of reactions. One of these is highlighted in this rule, namely, a malaise of apathy that could arise

---

[113] Fourteenth Rule, *Spiritual Exercises* 366.

[114] Fifteenth Rule, *Spiritual Exercises* 367.

[115] The actual doctrine is much more complex than stated above. Predestination in its broadest meaning is every Divine decree by which God, owing to his infallible prescience of the future, has appointed and ordained from eternity all events occurring in time, especially those which directly proceed from or at least are influenced by human free will. Theology restricts the term to those Divine decrees which have reference to the supernatural end of rational beings, especially human beings. Considering that we do not know all human beings reach their supernatural end in heaven but that some may be eternally lost through their own fault, there must exist a two-fold predestination: (a) one to heaven for those who die in a state of grace; (b) one to the pains of hell for all those who depart in sin or under God's displeasure. According to current use, however, it is more accurate to call the second option Divine "reprobation" so that the term "predestination" is reserved for the Divine decree of happiness of the elect.

as people say: "Whether I am to be saved or damned is already determined and this cannot now be changed by my doing good or evil."[116] The concern of Ignatius was that such an attitude could result in individuals ceasing to apply themselves to good works and growth in virtue. This doctrine also underlined the Reformers' claim that good works were useless[117] as it was only by faith, which is a gift of God, that anyone is justified.

In our contemporary times the spirit of fatalism can breed a similar lethargy. One with a fatalistic attitude can see the whole of life as prede-termined by fate, thus an individual's own actions whether good or bad have no determinative influence on life. Without the evangelical belief of the Reformers, this attitude can produce similar results in terms of apathy. There is an ongoing need for prudent clarification in every generation. Although each one of us has been chosen by grace we are expected to co-operate in our spiritual growth through our consistent choice of what is good.

The Sixteenth Rule—The Importance of Discreet Encouragement

A key principle for the Reformers was the understanding of "justification by faith" alone. This meant that human beings are justified in God's eyes by faith in Christ, which is a gift of God. There is no way in which human persons merit such a gift of grace and no way in which they can earn it, since the grace of God is utterly gratuitous. Here, as in the previous two rules, Ignatius is looking to a balanced approach which will provide discrete encouragement.

Faith is certainly important and to be acknowledged as a gift of God. Too great a focus on faith alone, however, can lead persons to neglect the importance of good works which further the work of faith. Ignatius speaks of it as making people lazy.[118] By contrast the Church calls human persons to be aware that it is not enough just to believe, and to have faith. The Lord

---

[116] Fifteenth Rule, *Spiritual Exercises* 367.

[117] Also note Luther's comments in his preface to his *Commentary on Romans,* where he states, "It is impossible that faith ever stops doing good. Faith doesn't ask whether good works are to be done, but, before it is asked, it has done them. It is always active. Faith is a living, unshakeable confidence in God's grace; it is so certain, that someone would die a thousand times for it. This kind of trust in and knowledge of God's grace makes a person joyful, confident, and happy with regard to God and all creatures. This is what the Holy Spirit does by faith. Through faith, a person will do good to everyone without coercion, willingly and happily; he will serve everyone, suffer everything for the love and praise of God, who has shown him such grace." Martin Luther, preface to the *Commentary on Romans.*

[118] Such "laziness" would arise from a sense of fatalism, such that individuals might argue—since I am unable to change my eternal destiny I should make the most of my present life

calls us to actions to express that faith; actions on behalf of others as we realize we belong to a community of faith. So both faith and good works are important and able to be seasoned with the grace of true charity.[119]

The Seventeenth Rule—The Intricacies of Grace

Always conscious of endeavoring to maintain a balanced teaching, Ignatius in this rule emphasizes the prudence necessary in dealing with the subject of grace and free will.[120] In no way is Ignatius trying to underplay the

---

enjoying that to the full for I do not know what the future may hold but that it has been predetermined already so there is nothing I can do to change it by my actions good or bad.

[119] Here Ignatius stresses again the importance of good works on behalf of others, not just in recognition of the communal dimension of our membership of the Church but also because "charity" of its very nature as we have already seen in terms of the inter-relationship with faith and good works is outgoing in actions that bring good to others.

[120] In the controversy over grace and free will Erasmus and Luther were drawn into a significant engagement. "Erasmus at first affirmed much in Luther, but increasingly objected to his 'extremism and rough manners.' The years 1517 and 1520 brought serious estrangements. The humanist followers of Luther wished Erasmus on their side, especially Melanchthon, who remained an ardent admirer of Erasmus all his life. But Luther's three fighting challenges to authority, as it existed in the Europe of his day, the *Address to the German Nobility, The Babylonian Captivity of the Church* and *The Liberty of a Christian*, brought the breach with Rome. In the same year a Roman Bull, *Exsurge Domine* (1520), chastised Luther. He answered with the *Assertions,* which among other things, denied free will. Erasmus hated to be drawn into this controversy. The new Pope Adrian VI, an old school friend of Erasmus, was genuinely interested in reform and wanted to see Erasmus do something, even come to Rome. Erasmus tried to shield his 'neutrality' by suggesting both ill health and his favorite idea of a truce. A jury of independent scholars (including himself) ought to be able to settle the commotion with due reason. Luther, from the other side, sarcastically counseled Erasmus not to get involved and to disturb his love of peace. Erasmus replied to him that he greatly feared Satan's power might be deluding Luther. Finally, responding to both outward prodding and inner conviction ('At least I cannot be accused of abandoning the Gospel to the passions of men') Erasmus wrote in one sitting his *Diatribe sui collation de libero arbitrio,* a classic treatise against Luther. It appeared September 1, 1524 in Basel. The Pope, the Emperor, and Henry VIII (who himself had received the title 'Defender of Faith' for writing against Luther 1521), congratulated Erasmus. The world considered the little book a beautifully written and ingenious tract. The issue was joined. ... Luther finished his four-times-longer answer, *De servo arbitrio* (December 1525). The answer was as unsystematic as Erasmus' piece, but powerful in its conviction and denial of the freedom of the will. Erasmus was stung. His peace was gone. Luther must be answered. The resulting two lengthy volumes, *Hyperaspistes Diatribae adversus servum arbitrium M. Lutheri* (1526, 1527), are more careful than his earlier work. Luther is castigated as the destroyer of civil, religious, and cultural order and harmony. In a sense Erasmus offers a detailed explanation of Christian Humanism and humanistic theology, as he conceived both. But not even his conciliatory and pacific *On Restoring Concord in the Church* (1533), concluding with the admonition 'tolerate each other,' was able to bridge the enmity. His common sense and uncomplicated tolerance could not satisfy the committed seeker

primacy of divine grace. He emphasizes that it is important to teach this but to do so only with a clear sense of the leading of the Spirit and with the motivation *for the greater praise of the Divine Majesty*.[121] Ignatius saw a discerned motivation for any such conversation or teaching as crucial for the troubled times in which he lived. For it was vital that Church teaching on the importance of the human response to God, in terms of free will and good works, should be upheld as important and not seen to be *impaired*, or *thought worthless*.[122] All is grace and the Lord has also, by grace, granted human persons free will to respond to grace.

In the light of these last four rules we might consider the particular responsibilities of twenty-first century theologians. There is both the responsibility of research within the field of individual expertise and a responsibility towards the Church with regard to the promulgation of Church doctrines. It is important that there be a living and healthy tension between these two responsibilities with due accountability. "The caution is that our speech, even critical, is to be informed by faithful love for what God has done and is doing at the heart of the Church. Then we are more likely to present a balanced and impartial teaching."[123] When there is a true love

---

for truth. The conflict raged. ... Luther's part in the debate is the emphasis on Christianity as dogmatic religion. He wants to solve the issue theologically. For Erasmus Christianity is morality, a simplicity of life and doctrine. He wants to resolve the problem philosophically. In current terminology, Erasmus displays an anthropological concern, but employs essentially theological tools, without being or ever wanting to be a theologian. Luther fashions his own theological tools, without much interest in systematic structure. Erasmus has deep pastoral concern. Luther desires the truth to shine forth and the whole church to accept his witness to a personal commitment. The two protagonists became symbolic for two camps, unable to meet. Erasmus defines free will: "By freedom of the will we understand in this connection the power of the human will whereby man can apply to or turn away from that which leads unto eternal salvation." Luther says that man is unable to do anything but continue to sin, except for God's grace. The whole work of man's salvation, first to last, is God's. Both proceed from different vantage points. Luther's solution is 'faith alone sets us free.'... Erasmus tries to skirt the difficulties that Luther's problematic mind discovers in much of the Church's age old interpretation of this Christian paradox." Ernst F. Winter, "Introduction" in *Discourse on Free Will*, D. Erasmus and Martin Luther; "Milestones of Thought," in *The History of Ideas*, eds F. W. Strothmann and Frederick W. Locke (New York: Frederick Ungar Publishing Co. Inc., 1961), viii–xi.

[121] *Spiritual Exercises* 369, Cf. *Constitutions* and note *Ad Deus Maior Gloriam*—for the greater glory of God a key imperative of the Society of Jesus.

[122] Ibid.

[123] Kolvenbach, S.J., op. cit. Cf. "As for theologians, by virtue of their own proper charisms, they have the responsibility of participating in the building up of Christ's Body in unity and truth. Their contribution is needed more than ever, for evangelization on a world scale requires the efforts of the whole People of God [Cf. John Paul II, Post-synodal Apost. Exhort. *Christifideles Laici*, nn. 32–55: AAS 81 (1989): 451–9]. If it happens that they encounter difficulties due to the character of their research, they should seek their solution in trustful dialogue with the Pastors, in the spirit of truth and charity which is that of the communion of the Church." Congregation for the Doctrine of the Faith, *Instruction on the Ecclesial Vocation of the Theologian*, 1990, [40].

for the Church then the responsibilities of research and the responsibility of accountability to the Church are not in conflict. If theologians are truly grounded in love for the Church, as Ignatius advocates, then pertinent private critical points may be raised in full fidelity. There is a difference here between a disposition that is critical and constantly speaks criticism and a disposition of love for the Church which can perceive, and on occasion offer, a perceptive critical perspective.[124]

Some reflection on the above rules might prove fruitful for theologians. Ignatius was concerned that people not be led astray into doctrinal error. "For Ignatius, a genuine attitude towards the Church militant requires us not only to praise what God is doing in his Church but to speak out as the occasion demands as members of that Church."[125] As members of the Church, it is not enough to applaud the way God works in and through the Church, but it is also important to speak out as members of the Church in causes advocated by the Church.

---

[124] "The living Magisterium of the Church and theology, while having different gifts and functions, ultimately have the same goal: preserving the People of God in the truth which sets free and thereby making them 'a light to the nations.' This service to the ecclesial community brings the theologian and the Magisterium into a reciprocal relationship. ... There should never be a diminishment of that fundamental openness loyally to accept the teaching of the Magisterium as is fitting for every believer by reason of the obedience of faith. The theologian will strive then to understand this teaching in its contents, arguments, and purposes. This will mean an intense and patient reflection on his part and a readiness, if need be, to revise his own opinions and examine the objections which his colleagues might offer him. If despite a loyal effort on the theologian's part, the difficulties persist, the theologian has the duty to make known to the Magisterial authorities the problems raised by the teaching in itself, in the arguments proposed to justify it, or even in the manner in which it is presented. He should do this in an evangelical spirit and with a profound desire to resolve the difficulties. His objections could then contribute to real progress and provide a stimulus to the Magisterium to propose the teaching of the Church in greater depth and with a clearer presentation of the arguments. In cases like these, the theologian should avoid turning to the 'mass media,' but have recourse to the responsible authority, for it is not by seeking to exert the pressure of public opinion that one contributes to the clarification of doctrinal issues and renders service to the truth. It can also happen that at the conclusion of a serious study, undertaken with the desire to heed the Magisterium's teaching without hesitation, the theologian's difficulty remains because the arguments to the contrary seem more persuasive to him. Faced with a proposition to which he feels he cannot give his intellectual assent, the theologian nevertheless has the duty to remain open to a deeper examination of the question. For a loyal spirit, animated by love for the Church, such a situation can certainly prove a difficult trial. It can be a call to suffer for the truth, in silence and prayer, but with the certainty, that if the truth really is at stake, it will ultimately prevail." Congregation for the Doctrine of the Faith, *Instruction on the Ecclesial Vocation of the Theologian*, 1990, [21, 29–31].

[125] Kolvenbach, S.J., op. cit.

The Eighteenth Rule—A Paean of Praise and Filial Fear[126]

Lest there be confusion, Ignatius begins this rule with a clear affirmation of the importance of love. At the same time Ignatius wishes to stress the importance also of fear of the Lord which the psalmist says is the beginning of wisdom,[127] *we should also strongly praise fear of the Divine Majesty.*[128] Talk of fear as praiseworthy is alien to twenty-first century minds but would not have been contentious in a sixteenth century context. Ignatius delineates two types of fear, which he then considers. There is a *filial fear* that is a sense of reverence, awe and wonder at the graciousness of God, the kind of reverence a child might have for a parent. Alongside this, Ignatius raises the importance of *servile fear*, which he sees as instrumental not only in helping conversion from sin but also in making further spiritual progress.

The love of God is a doctrine widely promulgated and acceptable but a focus on the fear of God raises many psychological objections. Nevertheless Ignatius points to a very human reality. Most people have occasions in their lives when they are less than human in their response to God and others. At these times it may be that a lesser motive, namely, the fear of God, might be more conducive to maintaining a Christian outlook and prompt a return to that filial fear which is *wholly acceptable and pleasing to God our Lord, since it is inseparably united with love of him.*[129] This last rule for thinking with the Church echoes the theme of the Contemplation to Attain the Love of God[130] at the end of the *Spiritual Exercises*. Above all we are to value service that is offered to God out of pure love. It is in this way of service out of love that we live in relationship with the Son of God. We come to recognize our own sinfulness and yet know that we are called to be a brother or sister of Christ, a child of God. "This state lived in the Spirit helps us to keep in balance contradictory realities like love and fear and just and sinner, the lights and shadows of the Church."[131]

I have endeavored to show in this chapter that the object of these rules, namely—*sentire cum ecclesia*—to think, judge and feel with the Church—is as relevant to the contemporary Church as it was in the time of Ignatius. Far from being a set of prescriptive rules that oppress, they form a series of guidelines that free the individual in three ways. They free the person *from* becoming enmeshed in negativity that would undermine individual and communal faith. They free the person *for* the possibility of resolving

---

[126] Terence P. Reilly contributes the article on *temor* in *Diccionario de espiritualidad ignaciana*.
[127] "The fear of the Lord is the beginning of wisdom," Prov. 9.10.
[128] Eighteenth Rule, *Spiritual Exercises* 370.
[129] Ibid.
[130] *Spiritual Exercises* 230–7.
[131] Kolvenbach, S.J., op. cit.

issues that arise, particularly with regard to the exercise of authority, thus enabling widespread service in the mission of the Church by prudent teaching. Finally they free the person *to* grow in love for the Church in union with Christ for the greater praise and service of God. This intimate love forms the heart of the relationship with Christ and the Church and is a central focus of the *Spiritual Exercises* to which we now turn our attention.

The Texts Surrounding the Text

Though the Rules for Thinking with the Church come at the end of the Spiritual Exercises I presented in the previous chapter that they are integral to the text of the Exercises. This chapter will consider the place of these Church within the Exercises. In addition, there are other texts surrounding the text of the Rules that are relevant for our consideration of Ignatius' understanding of the Church and the ecclesial dimension that informed his relationship with the Church. In particular, we shall consider important references in the Constitutions of the Society of Jesus, in the Reminiscences or 'Autobiography', and in his correspondence. Before we look at these important documents, however, we shall explore the text of Ignatius' own life by considering relevant sections of his Autobiography and relevant interactions with authority during his time of study. Our aim throughout is to consider Ignatius' own developing ecclesial disposition.

The Text of Ignatius' Life

It is important to review not just the written articulation of Ignatius' understanding of the Church and its crucial for our dealings with regard to the first of the individual believer, but also to trace in his own life the practice of the principles he puts before readers in the Rules for Thinking, Judging and Feeling with the Church. These principles coalesce in a certain disposition that ignores mutability with regard to the Church, a disposition that is manifested also in his other writings.

An early event from the Autobiography serves some to pal insight. After the year that he spent in Manresa where he formulated the first draft of the Spiritual Exercises, Ignatius set out for the Holy Land. He arrived there in

2

The Texts Surrounding the Text

Though the Rules for Thinking with the Church come at the end of the *Spiritual Exercises*, I asserted in the previous chapter that they are integral to the text of the *Exercises*. This chapter will consider the place of the Church within the *Exercises*. In addition, there are other texts surrounding the text of the Rules that are relevant for our consideration of Ignatius' understanding of the Church and the ecclesial disposition that informed his relationship with the Church. In particular, we shall consider important references in the *Constitutions of the Society of Jesus*;[1] in the fragment of Ignatius' *Spiritual Diary*;[2] and in his correspondence. Before we look at these important documents however, we shall explore the text of Ignatius' own life by considering relevant sections of his *Autobiography*,[3] and relevant interactions with authority during his time of study. Our aim throughout is to consider Ignatius' own developing ecclesial disposition.

The Text of Ignatius' Life

It is important to review not just the written articulation of Ignatius' understanding of the Church and its crucial functioning with regard to the life of the individual believer, but also to trace in his own life the practice of the principles he puts before readers in the Rules for Thinking, Judging and Feeling with the Church. These principles coalesce in a certain disposition that Ignatius maintains with regard to the Church, a disposition that is manifested also in his other writings.

An early event from the *Autobiography* gives some initial insight. After the year that he spent in Manresa where he formulated the first draft of the *Spiritual Exercises*, Ignatius set out for the Holy Land. He arrived there in

---

[1]The edition used throughout the book is *The Constitutions of The Society of Jesus And Their Complementary Norms: A Complete English Translation of the Offical Latin Texts*, ed. John W. Padberg (St Louis: Institute of Jesuit Sources, 1996).
[2]The edition utilized here will be found in *Saint Ignatius of Loyola: Personal Writings*.
[3]Ibid.

September 1523. He tells us in his autobiography that: "his firm intention was to remain in Jerusalem, continually visiting the holy places; and, in addition to this devotion, he planned to help souls."[4] When he requested permission for this course of action from the Franciscan superior, the Franciscans being the guardians of the Holy places, he was refused. The Franciscan Provincial told him that it was not possible; he would have to leave with the other pilgrims.

Previously the Franciscans had problems relating to the ransoming of pilgrims who had been captured by the Saracens. Ignatius replied that he was firm in his purpose: "and was resolved that on no account would he fail to carry it out."[5] He was convinced that it was God's will for him to stay in Jerusalem. The Provincial responded that he had authority from Rome to excommunicate anyone unwilling to obey him.[6] Ignatius immediately responded that he would obey, he did not need to see the documentation, and he left the following day. In this particular case the voice of authority as Ignatius understood it, overruled Ignatius' own discernment.

Interactions with Authority

Within the *Autobiography* we encounter a number of occasions when Ignatius had interactions with authority for example: in Alcala,[7] in

---

[4] "Autobiography of St. Ignatius Loyola," [46] in ed. Joseph Munitiz S.J. and Philip Endeau S.J., *Saint Ignatius of Loyola: Personal Writings*, trans. with intro and notes London: Penguin Classics, 1996.

[5] Ibid.

[6] "...the Provincial told [Ignatius], using kind words, how he had learned of his good intention of remaining in those holy places, that he had thought a good deal about the matter, and that, from the experience that he had of others, it was his judgment that it would not be appropriate. For many people had had this desire, and then one had been taken prisoner, another had died, and then the order had been left having to ransom the prisoners. [Ignatius] should therefore get ready to go the following day with the other pilgrims. To this [Ignatius'] reply was that he was very firm in this intention, and that in his judgment on no account should he refrain from putting it into practice; politely he made it clear that, although the Provincial did not think it a good idea, he would not abandon his intention on account of any fear unless it was a matter of obliging him under pain of sin. To this the Provincial said that they had authority from the Holy See to make anyone leave there or stay there whom they saw fit, and to be able to excommunicate anyone who was not willing to obey them. And in this case, it was their judgment that he mustn't remain etc. When he wanted to show [Ignatius] the bulls on the strength of which they could excommunicate him, he told them that there was no need to see them: he believed their Reverences, and since this was their judgment, with the authority they had, he would obey them." Ibid. 34–5 [44–7].

[7] In Alcala, Ignatius and his companions accepted various injunctions put upon them by the Inquisition, *viz.*, about the clothing they were to wear, not looking religious, and about not talking or teaching about matters of Christian doctrine until they had studied for at least four years. Cf. ibid. [58], 41.

Salamanca,[8] and in Venice.[9] On each of these occasions we see that honesty, discretion and a concern for decisiveness characterize Ignatius' words and actions.[10] What is evident is that Ignatius has a deferential disposition towards authority and that these events indicate interactions not confrontations. At each point, Ignatius is concerned to be publicly exonerated if public charges have been made, and to receive a testimony to his orthodoxy, in order that there should be no stain of heresy on himself or his companions.

In his early years in Rome, Ignatius also approached Pope Paul III in August 1538 about other trumped up charges that had been made against him and his companions, seeking a formal judgment.[11] He received a favorable hearing: "The Pope, even though he had cause for suspicion reacted favorably to what I told him, praising our talents and the use we made of them for good. He then made us a short exhortation, speaking to us, indeed, as a father and a true shepherd."[12] This concern for concrete papal approval was characteristic of Ignatius' relations with the different Popes he encountered through the rest of his life in Rome. Clearly he was committed to the service of the Church and to the person of the Pope who had the responsibility for the universal Church. At the same time he was concerned that the interactions with the Papacy needed to be based on true factual information about himself and his companions. The culmination of this approach was in November 1538 when Ignatius and the first companions approached the Pope to put themselves at his service for the good of the Church. Thereafter the Pope began to send the companions on mission[13] and, in 1539, the Deliberations of the First Fathers (*Deliberatio*

---

[8] Ibid., [66], 45.

[9] Ibid., [86], 55.

[10] Ibid. "As the pilgrim was on the point of leaving [Venice] he learned that they had accused him before the Inquisitor and brought a case against him. Hearing this, and seeing as they were not summoning him, he went to the Inquisitor and told him what he had heard. He was on the point of leaving for Spain and he had companions: his request was that he should be so kind as to give a verdict. The Inquisitor said that it was true that there was an accusation, but that he didn't see any matter of importance in it. He just wanted to look at his writings on the *Exercises*. On seeing them, he was very complimentary about them, and asked the pilgrim to leave the copy of them with him. So he did; nevertheless, he renewed his insistence that the proceedings be gone ahead with, right up to the verdict. The Inquisitor was making excuses, but he went to his house with a public notary and witnesses for his case, and he got a sealed statement on all this."

[11] "I talked alone with His Holiness in his apartment a whole hour. Then, while speaking at length to him about our designs and intentions, I related clearly how many times judicial proceedings had been taken against me ... I begged His Holiness in the name of all my companions, to have a remedy devised, in order that our doctrine and manner of life should be investigated and examined by whatsoever ordinary judge His Holiness would appoint: for if they found evil, we wanted to be corrected and punished; and if good, that His Holiness should extend his favor to us." Letter to Isabel Roser, December 19, 1538, in Hugo Rahner, S.J., *Saint Ignatius Loyola: Letters to Women* (Edinburgh and London: Nelson, 1960), 272.

[12] Ibid.

[13] "Pressures were brought to bear upon the Pope. Charles V wanted the early companions to go to the Spanish Indies, John III wanted them in the Portuguese Indies, the bishops and

primorum Patrem)[14] led to the decision to establish the Society of Jesus convinced as they were that such a foundation was clearly the leading of the Holy Spirit as they stated:

> God in his mercy graciously willed to assemble and to unite us, although we were weak and strangers to each other by virtue of nationality and mind. It is not up to us to break up that which God has united, but we must rather affirm and stabilize this unity by drawing closer into a single body, each having responsibility and understanding of the other; for courage itself when it is concentrated has more vigor and strength to accomplish all sorts of good but difficult deeds than when it is divided.[15]

---

princes of northern Italy who had witnessed the group's behavior in their first apostolates, wanted them to return to them. It was evident that the group was about to split apart; ... Would this be the end of the beautiful, informal, spiritual friendship which for five, seven and, in certain cases, ten years had gathered them around Christ? Such an important question had arisen, the companions undertook, as was their custom, a general deliberation." Ravier, S.J., *Ignatius of Loyola and The Founding of the Society of Jesus*, 81.

[14] These deliberations began in March 1539 and ended June 24, 1539 and were conducted in the evenings while the diverse ministries occupied the day. "Before the meeting, the point to be discussed would be chosen by the most competent members of the group. During the day, they would ask for divine enlightenment: each one, especially during Mass, would consider carefully and sincerely the pros and cons of each solution. And then they would take their time as generously as circumstances would permit: '*Per multos ... dies*': 'We decided to assemble for a number of days before separating in order to consider together our vocation and our way of life.' For what purpose? 'To arrive more quickly at the end which we had determined in advance for ourselves, and about which we were thinking.'" Ibid., 82. The companions were well aware of their differences in nationality and inclinations yet, "on one point all the companions were unanimous that was 'to seek the perfect will of God as he is pleased to reveal it to us, according to the aims of our vocation'. It was on the question of 'the means of proceeding so that our activities might be freer and more efficacious for us and for those we were serving, that there was a plurality of opinions.' This fact established, 'we desired to find a way of resolving this plurality. By means of care and attention, it was necessary to find a way out of this dead end so that we might offer ourselves as a holocaust for the praise, honor and glory of God, for whom we would give up all that belonged to us.' Such was the atmosphere of the undertaking. A first decision about which all were in agreement was that these deliberations would be above all a sincere and loyal questioning of God. The conditions were first to reinforce their habitual fervor in prayer, penance and meditation; then, to do all we could to succeed; as for the rest, to cast upon the Lord all our thoughts." Ibid., 83.

[15] "And the companions further added: 'In all that we have said and will say, we understand: we will take absolutely nothing from our own minds but will rely only on that, whatever it may be, which God will have inspired and which the apostolic See will confirm and approve.'" Ibid., 84. A further question centered on the importance of obedience: "To the vows of perpetual chastity and poverty which we had uttered under the hands of the papal apostolic nuncio at Venice was it fitting to add a third—that of obeying one of us? ... In order that we might be able with more sincerity and merit, to achieve during all of our lives the will of our Lord God, and to follow the wishes and orders of His Holiness to whom we have freely offered all that is ours: will, intelligence, strength, etc." Ibid., 85. "Finally, with the Lord's help, with unanimity and not a plurality of voices they concluded: 'It is better for us, it is necessary to promise obedience to one of our group.' And this will serve a triple purpose: 'That we might

The Society of Jesus was formally approved in 1540.[16]

The Determining Influence of the Cardoner[17] Experience

From the formative period of his time in Manresa, where his mystical experiences and consolations culminated in the illumination beside the river Cardoner, Ignatius had a renewed appreciation of the Church in the world. It was beside this river as Ignatius sat one day "with his face towards the river, which was running deep below. And as he was seated there, the eyes of his understanding began to be opened." He was enlightened with a singular grace that became known as the Cardoner experience. "Not that he saw some vision, but understanding and knowing many things, spiritual things just as much as matters of faith and learning, and this with an enlightenment so strong that all things seemed new to him." It was not possible to describe all the particular things he understood at that time, "though they were many: only that he received a great clarity in his understanding, such that in the whole course of his life, right up to the sixty-two years he has completed, he does not think, gathering together all the helps he has had from God and all the things he has come to know (even if he joins them all into one), that he has ever attained so much as on that single occasion." The effect of this was that it "left him with the understanding enlightened in so great a way that it seemed to him as if he were a different

---

be able to realize better and in a more exact fashion our primary purpose of accomplishing (by our every action) the will of God; then, that the Society might be more reliably preserved and, finally, so that everything might be correctly provided for whatever might happen to each one—be it temporal or spiritual.' The ministries, the body of the Society, the personal contact of the Superior with each of the members were the three goals to which the ten early Fathers sacrificed the dear, relished, fruitful liberty of the earlier companionship. It was a historic moment." Ibid., 87. Cf. also John Carroll Futrell, S.J., *Making An Apostolic Community of Love: The Role of the Superior according to St. Ignatius of Loyola* (St Louis: Institute of Jesuit Sources, 1970), 222

[16] John Padberg, S.J., "Ignatius, the Popes and Realistic Reverence," *Studies in the Spirituality of the Jesuits*, (May 25, 1993): 1–38 makes the point that two historical factors need to be borne in mind: "Ignatius and the early Society needed the constant support of the Pope, and the popes in turn had in the Society an extraordinary instrument directly at hand for their projects. The Society needed papal protection. It was new and small and utterly surprising in some of its features, so unlike those traditionally associated with religious life. Ignatius wanted the assurance of continuing papal approval, both because he felt the need of a bulwark against the objections that would continue to be raised even after his death and also because he genuinely saw in these papal documents the sign of divine approval. Experiencing this unexpected phenomenon in the Rome of that time, a new body of highly educated, fervent, mobile men who deliberately eschewed place and privilege, the Pope was happy to solidify and protect their structure and work as he made use of them."

[17] The river Cardoner runs through Manresa.

person, and he had another mind, different from that which he had before."[18] It is clear that after the Cardoner illumination Ignatius saw the Church, in Hugo Rahner's words, as "the rule for measuring enthusiasm."[19] The Church is seen as the place of apostolic service. This is why it was inconceivable for Ignatius that anyone should make a choice about a matter that was contrary to Church teaching. For Ignatius a truly authentic choice [election][20] involves coming to a deeper union with Christ, which means also being united with the Church, in her continual struggle against all that undermines the truly human.

These sentiments marked his own life and were part of the practical advice he offered through spiritual direction. So, for example, many years after the illumination beside the Cardoner, Ignatius wrote to the Benedictine nun Teresa Rejadella: "Every internal experience that comes directly from God must be in humble harmony with the prescriptions of the Church and with obedience."[21] He was convinced that the Spirit of God promised by Christ to the disciples and to the early Church was still operative within the Church of his own time, and would continue throughout all time. Love for the Church was for Ignatius, as we have seen, an extension of his love for Christ.

The Origin of the Rules in the *Spiritual Exercises*

The *Spiritual Exercises* make no sense as a book to be read. They are something to be "made." The book itself is primarily a manual for the director, the one who gives the *Spiritual Exercises*, not for the retreatant who makes them. The essence of Ignatian spirituality is a growth in an interior freedom that leads to the service of Christ and his kingdom. The *Spiritual Exercises* are essentially a process of discernment and of a reorientation of an individual's freedom so as to allow them to make an option for the kingdom of Christ. It is a discernment made in the light of Christ's life in order to help a person know and put into practice God's will for him or her. For Ignatius, discernment always involves an ongoing conversion—an option of love; it is the root of Christian commitment and praxis. The *Spiritual Exercises* are meaningful only in the measure that they help

---

[18] *Saint Ignatius of Loyola: Personal Writings*, 27, [30].

[19] Hugo Rahner, *The Spirituality of St. Ignatius Loyola* (Maryland, MD: Newman Press, 1953), 58.

[20] The "election" or Choice of a Way of Life is a key component of the *Spiritual Exercises* and will be considered in more detail later in this chapter.

[21] Ignatius Loyola, letter to Sister Teresa Rejadella, June 18, 1536, cited in Rahner, *The Spirituality of St. Ignatius Loyola*, 58.

Christians grow in the freedom of love. They help the person making them to attain true freedom in God through a process that is structured in weeks and days, preludes and points, examens and repetitions and rules—all with this one aim in view. It is within this dynamic that the Rules for Thinking, Judging, and Feeling with the Church have their place. Indeed, the Church has a vital function in the radical encounter with God that is the heart of the *Exercises*.

Ignatius was always concerned to emphasize the primary freedom and initiative of God in the entire life of faith and grace. It is God's sovereign freedom that calls forth our response of freedom. God "became a human being in order to save the human race."[22] As human persons we are called to respond to God's redemptive work by living that reality in the particular "state or way of life he may call us to in his service."[23] Here we see the empirical nature of Ignatius' thought. He always preferred the concrete to the abstract. We are called to serve the Lord and that life of service is to be lived in union with the Church, the spouse of Christ.[24] Always Ignatius stressed that love is expressed more in deeds than in any words of love. So love of Christ is inextricably linked with love of the Church and must be expressed in acts. "'Loving union with God': these are the last words of the Rules for Thinking with the Church and the final words of the *Spiritual Exercises* themselves. This union cannot be lived independently of the Church."[25]

The Operative Dynamic in the *Spiritual Exercises*

The dynamic at work within the *Spiritual Exercises* involves the free loving invitation of God to an intimate relationship that draws forth a free loving response from human persons. Because this is not an abstract but a concrete reality, that individual human response is located within a community—the Church. It is the Church that is the gift of God to the individual and the place where the human response of service may be made manifest. All this presupposes the action of the human person in freedom. Our desires, however, are often ambiguous. We are not free. We can desire to be free and certainly God wants us to be free. This movement to growth in freedom

---

[22] Ignatius Loyola, *The Spiritual Exercises: A Translation and Commentary*, George E. Ganss, S.J. (Chicago: Loyola University Press, 1992), 102.
[23] Ibid., 135
[24] Ibid., 365
[25] Kolvenbach, S.J., "The Rules for Thinking, Judging, Feeling in The Post-Conciliar Church," 19–27.

is the content of the first week[26] of the *Spiritual Exercises*. During this week there is a striking encounter and dialogue with Christ on the Cross. Entering into this conversation with Christ on the Cross helps to focus both the gratitude and sorrow that true awareness of sin brings.[27]

In the movement into the second week, a growing freedom emerges and the desire to respond to Christ by sharing in his redemptive work. The nature of this service gradually becomes clearer through an ongoing engagement with the mystery of Christ's life in prayer. Here, the Church has a profound importance—for Ignatius a taken-for-granted importance—in the internal structure of the *Spiritual Exercises*. So he indicates in the directive concerning the election or choice of a way of life: "It is necessary that all the things about which we want to make an election be morally indifferent or good in themselves, and that they are on the side of our holy mother, the hierarchical Church and are not bad or opposed to the Church."[28]

Configured to Christ and the Church

The content of the second week of the *Spiritual Exercises* involves a series of contemplations on the life of Christ from his conception and birth through scenes from his active ministry. There are two episodes from Christ's life each day, plus repetitions.[29] In spending this time in prayer the individual is asking for the grace to be drawn into a deeper relationship with Christ—to be, as it were, configured to Christ. And because of the

---

[26] The *Exercises* after a preliminary meditation on the "Principle and Foundation" are divided into four weeks, or periods of time. The first week focuses on the growth in freedom via a consideration of sin and the redemption accomplished in Christ. The second week is a consideration of the life of Christ and includes key meditations assisting the one making the *Exercises* towards a certain choice of a way of life. The third week is a prayerful consideration of the Passion of Christ and the fourth week focuses the resurrection and concludes with the "Contemplation to Attain the Love of God."

[27] "Imagine Christ our Lord present before you upon the cross, and begin to speak with him, asking how it is that though He is the Creator, He has stooped to become man, and to pass from eternal life to death here in time, that thus He might die for our sins. I shall also reflect upon myself and ask: What have I done for Christ? What am I doing for Christ? What ought I to do for Christ? As I behold Christ in this plight, nailed to the cross, I shall ponder upon what presents itself to my mind." *Saint Ignatius of Loyola: Personal Writings*, 296, [53].

[28] Ibid., 316, [170].

[29] For example there is a pairing of the Presentation of the child Jesus in the Temple and the Flight into Egypt. The first prayer period of a day would be the Presentation, the second the Flight into Egypt, the third would be a repetition of a point where the one praying experienced particular consolation or desolation. The fourth period of prayer would be another repetition and finally the fifth period of prayer would be an application of the interior senses to a particular point that had arisen for the one praying through the day. Such a format leads to a deepening experience of prayer.

intimate link between Christ and the Church the individual also becomes, as it were, configured to the Church. In making the *Spiritual Exercises* one becomes: "configured to the Church in its fundamental service and intimate experience of Christ, even more, that one comes to participate in that service and experience."[30] By God's gracious invitation and gift we are enabled to offer all the circumstances of our lives, the activities, joys and sorrows, happiness and suffering to the Lord for the redemptive work of God which continues throughout all time.

In this way, in the one making the *Spiritual Exercises,* the Church realizes through that individual's experience its own radical nature as the beloved of Christ—as spouse of Christ. Also, it is in and through the individual's experience that the Church re-appropriates her mission to be part of the redemptive work of Christ. It is through her individual members that the Church continues to participate in the struggle for human salvation. Thus there is a profound reciprocity between the individual and the Church, as the individual is configured to the Church and the Church realizes more deeply its own reality through the experience of the individual.

The Importance of the Election

The word Church rarely appears in the *Spiritual Exercises.*[31] But crucially it does appear at the focal point of the text namely at the time of the election, and here the Church is clearly identified. Ignatius frames the subject matter for the election within two criteria. First, such subjects must be "either indifferent or good"[32] in themselves. Secondly, such subjects must also "function constructively within our Holy Mother the hierarchical Church."[33] To give added weight to what Ignatius considers to be essential prerequisites for any choice of a state of life, he restates these criteria negatively. The subjects for an election should not be 'bad' as opposed to indifferent or good; nor should they be "opposed to her"[34] [the Church]. No election could be made about something that was contrary to Church teaching, or that would lead to the "absurdity" of leaving the Church.

It is abundantly clear, therefore, that Ignatius is locating the choice of the individual within the redemptive work of Christ that engages the

---

[30] Buckley, S.J., "Ecclesial Mysticism in the *Spiritual Exercises,*" 441–61.
[31] Ibid. "Perhaps fifteen times and initially in a very minor way. Thus the precepts 'of the Church' are four times acknowledged [*Exercises* 18, 42, 229]. Four times the term designates a building of Catholic worship [*Exercises* 88, 355, 358, 360]. Seven times it refers to the community, "independent of buildings and precepts."
[32] Ignatius Loyola, *The Spiritual Exercises: A Translation and Commentary,* 170.
[33] Ibid.
[34] Ibid.

Church. Indeed, it is participation within this mission of the Church that conditions the legitimacy of any choice of a way of life, whether religious, lay, or clerical. Within the *Spiritual Exercises* there is no provision for the 'ecclesially indifferent' and their very structure assumes a commitment to the Church. Already, during the transition from the first week to the second week, in the meditation on "The kingdom of Christ,"[35] that commitment to respond to the call of Christ through a life of service has been proposed to the individual. The underlying presupposition is that it will be service within the Church. In that meditation also, the reality of the struggle that Christ is engaged in with those who oppose his kingdom is identified.

The Struggle of Christ is the Struggle of the Church

The key meditations of the second week of the *Spiritual Exercises* bring into sharp focus the nature of this struggle in which Christ and the Church are engaged. Ignatius saw this struggle at the heart of human history. In the meditation on the Two Standards he gives a graphic description of the standard of Satan. "Imagine the leader of all the enemy, in that great plain of Babylon.[36] He is seated on a throne of fire and smoke, in aspect horrible and terrifying." [37] And he details the different ways in which evil deceives and draws to a dependence on riches, honor and pride leading to "all the other vices."[38] The satanic, the diabolical is the antihuman, the humanly destructive, and this sense of relentless, cosmic struggle re-appropriates

---

[35] The Kingdom of Christ is a meditation made on the transition day between the first and second week involving the call of an earthly king and then more importantly the call of Christ. The grace sought is not to be deaf to the call of Christ "but alert to fulfil His most holy will to the best of my ability." The movement of the prayer is towards an offering of the whole person, "going against their sensuality and their carnal and worldly love." *Saint Ignatius of Loyola: Personal Writings*, 303–4, [91, 97].

[36] The use of "Babylon" as a personification of evil is found, first and foremost, in the Bible itself (Isa. 13.19, 21.1–10; Jer. 51.37; Rev. 18.10–13, 19.2). Beyond this, it is picked up by many of the Church Fathers, particularly Origen, Ambrose, Augustine, and Gregory the Great. For St. Augustine the Babylonian captivity is "our captivity," Israel's deliverance "our deliverance." Jerusalem and Babylon are to be contrasted, the "vision of peace" vs. "confusion." Augustine associates the two cities with two loves—the love of God, or charity, with Jerusalem and the love of the world, cupidity, with Babylon. Drawing on the experience of the captive Hebrews, he argues that one can be a true citizen of Jerusalem even while a captive sojourning in Babylon. Augustine's *City of God* gives further elaboration. *A Dictionary of Biblical Tradition in English Literature*, ed. David Lyle Jeffrey (Grand Rapids, MI: Wm B. Eerdmans, 1992), 69.

[37] *Spiritual Exercises* 140.

[38] Ibid., 142.

within the *Spiritual Exercises* the Pauline understanding of the conflict that lies at the heart of human history.[39]

It is Christ, however, who stands against the "enemy of our human nature" as Ignatius often referred to the devil. In the Two Standards meditation the depiction of Christ is in stark contrast to the depiction of Lucifer. "Consider how Christ our Lord takes his place in that great plain near Jerusalem, in an area which is lowly, beautiful and attractive."[40] The characteristics of Christ are to invite to poverty, as opposed to riches [and especially spiritual poverty]; reproaches and contempt as opposed to honor from the world; and humility as opposed to pride; "then from these three steps they should induce people to all the other virtues."[41]

The *Spiritual Exercises* understand the Church as the community gathered around Christ engaged in this mysterious and fundamental struggle that lies at the heart of human history. This is the intractable conflict between the call of Christ and the influences of the antihuman. The Church, both in Paul's letter to the Ephesians and in the *Spiritual Exercises,* is a community in struggle, indeed, is the *principal agent* in this struggle with the antihuman. This engagement of the Church means that any serious election must assess the contribution that any state of life may make to the Church in this struggle. Accordingly, the election made by an individual is never for or about the individual alone but always the individual within the Church and the contribution of that individual to the struggle in which the Church is engaged.

The Contradiction at the Heart of Human History

Within the twenty-first century we have lost much of the dynamic insight that Ignatius puts before us in these central meditations of the *Spiritual Exercises*. Ignatius came to interpret and to symbolize the profound contradiction that lies central to all human history, not as a struggle between social or even religious forces, but between impersonal forces as our society might interpret this contradiction today. He saw it primarily as a battle between persons and even communities. This enormous and continual struggle in history is not between human beings but about human beings and the very

---

[39] Eph. 6.11–18.

[40] *Spiritual Exercises* 144. The contrast with the base of Lucifer's operations is strongly marked here and evocative once more of the contrast between Babylon and Jerusalem noted above.

[41] Ibid., 146. The contrast of virtues and vices are clearly outlined in this depiction of the different strategies of the rival groups. Again Ignatius underlines the serious nature of this battle within the heart of all human persons of the human versus the antihuman.

destiny of human life. Fundamentally it is a struggle of the human versus the antihuman and the battle field is the human heart.

Through the election the individual is drawn into a union with Christ in a life that struggles against the "enemy of our human nature"—acknowledging that the definitive victory of redemption has been won by Christ. At the same time, Christ's redemptive work continues in our world in and through the Church. The Church makes known the saving grace of Christ and calls her members to share in the struggle against all that seeks to undermine human relationship with God.

Ignatius' insistence that the diabolical is the antihuman[42] leads to a radical critique of culture. If the Church is to be true to itself in any culture it will be on the alert, not beguiled into an inauthentic peace. In any sound election the individual comes to participate in the Church's struggle. Such participation unites the individual to the Church and because the Church is configured to Christ, so the individual is united to Christ in his redemptive work. In this way the struggles of men and women against all that dehumanizes carries forward the mission of the Church. They embody this radical commitment of the Church to its mission, as this understanding of the Church clarifies the election and thus the purpose of the *Spiritual Exercises*.

The Cutting edge of the Triple Colloquy

This understanding of human life and the urgent religious impetus to enter into Christ's struggle for the soul of the world is alien to a twenty-first century, more domesticated Christianity. For our contemporary culture there is little or no sense of the Church in conflict with the enemy of our human nature.[43] The primary focus of Christians within the North Western hemisphere in recent years appeared to be upon individual religious experience as a means of security and the provision of a consoling affective life. Even our theological interpretation of the Church according to the different models of herald, servant, mystery, people of God or hierarchical institution, does not generally include the understanding of a Church in struggle.

The contrast with Ignatius' understanding could not be more dramatic. He saw an inherent struggle within each human person between two contradictory vocations, one a call from Christ to salvation and the other a

---

[42] The very title of this meditation cites "Lucifer, the deadly enemy of our human nature," *Spiritual Exercises* 136.

[43] The "enemy of our human nature" is not a term generally utilized in contemporary Church culture. This does not mean there is not an awareness of the destructive power of evil. There is perhaps a greater focus on parts of the world where there is clear anti-Christian and anti-Catholic sentiment which expresses itself in violence against Christians and particularly Roman Catholics. The persecution of Christians by ISIS would be a classic expression of this.

call to destruction. The meditation on the Two Standards clearly illustrates this understanding. The calls are to two contradictory communities, one the community of the Church surrounding Christ and the other to a community that would undermine all that is truly human. A choice is set before the individual and, though this call into conflict may be a source of scandal to some, a choice must be made—not to choose is to choose!

Against this subtext of a Church in struggle Ignatius proposes a crucial prayer for enlightenment, asking for the grace of knowledge of the deceptions of the enemy of our human nature in order to reject them and knowledge of the way Christ is calling in order to follow him more closely.[44] This prayer is, indeed, the cutting edge for ongoing conversion to the call of Christ. It is the prayer of the Triple Colloquy. [45] The importance of this prayer is emphasized by its solemn, even ritualistic nature, made first to Our Lady, then to Christ and finally to the Father.

Ignatius invites us to behold our lives in the world through the lens of this prayer. It is a constant learning process. The prayer is an expression of that desire to see the way in which we are deceived by the enemy of our human nature in order to resist such deceits. It is also a desire to see the way in which the Lord leads in order to be more intimately united with him. It is to see the way in which our deeper and more subtle attachments induce us to cling to what is familiar and safe "always looking on, quieting your imagination, being sensible, marking time, being sage before the risks of deciding, fearful of creativity."[46] By contrast the divine initiative often moves the individual and the Church beyond rationality, into areas of the mission which do not always fit with human prudence. It is not that the divine initiative calls us to a course of action that is less than rational. Rather, divine prudence is infinitely creative and can enable the fulfillment of the mission far beyond what human beings initially considered themselves capable of undertaking. How often in our own experience have we accomplished

---

[44] The Triple Colloquy is the culmination of this meditation on the two standards of Christ and Lucifer and so important are the graces that Ignatius encourages the exercitant to ask for that he suggests the continued use of this colloquy during the key meditations of the Three Classes of Men and also the Three Kinds of Humility and the remaining periods of prayer of this second week.

[45] "A Colloquy should be made with Our Lady. I beg her to obtain for me grace from her Son and Lord that I may be received under his standard; and first, in the most perfect spiritual poverty; and also, if his Divine Majesty should be served and if he should wish to choose me for it, to no less a degree of actual poverty; and second, in bearing reproaches and injuries, that through them I may imitate him more, if only I can do this without sin on anyone's part and without displeasure to the Divine Majesty. Then I will say a Hail Mary. A Second Colloquy will be to ask the same grace from the Son, that he may obtain it for me from the Father. Then I will say the Soul of Christ. A third colloquy will be to ask the same grace from the Father, that he may grant it to me. Then I will say an Our Father." *Spiritual Exercises* 155.

[46] Joseph Veale, S.J., "St. Ignatius Asks, 'Are you sure you know who I am?'" *Studies in the Spirituality of the Jesuits* 33/4 (September 2001): 1–38.

things with prayer and reliance on the Lord that we knew to be far beyond our own sense of our capabilities?[47]

Purification and the Passion

The prayer of the Triple Colloquy is vital since the experience of the *Exercises* helps the individual to see the many subtle variations there are in personal "riches" and "honors." Virtually anything, which is not God, can become riches. We need always to be on the alert. "The more the enterprise is selfless, idealistic, and noble, inescapably what justice or truth demands, the more it needs scrutiny, needs the scrutiny of the Spirit."[48] There is, therefore, an ongoing need for purification,[49] not just of reason and will and desire, but also of the very spirit of a human person. Such purification is vital not just for the individual, but so that the body of Christ, the Church, might be healthy also. The wellbeing of the Church, and the truth and integrity of her living, depends on the way in which individual members are faithfully living in Christ.[50]

The Triple Colloquy is a prayer that asks for the individual to be drawn, at an ever deeper level, into the experience of Christ. We are actually praying to enter into Christ's work and his way. This prayer is also expressing a willingness to enter into the consequences of walking in this way. During the third week contemplations on the Passion of Christ,[51] these consequences become clearer. And in the fourth week contemplations on the Resurrection,[52] it becomes evident that the way of Christ is always through death to resurrection. The *Exercises* when well made lead to a greater freedom. "You cannot be more free than to choose what is more according to the mind of Christ."[53] And always the final hermeneutic is the Cross without which there can be no Resurrection.

---

[47] Such awareness leading to a greater dependence upon God would also be the experience of the saints. Here St. Therese of Lisieux is a classic example when she considers herself as a child in the arms of her father. 'I tell you that it is enough to recognize one's own nothingness and to abandon one's self like a child in the arms of God our Father." St. Therese of Lisieux, *Autobiography of a Soul* (New York: Doubleday, 2001).

[48] Joseph Veale S.J. Ignatius Asks, "Are You Sure You Know Who I am?".

[49] The spiritual tradition makes clear that any growth in holiness requires a purification of mind and heart. Here the emphasis is on a deeper purification even of the very spirit of the person.

[50] Cf. *instrumenta conjuncta cum Deo* [cf. *Constitutions* 813].

[51] The third week consists of a series of contemplations from the Last Supper through the events of the Passion and death of Jesus up to his burial.

[52] The fourth week consists of a series of contemplations of the appearances of the resurrected Jesus up to and including the Ascencion.

[53] Veale, S.J., op. cit.

Union of Christ and the Church

This emphasis on struggle and conflict may give rise to an image of the Church as an army, and certainly as we have seen this has scriptural resonance in Paul's letter to the Ephesians. This is not, however, the primary image of the Church in the *Spiritual Exercises*. Rather, as we explored when examining the Rules for Thinking, Judging, and Feeling with the Church, the primary images for Ignatius are the intimate ones of "spouse" and "mother." These are both feminine nouns and unitive metaphors. As "Spouse" the Church embodies a union with Christ and as "Mother" the Church embodies a union among all believers. So we have the nuptial mysticism of loving union present through the image of "Spouse" and the fruitfulness of this in the use of the image of "Mother." In addition, there is the humble loving service which the Church's "children" are to espouse. In this way we may see continuity between a "mysticism of union" and a "mysticism of service."[54]

Accordingly, for Ignatius the whole life of the individual—in whatever state that may be: religious, lay or clerical[55]—and all activity are within the life of the Church which Christ has made his spouse. This is the reason why there is a call to a union amongst believers in terms of doctrinal orthodoxy and ecclesiastical obedience. If the Church is spouse and mother, then the disposition of mind of the individual will always be "a spirit open and prompt to obey in all things."[56] For the Spirit of God, which unites the Church with Christ and is the guiding force in the way the Church is governed, is the same Spirit operative in the heart of the individual making the *Spiritual Exercises*.

---

[54] De Guibert, *The Jesuits: Their Spiritual Doctrine and Practice,* 50. De Guibert distinguished Ignatius' "mysticism of service" from a "mysticism of union" because Ignatius made no reference to the "spiritual marriage" or "transforming union" *per se*. Rather Ignatius focused on the humble and loving attitude of a servant before the Divine Persons. The very fact that he did not consider the Rules for Thinking, Judging, and Feeling with the Church in any detail I am suggesting raises a distinctive possibility of uniting these two distinct forms of mysticism both with one another and more significantly with the institutional Church.

[55] These were the three states envisaged by Ignatius, we find the same three states depicted in Hans Urs von Balthasar, *The Christian State of Life,* trans. Mary Frances McCarthy (San Francisco: Ignatius Press, 1983). There is no indication given of a single "state". A single person for Balthasar—and possibly also for Ignatius—is a person on the way to discovering the state to which they have been called either to marriage, religious life or the priesthood. Both Ignatius and Balthasar envisage that the majority of people would be married.

[56] *Spiritual Exercises* 91. The presumption is of a loving obedience due to a spouse or a mother that would prompt a loving desire to obey.

Union in Guidance and Governance

The union of guidance and governance lies at the heart of the *Exercises*. Within the depth of this union is the life-giving consoling Spirit of Christ, expressly mentioned in the fourth week of the *Spiritual Exercises* as the one who is the source of consolation during contemplations on the Resurrection.[57] This gift of consolation lies also at the heart of the guidance and governance that the Spirit brings to the individual through the Church. Here, the Spirit guides through the various hierarchical authorities in the Church, through Sacraments and Scripture and Tradition.[58] In addition the Spirit guides by the change effected within human subjectivity. In particular, through a deepening love and friendship with Christ that transforms an individual's affectivity. The effect upon the human person is that the guiding presence of the greater love of the Spirit at work interiorly within the person brings order to the lesser external loves.

Accordingly, from the very beginning of the *Spiritual Exercises,* this fundamental experience of the loving guidance of the Spirit is operative, gradually transforming the human person from within. The fifteenth annotation[59] makes this clear when it speaks of the embrace in which Christ holds the soul of the person; and insists that this is the primary and pivotal experience fundamental to the *Spiritual Exercises*. It is this intimate and immediate communion in love that Ignatius seeks to preserve by warning the director of the *Spiritual Exercises* to be careful not to compromise this relationship by undue interference. This relationship is also the way in which the human person is configured to the Church in the Church's relationship to Christ.[60]

In a Nutshell

Within the *Spiritual Exercises,* the hierarchical or institutional Church is more than merely a context within which the human person comes to

---

[57] This is the "office of consoler" which Christ our Lord carries out.

[58] Detailed consideration was given to the guidance and governance work of the Spirit in consideration of the Rules for Thinking, Judging, and Feeling with the Church in the previous chapter.

[59] "... During these Spiritual Exercises when a person is seeking God's will, it is more appropriate and far better that the Creator and Lord himself should communicate himself to the devout soul, embracing it in love and praise, and disposing it for the way which will enable the soul to serve him better in the future. Accordingly, the one giving the Exercises ought not to lean or incline in either direction but rather, while standing by like the pointer of a scale in equilibrium, to allow the Creator to deal immediately with the creature and the creature with its Creator and Lord." *Spiritual Exercises* 15.

[60] "The soul participates in the mystical union marked between the Church, this concrete community of disciples, and Christ." Buckley, S.J., "Ecclesial Mysticism."

experience God. The very relationship between Christ and the Church becomes the paradigm for the individual's relationship with Christ and the embodiment within which that relationship is realized. "In a very real way, the Church realizes again its relationship to Christ in the exercitant's relationship to Christ; in a very real way, the exercitant comes to participate in the mission and the fundamental experience of the Church."[61]

It is in the light of the Church that the individual comes to experience the intimacy and intensity of the love of Christ and becomes aware of the guidance of the Holy Spirit in life. It is in the light of the Church also that the individual comes to understand and appreciate the election by which there may be a participation in serving Christ's kingdom, which stands against all that is antihuman. Finally, there is within the *Spiritual Exercises* a mysticism of service within the Church, united with Christ in the struggle. This is inextricably linked with a mysticism of loving union with the Trinity, in and through Christ, since the redemptive work of Christ is a divine mission with which all persons of the Trinity are engaged.

Thus in the "Contemplation for Attaining the Love of God,"[62] we become united in love and grace with the Lord. And we recognize that this same Lord is always bringing his redemptive work to fruition through all created things. As we share in the relationship between Christ and the Church we are brought to a deeper union with God. We are also drawn into a more profound participation in and personal embodiment of the mission of the Church. This gift of God's love and grace is consistently given to the Church across all generations. It is a gift that abides within the Church despite any sinfulness on the part of her individual members.[63]

---

[61] Buckley, S.J., ibid.

[62] *Spiritual Exercises* 230–7. The focus of this contemplation is that love ought to manifest itself by deeds rather than words and that love consists in a mutual sharing of goods. Thus as the one making the *Exercises* contemplates the way in which God gives all of creation, human gifts, and the gift of redemption in Christ they are drawn to respond with an entire gift of self in the *Summa Suscipe* which states: "Take Lord, and receive all my liberty, my memory, my understanding, and my entire will, all that I have and possess. Thou hast given all to me. To Thee, O Lord, I return it. All is Thine, dispose of it wholly according to Thy will. Give me Thy love and Thy grace, for this is sufficient for me."

[63] It is this gift which enabled the Conciliar Fathers at Vatican II to state that "The Church, whose mystery is set forth by this sacred Council, is held, as a matter of faith, to be unfailingly holy. This is because Christ ... joined her to himself as his body and endowed her with the gift of the Holy Spirit for the glory of God." This holiness, however, exists alongside the reality of a sinful church always in need of reform, composed of members who are called to constant conversion. "Therefore all in the Church, whether they belong to the hierarchy or are cared for by it, are called to holiness." "Lumen Gentium 39," *Vatican Council II: The Conciliar and Post Conciliar Documents*, ed. Austin Flannery, O.P. (Dublin: Dominican Publications, 1992), 396.

The *Constitutions*

The Spirit of God operative in guidance and governance is also found in important moments in the *Constitutions of the Society of Jesus*. Indeed, here, union with the Spirit of God is almost always seen in terms of guidance and governance. The Holy Spirit guides human persons especially through "writing and imprinting the interior law of charity"[64] within them. It is that work of the Spirit that we saw operative within the *Spiritual Exercises*. It is this same "law of charity" that unites the individual with the Lord. Thus both guidance and union come from the same Holy Spirit.[65]

It is this mystical participation in the union between Christ and his Church which continues to emerge in Ignatius' understanding of the Church as communicated to others. When the Society of Jesus was approved as a religious order in 1540,[66] the Formula of the Institute made it clear that service of the Church under the Roman Pontiff was an essential element of life in the Society of Jesus. So, in the final apostolic letter of confirmation of the Society in 1550,[67] the new redaction of the Formula describing the goal of the Society read:

> Whoever desires to serve as a soldier of God beneath the banner of the cross in our Society which we designated by the name of Jesus and to serve the Lord alone and the Church, His spouse, under the Roman Pontiff, the vicar of Christ on earth, should, after a solemn vow of perpetual chastity, poverty and obedience, keep what follows in mind.[68]

Here it is clear that Christ and the Church are the objects of the service of members of the Society of Jesus. The Roman Pontiff is the person under

---

[64] *Constitutions*, Preamble [134].

[65] "Categorically, to bring in a Rahnerian distinction, the Spirit governs through the hierarchical authorities, the prophets, preachers, confessors, and teachers in the Church, through commandments and precepts, through sacraments and Scripture and Tradition, through all of those external means which build up the Body of Christ. Transcendentally, the Spirit guides and governs by the change in human subjectivity, especially through the charity or love of friendship that draws and transforms into unity all human affectivity. "The love which moves me and makes me choose such a thing should come down from above [*de arriba*], from the love of God in such a fashion that the one who chooses should feel [*sienta*] first in himself that love which he has greater or less, for the thing which he chooses, is solely for the sake of his Creator and Lord". *Exercises* [184]. ... This experience of love transforms human affectivity and gives human choice/election its direction. It is the greater love that puts order into the lesser loves. And this is the effect of the Spirit of God within the human person." Buckley, S.J., "Ecclesial Mysticism."

[66] Apostolic Letter, *Regimini Militantis Ecclesiae*, September 27, 1540, Paul III.

[67] Apostolic Letter, *Exposcit Debitum*, July 21, 1550, Julius III.

[68] Formula of the Institute of the Society of Jesus, *The Constitutions of the Society of Jesus And Their Complementary Norms*, ed. John Padberg, S.J., (St. Louis: Institute of Jesuit Sources, 1996), 1.

whom the Society will serve the Church.[69] Thus from the first paragraph of the Formula of the Institute, the Jesuits identified the Church both as the spouse of Christ and as the focus for their service. Even more, the Roman Pontiff is identified not only in terms of his relationship to Christ as vicar, but also as the one who is the primary source of sending on mission the Jesuits in their service of the Church.[70]

A Particular Intimacy

It is this metaphor of spouse that again, as with the *Spiritual Exercises,* is a key term. It is this intimate union of "spouse" that links the Church to Christ, just as the term "vicar" links the Roman Pontiff to Christ. Indeed there seems to be an implied parallelism suggested: "just as to understand the nature and function of the Roman Pontiff, one must above all understand that he is the vicar of Christ, that he represents Christ's care for the whole Church, so in order to understand the nature of the Church one must understand it as the spouse of Christ."[71] It also implies a particularity of "intimacy" between the Pope as Vicar of Christ, and the Society of Jesus.[72]

---

[69] On August 15, 1534 Ignatius and six companions (Favre, Xavier, Lainez, Salmerón, Rodrigues and Bobadilla) climbed to Montmartre. "There, a chapel with a crypt had been dedicated to the martyrs. The companions stopped there. The dawn rose over Paris. The place was deserted and at some distance from the city. ... Favre was the only priest in the group, having recently been ordained (on May 30). He celebrated the Mass. At the moment of communion, each pronounced his vows – so carefully studied and perfected. Favre gave the Eucharist to his six companions." Ravier, S.J., *Ignatius of Loyola and The Founding of The Society of Jesus,* 72. They made a joint commitment at Montmartre "to go to Venice and Jerusalem and to spend their lives in what was beneficial to souls. And if permission was not given them to remain in Jerusalem, they were to return to Rome and present themselves to Christ's vicar, so that he could employ them wherever he judged to be more for the glory of God and the good of souls." "Autobiography of St. Ignatius Loyola," [85] in *St. Ignatius of Loyola: Personal Writings,* 54. On November 18, 1538 the companions in conscience put themselves totally and unconditionally at the disposal of the "Vicar of Christ in order to be sent wherever it seemed appropriate to him to send them and on whatever mission he chose." This "offering" of November 1538 is an important event because in it the companions had offered their obedience to the Pope in the fullest sense. In this act of obedience, they believed that they would find the sure discovery of God's will as a fecund apostolic source, the necessity of a universal apostolate, and total self-abnegation in the service of Jesus Christ through his Vicar—all this was included in the action of the first companions. Ravier, S.J., *Ignatius of Loyola and the Founding of the Society of Jesus,* 33–4.

[70] The Pope is the primary one who sends on mission and the superiors of the Society do so only under the delegated authority of the Pope. Cf. *Constitutions* 606.

[71] Buckley, S.J., "Ecclesial Mysticism."

[72] It is this bond of a particular intimacy rooted in the tradition of the Society that I appeal to later as also at the heart of the Ignatian ecclesial disposition. Thus we are dealing not just with a cerebral loyalty but a deep affective intimacy rooted in generations of Jesuits.

This spousal metaphor, and its emphasis on the union between Christ and his Church, also appears in Ignatius' correspondence. In his letter of 1555 to Claude, Emperor of Abyssinia, where he was explaining to the Emperor the primacy of the Roman Pontiff and the unity and authority of the Church, he wrote: "the Catholic Church is one throughout the whole world, and it is impossible for one to be attached to the Roman Pontiff and another to the Alexandrian. As Christ the Bridegroom is one, so the Church, His Spouse, is only one."[73] For Ignatius the Church must be one because she is the bride of Christ.

Loyalty to the Pope both Practical and Mystical

The commitment to the Holy Father, and the other Roman Pontiffs who would succeed him, was made explicit in terms of the mission of the Society. The most important source of the mission was the Roman Pontiff.[74] Ignatius considered that the Pope could best direct the members of the Society to where the need of the Church was greatest and therefore where there would be more universal service. This commitment to go wherever the Pope would send them became the foundation of a special fourth vow.[75]

The *Constitutions* that Ignatius drafted in his final years gave evidence that his attitude was to be totally at the disposal of the Pope. Part VII of the *Constitutions* focuses on the mission and ministries of the Society. The first chapter deals with missions from the Supreme Pontiff. Ignatius states that: "to treat the missions from His Holiness first as being most important, it should be observed that the vow which the Society made to obey him as the supreme vicar of Christ without any excuse meant that the members were to go to any place where he judges it expedient to send them for the greater glory of God and the good of souls."[76]

---

[73] Ignatius of Loyola to Claude, Emperor of Abyssinia, February 23, 1555, *Letters of Ignatius*, 369. There is also a letter from Ignatius to Francis Borgia dated September 20, 1548, where he urges him to refrain from physical mortifications which were a feature of religious life in the sixteenth century but rather "to seek more immediately the Lord of all, or, what comes to the same thing, seek His most holy gifts ... These gifts with His Divine Majesty as their end are an increase in the intensity of faith, hope and charity, joy and spiritual repose, tears, intense consolation, elevation of mind, divine impressions and illuminations, together with all other spiritual relish and understanding which have these gifts as their objects, such as a humble reverence for our holy mother the Church, her rulers and teachers." Ibid., 181.

[74] Cf. *Constitutions* 603, 605.

[75] "I further promise a special obedience to the sovereign Pontiff in regard to the missions according to the same apostolic letters [of the papacy to the Society] and the Constitutions." *Constitutions* [527], ibid.

[76] *Constitutions* [603].

Ignatius does not just consider the Pope a necessary help in discernment. Rather, as part of his own deep mystical sensibility, he considered His Holiness as Christ's vicar on earth. Thus, as the disciples gathered around Christ and were sent out on mission, so members of the Society would gather around Christ's vicar to be sent out on mission also.[77] The Church for Ignatius was the visible embodiment of the Lord, and the service of Christ was carried on under the direction of Christ's visible representative on earth.

Missions given by a superior also: "will consider the holy intention of the Pontiff for the service of Christ our Lord."[78] So the superior sends only in the Holy Father's place. Within this process of sending on mission, the voice of God is to be recognized in the voice of the superior but also in the individual's own soul. Jesuit obedience is not finished by the realization of the received order but it is always open to the call of the Lord for the greater glory of God.[79] This means that discernment is an ongoing process. The discernment of the individual and the discernment of the superior are both required. The practice of manifestation of conscience[80] made to the superior is, in part, in order that the discernment of the individual may be taken into consideration by the superior in the latter's own discernment. It also enables provincial superiors to have a deep knowledge 'in the Lord' of

---

[77] In the 'First Summary of the institution of the Society of Jesus' [*Prima Societatis Jesu Instituti Summa*] written in 1539 and reproduced in its entirety in the bull of institution of the Society [*Regimini militantis* 1540] the second chapter is very clear and eloquent: "Let all the companions know and may they remember, not only in the early days of their profession, but every day, so long as they may live, that this entire Society and all of its members fight the battle of God in faithful obedience to our most Holy father Paul III and to his successors and that they have submitted themselves to the authority of the Vicar of Christ and to his power of divine right, not only by virtue of the common obedience of all the clerics but also by the bond of a vow: in such a way that everything that His Holiness may order us to do for the good of souls and the propagation of the faith, we are bound to implement immediately without excuse and with all of our strength, whether he sends us to the Turks, to the new worlds, to the Lutherans, or to no matter what others—faithful or pagan." Ravier, S.J., *Ignatius of Loyola and the Founding of the Society of Jesus*, 103–4. The practical outworking of this was that the early companions were soon scattered as they were sent on mission by the Pope. In April 1541 when the companions made their final vows four out of the original ten were already missioned away from Rome.

[78] *Constitutions* [615].

[79] Cf. *Constitutions* [616].

[80] The first mention of 'manifestation of conscience' in the *Constitutions* occurs in the section devoted to the General Examen of candidates for the Society. "After pondering the matter in Our Lord, we consider it to be of great and even extraordinary importance in his Divine Majesty that the superiors should have a complete understanding of the subjects that by means of this knowledge they may be able to direct and govern them better, and while caring for them guide them better into the paths of the Lord" [91]. "Wherefore, whoever wishes to follow this Society in our Lord or to remain in it for his greater glory must be obliged to the following. ... he must manifest his conscience with great humility, transparency, and charity without concealing anything which is offensive to the Lord of all men" [93], see also [95, 97, 263, 424, 551].

the men under their care. This also indicates the very active, participative and responsible nature of the Jesuit vow of obedience.[81]

So important did Ignatius consider this commitment to the Holy Father that he incorporated into the *Constitutions* a mandate for each Superior General. When a new Pope took office, within a year of the election, the Superior General was "to manifest to His Holiness the profession and express promise which the Society has to be obedient to him, especially in regard to the missions, to the glory of God our Lord."[82] In this singular gesture the whole of the Society of Jesus through the action of the General renews this commitment and in particular the fourth vow of obedience to the Holy Father with regard to the mission.

The *Spiritual Diary*[83]

The *Spiritual Diary* records the intense inner life of Ignatius as he sought to discern God's will for the character of the new Society of Jesus. It gives a unique insight into the personal relationship of Ignatius with God. The *Spiritual Diary* is especially focused on the extent to which poverty will mark the Society.[84] Is poverty to be a partial or a complete reality? The

---

[81] The matter of obedience will be considered in more detail in the next chapter. Suffice it here to recall two paragraphs from the *Constitutions*. "In offering personal obedience, all should leave to superiors the full and completely free disposal of themselves, desiring to be guided, not by their own judgment and will, but by that indication of the divine will that is offered to us through obedience; and they should make their own the superior's command in a personal, responsible way and with all diligence "bring to the execution of commands and the discharge of assignments entrusted to them the resources of their minds and wills, and their gifts of nature and grace" [152]. "Obedience by its very nature and perfection supposes in the subject the obligation of personal responsibility and the spirit of ever seeking what is better. Consequently, he can, and sometimes should, set forth his own reasons and proposals to the superior. But a subject may not refuse to obey in those things where there is not manifestly any sin, because he thinks something better should be done or because he believes he is led along other lines by the inspiration of the Spirit" [153].

[82] Ibid., [617], 281.

[83] The *Spiritual Diary* is a document—one of very few—that is in the original handwriting of Ignatius. The title given to these sheets of paper (twenty-eight pages in all which are the result of Ignatius taking four to six pages at a time and folding them down the middle. Thus he did not use a formal notebook) is somewhat misleading: they are not a diary in the normal sense of the term. "Ignatius is keeping note of progress made during the process of making up his mind: he is making a choice or 'election' in the terminology of the *Spiritual Exercises*." "The Spiritual Diary of Ignatius," in *Saint Ignatius of Loyola: Personal Writings*, 67.

[84] "With the opening of the year 1544 (the *Diary* begins in February of this year) it seems that the first great wave of activity that had been carrying Ignatius forward ever since his arrival in Rome suddenly diminished. The house of St. Martha for the reform of prostitutes was founded in January, but then four months of extremely bad health crippled Ignatius' movements. ... it must have been clear that a period of consolidation, and above all of intense organization and planning was becoming increasingly necessary. The Society of Jesus was expanding rapidly

question is, should there be revenue or not for the churches of the Society and their sacristies?[85]

If the Society embraced a partial poverty it would more easily be able to maintain itself. Then it could concentrate on the mission and the different forms of apostolic work without being anxious about financial concerns. If, however, it accepted complete poverty, there too would be advantages. Members of the Society would gain greater spiritual strength and increased devotion by trusting their welfare to the Lord alone. Such a stance might lead other people to be edified by the Society's witness. The eventual result is that Ignatius decides against revenue so that the Society could embrace a complete poverty.[86]

To discern God's will with regard to poverty, Ignatius began a very intensive period of prayer and reflection upon the graces he received.[87] In seeking God's will for the Society, Ignatius maintained both an active

---

in numbers and in the diverse directions of its personnel and their occupations. Attached though Ignatius was to the 'inner law of divine love' as the guiding principle for himself and his subjects, mounting pressure from his companions and from the papacy, together with the evident dangers of dissipated energy, impelled him to begin the unwelcome task of composing the *Constitutions*. The problem became crucial with the need for a decision concerning poverty [which is the subject matter of the *Spiritual Diary*]: Ignatius realized that the principles involved were of radical importance. First, there was the complex question of poverty itself: he was sufficiently aware of life's realities to appreciate that absolute poverty might spell the end of the new order by any normal calculus of human probability. Secondly, his own authority would be particularly tested: for the first time he would have to exercise on a grand scale the power so gladly entrusted to him and so reluctantly accepted." Ibid., 67–8.

[85] This issue "appeared to be one in which he would have to revoke a decision already approved by the early companions. In the spring of 1541 a commission (consisting of Ignatius himself and Codure) had examined whether the sacristies of churches should be allowed to possess income; this was normal even in orders of strict observance, like the Franciscans. Guided by the commission, all had agreed. But now Ignatius was asking if this decision should be set aside because it seemed to lessen the complete poverty to which they were committed. Only if the *Diary* is seen against this background can one understand the apparently excessive hesitation over such a relatively minor matter." Ibid., 68.

[86] Ignatius was subsequently overruled.

[87] The *Spiritual Exercises* provide the key to understanding what is happening in the *Spiritual Diary*. "The *Spiritual Exercises* revolve around the central axis of reform. At the heart of the second week the exercitant is provided with a series of considerations and methods that will help a person to see what changes are required and how to choose them. Ignatius outlines three possible scenarios, which he had discovered by personal trial and error. The first is when one receives the sort of illumination that admits of no doubt... The second and third are more protracted and complicated. The third, which is explained more fully, is dominated by the notion of the 'reasonable'. Here there are two possibilities: first, one can draw up a list of pros and cons that concern the matter at issue; secondly, by imagining different situations one can try to gain some distance from the problem, and thus study it more objectively. ... There is clear proof that Ignatius was using the first of these techniques to help him: we have the list of *pros and cons* that he drew up and mentioned at several points in his reflections [February 8, 10, 11, 16]. However, the second of the three scenarios mentioned is the most distinctively Ignatian. He describes it as: "At time when sufficient light and knowledge is received through experience of consolations and desolations, and through experience of the discernment of

and a receptive disposition. The character of the Society and its characteristic "way of proceeding" was to be established by God Himself, not
by the opinion of others. He determined to wait upon the Lord in prayer
for guidance. It is a time when he experienced great consolations and
Trinitarian visions.[88]

Eucharist—The Realization of the Union of Christ and the Church

Within the fragment of the *Spiritual Diary* that still remains, Ignatius gives
a primary place of importance to his celebration of Mass. It is here at the
Mass that he receives many of the graces that he records in this fragment. It
is important that we consider the vital nature of the celebration of the Mass
in Ignatius' discernment. We have already seen that Ignatius understood the
intimate link that exists between Christ and the Church, and also understood the profound reciprocity between the individual and the Church, as
the individual is configured to the Church and the Church realizes more
deeply its own reality through the experience of the individual, in the
making of the *Spiritual Exercises*.[89]

It is then no surprise that it is also within the context of the celebration
of the Eucharist – the central act of Ignatius' day—that his discernment
takes place. The daily Mass is the focal point of the graces he receives. The
Eucharist[90] brings into sharp focus, for the eyes of faith, the action of the
Trinity in the sacrifice of Christ. In the offering of Christ to the Father, in
the power of the Spirit, Christ offers also the Church to whom he is inextricably conjoined.

Thus, although the institutional Church is not directly mentioned in
this fragment of the *Spiritual Diary*,[91] she is involved both as the context

---

different spirits [Exx. 176]. It is clear that the *Spiritual Diary* is the record of such a time of
'discernment' with the 'consolations and desolations' duly noted." Ibid., 69.

[88] "Tranquility and extraordinary lightness," he noted on February 19, 1544, "to the point of
feeling my intense love which I felt for the Most Holy Trinity." Cf. also his prayer "Eternal
Father, confirm me; Eternal Son, confirm me, Eternal Holy Spirit confirm me; Holy Trinity
confirm me; my God who is the only God, confirm me," February 18, 1544. Ibid., 81, 82.
Ignatius appeared to attach more importance to Trinitarian revelations. At Manresa he had
received significant illuminations of the mystery of the Trinity. Throughout his life, he said that
he had a feeling of great devotion when praying to the Trinity.

[89] Cf. the section on the *Exercises* in the earlier part of this chapter.

[90] Ignatius had a great devotion to the Eucharist and we have already seen in Chapter 1 looking
at the Rules for Thinking, Judging, and Feeling with the Church that he advocated a more
frequent attendance at mass and reception of holy communion than was the normal practice
of his time.

[91] Except for example on the March 6, where Ignatius indicates that he went to St Peter's and
prayed before the Blessed Sacrament, and then attended a Mass said by one of the Cardinals.

and in the content of the discernment. Not only will the result of Ignatius' discernment affect the future of the Society of Jesus, but also the entire Church. In addition, as the Eucharist is offered by Ignatius, and is made acceptable by Christ as an offering to the Father in the power of the Spirit, so Ignatius and the entire Church in the mystery of the body of Christ are offered. The intrinsic link between Christ and the Church ensures that every celebration of the Eucharist, with however many or few in attendance, involves the whole of the Church.

The importance of this understanding of the Eucharist has been somewhat overlooked in our contemporary times. Members of the Church have sometimes tended to focus on individual attendance at the Mass. This has contributed to a loss of corporate understanding of the Church and a 'distancing' of the individual both from the community as gathered and, more particularly, from the institutional Church. It has also contributed to a way of seeing discernment as a very individual enterprise rather than as something that can only genuinely be undertaken in relationship to the Church. The *Spiritual Diary* clearly indicates that for Ignatius discernment was always a process undertaken within the context of the Church and particularly in the context of the Church gathered at the celebration of the Eucharist.

It is within this context then of the celebration of Mass[92] over a period of days and his prayer and reflection before and after the Mass throughout the day that Ignatius comes to know his way forward. Throughout the fragment Ignatius devotes his celebration of the Eucharist to: Our Lady, the Trinity, the Holy Spirit and the Holy Name of Jesus. His primary intercessors are the persons of the Holy Trinity and Our Lady. This recalls the prayer of the Triple Colloquy, which we considered earlier, and again there is the same entreating for the grace and favor of a knowledge that will be more to the glory of God and that will be life giving for the Society and the Church. The importance of the request for insight that he is making is underlined by the solemnity of his prayer and the dedication of each mass to his most important intercessors.

---

[92] So for example he notes the particular mass that he celebrates: On Friday April 25, 1544 the Mass of St Mark; on Saturday April 26 the Mass of the Holy Spirit; on Sunday April 27 the Mass of the day; between Monday April 28 and Sunday May 11 he celebrates each day the Mass of the Trinity; on Monday May 12 the Mass of All Saints etc. The context of the mass is where also he experiences the consolation of tears and other phenomena. On Sunday May 11, he writes: "Tears before mass; very many and continuous divinely granted, as I had prayed for it this very day because during the week I had sometimes experienced the external *loquela*, and sometimes not, but the internal more rarely, although on Saturday I found it a little more clear. So also during all the masses of the week, although I was not so visited with tears, yet I experienced greater quiet or contentment throughout the mass from the pleasure of the *loquelas*, with the devotion I could feel, than at other times when during part of the mass I had tears." "The Spiritual Diary of Ignatius," in *Saint Ignatius of Loyola: Personal Writings*, 107.

During the course of the discernment period, Ignatius recalled the illumination at La Storta,[93] a Church outside Rome, where he had a vision of the Father placing him with the Son.[94] Accordingly, on one occasion in the discernment he spoke of the grace he received as follows: "It seemed in some way to be from the Blessed Trinity that Jesus was shown or felt, and I remembered the time when the Father put me with the Son."[95] Within virtually all of these times of grace, Ignatius' fervor and devotion reveals itself also in an abundance of tears.

> I entered the chapel and while praying felt, or to put it more exactly, I saw not by natural power, the Blessed Trinity and also Jesus who was representing me, or placing me before the Trinity and also acting as mediator close to the Blessed Trinity, that I might communicate in that intellectual vision. On feeling and seeing in this way I was covered with tears and love, but with Jesus as the object; and toward the Blessed Trinity, a respect of submission.[96]

This intensely intimate, personal, affectionate and familiar disposition of faith is the core of Ignatius' relationship with Christ. This relationship informs his prayer and is the source of his love for the Church. From this

---

[93] A Church some fourteen kilometres from Rome.

[94] See "Autobiography of St. Ignatius," in *Saint Ignatius of Loyola: Personal Writings*, 60. This is commonly referred to as the "vision of La Storta." "In fact, what is called *the vision* of La Storta should be called the *visions* of La Storta. If one refers to the most certain non-Ignatian sources of this event [Nadal (four accounts), Polanco, Ribadeneyra (two accounts) and Canisius], that is to Laynez's report to all the Fathers in Rome in 1559, calling to mind the *recent* confidences of Ignatius, it is necessary to distinguish at least two successive times in this revelation. First during several days, an interior *word* of the Father which *imprinted itself in the heart* of Ignatius, in the course of the Mass: 'I shall be favorable to you in Rome' [you in the plural]; and another time it was undoubtedly the episode of La Storta 'it seemed to him that he saw,' said Laynez 'Christ with his Cross, on his shoulder and near him the Eternal Father who was saying, 'I want you to take this one as your servant.' And thus Jesus took him and said; 'I want you to serve us.' This time the words (you in the singular) and the gestures concerned only Ignatius. This testimony by itself thus leads us not to talk as if it all took place in the chapel of La Storta at one single time." Ravier S.J., *Ignatius of Loyola and the Founding of the Society of Jesus*, 425.

[95] *Spiritual Diary*, February 23, 1544, in ibid., 84–5. "'He had decided' the *Autobiography* tells us, 'to remain one year without saying Mass, preparing himself and asking the Madonna to be willing to unite him to her Son.' A longtime desire which dated from June 1537, and about which he had frequently besought the Virgin. 'And one day when he found himself in the church saying prayers—it was a few miles before arriving in Rome – he felt such a change in his soul and he saw so clearly that God the Father was uniting him with Christ his Son, that he would never dare doubt that God the Father had united him with his Son.' Then there was first a transforming illumination which provoked in him a profound emotional shock. This illumination was accompanied, without being part of it, by a 'vision': Ignatius did not specify whether it was an 'exterior' or an 'intellectual' vision." Ibid.

[96] Ibid., February 27, 1544, 87.

foundation, rooted in faith and love for Christ and his Church, Ignatius approached the many practical issues that he was called upon to face as General Superior of the Society of Jesus. One such practical difficulty was the question of whether Jesuits should accept ecclesiastical honors within the Church. Could this be countenanced under the *Constitutions* and was it according to the way of proceeding that the Society understood in the initial foundation? This vexed question was raised on a number of occasions as Ignatius was asked to allow certain of his men to be designated Bishop.

The Problem of Ecclesiastical Honors[97]

Much later in Ignatius' life while he was General Superior of the Society a difficult situation confronted him. In 1546, King Ferdinand I, who would later succeed Charles V as the Holy Roman Emperor, wanted to have one of Ignatius' early companions, Claude Le Jay, appointed bishop of Trieste. Ignatius was strongly opposed to Jesuits assuming any ecclesiastical dignities believing that this would diminish the man's availability for the mission. Ignatius intervened with the King and then directly with Pope Paul III to block the appointment.

The Pope though kindly disposed to the Jesuits replied that he had already decided to make the appointment being convinced that his decision was from the Holy Spirit. He sent Ignatius away urging him to pray. Ignatius did pray but he also used every human means and every available influence, visiting a number of Cardinals in Rome asking them to urge the Pope and King to change their minds. In the end the Pope delayed the matter and the King capitulated. Le Jay never became a bishop. The initial clear decision of the Pope was not implemented.

This episode from the life of Ignatius indicates that he was a person who loved the Church while at the same time being a shrewd observer of human nature and a man of keen political sense. There was no question other than that Ignatius would obey the Pope. This was integral to his understanding both of obedience and of the special bond that linked the members of the Society with the Pope. At the same time he often seemed to go beyond representing his own opinion to use every available human means if he believed his opinion was right.

Another example of this is the three attempts that were made, by Charles V and then Philip II, to have Francis Borgia made a Cardinal. On each occasion Ignatius both prayed and urged the Society to pray and also endeavored through friends to resist the appointment. In each case the attempts to make Borgia a Cardinal failed. In a letter to Francis Borgia in

---

[97] This primarily referred to requests coming to Ignatius that members of the Society of Jesus should be made Bishops.

June 1552, Ignatius explained how he came to his conviction but at the same time how he ultimately stood "indifferent'" ready for whatever God's will might affirm.

> I have felt, and now feel, that it is God's will that I oppose this move. Even though others might think otherwise, and bestow this dignity on you, I do not see that there would be any contradiction, since the same Divine Spirit could move me to this action for certain reasons and others to the contrary for other reasons, and thus bring about the result desired by the Emperor. May God our Lord always do what will be to His greater praise and glory.[98]

This process of following the firm conviction he discerned, while being willing to obey[99] the final authoritative word of the Pope, was for Ignatius fully in accord with his understanding of obedience and loyalty.[100] What these incidents do reveal is that in the life of Ignatius, the lived relationship he had with the Papacy, though always reverent and obedient, was also somewhat complex.

The complexities, however, arose from the circumstances and occasions of interaction, not from the inherent disposition of Ignatius towards the Pope and his love for the Church. What does seem clear from the citation noted above is that Ignatius continues to maintain a certain outlook contained within the presupposition of the *Exercises*[101] and implied within the Rules for Thinking with the Church. He endeavors always to put a good construction on the words and actions of the Pope.

---

[98] Ignatius Loyola, Letter to Francis Borgia, June 5, 1552, in *Letters of St. Ignatius*, selected and trans. by William Young, S.J. (Chicago, University of Loyola Press, 1959), 258.

[99] Clearly obedience is for Ignatius a key characteristic of the society. The following two extracts from the *Constitutions* make it clear that such obedience is ultimately to Christ and to be undertaken in love not fear. See *Constitutions* [284, 547].

[100] "Representation may well be made, and even should be, through the prelate or person through whom His Holiness issues the command to go somewhere, by asking how he wishes him to make the journey and stay in the place, namely by living on alms and begging for the love of God our Lord, or in some other manner. This is so that what His Holiness deems best may be done with greater devotion and security in our Lord." *Constitutions* [610].

[101] "That both the giver and the maker of the *Spiritual Exercises* may be of greater help and benefit to each other, it should be presupposed that every good Christian ought to be more eager to put a good interpretation on a neighbor's statement than to condemn it." *Spiritual Exercises* 22. This presupposition of the *Exercises* sets the context for the interaction between the one who gives the *Exercises* and the one who makes them. It enables a relationship of trust to develop and therefore enables the one making the Exercises to speak with a freedom and openness that disposes them to be receptive to grace. In the context of this paragraph I am endeavoring to show that Ignatius has this same disposition of the presupposition with regard to his attitude towards the words and actions of the Pope. It is natural to Ignatius to strive always to see the good in what the Holy Father was saying to him or in the actions the pontiff undertook.

Ignatius' behavior illustrates his own conviction that the Holy Spirit continues to work in the Church both through individuals and through the directives of authority. These two modes of action of the Spirit may come into conjunction through spontaneous approval by authority; through the presentation of additional data for discernment to authority; or there could be, as Ignatius indicates above, the inspiration of the Spirit in different ways.[102] What is significant is Ignatius' conviction that the will of God is most coherently known and followed through active obedience to superiors and primordially to the Vicar of Christ. He trusted that Christ continues to guide his Church through this means across generations whatever the defects of individuals may be.

A Final Word

Ignatius' Rules for Thinking with the Church, as we have seen, are firmly rooted in the experience of the *Exercises* and are congruent with the dynamic found there. His understanding of the inextricable connection between love for Christ and love for the Church drives his whole process of election in the *Spiritual Exercises* and the section on mission in the *Constitutions*. Within the *Spiritual Diary* we can glimpse how his reverence for the Eucharist fuelled this vision of the Church rooted in the Trinity and at the service of the world. Within the text of his own life story, through his *Autobiography*, letters and the history of his time in Rome we have perceived some of the complexities of the situations that he faced and his response rooted in a constant loyalty to the Church. There is a clarity and consistency about his attitude to the Pope and the Church. Amidst complex circumstances, there is the simplicity of a genuine true principle—Christ and the Church are conjoined. It is these characteristics of what I am calling Ignatius' ecclesial disposition that I shall explore in the next chapter.

---

[102] Cf. Jules Toner, *Discerning God's Will: Ignatius of Loyola's Teaching on Christian Decision Making* (St. Louis: Institute of Jesuit Sources, 1991).

3

Ignatius' Ecclesial Disposition

It was clearly asserted in the previous chapter that Ignatius does not envisage the Church as other than conjoined to Christ. This awareness of an indissoluble bond lies at the heart of his ecclesial disposition. His love for Christ was mirrored in his love for the Church. Ignatius saw the two as inseparable and this was the basis of his love shown in action. It is essentially, I have argued, a coherent principle underpinning his relationship with the Church and orienting his loyalty to the Roman Pontiff. This disposition clearly reflects a certain perception of the Church. But it is not an understanding confined to the subject of the Church in isolation. It is a perception of the Church as the body of Christ, so clearly there is an impact on any Christological understanding. If the Church is conjoined to the second person of the Trinity then there is also though less well articulated an engagement with Trinitarian relations.[1] Let me be clear here. Ignatius was not a systematic theologian neither did he make any original theological contribution. What he did do through graced insight was to insist on a simple understanding of the Church in relation to Christ and the Trinity in a way that emphasized the ongoing work of the spirit of God within her.[2] Today we might designate such an appreciation as a core understanding of the organic unity of the central tenets of the faith.[3]

This chapter will attempt to illustrate the way Ignatius came to this appreciation primarily by drawing from his mystical experiences at Manresa and his later spiritual diary. The *Spiritual Exercises* will remain a privileged source of inspiration as the 'Rules for Thinking, Judging, and Feeling with the Church"—the springboard of this investigation—are contained within this text, but the other texts that were the subject of Chapter 2 all figure in this consideration. It is the unity of these central

---

[1] We have already seen in the previous chapter in the *Spiritual Diary* the way in which Ignatius considers the Trinity to be actively engaged in his work for the Church.
[2] Cf. *Spiritual Exercises* 365.
[3] This might be particularly illustrated through the event of the Cardoner illumination detailed later in this chapter. Cf. Gill Goulding, C.J., "The Cardoner Imperative," *The Way* 47 (1/2) (2008): 243–59.

texts with tenets of the faith that form the heart of what I have called the ecclesial disposition of Ignatius. Why this is so important to emphasize is that when we consider Ignatius' ecclesial disposition we are looking at an organic appreciation. Ignatius' attitude to the Church is the result of an integrated faith; therefore, it involves also his understanding of Christ, the Trinity and the reality of human persons.

Accordingly, when we cite Ignatius' ecclesial disposition as a distinctive entity it will still be within the wider context of this integrated approach. So we shall explore the different influences on Ignatius that helped to form this disposition. We shall consider first the influence of his own time and cultural milieu. Then we engage with the seminal experience at Manresa. In every area of exploration we find that Ignatius' primary focus is on Christ; that he comes to a deep understanding of his relationship with the Trinity through Christ. Finally he comes to a profound appreciation of the human person graced by God and called to a deep relationship with God and a share in the redemptive mission of Christ.[4] Foremost throughout the chapter we will be seeking resonances of the motives with which Ignatius desires to give his life to God, and the service of the Church then to observe how he views this in terms of obedience.

The Influence of his own Time

During his early life Ignatius had great dreams and desires for adventure and romance, and these fuelled his imagination. Indeed, some of the values that shaped his life were rooted in these experiences. There were certain feudal values such as fidelity, courage, friendship and generosity that were at the heart of the relationship between great lords and those who served them.[5] A desire to serve and a willingness to suffer in a noble cause were also hallmarks of this relationship. Ignatius stood—as it were—on the cusp between the Middle Ages and the Renaissance. Joseph de Guibert gives the classic statement on Ignatius' place as one of being between two

---

[4] In many ways this mirrors the progress through the *Spiritual Exercises* as the exercitant is drawn through a developing relationship with Christ to a deeper engagement with the Father, and this growth in relationship with Christ and the Father is all within the dynamic of the leading of the Holy Spirit.

[5] "Joseph de Guibert limits the concept of the 'military' in St. Ignatius' spirituality to the *servitium per amorem*, the service of love, in opposition to all false images of narrow, sergeant-major type of discipline, of noisy flag-waving, of the spirit of the barracks, and of modern militarism. ... Yet the breath of knighthood rests on this "service of love," the breath of struggle, of daring, of readiness to act at any moment." Hans Wolter, "Elements of Crusade Spirituality in St. Ignatius" in ed. Friedrich Wulf, S.J., *Ignatius Loyola His Personality and Spiritual Heritage 1556–1956* (St. Louis, Institute of Jesuit Sources, 1977), 97–134 [98]. It is clear from this article that Hans Wolter makes a strong case for the connection between Ignatius' values of chivalry and those of Crusader Spirituality.

worlds. "Ignatius was the opposite pole from his contemporaries of the Renaissance. He was a man from the Middle Ages who had strayed into the sixteenth century in the height of its development. This statement is not true in the sense that he failed to understand his own times, because, on the contrary, he had insights of genius into the most serious needs of his era. But the statement does hold true in this sense: Ignatius' tastes, his tendencies, his uncompromising and serious supernaturalism placed him in violent opposition to the naturalism and skeptical dilettantism of so many humanists."[6]

He was a medieval man with all that he drew from that period that shaped his ideals and sensibilities.[7] Yet at the same time he was able to move into the new world that was emerging in Renaissance life. The values that he brought from the past shaped his response after his conversion. He committed himself to following Christ in his Church under the Roman Pontiff. Just as a knight was faithful in serving his king and a vassal in serving his lord, so Ignatius desired to be faithful in serving Christ in his Church. He was truly zealous in this service.[8]

Already we have seen how Ignatius' background influenced his way of framing the meditations in the *Spiritual Exercises* of the "Call of the King" and the "Two Standards" referred to in the previous chapter. He draws on

---

[6] De Guibert, S.J., *The Jesuits Their Spiritual Doctrine and Practice*, 71. This view, however, has been tempered in recent scholarship e.g. John O'Malley, S.J. who wishes to see Ignatius as complexly immersed in a culture which had become imbued with Humanistic thought such that there was a profound and lasting impact on both Ignatius and the Society of Jesus. "The historiography of the relationship between Renaissance Humanism and the first generation of Jesuits emits conflicting signals. Most studies of Ignatius Loyola affirm that he embraced for his new religious order that aspect of Renaissance culture known as Humanism, sometimes seeming to imply he was himself a learned exponent of it. We know, however, that his own and his early companions' education and culture were basically eclectic and late-medieval. ... My thesis is simple: Renaissance Humanism, despite reservations some of the Jesuits entertained about certain aspects of it, had a profound and determinative impact on the Society by the time Ignatius died in 1556, and we shall never understand the subsequent history of the Society unless we take that impact into account. I believe that the first Jesuits, including Ignatius, were not always fully aware of the consequences of their attitudes and decisions regarding Humanism; but that fact does not mitigate the immensity of its influence henceforth on the Society." John W. O'Malley, S.J., "Renaissance Humanism and the Religious Culture of the First Jesuits," *Heythrop Journal*, XXXI (1990): 471–87, [471].

[7] Jan Huizinga makes notable observations about such sensibilities: "wherever the purest form of the knightly ideal was promoted, asceticism was emphasized (103); the noble warrior owned no property (103); and was a hero for love's sake (104)." Jan Huizinga, *Herbst des Mittelalters. Sudien über Lebens und Geistesformen des 14. Und 15. Jahrhunderts in Frankreich und in den Niederlanden*, 3rd edn. (Leipzig: Brill, 1930), 132–3, cited in Hans Wolter, 97–134, [105].

[8] It is perhaps helpful here to note that Ignatius and his companions had no sense of the democracy which is common currency in our understanding of political and social life today. Yet, it is also important to recognize that this call to be a faithful, fervent servant of the Lord is one that resonates in the hearts of human persons across the generations.

his understanding of chivalry and the importance of the one to whom an individual swears his fealty, his allegiance.[9] Is it to Christ or to someone else? His understanding of loyalty also helped to form the way in which he expressed his devotion to Christ through his commitment to the Church and the Pope as Vicar of Christ.

Ignatius considered himself a disciple of the risen Christ—the living Lord. He wanted to respond to his Lord in every conceivable circumstance. He pondered what we would later call "the signs of the times." He was aware that he stood at a momentous period in history. The discovery of the New World in the North American Continent[10] and also of a passage east to India[11] opened up enormous missionary possibilities. It was now realized that there were literally millions of people who had not heard the gospel and who might be converted to Christ.

Within Europe, the Protestant Reformation in Germany and Switzerland[12] posed a significant challenge to the Church. Ignatius and his early companions felt called to respond to the questions being raised by the Reformers[13]. Alongside this, there was a need to address the

---

[9] The oath of Fealty from the Latin *fidelitas* was a solemn pledge of allegiance of one person to another usually between a subject and his Lord. It was generally made with a hand laid upon an altar, or relics of a saint or saints—often those contained in an altar. Examples of such oaths of fealty may be found in Brian Pullan, *Sources for The History of Medieval Europe from the Mid-eighth to the Mid-thirteenth Century* (Oxford: Blackwell, 1966), 20–3.

[10] Christopher Columbus' three voyages to the Americas, 1492, 1493–6, 1498–1500; two voyages of Amerigo Vespucci to South America, 1499–1500 and 1501–2. In 1513 Balboa discovers the Pacific Ocean. Cortés' conquest of Mexico 1519–21. Magellan's voyage of circumnavigation 1519–22. Jacques Cartier's voyages to North America, 1534 and 1535–6. From Chronology in Ronald H. Fritz, *New Worlds: The Great Voyages of Discovery, 1400–1600* (Stroud: Sutton, 2002). A Jesuit mission led by Manuel de Nóbrega arrived in Brazil in 1549.

[11] Bartolomé Dias discovers the Cape of Good Hope, 1487–8. Vasco da Gama's first voyage to India, 1497–99 reaching there May 1498, makes a second voyage to India 1502–3 and a third in 1524, dying there on Christmas Eve. Ibid. Jesuits were soon sent to these lands by the Pope—Francis Xavier arrived in India in 1542; Manuel de Nobrega in Brazil in 1549; Matteo Ricci in China in 1583; and Robert de Nobili in Southern India in 1607.

[12] Germany and Switzerland, as we know them today, did not exist. There were various autonomous principalities in the area we know as Germany. Unification only came in 1870. In Switzerland the various cantons were also autonomous.

[13] Initially the early companions saw the Reformation as primarily a lapse in morals and did not really appreciate the power of the Reformers' theological positions. This changed very quickly, however, and in 1550 "the Jesuits officially added 'defense of the faith' to the stated purposes of their order, an indication of their growing commitment to opposing the Reformation and perhaps especially to strengthening wavering Catholics ... In the 1550s and 1560s their most concentrated efforts to deal with the impact of Protestantism took place in German-speaking lands, where they were warmly supported by rulers like Emperor Ferdinand I (1558–64) and Duke Albert V of Bavaria (1550–79). Leading the Jesuits in these territories was Peter Canisius, to whom was due in considerable measure Catholic success in south German lands. By 1555 there were about fifty Jesuits in the empire, some fifteen in Cologne and practically all the rest in Vienna. By the turn of the century, there were about 1,700. In efforts to stabilize

decadence of the Church in many parts of Catholic Europe. The ignorance and worldliness of numbers of priests and religious called for a vigorous apostolate of religious education and spiritual renewal and reform. These were challenges facing the Church, and Ignatius, in his love for the Church, utilized the energies and the resources of the embryonic Society of Jesus over time in responding to them. During Ignatius' own lifetime most of his energies went into pastoral initiatives [including education] and the [foreign] missions. "Besides teaching in their own institutions, Jesuits soon came to hold positions on theological faculties of universities like Cologne, Trier and Mainz."[14] It was well-trained clergy from faculties such as these who became influential pastors in the renewal of the Church.

As we have seen, Ignatius wished to put his newly founded order at the disposal of the Pope. In his devotion to the Church he saw in the papacy, as Hugo Rahner puts it, "the supreme instance of that visibility which was both a mark of the Church and a necessary yardstick for measuring the invisible."[15] Ignatius was concerned that the mission of the Society of Jesus should promote the universal good. He believed that the Pope could best discern what was needed by the Church for the Church as a whole[16] for the promotion of her mission. Ignatius was always on guard against the possibility of self-deception. This was why he was convinced that obedience to legitimate superiors was the best protection against delusion. His understanding of obedience[17] was closely connected to his love for Christ crucified who, for the sake of human beings, had become obedient even unto death.[18]

The circumstances of Ignatius' own time ensured that the ecclesial disposition he began to form would require certain clear characteristics. These would include: a sense of fidelity to the Church and loyalty to the Pope; generosity in a willingness to go wherever the Church might need to be served; courage in the openness to suffer in the service of the Church. Finally this disposition was to be manifested through an active obedience

---

or win back Catholics, they employed the same ministries as elsewhere but gave them a more apologetic and polemical orientation. A few Jesuits used their role as confessor to monarchs to influence politics, as did Wilhelm Lamormaini with Ferdinand II. The backbone of their efforts, however, was formal education. In 1552 at Vienna they established their first school in German lands, where by 1600 the number of schools had grown to forty. The enrollments in these basically secondary institutions were often large (700–1000). By the later part of the century, the Collegio Germanico, which Ignatius established in Rome in 1552 for the training of diocesan clergy for northern Europe, began to bear fruit, and from the alumni came a number of especially well-trained pastors and theologians." John W. O'Malley, S.J., encyclopedia article "Jesuits."

[14] Ibid.

[15] Hugo Rahner, *Ignatius the Theologian* (New York: Herder & Herder, 1968), 219–20.

[16] Cf. *Constitutions* [605].

[17] Obedience became a defining characteristic of the Society of Jesus. Ignatius' understanding of obedience is considered in more depth later in the chapter.

[18] Phil. 2.8.

modeled after the example of Christ. Ignatius added to this foundation through the insights he received at Manresa.

The Seminal Experience of Manresa

Ignatius' own theological insights arose in the most part from his own mystical experiences, particularly those that occurred during his time at Manresa.[19] The most intense of these experiences took place beside the river Cardoner. Here, Jerome Nadal, one of Ignatius' early companions recalls that Ignatius received: "a sublime illumination in which the supreme truths [were] all united together in one single embracing vision."[20]

> Once he was going in his devotion to a Church, which was a little more than a mile from Manresa [I think it is called St. Paul's], and the way goes along by the river. Going along thus in his devotions, he sat down for a little with his face toward the river, which was running deep below. And as he was seated there, the eyes of his understanding began to be opened: not that he saw some vision, but understanding and knowing many things, spiritual things just as matters of faith and learning, and this with an enlightenment so strong that all things seemed new to him. One cannot set out the particular things he understood then, though they were many: only that he received a great clarity in his understanding, such that in the whole course of his life, right up to the sixty-two years he has completed, he does not think gathering together all the helps he has had from God and all the things he has come to know [even if he joins them all into one], that he has ever attained so much as on that single occasion.[21]

The context of this extraordinary revelation was the period of Ignatius' spiritual formation at Manresa. Here, he later insisted, the Lord took him by the hand and taught him as a teacher teaches a child. He had come to Manresa fresh from his conversion during his convalescence at Loyola.[22] That time of physical suffering and recuperation was a prelude to the intense spiritual preparation he then underwent.

---

[19] Ignatius was at Manresa 1522 to early 1523. "At this time God was dealing with him in the same way as a school teacher deals with a child, teaching him." *Autobiography* [27]. During this time Ignatius received significant insights concerning the Trinity; the way God had created the world; the presence of Christ in the Eucharist and the humanity of Christ.

[20] Nadal, cited by Hugo Rahner, *Ignatius the Theologian*, 10.

[21] Ignatius Loyola, "Autobiography of St. Ignatius Loyola," [30] in *St. Ignatius of Loyola: Personal Writings*, 26–7.

[22] Ignatius was wounded in 1521 when taking part in the defence of Pamplona. His right leg was shattered; he suffered an operation and then convalescence at Loyola.

The sojourn at Manresa was not part of Ignatius' original plan. He had envisaged spending only a few days there, but when it became apparent to him that the Lord was working profoundly with him, the days extended to weeks and then to months. He lived for ten months outside the town, spending hours each day in prayer and also working in a hospice. It was while he was here that the ideas for what are now known as the *Spiritual Exercises* began to take shape. In particular he received significant illuminations concerning the Trinity. [23]

So significant were these experiences that Ignatius maintained a life-long devotion to the Trinity. The experience beside the Cardoner was the pinnacle of all the mystical graces that Ignatius received at Manresa. Though the details in the *Autobiography* are sparse, there is an indication of the scale of the organic insight which enabled Ignatius to see all the truths he had previously learned in a new and integrated light. From this time onward he adopted the principle of contemplative discernment as crucial for all action. The Cardoner experience formed a touchstone for his whole life, and for the writing of the *Spiritual Exercises* and the later *Constitutions*.

The language is bare of description but rich in implication. Ignatius' description is reminiscent of some of St. Paul's letters where he speaks of all things being united in Christ.[24] This architectonic insight of the truths of the faith followed from previous insights he had received concerning the humanity of Christ, how God created the world and how Christ is present in the Eucharist.[25] "The person of Jesus Christ became for Ignatius the very way in which, and against which, everything took its ultimate meaning. Ignatius mystically tasted that all things hold together in Christ."[26]

This singular organic vision could not be transmitted to those who followed Ignatius. What could, however, be shared was a certain perspective, a certain "horizon" against which all else is seen. Harvey Egan, S.J. wrote

---

[23] "He used to have great devotion to the Most Holy Trinity, and so used to pray every day to the three persons separately. And as he was also praying to the Most Holy Trinity as such, a thought used to occur to him: how was he making four prayers to the Trinity? But this thought troubled him little or not at all, as something of little importance. And, one day, while praying the office of Our lady on the steps of the above-mentioned monastery, his understanding began to be raised up, in that he was seeing the Most Holy Trinity in the form of three keys on a keyboard, and this with so many tears and so many sobs that he could not control himself. And on walking that morning in a procession which was leaving from there, at no point could he restrain his tears until the mealtime, nor after the meal could he stop talking, only about the Most Holy Trinity, and this with many comparisons, a great variety of them, as well as much relish and consolation, in such a way that the impression has remained with him for the whole of his life, and he feels great devotion when praying to the Most Holy Trinity." "Autobiography of St. Ignatius Loyola" [28].

[24] Cf. Col. 1.15–20.

[25] "Autobiography of St. Ignatius Loyola" [28, 29].

[26] Harvey Egan, S.J., *The Spiritual Exercises and the Ignatian Mystical Horizon* (St. Louis: Institute of Jesuit Sources, 1976), 98.

of a certain "mystical horizon"[27] that inspires the thought of Ignatius. I shall argue that this horizon is one in which Christ is central and also revelatory of the work of the Trinity. The experience beside the Cardoner led to a graced human understanding whereby Ignatius saw God at work in creation especially through the lives of human persons. It is in and through such lives freely offered to God and bearing witness to the integration of intellect and affectivity that God continues the work of salvation. Within Ignatius himself there was "a harmonious union between Ignatius' driving love and his strong power of reasoning, and this combination was devoted to the service of Christ. That balanced union of the intellectual and volitional powers is perhaps the most characteristic trait in Ignatius' spiritual personality."[28] From this integrated perspective there is a clear implication, which is developed in the *Spiritual Exercises,* [29] that the individual is part of the community of the Church, the body of Christ. United with Christ in and through the Church the individual is called to take part in the redemptive work of Christ.

From this seminal experience at Manresa, beside the river Cardoner, Ignatius brought to his foundational ecclesial disposition an awareness of the importance of contemplative discernment. Such discernment could, by divine grace, enlarge the understanding to perceive the Trinitarian horizon within which all else might be viewed. Accordingly, all the events of Ignatius' own life were thereafter seen by him within this Trinitarian horizon, focused in and through the person of Christ.

The Centrality of Christ

A key characteristic of Ignatius' ecclesial disposition is the central place which Christ holds. The clarion call of Christ resounds through the *Spiritual Exercises* of St. Ignatius Loyola.[30] It is a call to enter into the mission of Christ. Even in the first-week meditations on sin,[31] the trajectory of the meditations is towards a dialogue with the crucified Lord where the retreatant is faced with the questions—"What have I done for Christ? What am I doing for Christ? What ought I to do for Christ?"[32] This mediation can

---

[27] Ibid.

[28] De Guibert, S.J., *The Jesuits: Their Spiritual Doctrine and Practice,* 73. It is this powerful graced intellect united to a passionate love for Christ which moves him to embrace all things in order to be associated with Christ in His redemptive work of reconciling the world to the Father.

[29] In particular at the time of the Election. *Spiritual Exercises* 170. The election then becomes a seeking to discern what is the specific role that this particular individual is called to play in the redemptive work of Christ as executed by the Church.

[30] Cf. *Spiritual Exercises* "The Call of the King," [91–5]; "The Two Standards," [136–48].

[31] *Spiritual Exercises* [45–90].

[32] *Spiritual Exercises* 53.

provoke the first stirrings of reason concerning one's disposition towards Christ in real life. What emerges from a careful reading of this exercise and others is that Ignatius uses, above all, appeals to human reason and affectivity to convince the retreatant of the attractiveness of following Christ. The underlying motive that informs Ignatius' ecclesial disposition, while not always explicit, is his ardent Christian love—*caritas*. It is a love for the person of Christ, the Son of God, and is fostered by his use of, and exhortation to use, one's reason and affectivity. This remains constant throughout his writings, but has been exemplified here.

The twin dynamic of reason and affectivity continue to be appealed to in *The Call of the Earthly King*.[33] Above all, one reflects on the reasons for answering his call: the king's generosity and noble-mindedness, and that if anyone were to refuse such an offer, how worthy of condemnation he would be. When applied to Christ, we reflect on how much more sensible following the Eternal King would be. There is clear freedom in the equation: Christ is calling only "Whoever wishes to join" him. But *Spiritual Exercises* 96 makes it explicit that this is a reasonable affair: we "consider that all persons who have judgment and reason will offer themselves entirely for this work." It further becomes a question of giving "greater proof of love," Ignatius's *magis* that impels all Christians to give ever more of themselves to God's service, but that expects it par excellence of those who desire to follow him more closely.

The imperative call of Christ is evident also when Ignatius invites one making the *Spiritual Exercises*, in the meditation on the Kingdom of Christ, to ask for the grace to be attentive to this call of Christ—"I will ask of our Lord the grace not to be deaf to His call but prompt and diligent to accomplish His most holy will."[34] It was this call of Christ which caused Ignatius to write the *Spiritual Exercises*, and in company with the first companions, to found the Society of Jesus.[35] The call of Christ implies a choice, primarily God's choice of the individual and then the human response of choice, which disposes the individual to enter more deeply into the mission of Christ in the world.

In the prayer of offering at the end of the Call of the King[36] we pray for the desire for "poverty" and "abuse" in following Christ, but in complete freedom ("my earnest desire and my deliberate choice") and subject to one necessary and all-important caveat: that "provided only it is for Thy greater service and praise." To avoid the misinterpretation of either a narcissistic longing for

---

[33] *Spiritual Exercises* 91–8.
[34] *Spiritual Exercises* 91.
[35] On August 15, 1534 the following men bound themselves "to the service of Christ and his vicar: Favre, Xavier, Laynez, Salmerón, Bobadilla, and Rodrigues, along with the three who joined them a short time later, LeJay, Broët, and Codure." De Guibert, *The Jesuits: Their Spiritual Doctrine and Practice*, 77.
[36] *Spiritual Exercises* 98.

suffering, or the voluntarist following of a Pelagian or semi-Pelagian kind, it is essential to delineate Ignatius's true motive for desiring poverty and suffering. The key motive here is again his great chivalrous love. It is implicit in his appeal to the noble ruler and his appealing attributes. It is behind the desire to follow anywhere—even to the ultimate end. This is not suffering for suffering's sake, but for the sake of the Beloved. It trumps even the motive of "so entering into his glory"—glory for the sake of glory, which might have been an old temptation for the former soldier Ignatius. What has emerged is the directionality of Ignatius's regard: that all things are directed to God's service and praise, so that God might increase (while Ignatius decreases).[37]

What is it about Christ that causes Ignatius to love him to the extremes of poverty and insults? The meditation on the Standard of Christ[38] directs us to consider him like this: "His appearance beautiful and attractive." This is an affective appeal, to be sure, but one that has us look at him in himself— and see his beauty and goodness (that which draws). Thus the motives for Ignatius' obedience are love of Christ, which finds resonance in both his reason and affectivity, the latter is drawn though perceiving Christ's beauty and goodness. There are other motives at work, such as the mere fact that Christ calls people and missions them[39] and that he attracts them to spiritual and actual poverty, insults and contempt, since these lead to humility, and humility is the one disposition from which one truly sees oneself, and sees Christ for who he is. It is almost a prerequisite for love, and, as Ignatius writes, a virtue that leads to all other virtues; he himself is its great exemplar.[40]

The divine call of love is focused in the call of Christ. The contemplations on the life of Christ in the second and third weeks of the *Exercises*[41] are primarily contemplations of Christ's call and his living out of that call in terms of his mission, which leads to his passion, death and resurrection. As previously indicated in the last chapter, it is against this background that during the second week Ignatius prompts those making the *Exercises* to "begin to investigate and ask in what kind of life or in what state his Divine Majesty wishes to make use" of them, and how they ought to "prepare (themselves) to arrive at perfection in whatever state or way of life God our Lord may grant (them) to choose."[42]

---

[37] Cf. Jn 3.30.

[38] *Spiritual Exercises* 136.

[39] *Spiritual Exercises* 145.

[40] Perhaps to understand Ignatius' devotion to the Church, it is helpful to have the insight of a twentieth century "Ignatian" theologian. In the *Book of All Saints*, Urs von Balthasar writes: "Ignatian obedience (which was always understood in the *Suscipe* as love) will now be interpreted in the context of Johannine love; this love gives its stamp not only to Christology, but (which is ultimately the same thing) also penetrates the very heart of the doctrine of the Trinity." Adrienne von Speyer, *The Book of All* Saints, intro. Hans Urs von Balthasar (San Francisco: Ignatius Press, 2008), 3.

[41] *Spiritual Exercises* [101–17].

[42] *Spiritual Exercises* 135.

In this election, the one chosen by God enters—as it were—into the union between Father, Son and Spirit.[43] This drawing into the life of the Trinity is crucial to an understanding of mission as Ignatius conceived it. Every mission, every genuine calling within the Church proceeds from the Father. The call proceeds from the Father and through the Spirit leads the one called to the Son, who has been called from all eternity by the Father. This leads to a desire for union with the will of God.[44] Union is the goal of this call: union with Christ and his body—namely the Church; union with the Spirit operative in the individual and in the Church; union with the Father the initiator and fulfillment of all creative union.[45]

Ignatius speaks of Jesus as both a "friend" and as our "Creator and Lord." He envisages the Incarnation as the saving work of the Trinity. He sees it focused in the eagerness of the Second Person to become a human being, as witnessed in the points for the contemplation on the Incarnation.[46] This, for Ignatius, is the central event of history. In Christ, God's love becomes present in our midst. In speaking of Christ, Ignatius is always careful to insist on both his humanity and his divinity, while safeguarding the distinction between the two.[47] For Ignatius, Christ is both "our Creator and Lord," and the friend with whom he asks the retreatant in the *Spiritual Exercises* to enter into colloquy.

The goal of history is the establishment of the Kingdom of God. This is to be accomplished through the mysteries of Christ's life by which he is united to humanity in the Incarnation. It is through the events of his life, passion, death and resurrection and finally in the Ascension that Christ brings that same humanity, which he has redeemed through his saving passion, into relationship once more with the Father. It is in and through the paschal mystery that God is glorified and humanity redeemed. The mystery of this unfathomable love of God, irrevocably committed to humanity, attracts individuals to risk the surrender of their lives. In this self-surrender they find their lives transformed.

---

[43] For Ignatius the election involves the individual coming to understand the particular part she has to play in the mission of the Church which is the outworking of the redemptive mission of Christ in the world. In consenting to this mission the individual is drawn deeply by grace gift into the love of the Trinity.

[44] Within the Spiritual Diary we find the constant pursuit of the will of God. So we have referenced on April 6 and April 7, 1544. "Sunday 6 April. Tears before mass: during the mass, after the passion, they were abundant and continuous: they led me to conform my will to the Divine; so also, tears after mass. Monday 7 April. Many tears throughout mass, drawing me to conform my will to the Divine." *Spiritual Diary* [21–2].

[45] A masterly exposition of the importance of the Trinity in the life and work of Ignatius is that written by the former Superior General Fr. Pedro Arrupe, S.J., "The Trinitarian Inspiration of the Ignatian Charism," *Studies in the Spirituality of the Jesuits* 33/3 (May 2001): 1–49.

[46] *Spiritual Exercises* 101–9.

[47] Cf. The Council of Chalcedon 451 AD.

It becomes clear in this process that Christ as the divine Word is in a continual momentum of self-communication to human persons. In Christ's Incarnation is revealed something of the very life of the Trinity. In the person, work, passion, death and resurrection of Christ this revelation is expounded. At the same time Christ also reveals to human persons the true meaning of human existence. The life Christ lived was a pattern of loving trust and obedience to the one he called "Abba."[48]

The implication of this for human persons is that the deepest truth of humanity is grounded upon the irrevocable and consistent love of the Father. An acknowledgment of this reality is the source of real transformation and hope, as Ignatius indicates in the "Contemplation to Attain the Love of God."[49] This transformation is effected by an ongoing refinement of spirit, as there is a deepening companionship with Christ in prayer. This companionship is not a self-referential activity. Rather it is always a companionship with Christ and the Church.[50] The individual never prays alone, even when physically apart from others.[51] The prayer of one is always also the prayer of the Church, the indissoluble bond between Christ and the Church ensures that this is so.

The *Spiritual Exercises* are not just devout contemplations of the gospel, nor a series of prayer meditations, they are not even a summary of the spiritual life. Their meaning emerges only in the light of their ultimate purpose, namely to present the one making them with a choice to serve

---

[48] "Many emphasize the *Abba* experience of Jesus [as] a major source of his message and manner of life (see R. Hamerton-Kelly, *Concilium* 143 [3, 1981] 95–102; J. Jeremias, *Abba* [Göttingen, 1966], 15–67) ... this approach stresses that Jesus enjoyed a deep experience of God as his own father, He dared to address God with the intimate but reverent Aram '*Abbā*' ('my own dear Father'). Though we know next to nothing about the private popular piety of Aramaic-speaking Galilean Jews of first century AD ... On the whole, one is justified in claiming that Jesus' striking use of *Abba* did express his intimate experience of God as his own father and that this usage did make a lasting impression on his disciples." John P. Meier, "Jesus of History: Origins and Ministry" in *The New Jerome Biblical Commentary*, eds Raymond E. Brown, Joseph A. Fitzmyer and Roland E. Murphy (London: Geoffrey Chapman, 1993), 1323, [78: 30, 31].

[49] *Spiritual Exercises* 230–7.

[50] "[The] mysteries of Christ are not realities of the past; they are continuing even in the present. The Christ of St. Ignatius, is the risen Christ, living now, continuing to accomplish His work until the Parousia. The Christ of the Kingdom is the Christ of glory, spreading the Kingdom of the Father over the entire human race. But where is the Christ of glory actually working now? In the Church. Therefore it is in the Church and in obedience to the Holy Father that Ignatius looks for Christ. His attachment to the Church is the direct result of his attachment to the risen living Christ." Jean Daniélou, "The Ignatian Vision of the Universe and of Man," in *Revue D'Ascetique et Mystique* (1950), 5–17 [7].

[51] "There is a perpetual prayer of the Church, of the individual in her, to God, which rings out like a kind of heavenly music. It is always heard and received in Heaven. Sometimes you are too tired to pray. ... You make up your mind to pray and you do, and suddenly you are no longer alone but singing in harmony with the universal melody of prayer." Adrienne von Speyer, cited in John Saward, *The Mysteries of March: Hans Urs von Balthasar on the Incarnation and Easter* (London: Collins, 1990).

God that will transform the individual's life.[52] In this process of choice the individual looks to find in peace the will of God "conforming himself, as far as he possibly can in his particular situation to the life laid down by Christ."[53]

The two central meditations that reveal the important Christology of the *Spiritual Exercises* are the Call of the King and the Two Standards. These two really form a unity. Both are fruits of the mystical graces that Ignatius received at Manresa and then later at La Storta.[54] It is vital that the one making the *Spiritual Exercises* comes to deeply appreciate that Christ the King is alive, he is fighting against the enemy of our human nature and that he is looking for collaborators in his redemptive work.[55] These collaborators form the reality of the Church.

Accordingly, the mysteries of Christ are not consigned to the past, but are continuing realities of the present. The Christ of Ignatius is the risen Christ, living now, continuing to accomplish his work until the end of

---

[52] "Our objective should be in the first place the desire to serve God, which is the end ... To sum up, nothing ought to induce me to take up or reject [any] means except the service and praise of God Our Lord and the eternal salvation of my soul." *Spiritual Exercises* [169].

[53] Hugo Rahner, *Ignatius the Theologian*, trans. Michael Barry (London: Geoffrey Chapman, 1990), 55.

[54] It is in the vision of La Storta that we see the way in which Ignatius is drawn through his intimacy with Christ into a deep appreciation of the Trinity. He understood that God the Father had communicated with him that he was truly and definitively "placed with Christ." This illumination was—as it were—the grace sought for in the meditation on the Two Standards in the *Spiritual Exercises*. Rahner says of this vision at La Storta: "Here the eternal Father stands in the center of the vision. He it is who speaks the blessed words to Ignatius. He it is who grants and carries out the final fulfillment of the prayer to be placed with Christ. And for the first and only time, here we learn with what words the placing with Christ was done: 'I want you to take this man as your servant' – 'I want you to serve us.' So presented, the vision is in fact the answer to the prayer of the meditation on the Two Standards, that ends by begging the eternal Father, that He grant what we have prayed for through Mary and Jesus: to be received into the service of Christ and under his standard." Hugo Rahner, *The Vision of St. Ignatius In The Chapel of La Storta* (Rome: Centrum Ignatium, 1975), 63.

[55] Ignatius saw history as a place of dramatic conflict as illustrated in the meditation on the "Two Standards" in the *Spiritual Exercises* and the "Rules for the Discernment of Spirits." "In contrast to the history which God is fashioning, there is that which the devil is making. In the background of human history there is a spiritual catastrophe which Ignatius makes us contemplate [in the first week of the *Exercises*] The diabolical world is for him always a complete reality, made up of evil spiritual powers who seek to turn man away from God. The meditation on the "Two Standards" shows us the action of the devil trying to ensnare souls. The "Rules for the Discernment of Spirits" describe for us in a remarkable way the present situation of the devil in History. He has been conquered since the Resurrection of Christ; he no longer has power over souls. He tries to frighten them by making out that Christian life is impossible. It is important therefore to know his deceits in order not to be duped by them. ... [Thus for those who would collaborate with Christ] there is a spiritual conflict against the powers of evil with the weapons of prayer and fasting." Jean Daniélou, "The Ignatian Vision of the Universe and of Man," 5–17 [8–9].

time. The Christ of the "Kingdom Exercise"[56] is also the Christ of glory, spreading the kingdom of the Father throughout all human reality in every generation. Specifically Ignatius sees Christ in glory working through the Church. Therefore, it is in the Church and in obedience to the Holy Father[57] that Ignatius looks for Christ. His attachment to the Church is the direct result of his attachment to the risen living Christ.

The call of Christ, therefore, implies the grace of vocation and the consequent grace of freely imitating and following Christ. By divine grace, the realization of the Kingdom of Christ will be established through the labors of individuals who offer themselves unreservedly in response to the call of Christ. Also, because Christ conquered through the Cross, only those willing to embrace the Cross in their lives will be able to help build up the Kingdom.[58] Indeed, because the place of victory over the enemy of our human nature is the Cross, the way of the struggle of the Church will always be this way of the Cross. The way of possession, self-affirmation and love of self are always the temptations to draw back from the humiliation of the Cross.

In Summary

Ignatius lived a certain mysticism that linked Christ, the world and the Church. All creation is intrinsically in relationship to Christ. The true meaning of all creation, and especially human creation, is disclosed in its relationship to Christ who is the concrete center of all that is.[59] This focus

---

[56] *Spiritual Exercises* 91–8.

[57] In 1537 Ignatius and his companions "placed themselves at the disposal of the pope, who by this time knew them and knew what their mode of life was. ... as Favre wrote, 'All of us who have bound ourselves together in this Society have offered ourselves to the supreme pontiff, since he is the lord of Christ's whole harvest. When we made this offering of ourselves to him, we told him we were ready for anything that he might decide in Christ for us to do. ... Our reason for placing ourselves in this way under his will and judgment is that we know that he has a better understanding of what is best for the whole Church.'" Idigoras, *Ignatius of Loyola, The Pilgrim Saint*, 409. Buckley emphasized later in this work: "The Romanism that is so characteristic of the Society of Jesus is not the result of carefully construed blueprint. Rather it has come about as a result of the vagaries of history. It is not the end product of ambition but of the will to serve. It does not mean allying oneself with the power base of the Church, but it means accepting scrupulously the benefits of being directed by the head of the Church." Ibid., 411.

[58] Cf. Mt. 16.24; Lk. 9.23; Mk 8.34. Cf. also Ignatius' understanding of the outworking of these texts in the Society of Jesus as revealed in the General Examen of candidates who wish to enter the Society. *Constitutions* [101].

[59] Cf. the letters of St. Paul where it is clear that Paul considers Christ to be the criterion for understanding what it means to be a human person: Rom. 5.15–21; Eph. 2.1–10, 4, 7–16; Phil. 2:5. Cf. also "The truth is that only in the mystery of the incarnate Word does the mystery of man take on light. Christ, by the revelation of the mystery of the Father and His love, fully

on Christ sustained Ignatius' ecclesial disposition. For him, the Church was not an external organization or a structural framework in which he set himself and his order. Nor was it a body to which he had some loose association and of which he was highly critical. Primarily the Church for Ignatius was the visible embodiment of Christ himself. And it was to Christ, our Creator and Lord, and to his greater glory that he offered his service and that of the members of his order. In this manner Ignatius wrote to the entire society in 1553 "we should love the whole body of the Church in her head Jesus Christ."[60]

Trinitarian Mysticism

Ignatius had a deep devotion to the Holy Trinity. In his life Ignatius received from each of the divine Persons different graces. This becomes clear during his time at Manresa, and later during his deliberations about poverty as recorded in the *Spiritual Diary*. A Trinitarian mysticism necessitates a Trinitarian vision. Ignatius appeared to have a sense of how everything came from the Father by the working of the Spirit in the act of creation; and returned to the Father through Christ in the power of the Spirit in a mysterious circular fashion.[61] For Ignatius, the Trinity was

---

reveals man to man himself and makes his supreme calling clear. For by His incarnation the Son of God has united Himself in some fashion with every man. ... All this holds true not only for Christians, but for all men of good will in whose hearts grace works in an unseen way. ... Such is the mystery of man, and it is a great one, as seen by believers in the light of Christian revelation." *Gaudium et Spes: Pastoral Constitution on the Church in the Modern World*, [22] December 1965, http://www.vatican.va/archive/hist_councils/ii_vatican_council/documents/vat-ii_cons_19651207_gaudium-et-spes_en.html (accessed April 4, 2013).

[60] Ignatius Loyola, "Letter to the Whole Society, July 23 1553," in *Letters of St. Ignatius of Loyola*, selected and trans. William Young, S.J. (Chicago: Loyola University Press, 1959), 301.

[61] Cf. the Patristic tradition of emanation and return within the Trinity. Aquinas refers to creation as "the emanation of things from the first principle" (*Summa Theologiae* [ST] I:45) Emanation for Aquinas refers to the active self-expression of a nature in relation to others in the production of another self. "Perfect emanation is found in God whose intellect and act of understanding, unlike those of angels are identical with his being. ... Aquinas goes on to maintain that God's self-knowledge, although perfect, unitary and eternal, still maintains distinction. This distinction consists in the God who expresses his self-knowledge in himself and the God who is expressed or conceived, namely the Son, who is the expression of the self-knowledge of the Father. The former is a perfect emanation of the latter in such a way that the being of both is identical and the emanation remains entirely immanent. ... Aquinas goes on to describe the place of the Spirit within the divine emanations and creative act. He seeks to make clear what we must understand of the Spirit with regard to God's immanent life and act of creation. ... Coupled to the emanation of the Word must be a love whereby the lover dwells in the beloved, both in God's knowing and in that which is known. The love by which God is in the divine will as a lover in the beloved "proceeds both from the Word of God and the God whose Word he is" (*Summa Contra Gentiles* IV, 19, 8). It is the Holy Spirit. It is as if the Father is the love and the Son the beloved, but immediately and in eternity this is returned

present to all things: the Church, the Eucharist, the understanding of poverty, the election. Indeed, the very structure of the *Exercises* derives from this Trinitarian perspective. In addition Ignatius also gives importance to the figure of Mary whom he links as a close collaborator with the work of the Trinity and a powerful intercessor with her son for the needs of human persons.

Within the *Spiritual Exercises* certain central meditations involve key graces which are the focus of the retreatants prayer.[62] At these times a particularly solemn and ritualistic form of prayers is suggested. The prayer of the Triple Colloquy[63] cited in the previous chapter is one such example and it indicates this movement within the Trinity and includes a relationship with Mary. There is an appeal first to Mary, then to Christ and finally to the Father all in the operative power of the Holy Spirit. The grace being requested involves "the highest spiritual poverty" seen as the greatest good that could be bestowed upon the retreatant, the grace of knowing one's utter dependence upon God and living in the truth of one's creaturely identity. Alongside this there is a clear value set on actual poverty and on all that militates against pride in terms of insults, contempt and humiliation. These are seen by Ignatius to have real value in the life of a Christian. The very mysticism of the Triple Colloquy is an expression of Ignatius' mystical prayer life. References to the Holy Spirit proliferate in the *Spiritual Diary* underlining the importance of the Holy Spirit in Ignatius' mystical life. Within Ignatius' own personal writings, including his letters there is a link between the Holy Spirit and his experience of consolation, desolation and confirmation.

Ignatius is clear that Christ configures the wills of human persons to the will of the Trinity. Christ's humanity is often an entry point for Ignatius in prayer.[64] Christ is the one who is both the mediator to the Father and the

---

so that the Son is the love and the Father the beloved. This introduces a kind of circular dynamism to the inner divine life which Aquinas refers to as kind of intellectual "motion." (*Summa Contra Gentiles* IV, 19, 12). ... It seems therefore, that God's knowledge becomes the cause of creation and the ground of the continual subsistence of the cosmos, while the Holy Spirit, which proceeds from the Father and the Son by way of love, is properly described as the principle of the motion of nature. This means that what moves all things to their characteristic operation is love, namely a desire for fulfillment [or return] in the beloved." Simon Oliver, "Love Makes the World God 'Round: Motion and Trinity," in ed. David L. Schindler, *Love Alone is Credible: Hans Urs von Balthasar as Interpreter of the Catholic Tradition*, Vol. 1 (Grand Rapids, MI: Wm B. Eerdmans, 2008), 177–88, [177–81].

[62] I am thinking here of the key meditations on the "Two Standards," "The Three Classes of Person," and the "Three Kinds of Humility."

[63] *Spiritual Exercises* 147.

[64] Ignatius from his time in Manresa had an ongoing sense of the near presence of the humanity of Christ and this also influences his writing of the *Spiritual Exercises*, cf. "consider what Christ Our Lord suffers in His human nature, or is willing to suffer, depending on the episode that one is contemplating;" and again "consider [how] he allows Himself in His sacred human nature to suffer most cruelly." *Spiritual Exercises* 196.

reflection of the beauty of the Father. He it is who is the way to the Father.[65]
He it is who brings the Church into being as inextricably linked to himself,
the head, and who draws followers to serve within the Church.[66] Over time
this ecclesial sense became more coherent for him as he was transformed
from Ignatius the pilgrim into Ignatius the man of service to the Church.[67]

The way Christ leads to the Father is always by way of the Cross.
Ignatius sees the Cross in its Trinitarian implications. The crucified one
is the obedient Son, the essence of all service to the Father. The Father's
will to reconcile the world encompasses the paschal mystery and the Spirit
maintains the unity that is stretched to its zenith in the unfolding of passion
and death. The sign of the election is to suffer with—compassion[68]—the
crucified Christ. For Ignatius also it becomes clear that this is both an
individual and a communal experience for the Church. As we have seen
in the previous chapter, for Ignatius, it was in the sacrifice of the Eucharist
that union with Christ found its most profound communal expression.[69]

---

[65] Cf. Jn 14.6.

[66] Cf. Pope Paul VI wrote: "The first benefit which we trust the Church will reap from a
deepened self-awareness, is a renewed discovery of its vital bond of union with Christ. This
is something which is perfectly well-known, but it is supremely important and absolutely
essential. It can never be sufficiently understood, meditated upon and preached." *Ecclesiam
Suam*, August 6, 1964, [622].

[67] When accused in 1537 of being heterodox, which happened to Ignatius on numerous
occasions, he was as always exonerated. Even though he was used to humiliations and insults
and to forgiving others, he would never give an inch when he was accused of not having
doctrinal rectitude or not living honestly. He was not merely satisfied with being declared
innocent, he took further steps by having a number of copies of the authentic transcripts of
the decision made, and he sent one of these copies to his friend Pietro Contarini. The reason
for his attitude was clearly explained in the covering letter, written in Latin, that he wrote to
Contarini, from which we translate the following paragraph: "We shall never be disturbed if
we are called ignorant, rude, unskilled in speaking, or even if we are called wicked, liars, and
unstable men. But we were grieved that our teaching was considered unsound in this affair
and that the *way* we have been following was thought bad. Neither the one nor the other
is from ourselves. They belong to Christ and His Church." The sense of the ecclesial was
becoming more and more centralized in his thinking, and as time went on, it would become
more coherent." Idigoras, *Ignatius of Loyola The Pilgrim Saint*, trans. and ed. [with a preface]
Cornelius Michael Buckley, S.J. (Chicago: Loyola University Press, 1994), 407–8.

[68] The compassion that Ignatius suggests that retreatants pray for is both a share in Christ's
apparently fruitless love for a sinful world and the compassion that is a source of strength as
the *Anima Christi* prayer states, *passio Christi conforta me*. Such prayer is both an opening to
the graced reality of Christ's passion and by grace drawing from this experience the strength
to live fully a life which will inevitably involve suffering.

[69] Devotion to the most Blessed Sacrament took deep root in St. Ignatius' soul from the earliest
days of his "conversion" in the paternal castle of Loyola. Soon he began to recommend it
earnestly to his fellow-townsmen of Azpeitia. During the providential sojourn at Manresa,
before finding means to embark at Barcelona for the Holy Land, he heard Mass every day
with great fervor and tenderness of soul. Certain it is that our Lord rewarded his devotion
with a very special grace. According to Father Ribadeneira: "One day in the church of that
monastery he was hearing Mass with deep reverence and devotion. At the moment when the
host was raised and shown to the people, he saw clearly with the eyes of his soul in what

Eucharistic devotion is also evident within the letters of St. Ignatius, for example a letter he wrote to the people of the town of Azpeitia, dated September 1540, on the occasion of a Papal Bull to establish the Confraternity of Minerva.[70] "I beg of you strongly and entreat you with all my heart for the love and reverence of God our Lord to bend every effort towards honoring, pleasing and serving His only-begotten Son, Christ our Lord, in this gift of the most Blessed Sacrament."[71] In a letter to Sister Teresa Rejadell from November 1543, Ignatius replies in the affirmative to her enquiry as to whether she should receive communion on a daily basis.[72]

---

way our Lord, Jesus Christ, true God and true Man, is truly hidden in that divine mystery beneath that veil and species of bread. Through this divine favor, doubtless, devotion to the adorable sacrament of the altar increased greatly in St. Ignatius' soul. The supernatural knowledge granted him of the way in which our Lord, Jesus Christ, is really and truly present in the consecrated host kindled more and more ardently in his breast the longing to unite himself with Him in holy communion as often and as intimately as possible. ... despite the almost universal custom of the times, we find Ignatius already confessing and communicating every week. ... From the beginning of his conversion St. Ignatius became so enamored of this practice that he insisted on it constantly for the rest of his life. This is evident especially in his letters, the Spiritual Exercises and the Constitutions of the Society of Jesus. ... He recommended this salutary practice to others wherever he went. In Alcalá an unusual change was observed in the university and the town, with much frequentation of the sacraments. ... In Paris, as Father Laynez wrote on this point to Father Polanco in 1547: 'As to spiritual things, at all times wherever he (Ignatius) has been, it seems that through him our Lord has moved many souls. ...' In Rome we find him carrying forward his Eucharistic mission by means of letters to persons of different stations in life and in different places. By this means he extended his Eucharistic apostolate in an extraordinary way to hundreds and thousands of the faithful, clerics as well as lay." P. Justo Beguiriztain, S.J., *The Eucharistic Apostolate of St. Ignatius Loyola,* trans. John H. Collins, S.J. (1955), 3–13.

[70] "[or] of the Blessed Sacrament. This Confraternity has existed down to the present moment (1955)." Ibid., 14.

[71] This continues "Therein His divine Majesty, in His divinity and humanity, is as great and as entire, as mighty and as infinite as it is in heaven. ... St. Ignatius closes his beautiful Eucharistic letter to his fellow—Azpeitians with this further burning request: 'Because I hope that God our Lord in His wonted infinite goodness and mercy will for your clear and manifest service shower down His most holy grace abundantly on the souls of all, I close by begging, entreating and imploring you, by the love and reverence you bear Him, to grant me always a share in your prayers, especially in those to the most Blessed Sacrament. All of you will at all times have the whole of mine, poor and unworthy though they be." Ibid., 16.

[72] "As for communicating daily, I recall that in the early Church everyone communicated daily. From that time till now there has been no ordination or written pronouncement of our Holy Mother Church or of the saintly scholastic doctors or positive theologians, which says that those who are moved to it out of devotion may not communicate daily. ... Wherefore, although you may not receive any great signs or trustworthy inspirations, the best and most complete testimony is the dictate of your own conscience. If, free from what are clearly mortal sins or what you may be able to judge such, you think that your soul is helped more and inflamed with greater love of our Creator and Lord; if you communicate with such intention, finding from experience that this most holy spiritual manna sustains you in peace and quiet and by keeping you in such dispositions, helps you to greater service, praise and glory, you need have no doubt that it is lawful and that it will be better for you to communicate every day." Ibid., 18.

In a letter to Francis Borgia in 1545 when the latter was still Duke of Gandía, Ignatius is delighted to hear that Borgia communicates frequently. "I give great thanks to His Divine Goodness that your Lordship, from what I have heard, receives Him frequently. In addition to the great increase of grace the soul obtains in receiving its Creator and Lord, this frequent reception is the chief reason why He does not allow the soul to remain obstinate in sin."[73]

The Ignatian vision is always that of the Trinity working in the world. In response to this dynamic activity of the Trinity, we are called as human persons to let go of self-centeredness in order to offer ourselves as willing participants in the divine mission. This is not an individual enterprise. Rather, it is in and through the Church that the redemptive work of God is enacted. As we experience the presence of God within, we are led to a deeper union with God and the Church. In addition we are also energized for the ministry we are called to undertake as members of the Church in participating in God's redemptive work.[74] Here is where contemplation in action is revealed in its fullness.

To the heart that is focused on God, everything becomes a spiritual experience because there is an openness to perceive the presence of God in all circumstances. In this way God may be spoken of as present in all things. Ignatius affirmed in this way of proceeding that Christian mystical union is essentially a union of love. Accordingly, there is always the possibility of our being conformed to the divine will in any circumstances if we desire to maintain that union.[75] It is the mission of the Holy Spirit to assist that life of the Spirit within. When a soul is filled with God then everything leads to God. Thus, a key characteristic of Ignatius' ecclesial disposition is an appreciation of the importance of the Trinity at work in the world. There is also a deep awareness of being called to a union of love with God and the Church. Finally, there is through this union an energized involvement

---

[73] "As soon as it falls into sin, even in things which are quite small (granted anything can be called small, when the object is infinite, the Summum Bonum), He straightway lifts it up stronger and more firmly resolved to serve its Lord better." Ibid., 19.

[74] Here we find contemporary resonances with the documents of Vatican II, particularly *Lumen Gentium*. For example "[Christ] continually distributes in His body, that is, in the Church, gifts of ministries in which by His own power, we serve each other unto salvation so that, carrying out the truth in love, we might through all things grow unto Him who is our Head." [7]; "Upon all the laity, therefore, rests the noble duty of working to extend the divine plan of salvation to all men of each epoch and in every land. Consequently, may every opportunity be given them so that, according to their abilities and the needs of the times, they may zealously participate in the saving work of the Church." [33]; see also paragraphs [8], [9], [17], [41]. All in Flannery, O.P. (ed.), *Vatican Council II: The Conciliar and Post Conciliar Documents*, 350–426.

[75] A way of maintaining that union is through the Contemplation to Attain the Love of God, *Spiritual Exercises* 230–7.

with the redemptive work of God both at an individual level and in the communal experience of the Church.

The Graced Human Person

The first word of the "Principle and Foundation"[76] in the *Spiritual Exercises* is 'man'—the generic reality of the human person. Ignatius' emphasis is not on the human person alone. For the rest of this first consideration calls the one making the *Spiritual Exercises* to consider that the true vocation of the human person is the praise, reverence and service of God. It is the mystery of the Trinity that is the center of the Ignatian vision, as we have seen already. It is this working, laboring, God in three Persons who accomplishes creation and the redemption of the world.[77] It is the wonder of God's working that Ignatius contemplates. God works, and labors, and thus anyone called to discipleship will need to work also. The place of that working will be the mission of the Church—a share in the redemptive mission of Christ.

The place of human endeavor is human history. It is here that the individual is called within the Church to labor. Through preaching and the sacraments the Church continues the mission of Christ in every age. It is a dramatic mission, as we have seen, since it means participation with Christ in the struggle against the enemy of our human nature. Here, Ignatius focuses on the deep reality of spiritual captivity. We are so often ensnared by our own particular form of "riches" and "honors" that lead inevitably to pride.[78] Only Christ can liberate the human person from this form of

---

[76] *Spiritual Exercises* 23.

[77] Here we might note the way in which the "Principle and Foundation" is recapitulated in the "Contemplation to Attain the Love of God." In completing the *Exercises* the retreatant is sent back into his or her ordinary life and occupations endeavoring to seek the love of God present in all things and thus live out the fullness of a creaturely vocation, namely to praise reverence and serve God and to keep this as a focus through all involvement with people and material things. The active grace of Ignatian "indifference" is a grace to be ongoingly prayed for.

[78] See The Two Standards, *Spiritual Exercises* 137–48. Feminist critique of this triad of prides, riches and honor and the opposing stress on humility outline significant issues for some women. "Such emphasis on the traditional categories of pride and capital sins, besides presenting reproach and contempt as desirable, raises negative responses in some contemporary women. ... Humility too, is an ambiguous virtue, especially if presented as the desirable result of reproaches and contempt. Often the expectations for humility reflect a gender bias with differing written and unwritten norms for women and men. Some women associate humility with patriarchal obedience and submission to father, husband or priest. Humility has frequently been equated with passivity, hiding, and low self-esteem, all of which have been detrimental to women's responsible adult development." Katherine Dyckman, Mary Garvin, Elizabeth Liebert (eds), *The Spiritual Exercises Reclaimed: Uncovering Liberating Possibilities for Women,* (New York and Mahwah: Paulist Press, 2001), 196–7. This author would want to reclaim the positive understanding of the importance of humility.

captivity. Such liberation is the will of the Father and Christ accomplishes this in the power of the Spirit.

The graced human person, as Ignatius envisages, is one who is magnanimous in leaving behind one's own ways of self-absorption and who desires to enter into the way of God. Such a loving disposition in a soul will enable one to be of outstanding service in the struggle. Ignatius desired, above all, that those who entered the Society of Jesus were capable of doing something great for love of God and indeed in the choice of ministries the principle of the more universal good and the multiplying effect—to help those first who had the possibility of passing on to many others the result of such graced assistance—was to be operative.[79] Such great actions are only possible for those who depend entirely on the grace of God at work within them, and not on their own natural capabilities. This is possible, by God's grace, for any individual.

It follows that such dependence upon the Lord encourages the growth of obedience. The goal of obedience is a will so focused on the divine will that it is not impeded by a contrary human will.[80] Obedience here is not only a matter of conformity to the will of God but is also a condition for union

---

[79] "To make the best choice in sending persons to one place or another while having the greater service of God and the more universal good before one's eyes is the guiding norm. ... consideration should also be given to where greater fruit is likely to be reaped through the means usual in the Society; as would be the case where one sees the door more widely open and a better disposition and readiness among the people to be profited. ... The more universal the good is, the more is it divine. Hence preference ought to be given to persons and places which, once benefited themselves, are a cause of extending the good to many others who are under their influence or take guidance from them. For that reason, the spiritual aid which is given to important and public persons ought to be regarded as more important, since it is a more universal good. This holds true also of spiritual aid given to persons who are distinguished for learning and authority, for the same reason of the good being more universal." *Constitutions* 622, 623.

[80] "It is very helpful for making progress and highly necessary that all devote themselves to complete obedience, recognizing the superior, whoever he is, as being in the place of Christ our Lord and maintaining interior reverence and love for him. They should obey entirely and promptly, not only by exterior execution of what the superior commands, with due fortitude and humility and without excuses or complaints, even though things are commanded which are difficult and repugnant to sensitive nature, but also by striving interiorly to have genuine resignation and abnegation of their own wills and judgments, bringing their wills and judgments wholly into conformity with what the superior wills and judges in all things in which no sin is seen, and regarding the superior's will and judgment as the rule of their own, so as to conform themselves more completely to the first and supreme rule of all good will and judgment, which is the Eternal Goodness and Wisdom." *Constitutions* [284]. Cf. "Consequently, in all things into which obedience can with charity be extended, we should be ready to receive its command just as if it were coming from Christ our Savior, since we are practicing the obedience [to one] in his place and because of love and reverence for him. Therefore we should be ready to leave unfinished any letter or anything else of course which we have begun, and in the Lord to bend our whole mind and energy so that holy obedience, in regard to the execution, the willing and the understanding, may always be perfect in every detail, as we perform with great alacrity, spiritual joy, and perseverance whatever has been commanded us." *Constitutions* [547].

with God. This is a way of self-abnegation,[81] which enables the purification and transformation of the human will into the divine will. Lest I give the impression here that the human will somehow "disappears" leaving a kind of monism I would simply reiterate that the focus of Ignatius' attention to obedience is on a union of will with the Lord such that one might say "I will what God wills," "I want only what God wants." It is this bond of a particular intimacy—not just a cerebral loyalty but a deep affective intimacy—that lies at the heart of Ignatius' understanding of obedience and that is central to the Ignatian ecclesial disposition.

It is this level of obedience that Ignatius seeks for members of the Society of Jesus and it is in these terms that he writes to the Jesuits of Portugal, "Try to see who it is you are obeying ... Christ, the supreme wisdom, immense goodness, infinite love ... You have the certainty that it is out of love for Him that you have placed yourselves under obedience, submitting to the opinion of a superior in order to be most in agreement with the will of God."[82] Clearly this is easier to write about than to undertake. Such union of our wills with the will of God, however, by the grace of God is a real possibility. Belief in this God-given freedom and the call to dependence and union with God is another key characteristic of Ignatius' ecclesial disposition. For Ignatius freedom and obedience were integrally linked. "Try then, dear brothers, to set aside completely your own wishes.

---

[81] "The better to arrive at this degree of perfection which is so precious in the spiritual life, his chief and most earnest endeavor should be to seek in our Lord his greater abnegation and continual mortification in all things possible; and our endeavor should be to help him in those things to the extent that our Lord gives his grace, for his greater praise and glory." Constitutions [103]. Such self-abnegation was considered to be fundamental to the lives of those called to the Society of Jesus.

[82] Ignatius Loyola, letter to Jesuits of Portugal, March 26, 1553. See also "It is not because superiors happen to be very prudent or very good people, nor because they are endowed with any other gifts of God our Lord, that they are to be obeyed, but because 'He who listens to you listens to me; he who despises you, despises me' ... [superiors] are representatives of the One who is infallible Wisdom and who makes up for whatever may be lacking in His ministers. ... So no matter who your superiors are, I would like you all to practice recognizing in them Christ Our Lord, and to reverence and obey in them His divine Majesty with complete devotion. ... Given the exceptional value of our wills, the sacrifice of them, offered in obedience to their Creator and Lord, is correspondingly great ... . Obedience is nothing less than a holocaust. It is there we can offer ourselves completely, without excluding any part of ourselves, in the fire of love to our Creator and Lord at the hands of His ministers. By obedience one puts aside all that one is, one dispossesses oneself of all that one has, in order to be possessed and governed by divine Providence by means of a superior ... . My request to you, for the love of Christ Our Lord, who not only gave the precept but led the way with his example of obedience, is that you should all make a great effort to attain obedience by winning a glorious triumph over yourselves ... . Then the true knowledge and love of God Our Lord will be able to take possession and control of your inner souls during all this pilgrimage, until the day when He leads you, along with many others won through your means, to the final and most blessed goal of eternal happiness." Ibid.

With great liberality, offer the liberty that He gave you to your Creator and Lord present in His ministers. Consider that it is no small privilege of your freedom of will to be able to return it completely in obedience to the One who gave it to you. You do not destroy it in this way; rather you bring it to perfection as you put your own wishes in line with the most sure rule of all rightness, the will of God."[83]

Unity and Tension

Ignatius' vision of union with God has inspired generations of men and women. A mysticism of union and service brings together prayer and work in one integrated whole. It links both personal creativity and obedient submission as we have seen in Ignatius' own focus upon obedience detailed above. It values the gifted nature of the individual and sees the individual always as a member of the body of the Church.

This sense of personal service in the Church has real positive potential. It can stimulate the adaptation of Roman Catholicism to every present situation and we see many examples of this in the Church's long history of evangelization. This Ignatian ecclesial disposition can instill a healthy recognition that intelligence and will, theory and practice, theological conviction and ecclesiastical policy, can never be unrelated. Holy thoughts must arise from a well-ordered and discerning love and must serve to build up the Church as the community of love. As an example, theology is not to be a matter of the mind alone; rather it involves also the affectivity and the imagination, which together with the intellect, form one harmonious response as faith seeks an ever greater understanding through the field of study. Theories and concepts should always point beyond themselves to a reality that is divine.

A characteristic position of the Society of Jesus is the transparency of representation.[84] This is revealed in the practice of manifestation of conscience.[85] Here an individual shares with the superior where he has a

---

[83] Ibid.

[84] At the very heart of the process of governance of the Society of Jesus is this transparency of representation between members of the Society and their legitimate superiors. Such transparency is central to an understanding of the vow of obedience. It is seen as vital that each member of the Society make known to the superior the way in which the Lord is guiding their own discernment. The practical manifestation of this transparency is through the manifestation of conscience.

[85] The "Jesuit Constitutions" (paras 91 and 92) in the *Examen* indicate Ignatius' attitude which forms the contextual background for our understanding what he has to say regarding manifestation of conscience or interior dispositions. He states: "It is a matter of great and even extraordinary importance that the superiors should have a complete understanding of the subjects, that by means of it they may be able to direct and govern them better, and while looking out for the subjects' interests guide them better into the paths of the Lord" [91]. And

sense of the Lord leading him in prayer and work. Such a transparency of representation sees the individual in the Church and the Church in Christ. Christ himself here leads into the fullness of Trinitarian relations. Thus, the man "making manifestation" is entrusting himself to Christ "in the person of the superior." The superior receiving manifestation is enabled, by his interior knowledge of the man for whom he is responsible, to make a wise decision concerning the man's part in the mission of the Society of Jesus. In this way the Church is well served.

The Ignatian focus of personal service towards the ever-greater God turns out, in the end, to be the surest path to truth and freedom. It is undertaken with many other companions in the community of the Church. It is an application of that scriptural principle of the Kingdom of God whereby the loss of life for Christ is the gain of life. For the truth of God's love and redemptive work reigns supreme. Thus an attempt to promote the glory of God in whatever field is always a work of reverent service with Christ.

The Heart of the Ecclesial Disposition of Ignatius

Ignatius was filled with a sense of God's exalted mystery, a man—as it were—intoxicated by God. In the Contemplation to Attain the Love of God,[86] Ignatius directs the one making the *Spiritual Exercises* to ponder how all limited perfections come from the supreme and infinite power

---

again "Likewise the more completely the superiors know these subjects; interior and exterior affairs, just so much the better will they be able, with greater diligence, love, and care, to help the subjects and to guard their souls from various inconveniences and dangers which might occur later on. ... To proceed without error in such missions, or in sending some persons and not others, or some for one task and others for different ones, it is not only highly but even supremely important for the superior to have complete knowledge of the inclinations and motions of those who are in his charge, [and that] while keeping to himself what he learns in secret, may be better able to organize and arrange what is expedient for the whole body of the Society" [92]. "Wherefore, whoever wishes to follow this Society in our Lord or to remain in it for His greater glory must be obliged to the following. ... he must manifest his conscience with great humility, integrity, and charity, without concealing anything which is offensive to the Lord of all men. ... in order that better provision may be made in the Lord for everything. Thus with His more abundant grace the candidate is helped more in spiritual progress, to the greater glory of His Divine Goodness." [93]. *The Constitutions of the Society of Jesus* 91, 92, 93. In addition it might be remarked that "manifestation of the interior state of one's soul was a common practice in religious life from the time of St. Anthony (d. 356). Until approximately 1000 it was used solely for the spiritual progress of the individual. St. Bonaventure (1221–74) approved superiors' use of the resulting knowledge to adjust religious observances to the subject's capacities. St. Ignatius notably expanded this use of the manifestation as an instrument to further the subject's spiritual welfare, the government of the Society, and its apostolic works." Ibid., fn. 19.

[86] *Spiritual Exercises* 230–7.

above as rays of light descend from the sun.[87] This sense of reverence and wonder was central to Ignatius' understanding of God. Yet reverent though he was in the presence of God, Ignatius was also convinced that God was never distant. He had a clear sense of intimacy with the Lord. He saw that God dwells in all creatures, especially human persons, giving life and intelligence,[88] and making them temples of the Holy Spirit. One of the early companions of Ignatius, Pedro Ribadeneira, said of him, "We often saw how even the smallest things could make his spirit soar upward to God."[89] In this way Ignatius saw that every created thing is, in its inmost being, transparent to the divine. This unity of reverence and intimacy is an essential ingredient of Ignatius' ecclesial disposition.

United to God in the depths of his soul, Ignatius never lost his sense of the divine presence when engaged in the different activities of daily living. He had, and wished his followers to have, the grace to find God in all things. In the famous phrase of Nadal, he was: "contemplative in the midst of action."[90] We have already seen something of the demanding nature of this principle. Christ and the following of Christ, in union with the Church and embracing the Cross, is the way of discipleship.

This ecclesial disposition is the one that informs all the rest of his writings. It is the context and subtext of his conversion trajectory as outlined in the *Autobiography*, where the illumination of his reason (mystically as at Manresa, and more naturally as his ongoing studies at Alcala, Barcelona and Paris indicate) and his deeper affective union to Christ and the Trinity which begins at his convalescence bed in Loyola, where he first observes his consolations, and continues to Rome many years later, as evidenced in *The Spiritual Diary*, in which he relates his "affectionate awe, closer to reverential love."[91] For Ignatius, along with his many motions and tears, intellectual illumination and affective devotion are continuously together in his spiritual life.

What is distinct and unwavering is his humble submission to the authorities of the Church that enter his life, even when he is imprisoned awaiting judgment. It is a waiting entirely bereft of bitterness or rancor, despite a certain "injustice" known only to the logic of his love for Christ and his Church.[92] He submits to the Franciscan authorities in the Holy Land, to the Dominican authorities and the judgment of the ecclesiastical court in

---

[87] *Spiritual Exercises* 237.
[88] *Spiritual Exercises* 235.
[89] Cited in Rahner, S.J., *Ignatius the Theologian* 23.
[90] *Simul in actione comtemplativus.*
[91] *Spiritual Diary* [26].
[92] As we shall see in later sections this kind of Ignatian *submission* to the judgment of the Church is echoed in the lives of later Jesuits. In particular we might cite Henri de Lubac's period of "silence" during which, like Ignatius, he waited patiently while refusing to use the advocacy of influential friends on his behalf. Each could be considered true *"vir ecclesiasticus"* in this regard.

Salamanca (and is imprisoned for twenty-two days), and asks the inquisitor to pass judgment on him and his writings in Paris. This submission reaches its apogee when the fledgling society decides to go to Rome and "present themselves to the vicar of Christ, so that he could make use of them whenever he thought it would be to the greater glory of God and service of souls."[93] Obedience, for Ignatius, can be seen for what it was: true listening ("*oboedire*"—to listen to), a discernment of the will of God, and a desire to fulfill it through action.

In July 1547, Ignatius wrote to the Jesuits of Gandia[94] about obedience, and reminded them of the convincing example of Christ, obedient to his parents in Nazareth, then deigning to be superior of the disciples as they lived together. He then relates that "when he had to depart from them physically, he left them St. Peter to be superior over the others and over his whole Church, entrusting their governance to him: 'Feed my sheep.'"[95] There is no question that Ignatius sees in the Petrine office the legitimate superior of the Church and of the Society, according to the desires of Christ himself.

It is perhaps in his letter to the Fathers and Scholastics at Coimbra[96] that the motive behind Ignatius' desire to think with the Church is best articulated, although by analogy, since he is writing about obedience within the Society.[97] He gives several rational reasons for instituting obedience

---

[93] "Autobiography." [85].

[94] The letter is dated Rome, July 29, 1547. Ignatius is here writing to a community of scholastics at Gandia, which was one of the earliest Jesuit houses in Spain. Ignatius in his first major text on religious obedience, details the advantages of living under such obedience; then, as a temporary expedient until a professed Jesuit is present and the *Constitutions* are promulgated, he instructs them on how to elect a superior for themselves. The person whom they chose was Andrés de Oviedo. Many of the themes advanced here will appear later and in greater detail in Ignatius' great letter on the subject, written in 1553 to the Jesuits in Portugal. Martin E. Palmer S.J., John W. Padberg S.J., and John L. McCarthy S.J. (eds), *Ignatius of Loyola Letters and Instructions* (St. Louis: Institute of Jesuit Sources, 2006), 195.

[95] Jn 21.17.

[96] To the Members of the Society in Portugal, the letter is dated Rome, March 26, 1553, "Generations of Jesuits heard [this letter] read at table once a month in their refectories. The letter was written in the context of the split in the province between the supporters and the opponents of the former provincial, Simão Rodrigues, and of the tension brought about by his successor, Diego Miró, a good but rigid individual. Even an official visitor sent by Ignatius, Miguel de Torres, could not re-establish peace and unity. About thirty men left the Society during this restless period. At one point Ignatius even asked Gonçalves da Câmara, 'Who is provincial?'" This is the fullest of Ignatius' several treatments of the subject [of obedience]. *Ignatius of Loyola Letters and Instructions*, 412.

[97] Ignatius extols obedience above every other virtue. "This is not only because of its own extraordinary worth, so emphasized by word and example in sacred Scripture, both Old and New Testaments, but because, as St. Gregory says, obedience is a virtue which alone implants all the other virtues in the mind and preserves them once implanted. To the extent that this virtue flourishes, all the other virtues will be seen to flourish and produce in your souls the fruits which I desire and which are demanded by him who through his own obedience

within the fledgling order, including the human need for authority, and the precedents within the life of the Church. He calls for a fervent life of service, evoking the reward of eternal life that awaits the faithful servant, citing passages of scripture to back up his case.[98] But these considerations being given, he turns to his ultimate reason for disposing his life to the good of souls in the Church: "But above all I want you to be stirred up by the pure love of Jesus Christ, by a longing for his honor and for the salvation of the souls he has redeemed."[99] This ultimate motive is behind the entire "figure" of Ignatius' desire to think with the Church.

Our exploration of Ignatius' ecclesial disposition in this chapter has led us to a rich understanding. This disposition is no mere vacillating attitude, nor a strident ideology. Rather, it is a graced gift. It involves an avowed belief in the work of the Trinity within the world, drawing human persons towards union. Christ is central here as Christ is the one who calls us into this union and to share in the redemptive work of God through the Church. Christ and the Church are conjoined. Ignatius' ecclesial disposition recognizes that human persons, graced by God, are able to respond to God in magnanimity, with courage, with generosity and employing the way of contemplative discernment. Willingness to embrace the Cross in imitation of Christ is clearly a part of this disposition and ensures a certain "tension" of being totally dependent upon God and fully and actively engaged in the mission. Finally, the concrete outworking of Ignatius' ecclesial disposition is always in faithfulness to the Church and loyalty and obedience to the Pope.

As we turn now to consider sixteenth and seventeenth century exemplars, we have a clearer sense of the ecclesial disposition that we are looking to find in the witness of their lives and writings.

---

redeemed the world which had been lost through lack of it, becoming obedient unto death, death on a cross. [Phil. 2.8]" Ibid., 413.

[98] "We may let other religious orders outdo us in fasting, night-watches, and other austerities which each one, following its own institute, holily observes. But in the purity and perfection of obedience, with genuine resignation of our wills and abnegation of our judgment, I am very desirous, dear brothers, that those who serve God in this Society should distinguish themselves, and that its true sons may be recognized by this – never looking to the person whom they obey, but in that person, to Christ our Lord, for whose sake they obey." Ibid.

[99] Ibid., 415.

PART TWO

Sixteenth and Seventeenth Century Exemplars

Introduction

In the last chapter we clarified our understanding of Ignatius' ecclesial disposition as a graced gift. We came to see that his disposition towards the Church was clearly grounded in his understanding of revelation. Therefore it was dependent upon his perceived understanding of the relationship between the Trinity and human persons. We noted the centrality for him of a profound relationship with Christ who draws individuals to union with the Trinity. We considered the importance of the sacramental life of the Church particularly the Eucharist and the sacrament of penance. We explored key characteristics that give color and depth to this disposition such as courage and generosity. We affirmed the importance of contemplative discernment as a mode of living and relating in this disposition and as a way of embracing the reality of the Cross in life. We concluded by emphasizing that the concrete manifestation of this disposition was in a clear love for the Church and faithfulness to the Church expressed in obedience to the Holy Father and to legitimate superiors.

In this section we shall engage with two historical exemplars of this ecclesial disposition, a man and a woman. Amidst turbulent times the spirit and intention underpinning this ecclesial disposition are given expression in the lives of an early Jesuit, the first under consideration is one of Ignatius' companions[1] Pierre Favre (1506–46), and the foundress of a new religious order, Mary Ward (1585–1645). Through their words and actions, they gave witness to Ignatius' will for all Jesuits, and indeed for all believing Catholics, concerning their disposition towards the Church, its practices, thought and authority. None of the figures chosen replicates exactly Ignatius' own ecclesial disposition. It would be impossible so to do as we are considering unique individuals not cloned human persons. What we do find, however, is that each of the individuals manifest within their lives and writings certain key aspects of the ecclesial disposition in conjunction with the central dynamic of the disposition namely a profound relationship with Christ. It is, above all, their personal sanctity that shines forth, giving strongest testimony of this witness.

Pierre Favre was from the Duchy of Savoy. Mary Ward was an English woman whose life bridges the sixteenth and seventeenth centuries. She outlived Favre and her legacy was the formation of a religious order for women formed by the *Spiritual Exercises* and ultimately taking the same *Constitutions* of the Society of Jesus. We shall explore the lives and writings of these two exemplars seeking evidence of Ignatius' ecclesial disposition in: that ardent love for the person of Christ that is fostered by his use of, and exhortation to use, one's reason and affectivity, emphasizing the union of learning and holiness; in a renewed emphasis on sacramental practice; and in the lived reality of obedience.

---

[1]The early companions included: Francis Xavier, Alfonso Salmeron, Diego Lainez, Nicholas Bobadilla (all Spaniards); Simon Rodrigues, Portugese and Pierre Favre, a Savoyard. Later they were joined by Jean Codure and Paschal Broët, both French, and Claude Le Jay, another Savoyard.

4

Saint Pierre Favre, S.J.

Within our exploration of the life and writings of Pierre Favre we find that a devout Catholic upbringing and education was the fertile ground for a deep personal commitment to Christ and his body—the Church. The ecclesial disposition is particularly manifested through his emphasis on the centrality of sacramental life; the importance of devotions in assisting consciousness of the presence of God and the operative practice of obedience.

The Witness of Life

It was in the village of Villaret, in the Grand Bornand, a valley of the Savoy Alps[1] that Pierre Favre was born April 13, 1506. This new Savoyard[2] was

---

[1] "The mountains confront the Savoyards at every turn: summer and winter they impose a way of life on them. It is a pitiless struggle—a struggle that has bred in them the qualities that mark their character: courage, foresight, ingenuity, a tenacious effort that refuses to slacken until victory is assured." *The Spiritual Writings of Pierre Favre*, eds Edmond C. Murphy, S.J. and John W. Padberg, S.J. (St. Louis: Institute of Jesuit Sources, 1996), 8.

[2] Situated in the western Alps with its capital at Chambéry, the duchy of Savoy began as a county of the Holy Roman Empire in the Middle Ages. During the reign of Amadeus VIII (1391–1436), the duchy acquired significant territory in Piedmont, east of the Alps, and its ruler was promoted to the status of duke by the Holy Roman emperor in 1416. In the fifteenth century, the duchy of Savoy included both Nice and Geneva, but by the sixteenth century the focus of the duchy turned east of the Alps. Savoy and the other western territories were difficult to defend against the powerful neighbor state of France. The plains of Piedmont offered more fertile land, greater population, and more possibility of expansion. Turin, the largest city in Piedmont, became the capital of the duchy in 1560. The survival of the duchy as an independent state was precarious throughout the sixteenth century. In general, France and Spain recognized that Savoy provided an important buffer between their states, and the game of diplomacy often worked well for Savoy. At others times, it caused disaster. During the Italian Wars of the sixteenth century, France overran and occupied the state in 1536. Duke Emanuel Filibert, through an alliance with Spain, managed to reconstruct the Savoyard state in 1559 in the peace of Cateau-Cambrésis. Subsequent dukes were less successful, and once again, Savoy was reduced to the status of a French satellite until the late seventeenth century.

the eldest child of a poor devoutly Catholic family.[3] At the time of Favre's birth Savoy was still rooted in medieval spirituality, there was no hint of the religious ferment that was to erupt in that area during his adult life.[4] With such a devout family[5] Favre had a very religious upbringing, in which the liturgical seasons of the Church and the seasons of the countryside formed a harmonious pattern of life for him. Indeed, we can see that his home environment was such that it inclined him naturally toward an acceptance of faith and to participation in the Church as part of the very fabric of his being. In the *Memoriale* he states: "Even about the age of seven, and this is a sign of an additional grace from God, I felt some especial movements of devotion. So from that time on, the Lord and spouse of my soul willed to take possession of the depths of my soul." [6]

Major Influences on Favre's Early Life

Favre spent part of his early life, from the age of seven to ten, as a shepherd.[7] He came to read the signs of weather, nature and season, and

---

[3]The village was at that time in an area that was predominantly Roman Catholic. "Catholicism has marked the Savoyards: the example and inspiration of the saints, the spiritual blessings that flow from the shrines of Our Lady dotting the land. It was a region of strong traditional piety—not just a matter of pious observances—that linked family to family. The Confraternity of The Holy Spirit, a branch of which had been established in nearly all parishes by Favre's day, included members of every family in a parish. From each person they collected offerings of crops, firewood, fleeces, meat, and other necessities of life for distribution among the needy, the sick, widows, orphans and the aged. The poor were not neglected: there were special boxes for the collection of alms to be distributed to them." *The Spiritual Writings of Pierre Favre*, 12.

[4]"Records of the passing scene left by contemporary travellers show that there was little scepticism and no general revolt against Christian teaching and principles. Festivals, sacred as well as profane might sometimes be marked by grossness, immorality and brutality, but on the whole life was anchored in a profound if not always well-instructed faith. Denial of dogma, sacrilege, failure to receive the sacraments at Easter, prolonged absence from Mass were rare." Mary Purcell, *The Quiet Companion* (Chicago: Loyola University Press, 1970), 13.

[5]Favre himself says of his family: "Our Lord ... gave me the grace to be baptized and to be brought up by good and very pious Catholic parents [Louis Favre and Marie Perissin] ... My parents brought me up in the fear of God our Lord in such a way that I began, while yet quite young, to be conscious of myself." Pierre Favre, "The Memoriale of Pierre Favre" [1 and 2], in *The Spiritual Writings of Pierre Favre*, 60–1. This sense of being conscious of himself was being conscious of his own behavior and any wrongdoing in his actions. "Favre means that he was fearful of transgressing the law of God as taught him by his parents. In this they showed their wisdom: fear of God is the heart of any genuine religious disposition. At an early age he had begun to take stock of his behavior, to examine his conscience; this is surely the beginning of a life-long habit of introspection." Ibid., 61 fn. 9.

[6]*Memoriale* [2]. Ibid., 61.

[7]*Memoriale* [3] makes this clear "The Favre family were farmers and shepherds, the only way to survive in those alpine regions. During the winters, when deep snow covered the hamlets and villages, little movement was possible. But from about May until autumn, one

knew what action to take to protect the animals in his charge. This sensitivity to nature was a trait that marked his later life, enabling him to use images and examples from nature to illustrate the points he wished to make in teaching and in writing.[8] He was an intelligent boy and when the possibility of a good education was offered to him, he seized the opportunity eagerly.[9] He had a quick and retentive memory and following an initial tutoring for the basics of education, he was sent to La Roche-sur-Foron. Here he came under the tutelage of a priest, Pierre Veillard[10], whose formative influence was life-long.[11] In particular, he helped Favre both to read classical works in the light of the gospel and to understand the close connection that should exist between learning and holiness. Favre remained at La Roche-sur-Foron until he was nineteen when he set forth for Paris.

---

member of each household in the valley, usually one of the children, climbed to the high meadows with the family livestock. Pierre was given this task for the first time at the age of seven, and learned to live this tough and responsible outdoor life in the company of the other shepherds of the area. Brian O'Leary, S.J., *Pierre Favre and Discernment* (Oxford: Way Books, 2006), 9. Later while at school in La Roche, he occasionally "helped to guard the flocks." *Memoriale* [4].

[8]The following are a few places where Favre draws his imagery from nature all within the *Memoriale*: [108]. The imagery of stream, fountainhead and water: "If it is given to you to draw somewhat from that fountainhead which is the Savior himself, beware lest you disdain or do not value as highly as you should those streams that flow from it through the Mother of God, through his saints, or through all the virtues that flow from other creatures, as I said."; [206] where we find a seasonal metaphor applied to the soul: "A holy desire led me to wish that my soul might have four spiritual seasons during this coming year: a winter, so that the seeds sown in the soil of my soul by God might be tended and so be enabled to put down roots; a spring so that my piece of earth might germinate and grow its crop; a summer, so that the fruit might ripen into an abundant harvest; and an autumn, so that the ripe fruit might be picked and gathered into the divine barns for safekeeping less any of it be lost."; and [280] where there is a lengthy inverted tree metaphor: "Up to the present you found more consolation in the splendor of the tree, which proceeds from divine grace, than in its root, where abides its vigor and its power. ... By its root and not by its fruit will you be led to the glory of this tree."

[9]Favre mentions that when he was ten he had a real desire to study despite the fact that he was only a shepherd. He used to "weep with longing to go to school. And so my parents were compelled against their plans, to agree to send me to school. And when they saw the notable progress I was making in understanding and memory, they could not prevent me from continuing my studies." *Memoriale* [3].

[10]"Master Pierre Veillard, a person whose instruction was not only Catholic but holy as well. His life was one of ardent sanctity." Pierre Favre *The Memoriale*, 3 in *The Spiritual Writings of Pierre Favre*, "Introduction," Edmond C. Murphy, S.J. and John W. Padberg, S.J., "The Memoriale," trans. Edmond C. Murphy, S.J., "Selected Letters and Instructions," trans. Martin E. Palmer, S.J. (St. Louis: Institute of Jesuit Sources, 1996), 61.

[11]There is very little recorded about this priest: "In 1517, while at Cluses he published a book, *Modus componendi epistolas* [How to Write Letters]. He seems to have begun his Latin school at La Roche in 1517 or 1518, about the time Favre became a pupil there. Velliard taught him Latin literature, some Greek, a little theology, and by word and example the fear of God. Favre never forgot this good man and in after years revered him as a saint." Ibid., fn. 12, 61–2.

Another life-long formative influence on Favre was his connection with the Carthusians. During the time of the Reformation it was said of the Carthusians that they alone among the orders did not need to be reformed.[12] This was attributed to a three-fold practice: they lived in silence for most of their days; they spent the majority of their time in solitude, coming together for the praying of the Divine Office and the celebration of Mass; and they lived the principle of stability in that they did not move out of their monasteries. Favre had an uncle who was a Carthusian prior in a monastery less than ten miles away from his home village.[13] Favre's contacts with the Carthusians stimulated both his intellectual and spiritual growth to maturity.

In later years Favre, Ignatius, and the early companions spent time in reflection and prayer at Carthusian monasteries.[14] The family ties aided by Favre's own developed intellectual understanding and a deepened affectivity and spiritual growth led him to esteem religious life. During his travels, as a professed member of the Society of Jesus, Favre regularly made contact with the nearest Charterhouse and stayed when he could. Later in his life, this close connection between the Jesuits and the Carthusians was further cemented. In 1544, at the General Chapter of the Order at the Grande Chartreuse[15] in France, the delegates voted that the Carthusians would become co-operators with the Jesuits in their apostolic work by offering for them masses, prayers, fasts, and mortifications. "And that their ancient Order and the Society of Jesus share the merits of the good works of both, 'in this life and the next.'"[16]

It was in Paris that Pierre Favre met Ignatius Loyola. Initially he shared rooms with Juan de la Peña and Francis Xavier and later Ignatius Loyola

---

[12] *Numquam reformatam numquam deformatam,* "The Carthusians have made no effort to extol the saints and spiritually mature men in their midst. That this order has always remained in good monastic observance is due in no small part to its having fled the favors and praises of men that arise from sanctity's signs and miracles." Nicholas Kempf, *De confirmation et regula approbata ordinis cartusiensis,* cited in Dennis D. Martin, *Fifteenth Century Carthusian Reform: The World of Nicholas Kempf* (Leiden: Brill, 1992), 1.

[13] His father's brother Dom Mamert Favre was Prior of the Carthusian monastery of Reposir about seven miles from Favre's home from 1508 and was succeeded by his mother's nephew, Dom Claude Perissin in 1522. The former gave the family guidance and advice and it was the latter who gave encouragement, advice and material support to Favre suggesting he should study in Paris and establishing a connection for him with the Carthusian monastery at Vauvert which was very close to the college of Sainte-Barbe. The *Memoriale* makes this clear in the entry for 1525.

[14] In this way we can see how, for Favre, there was a natural affinity to esteem religious life. Also it is interesting to note as Brian O'Leary, S.J. does that "it may well have been this example that prompted him at the age of twelve, to make a vow of perpetual chastity." Brian O'Leary, S.J., *The Discernment of Spirits in the Memoriale of Blessed Peter Favre* (Osterley: The Way Publications, 1979), 10.

[15] The mother house of the Carthusian order which was situated fourteen miles north of Grenoble. The first monastery was built by St Bruno in 1084 on this site.

[16] Mary Purcell, *The Quiet Companion: Peter Favre, S.J. 1506–1546* (Chicago: Loyola University Press, 1970), 144.

came to join them. Here was formed a companionship that deepened over time during this period of study. Indeed, Xavier and Loyola along with Favre were instrumental in the formation of the Society of Jesus. Favre's own studies went well; he was a good scholar and enjoyed his arts course. The subjects he studied were: grammar, dialectic, geometry, cosmology, literature and philosophy.[17]

At this time, though his intellect was expanding, his interior life was in turmoil. He said of himself: "I was always very unsure of myself and blown about by many winds: sometimes wishing to be married, sometimes to be a doctor, sometimes a lawyer, sometimes a lecturer, sometimes a professor of theology, sometimes a cleric without a degree—at times wishing to be a monk."[18] He had come to university from a small, settled, devoutly Catholic home and education and he had been plunged into the turbulent, boisterous, and radical atmosphere of student Paris. It was a shock to Favre's psyche and it brought to the fore a tendency to vacillate between elation and melancholy. As he came to the conclusion of his studies he was unsure which direction to take.[19]

---

[17] Cf. Chapter 2 and the discussion concerning Ignatius' time at the University of Paris and the different subjects studied by himself and the early companions.

[18] Pierre Favre, *The Memoriale* 14, *The Spiritual Writings* 67.

[19] The theological formation he received in Paris influenced his spirituality, and according to Murphy and Padberg, there are discernable traces of nominalism found in his writings. This current, following William of Ockham's insistence that God's absolute freedom means he could have ordained things otherwise, cast in doubt the absolute goodness and truthfulness of things, and submitted them to the primacy of the "will of God"—his mere intention, imbuing it with a kind of unstated arbitrariness. As a consequence of this, a separation between Will and Reason arose, and the moral order took on more of an aura of "obligation" and "prohibition." In theology a separation between reason and faith ensued. Against this backdrop, the importance of receiving spiritual "favors," indicators of God's unforeseen generosity and approval, becomes increasingly important. Like Luther's view, it's a largely voluntarist conception in which subjective experience is given primacy, but unlike Luther's formal expectation of God's mercy, Favre looks mainly to "God's action in the depths of one's being." It is perhaps this influence, Murphy and Padberg suggest, that contributed to his "anguished quest for certainty" as well as his temptations to pessimism and depression. Pierre Faber, *Spiritual Writings of Pierre Favre*, eds Edmond C. Murphy and John W. Padberg (St. Louis: Institute of Jesuit Sources, 1996), 23. In later years the temptation to vacillate erupted on other occasions, for example on June 10, 1543 in a long written entry in the *Memoriale* Favre states that "I was frequently troubled in mind and deeply depressed," *Memoriale* [328], in *Spiritual Writings* 256. Favre prayed "that he be relieved of his instability, that swaying backwards and forwards from extremes of optimism to extremes of pessimism. All this would not be such a problem if he were not so familiar with the causes and circumstances which beget and foster evil. But he pays so much attention to the power of sin and error that he forgets the virtues and the good that God has sown in men. If he would only look at these good things with a simple eye and not with an evil eye, he would achieve not merely a greater interior peace but also greater apostolic fruit." O'Leary, S.J., *Pierre Favre and Discernment*, 103.

Integration of Intellect and Affectivity

It was at this time that Ignatius Loyola came to his assistance. Favre had coached Ignatius in his early studies in philosophy. Now it was the turn of Ignatius to help Favre in particular to integrate his intellectual understanding and his affectivity. We saw already in the last chapter how this balanced integration of the intellectual and affective dimensions of life was characteristic of Ignatius and underpinned his ecclesial disposition.[20]Indeed, this union of a graced intellect and a passionate love for Christ and his Church was a reality that Ignatius encouraged in his companion.

Alongside his inability to decide about his future Favre also suffered from scruples[21] and temptations to impurity. He knew he needed some disciplined structure and practice to his life and had the humility both to ask for assistance from Ignatius and to follow the practice of docility to the direction he received. He readily followed the spiritual direction he received being convinced that God was leading him through the guidance of the spiritually more mature Ignatius.[22]

Favre said of Ignatius: "He became my master in spiritual things, and gave me a method of raising myself to a knowledge of the divine will and of myself."[23] Favre's willingness to let himself be guided by Ignatius reaped

---

[20] Cf. de Guibert, *The Jesuits: Their Spiritual Doctrine and Practice*, 73.

[21] "I was greatly troubled by other temptations to contemplate the defects of others, to suspect them, and to pass judgment on them. But in this matter the grace of my Consoler and my Teacher did not fail me, who set me on my first steps in charity toward my neighbour. At that time also and until I left Paris, I had scruples over every single one of countless imperfections that nobody knew." *Memoriale* [11]. Ibid., 66.

[22] Cf. *Memoriale* [12 and 13] "And so, knowing or judging or feeling something of these many bad spirits as regards myself or God our Lord or my neighbour, I saw that never did our Lord let me remain tied up or deceived in anything, as I think; but in everything, with inspirations and enlightenment from his holy angels and from the Holy Spirit, he would always free me at a time that seemed good to him and was opportune for me." Ibid., [12], 66. Edmund Murphy remarks: "These passages show Ignatius, with great delicacy, at work on the mind and heart of Favre. Antonio Araoz, one of the early Jesuits, who spent a long time in Spain with Favre and knew him very well, recounts that Ignatius kept Favre for two years like a novice, getting him to examine his conscience daily on his thoughts, words, and actions. Then he made him work hard to root out his bad habits, taking them one by one, beginning with those which gave scandal to others or hampered his own spiritual progress and giving special attention to the ones most deeply rooted in him." Ibid., 66 fn. 22.

[23] Pierre Favre, *Memoriale* 8, *Spiritual Writings* 64. Also "Firstly, he gave me an understanding of my conscience and of the temptations and scruples I had had for so long without either understanding them or seeing the way by which I would be able to get peace." *Memoriale* 9, Ibid., 65. Such scruples manifested themselves on occasions throughout his life. "From October to December 1543, Favre found himself in Louvain, where he immediately fell ill with the tertian fever. His physical recovery brought him a difficult case of conscience. He had received instructions from Ignatius to proceed to Portugal, but the Nuncio Poggio had been scheming to keep him in Germany. Favre had received word that the necessary powers had in fact arrived from the Pope. In his anxiety, Favre wrote again to Ignatius: 'I did not

the spiritual fruit of clear discernment and a more integrated life. Although Favre suffered from this temptation to vacillation periodically throughout his life, as can be seen within his spiritual journal, *Memoriale*, Ignatius helped him to know how to deal with these temptations and how to discern the will of God in concrete situations. Favre recognized within the guidance and governance that Ignatius provided the authoritative call of the Spirit of God, constantly present within the Church, which always seeks the good of the human person.[24]

Favre made the *Spiritual Exercises* with Ignatius shortly after receiving his first degree. Thereafter he was ordained to the diaconate and then the priesthood. He was the first priest among Ignatius' early companions.[25] Ignatius said of Favre in later years that he was the best director of the *Spiritual Exercises* amongst the early companions. With these friends in the Lord Favre dedicated his life to God on August 15, 1534, in a small chapel at Montmartre.[26] They vowed to go to Jerusalem and on their return to place themselves under obedience to the Pope. In embryo, this decision was the root of the fourth vow that became enshrined in the Jesuit *Constitutions*. It was a vow of obedience to the Roman Pontiff particularly with respect to being sent on mission.[27]

It is interesting to note, that when Ignatius had to return to Spain to recuperate from ill health in April 1535, he left Favre in charge of the small group of companions in Paris. Clearly Ignatius had seen signs of leadership in this sensitive and self-effacing Savoyard. When Ignatius returned eighteen months later, the now expanded group[28] set forth for Rome to obtain the

---

cease to be perplexed, seeing on the one hand the command of your Reverence, and on the other understanding the contrary will of his Holiness ... I say all this, not because I am inclined in my soul more one way than another, but so that your Reverence may know what is happening so secretly there ... Again I beg you for the love of Jesus Christ to make haste in sending me a definite answer.' It is very strange that Favre did not anticipate what the only possible reply of Ignatius could be: that is, that the Company was formed to be at the service of the Pope, whose will overruled even that of Ignatius." O'Leary, S.J., *Pierre Favre and Discernment*, 125.

[24] Cf. "that between Christ our Lord, the Bridegroom, and the Church, his Spouse, there is the one same Spirit who governs and guides us for the salvation of our souls." Thirteenth Rule, *Spiritual Exercises* 365.

[25] It was Favre who celebrated the mass at Montmartre.

[26] "At the communion of the mass said by Favre, each of the companions pronounced a vow of chastity, of evangelical poverty as soon as their studies at the university were completed, and of making a pilgrimage to Palestine if transport could be found within a year of leaving Paris. The vows though private, bound them strictly in conscience as engagements to God. There was an implied vow of obedience to the pope if they were unable to labor in Palestine for life." *Spiritual Writings of Pierre Favre*, 68. On the following two years, on the anniversary of this date, the companions "all returned to the same place to reaffirm our aforesaid resolutions and for this we received each time a great spiritual increase." *Memoriale* [15]. Ibid., 69. The grace they received at each renewal of their vows strengthened their certainty that they were doing the will of God.

[27] See Part I, Chapter 2, "The Texts Surrounding the Text."

[28] In addition to Ignatius, Francis Xavier, Pierre Favre, "Master Bobadilla, Master Lainez,

permission of Pope Paul III for their Jerusalem pilgrimage and that the non-clerical members of the group might be ordained.[29] Permission was speedily granted for their requests[30] but it proved impossible to make their way to Jerusalem. Due to the activities of the Turkish navy, boats were not sailing to the Holy Land. Consequently, a small group of the companions including Ignatius and Favre set off to walk to Rome.

In Rome, Favre, who had the reputation of a good theologian, was appointed by the Pope to lecture on scripture and positive theology and Lainez on scholastic theology in the University of Rome, "The Sapienza."[31] Peter Canisius was to say of him in later years: "I have never met a more learned or profound theologian, or a man of such lofty and unique sanctity. His only desire is to co-operate with Christ in the salvation of souls. In public or private conversation, and at table, his every word breathes of God and devotion to God, and that without irking or boring those present."[32] Favre's work as a theologian in Rome, however, was not without controversy.

Master Salmerón, and Master Simão," *Memoriale* 15, ibid. There were also in those two years additional companions. "Claude Jay, born at Mieussy in Savoy about 1500 was with Favre at La Roche under Velliard, whom he succeeded as principal of that school. Favre, who met him in Le Villaret in 1533, persuaded him to come to Paris and finish his theological studies there. He entered Sainte-Barbe in September 1534, gained his licentiate March 1536, and became Master of Arts the same year. Then, under Favre's direction, he went through the Exercises and made up his mind to join the little group. He took vows with them August 15, 1535. Master Jean Codure, born June 24, 1508, at Seyne in the diocese of Embrun, betook himself to Paris at the age of twenty-seven and entered the college of either Torcy or Lisieux. Tormented by a desire for holiness, he came to Favre for direction. He made the Exercises extending them to forty days, then joined the little community and took vows with them on August 15, 1536. Master Paschase Broët born at Bertrancourt in Picardy c. 1500, studied at Amiens and was ordained priest, most probably in 1524. He settled in Paris c. 1534 to complete his theology. Worries about orthodoxy haunted him. Through Claude Jay he got to know Favre, who advised him to make the Exercises. He took vows with the other companions. So, as a result of Favre's winning personality the nascent Society found itself with ten members." Ibid., 68–9 fn. 27.

[29] On April 3, 1537, they were received in audience by Pope Paul III.

[30] "Cardinal Pucci, the Pope's penitentiary empowered them by decree to seek ordination from any bishop they chose in the Patriarchate of Venice or elsewhere under the 'title of poverty.' On June 24 of that year, Ignatius, Xavier, Lainez, Codure, Bobadilla and Rodrigues were ordained priests in Venice; Salmerón, not yet twenty-three, could only be ordained deacon with the others. Favre, Lainez, and Ignatius then spent a month in solitude and prayer, followed by several months of pastoral work." Ibid., 70.

[31] "Favre began his lectures in November 1537 and continued them until May 1539. By April 1538 all the companions had arrived in Rome. On May 5 they were given faculties by Cardinal Vincenzo Carafa to preach everywhere, to hear the confessions of both sexes, to absolve from certain reserved cases, to distribute Communion, and to administer the other sacraments. The Romans were thunderstruck to hear them preaching: only in Advent and in Lent was preaching done in Rome." Ibid., 70.

[32] *Monumenta Historica Societatis Jesu*: Epp. Can [1] 76–7, cited in Purcell, *The Quiet Companion*, 125. It is useful to note also, that the term theologian in the sense used by Canisius is more focused on "that perception of mysteries which experience yields, the wisdom imprinted by piety and matured by discernment, reflection of a particular type born

Along with his companion and fellow theologian Diego Lainez, Favre became very concerned about the preaching of an Augustinian friar.[33] They perceived that there were traces of Lutheran doctrines in his preaching and Favre was determined to tackle him on this matter. It was Favre's fervent affective commitment to the Church combined with his intellectual awareness of the doctrinal controversies that enabled him both to identify the errors and gave him the fortitude to tackle the problem.

Favre and Lainez first met with him in private to put before the friar their concerns about his preaching and where they detected errors. Only when the friar proved obdurate and refused to listen to them did they begin to preach against the specific Lutheran doctrines they had detected. In this way we can see that Favre was exemplary of that ecclesial disposition of integrated affectivity and intellect and was acting in the spirit of the Rules for Thinking, Judging, and Feeling with the Church. He first clearly identifies the errors in the preaching of the Friar and then proceeds to address them. There is then an attempt in private to deal with the matter, and only afterwards recourse to a public denunciation of the doctrine that was being preached. At no time was there a personal attack on the friar himself.

We can also see that Favre was attentive to the need for discretion in handling this matter.[34] He was sensitive to the fact that great prudence was necessary in speaking about doctrine.[35] He has a clear concern that no one should be led into error through the preaching of the friar or the consequences that followed from the attempt of Favre and Lainez to deal with the matter[36] through preaching against the teaching of the friar. And finally, he is sensitive to the fact that it is vital not to baffle the ordinary people of the city who might be so confounded by matters of doctrine that they do not understand and that they just depend upon a vague sense of faith without seeing that continuing to live faithful lives of service in good works is also important.[37] The content of the preaching of the two Jesuits needed to take into account both a correction of the erroneous doctrine being preached by

---

of personal encounters with Jesus Christ and the moral attitudes those encounters engender." M. de Certeau, *Bienheureux Pierre Favre: Memoriale* (Paris, 1960), 25, cited in ibid., 54.

[33] Fra Mainardi de Saluces who had significant support in the city. In the face of the criticism offered by Favre and Lainez a campaign of slander was launched against Ignatius and his companions, until "In the end, the calumniators were forced to retract in the presence of the governor of Rome, Benedetto Conversini, and this official later put his signature to a document which completely vindicated the life and teaching of Ignatius and his followers." O'Leary, S.J., *Pierre Favre and Discernment*, 14.

[34] We might recall the content of the fourteenth to the eighteenth of the Rules for Thinking, Judging, and Feeling with the Church.

[35] Cf. Fourteenth Rule, *Spiritual Exercises* 366.

[36] Fifteenth Rule, *Spiritual Exercises* 367.

[37] Cf. "we should take care that we do not, by speaking and insisting strongly about faith without any distinction or explanation, give the people an occasion to grow listless and lazy in their works—either before or after their faith is informed by charity." Fifteenth Rule, *Spiritual Exercises* 367.

the friar, and the need to encourage those who listened to deepen their faith and practice of works of charity. Here we have exemplified that ecclesial sense of the importance of affirming good doctrine while having a care both for the friar who was expounding false doctrine and the people who might be led astray by it. There is a delicacy in Favre's manner of dealing with this situation which highlights both his faithfulness to the Church, and his compassionate pastoral practice.

Obedience to the Pope

In the last days of November 1538, when it had become clear that there was no realistic hope of being able to travel to Jerusalem, the companions decided to adopt their precautionary strategy and offer themselves unconditionally to Pope Paul III for whatever service he deemed most suitable for them. The Pope gladly accepted this offer.[38] The first companions then began to consider if they should take an additional vow of obedience to one of their number in addition to their vows of chastity and poverty. This vow would mean they would take on the responsibilities of a religious order, considering that in this way they might best serve the Church. There were long deliberations about the matter, as the second chapter made clear, and during these deliberations Favre acted as secretary.

In 1540 the new Society of Jesus received papal approval in the papal bull *Regimini militantis Ecclesiae*. In 1550 this approval was reconfirmed.[39] The first companions put themselves under obedience to the Pope to go wherever he might wish to send them. In the case of Pierre Favre, this was wherever a qualified theologian might be needed. Paul III had heard Favre in a disputation which the early Jesuits conducted in his presence one evening and had been impressed by the gentle introvert who could speak with such authenticity. Having identified Favre as a significant apostolic tool for the Church, the Pope began to use this exemplary priest to tackle the theological problems of the day. These consisted both in the ignorance of the Roman Catholic clergy and the evangelizing fervor of the Reformers.

In 1539 Favre was sent to Parma[40] and thus began the first of his many travels which continued until his death in 1546. Much of his work involved

---

[38] "Favre interpreted the event as the quasi foundation of the Society." *Spiritual Writings of Pierre Favre*, 70.

[39] Pope Julius III Papal Bull, *Exposcit Debitum*.

[40] April 1539, the Pope appointed Cardinal Ennio Flonardo as legate in Parma to administer that part of the Papal States known as the Legation which stretched across northern Italy from Genoa to Venice. It was a disturbed and contentious district, rapidly going over to heresy. The cardinal, dedicated to Church reform, asked the Pope for "two priests of reformed life" who by their preaching would defend the Catholic faith. For this task Favre and Lainez were chosen by their companions and left for Parma in May." *Spiritual Writings of Pierre Favre*, 72. It is

hearing confessions and giving spiritual direction as well as teaching and disputation. In particular, the Pope sent him to meetings with Lutherans at Worms[41] and Ratisbon,[42] and eventually he was appointed to the Council of Trent[43] but he died before arriving there. In between these meetings he traveled to Spain and Portugal, but he spent most of his time in Germany. He died in Rome en route for Trent, in 1546.

The Witness of Favre's Spiritual Writings

The primary focus of this section on the spiritual writings of Pierre Favre is the *Memoriale*, the majority of which consists of Favre's reflections on his experiences in prayer. Alongside this I draw from selected letters and various instructions that Favre wrote to other Jesuits. In April 1542, while in Speyer, Favre commenced his *Memoriale*. It was a spiritual journal in which he began to remind himself of the many favors and blessings he had received from God during his life and for which he owed God gratitude. Later the journal served a different purpose. He began to jot down after his meditations the thoughts that had occurred to him. In this way he began to distinguish his consolations and desolations and use Ignatius' Rules for the Discernment of Spirits.[44] His *Memoriale* then became for him a tool of discernment. It acted as an instrument for discovering the will of God in this regard so that he knew what he should undertake.

We have already seen that Pierre Favre was a gentle, sensitive, self-effacing man. His genuine simplicity made him attractive to all classes of

---

clear that Favre had already established a reputation as a priest who led a dedicated life and who was capable of defending the Catholic faith and the Church.

[41] 'The Emperor hoped that the Colloquy of Worms, which opened on November 25, 1540 and dragged on until January 18, 1541, might lead to doctrinal agreement between the Catholics and the Protestants. The Protestant side was united, the Catholic quite divided, so the colloquy came to nothing. At Worms Favre quickly realized that conferences, colloquies, and diets could not bring religious peace – among other things they were too open to power politics and to manipulation for purely secular aims." Ibid., 74 fn. 35. "Things went so badly in the assembly at Worms that the Emperor was forced to adjourn it to Ratisbon where he could be present in person and make efforts to restore religious peace in Germany. Favre accompanied Dr Ortiz from Worms to Ratisbon by way of Speyer. When they arrived at Ratisbon, Ortiz addressed the Emperor and his court twice daily. Favre heard confessions, engaged in spiritual direction and again gave the Exercises, his most effective pastoral ministry. The Catholic side was divided both politically and religiously, and had no idea how to communicate its position in the vernacular, a skill at which the Protestant side excelled. Catholics relied too much on the Fathers of the Church and too little on scriptural arguments. In July the Diet finally collapsed over questions concerning the sacraments, transubstantiation, and the authority of the pope." Ibid., 27.

[42] Later known as Regensburg.

[43] Council of Trent 1545–63, the most significant Roman Catholic council of the Reformation period.

[44] *Spiritual Exercises* [313–36].

persons and he was equally at home with the learned and the unlearned; in the court or in the field. Simon Rodriguez, S.J. in 1577, recalling his student days in Paris with Favre, wrote of him: "There was an especially rare and delightful sweetness and charm in his relations with other men which I must confess to this very day I have not discovered in any other. In some way or other, he so won the friendship of other men and gradually stole into their souls, that by his whole manner, and the gentleness of his words, he irresistibly drew them to a love of God."[45] These genuine human qualities grounded Favre's ecclesial disposition and enabled him to speak naturally about matters of faith, the sacraments and the doctrine of the Church. It is clear from the *Memoriale* that this naturalness was not dependent upon Favre's own human qualities alone—he was not an eloquent speaker—but because he also sought, in prayer, the grace of God and the intercession of the saints. So on an occasion when Favre was particularly concerned about the Dean of Speyer and wanting to help him to make the *Exercises* he took the matter to prayer "for a way to accomplish this seemingly impossible goal" and "a certain devotion came to me which I had not thought of before."[46] Favre then undertakes a series of prayers to the Father, Our Lady and the Dean's guardian angel, plus all the saints. This emphasis on prayer sustained both Favre's serenity and that openness to others so characteristic of his naturalness in dealing with anyone he encountered.

The Centrality of Sacramental Life

It was this authentic interest in others that enabled him also to draw them to an experience of conversion. For Favre, such conversion was best celebrated in the sacrament of confession.[47] Favre was renowned for his confessional practice; his natural gentleness and kindness made him a "specialist" of the

---

[45] Cited in O'Leary, S.J., *The Discernment of Spirits in the Memoriale of Blessed Peter Favre*, 20.

[46] *Memoriale* [34], *Spiritual Writings* 85, Favre continues "This consisted in praying first to the dean's heavenly Father, who was the first to gain him; secondly, to his Mother and Lady, the mother of Jesus; thirdly, to his guardian angel, his master and his instructor, so to speak; fourthly, to the men and women saints, who, like brothers and sisters, have a special spiritual affection for him. This practice seemed to me a good way of gaining a person's friendship. So I came to recite for the first-named person the Our Father, for the second a Hail Mary, for the third the prayer *Deus qui mior ordine angelorum* and the fourth by saying the prayer *Omnes sancti tui quaesumus, Domine* ... There occurred to me also something very necessary for retaining a person's goodwill, apart from what other things can be done for him: to have great devotion to all the guardian angels, for they can predispose people towards us in many ways and curb the violence and temptations of our enemies." Ibid.

[47] Cf. *Spiritual Exercises* 354, we have already seen in Chapter 1 how much the sacrament of confession came under attack from the reformers. What Favre also witnessed was the infrequent practice of confession amongst Catholics which he took in part to be due to the poor administration of the sacrament. Therefore he was always most particular in his own practice

confessional and many sought him out as their confessor. We have some understanding of his disposition in the confessional and his practice as a confessor in the letter he wrote to a Jesuit, Cornelius Wischaven in Cologne, in late January 1544. The letter is a detailed indication of the manner and matter of questioning of penitents, and the suggestions that might be offered to them with regard to spiritual direction and formation in doctrine. Towards the end of the letter the following passage appears:

> In hearing and handling confessions, you should always be meek and forbearing, preserving a spirit of gentleness, never giving admittance to the spirit of bitterness or any spirit of annoyance at a penitent's irritating behavior. You must never let this great and holy work become a source of annoyance to you, for we stand in the place of Christ, who bears the sin of the world. We must make sure that no sinner is ever made to feel bad in the very place where he came for the sole purpose of being examined, instructed, and judged by us, to whom he has come as the representatives of the gentle Christ. Let us avoid any Pharisaic supercili-ousness and a judgment which ends up alienating the person. So far as we can, we should never let a person leave us who would not willingly come back.[48]

Favre often proposed that new penitents should make a general confession as the foundation of a renewed life.[49] When he ministered in the confessional, showing mercy to a penitent brought tears to his eyes. As he ministered this sacrament he discovered anew the mercy God granted to Favre himself.

Within this focus on confession we can also see revealed the Christocentric character of Favre's focus and understanding. When reflecting on an

---

of administering the sacrament and also had clear convictions that he communicated to others about the practice of confessors.

[48] Letter from Pierre Favre to Cornelius Wischaven, on How to Hear Confessions, Cologne, late January 1544, MonFabri, 245–52, [Epist. 82], cited in The Spiritual Writings of Pierre Favre, 360. The letter continues with a reprimand for confessors who believed that the converted [i.e. regular penitents] should be treated with increasing severity. "Why should we be so austere? Do we not realize that God regards it as a great thing that anyone should come to us for frequent and regular confession? It is a great thing indeed, that a penitent should bare his soul to you. But it is a far greater thing that he looks forward to your admonishments. For he finds this humbling, but if he did not come to confession he would not have this opportunity of exercising humility and other concurrent virtues."

[49] For those whom Favre saw as frequent backsliders he suggested a series of possibilities: "the best help is frequent confession and Communion with the same priest. Also: a method for examining themselves on the particular sins together with their occasions. Also: some good works by way of mortification in the areas in which the temptations of the world arise. ... consider it well worth our while if we can keep within the boundaries of God's way a person who had been outside it. Christ would still die for this alone, and he comes to our soul. Why should we then be so demanding that we fail to realise that it is a great thing in God's eyes for a person even to come to frequent confession nowadays." Ibid., 360–1.

occasion where he was forced to wait for a young man who had promised to come to confession but had twice already failed to do so, he received an insight from the Lord in the face of his impatience. He began to compare his reaction to this young man's lack of punctuality and potential insincerity to Christ's reaction to Favre. He reflected: "How often do you make Jesus stand at your door? And yet you want him not to get discouraged, not to regret having waited; ... Be sure, then to treat his little ones in the same way. Act yourself as you know he would act if his humanity were visibly and locally present in visible flesh."[50]

What is implicit here and in other areas of Favre's spiritual writing and his life is that desire to imitate his Lord and to be united with him that is apparent in the meditations on the "Two Standards" and the "Three Kinds of Humility" in the *Spiritual Exercises*.[51] The example of Christ was always at the forefront of Favre's contemplation and action. In the *Memoriale* he prays that "would that my whole inner being, especially my heart, were so yielding to Christ coming in as to open up and leave to him the place in my heart's center."[52] He desired that his whole life of prayer and work would be lived in imitation of Christ.[53] United with Christ he knew he would be drawn into the depths of God, into the relations of the three persons of the Trinity.[54]

---

[50] *Memoriale* 429, *Spiritual Writings* 307. He continues: "Then there returned to me that devotion to each soul given me so often by the Lord, and with it there returned the resolve to suffer and labor for them not only in a universal or general way—which is less wearisome and more glorious—but also for each single soul, in that way imitating him who belongs wholly to each, who lived his entire life for each, and who suffered and died for each."

[51] See Part I, Chapter 2, "The Texts Surrounding the Text."

[52] *Memoriale* [68], *Spiritual Writings* 108.

[53] "O that the time may come when I contemplate and love no creature without God and, rather contemplate and love God in all things or at least fear him! That would raise me to the knowledge of God in himself and, in the end, all things in him, so that he would be for me all in eternity. To ascend by these degrees, I must strive to find Christ, who is the way, the truth, and the life, first in the center of my heart and below, that is, within me; then above me, by means of my mind; and outside me, by means of my senses." *Memoriale* [306–7]. Ibid., 244.

[54] Following fn 54, *Memoriale* [307] continues with an explicit reference to this Trinitarian perspective. "I shall have to beg power from the Father to do this, for he is said to be 'above'; wisdom from the Son, who on account of his humanity is said to be 'outside' in a certain way; and goodness from the Holy Spirit, who in some way can be said to be 'below,' that is, within us. Otherwise our interior cannot be laid open so that God may be inwardly beheld by a purified heart, nor can our superior part be elevated to the invisible mysteries of God which are above all things, nor can our members be mortified so as to experience him who is outside all things and who moves through all things." Ibid.

The Importance of Devotions in Assisting Consciousness of the Presence of God

Favre was a man who never lost his preference for the devotions of his childhood. This childlike, but not childish, preference for devotions led him to a deeper union with God. The feasts of Our Lord, Our Lady and the saints were all important occasions that he celebrated. He had a devotion to relics and was happy to make pilgrimages to shrines. He never forgot his devotion to his own guardian angel and to the angels who guarded the individuals, households[55] and towns through which he passed on his journeys.[56] Indeed, the notion of pilgrims and pilgrimages had fallen into disrepute, and was one of the many devotions ridiculed by Reformers. By contrast, Ignatius incorporated into the training of novices the practice of a pilgrimage. This not only emphasized a point of doctrine that Reformers decried, but it also tested the resources of courage, humility and endurance of a candidate for the new order. Favre saw the pilgrim as an itinerant apostle for God and much of his own life reflected this reality.[57] When travelling from place to place Favre used other devotions which were a great help to him as he walked through the mountains, fields, and vineyards on his journeys. "One can pray for the increase of good things like this, or ask forgiveness for those who are unable to recognize the spiritual meaning of those creatures or who do not know the One who has given all this to them."[58]

---

[55] April 1543, "On another day during the octave of that Easter, as I was settling into a house which I had rented, my mind and spirit were moved in various ways to desire that my entrance into that new dwelling place might be a happy one. So in every room and passage of the house I knelt down and said this prayer: 'Visit, we pray you, O Lord, this dwelling and drive far from it all the wiles of the enemy; may your holy angels dwell in it and keep us in peace, and may your blessing be always upon us through Christ our Lord.' ... I then invoked the angel guardians of the neighborhood, and I felt that this too was a fitting and praiseworthy thing to do when changing to a new locality. I wished also in a prayer that the wicked spirits in the neighborhood might be powerless to harm either myself or those coming to live with me in the house ... I also invoked SS. Ottilia, Jodocus and Lucy to whom the chapel beside my rented house was dedicated." *Memoriale* [282–4], *Spiritual Writings* 229.

[56] For Favre the sixth, seventh, and eighth of the Rules for Thinking, Judging, and Feeling with the Church were a natural extension of his own character, *Spiritual Exercises* 358, 359, 360.

[57] A pilgrimage was one of the experiments that Ignatius had included as part of the formation of Jesuit novices. It is still undertaken by Jesuits in the twenty-first century. It could be seen in Ignatius's time as a kind of preparation for becoming an itinerant apostle that many of the first companions lived, in imitation of Christ. In any generation it is an experiment that causes the novices to deepen their trust in God and be open to the vicissitudes of a life of dependency both upon God and the goodwill and charity of others.

[58] Favre continues, "I likewise used to pray to the patron saints of these different regions. I asked the saints to do what the inhabitants no longer knew how to do, namely, to thank God, to get his forgiveness for their sins, to ask for the graces they needed." Cited in Letter

In the face of those amongst the Reformers who dishonored or threw away statues and relics, and who ridiculed simple devotions like the Sign of the Cross and the use of holy water,[59] Favre dwelt on these things and included many references in his spiritual journal.[60] One day when he was in the Church of the Holy Cross in Speyer he decided to say the Mass of the Holy Cross.

> My reason was the presence in that Church of a certain crucifix which, once held in great veneration, had by the power of God rekindled faith and aroused devotion ... the Lord now gave me a very good spirit and a feeling of great devotion to that cross which led me to venerate it and, together with it, every standard and every sign of the cross. I perceived too with trustful faith the wonderful power of the cross against the demons, and therefore I desired it to be possible that I might always bear that cross in my soul, in a real but spiritual way through faith and hope. With faith I had the same wish about holy water and about everything sanctified by the word of God or marked with the sign of the cross; also about representations of the crucified Savior, the Blessed Virgin, and the saints, about the relics of their holy bodies, and about other things of that kind.[61]

Here, we have a clear sense that for Favre, these devotions of the Sign of the Cross and the use of holy water were not superstitious actions but a helpful recalling of the presence of God. There was suspicion of these devotions amongst the Reformers who saw scripture as their sole authority and who rejected anything that could not be seen to have a scriptural basis. Indeed, some Reformers regarded such devotions as a certain superstitious idolatry. For Favre, however, these were actions arising from his faith and giving greater insight into his faith. Accordingly, we see here an illustration of the ninth of the Rules for Thinking, Judging, and Feeling with the Church, where it is clear that veneration is given through such devotions *according to what they represent*.[62] In this way such devotions are clearly an aid to Favre's prayer and the growth of his interior life. It is from his experience that he recommends such practices to others.[63]

---

from Peter Canisius to Claude Aquaviva, January 1583, in Thomas H. Clancy, S.J., *The Conversational Word of God: A Commentary on the Doctrine of St. Ignatius of Loyola concerning Spiritual Conversation, with Four Early Jesuit Texts* (St. Louis: Institute of Jesuit Sources, 1978), 61.

[59] Cf. examples given in Chapter 1.

[60] For example in the *Memoriale* [118, 120, 123, 124, 129], in *Spiritual Writings* 136, 137, 139, 140, 143–4 respectively.

[61] *Memoriale* [130], in *Spiritual Writings* 144.

[62] Eighth Rule, *Spiritual Exercises* 360.

[63] On the occasion of the vigil of the Feast of the Assumption 1542, Favre went to the Cathedral of Our Lady of Speyer and here experienced much consolation through the different devotional

It is also important to note the particular veneration that Favre extended to the Blessed Virgin Mary. This is evident throughout the *Memoriale* but particularly focused on the feast days of Mary. For example on August 15, 1542, the Feast of the Assumption, Favre notes that after making his thanksgiving after Mass he was drawn to thank Our Lady for her intercession on his behalf and to ponder the working of the Holy spirit in the life of Mary.[64] After such consideration Favre seeks her intercession for interior renewal: "I asked God's Mother to obtain for me the grace of being fortified, refashioned, and reformed interiorly."[65]

Responding to a Church in Crisis

The middle of the sixteenth century was a time of religious ferment and political upheaval.[66] The Reformers had made great strides in Germany[67]

---

elements. He stated: "At first vespers of the Assumption I found great spiritual devotion when I was in the cathedral of our Lady of Speyer. This was because the ceremonies, the lights, the organ, the chanting, the splendor of the relics and the decorations – all these gave me such a great feeling of devotion that I could not explain it. I blessed the person who had placed the votive lights there, lit them, and arranged them in order, and also the person who had left an income for that purpose. Likewise I blessed the organ, the organist, the benefactors, and others, as well as all the priestly vestments that I saw had been laid ready there for the worship of God. So too the choir and the sacred music sung by the boy choristers, and I blessed in the same way the reliquaries and those who sought out relics and adorned them fittingly when found. In short, I was led by that spirit to esteem the least of these devotional activities, performed with a simple Catholic faith, more highly than a thousand degrees of that idle faith made so much of by those who will agree with the hierarchical Church." *Memoriale* [87], *Spiritual Writings* 118.

[64] "I reflected on the perfection that [our Lady] had always possessed in her own nature that she was under the unceasing and effective influence of the Holy Spirit, though not always, as I think, in the same way. For though she was at all times full of grace and though the Lord was with her and though she was blessed above all women, she was probably not affected at all times and to the same degree by the fervor and consolation which comes from the Holy Spirit. There was still room left in her for the most perfect humility, for a hunger and thirst to please the Almighty more and more, room too for a fear lest she might not serve God in accordance with his will. *Memoriale* [89], ibid., 121.

[65] Favre continues: "so that when later on it might be very just and necessary to withdraw from me the actual motion and sensible operation of the Holy Spirit, I should not then be so ready to squander, dissipate, and thus lose the gifts of God that filled me, nor should I be so slack, negligent, and carnal, so heedless in spirit with regard to spiritual things." Ibid. The day after this feast Favre notes, "with great devotion, faith, and hope I begged that our Lady would obtain for me, firstly, holiness and the purification that results from chastity, self-control, and total purity of body and spirit. Secondly, I asked for the grace to be guided to rule myself and direct my life according to the service of Christ her Son. Thirdly that she would obtain for me peace in this world by the practice of all the virtues and glory in the next." *Memoriale* [90], ibid., 121–2.

[66] See previous chapters.

[67] Of course Germany as we understand it in the twenty-first century did not exist until 1870. The Reformers had made significant progress amidst the different German principalities.

and indeed one of Favre's greatest fears was that the whole of Germany might be lost to the Reformers. "Then I pondered on that torment which has never left my mind since I first came to know Germany: the dread of its total defection from the Faith."[68] He was sent by the Pope to a series of meetings at Worms in 1540[69] and Ratisbon in 1541, and later he was appointed by Pope Paul III as a theologian to the Council of Trent.[70] However, he died before being able to take part in the discussions.

These meetings were extremely difficult for a man of such a gentle and self-effacing spirit as Favre. At Worms he clearly saw that the motives of the majority of participants were political and not religious. The German princes desired peace in the face of potential religious wars. Lutheranism had spread significantly throughout Germany. Favre had already come into contact with the effects of religious turmoil during his time at the University of Paris, where heated debates, and occasionally violent conflicts, had been common. There were also public executions of heretics which university students had been mandated to attend. Favre had then some familiarity with Lutheran teaching. Nevertheless, it was only when he arrived in Worms that he had a sense of the widespread nature of this teaching. The points made by the Lutherans who attended this meeting were clear and succinct. They affirmed justification by faith alone. They rejected the Mass, purgatory, pilgrimages, relics, indulgences and invocation of the saints. They desired the abolition of monasteries and convents, and denied that the papacy was of divine institution. Clearly what the Reformers rejected in these matters the Church affirmed.

The greatest difficulty for Favre, however, was the response of the Catholic members at the Worms meeting. He witnessed the defection of many Catholics including bishops, priests and religious. He saw a tendency to compromise on the Catholic side and a certain unhelpful vacillation.

---

[68] Favre continues. "May God prevent the realization of that thought, which has so often come to my mind, not from a good spirit, but rather from that spirit of diffidence that has harassed me in so many ways up to now. It strives particularly to bring me to outright despair of bearing any fruit, first by leading me to contemplate flight and then by provoking in me the desire to leave the Rhineland and so abandon the position entrusted to me." *Memoriale* [329], *Spiritual Writings* 256.

[69] Worms was most famous for the Diet of Worms 1521 where Martin Luther had been summoned by the Emperor Charles V and ordered either to renounce or reaffirm his views. Luther gave his famous speech: "Unless I am convicted by Scripture and plain reason – I do not accept the authority of popes and councils for they have contradicted each other – my conscience is captive to the Word of God. I cannot and will not recant anything for to go against conscience is neither right nor safe. Here I stand, I cannot do otherwise. God help me. Amen." In response the Emperor stated: "A single friar who goes counter to all Christianity for a thousand years must be wrong."

[70] Council of Trent 1545–63 convened in twenty-five sessions under two popes, Pope Paul III and Pope Julius III. The Council defined Church teaching in the areas of: Scripture and Tradition, Original Sin, Justification, the Sacraments, the Eucharist, and the Veneration of the Saints.

"Here in Worms Lutheran doctrine continues to be preached openly in the Dominican Church ... [the] citizens were deceived not so much by the seeming good preaching of the Lutherans as by the bad example of their pastors."[71] The public contrast of zealous preaching on the part of the Reformers and vague and half-hearted compromise on the part of the Catholic participants was a source of disillusionment for Favre. His real concern was the disservice that was done to the Church by those very members who were meant to be defending the Church.

Favre's reaction to these difficulties was typical: he had recourse to prayer. Here, he received an indication of the importance of praying for key figures in the religious conflicts of his times. He saw these men as having grave responsibilities and his compassion for them was stirred.

> I felt great fervor as eight persons became present to me along with the desire to remember them vividly in order to pray for them without taking notice of their faults. They were the sovereign pontiff, the emperor, the king of France, the king of England, Luther, the Grand Turk, Bucer and Philip Melanchthon. That came about through experiencing in my soul how severely these men were judged by many; as a result I felt for them a certain kind of holy compassion accompanied by a good spirit.[72]

Here we see an extraordinary ecumenical spirit operative within Favre. He was praying for Pope Paul III;[73] Charles V[74] the Emperor; Francis I[75] King of France; Henry VIII[76] King of England; Martin Luther;[77] Suleiman I[78] the grand Turk; Martin Bucer,[79] and Philip Melanchthon[80] leading lights amongst the Reformers. It is important to note here that he prays for them and their good, not against them and for their downfall. He brings them before the love of God which embraces all human beings.

Later in his *Memoriale* he speaks of the Lord giving him: "many feelings of love and hope for heretics and for the whole world."[81] We can see

---

[71] He continues: "Would to God that there were in each town of this land two or three priests not living openly with women or guilty of other notorious sins. If there were I feel sure that, with God's help, the ordinary people would turn back. I speak of towns and cities from which Church rule has not as yet been totally expelled." Cited in Purcell, *The Quiet Companion*, 81.
[72] *Memoriale* 25, *Spiritual Writings* 79.
[73] Pope Paul III 1534–49.
[74] Charles V Holy Roman Emperor 1519–56.
[75] Francis I King of France 1515–47.
[76] Henry VIII King of England 1509–47.
[77] Martin Luther lived 1483–1546.
[78] Suleiman first reigned 1520–66.
[79] Martin Bucer lived 1491–1551, a Protestant reformer based in Strasbourg.
[80] Philip Melanchthon lived 1497–1560, and was a collaborator of Martin Luther.
[81] *Memoriale* 33, ibid., 84.

how this focus on the love of God extended to all human persons.[82] In the moment of great disillusionment, Favre commends the most important figures in the conflicts that he perceived all around him, to the love and mercy of God. Here, we may catch an echo of Ignatius' Cardoner experience[83] when he perceived the organic unity of all things created and reconciled in Christ and in and through him brought into the reality of the Trinity. Favre's prayer betokens that sense of inclusivity that sees all persons being encompassed within the loving providence of God.

Favre continued his ministry as a confessor and spiritual director at these meetings. Increasingly he was involved with priest penitents. In Speyer and Ratisbon bishops also sought him out as a confessor and many of the Emperor's court were amongst his penitents.[84] It is clear that in and through his ministry of spiritual direction, Favre was able to exercise an influence that led to the conversion of many priests, bishops and officials from their previous reprehensible conduct. In a letter to Ignatius from Speyer dated April 27, 1542 he states: "the vicar general has returned to the beginning of the Exercises with a view to making a general confession with me. Bishop Otto Truchsess likewise started them from the beginning."[85]

It is clear that Favre prayed for his penitents as well as seeking to assist their conversion and spiritual growth. It is also in this spirit of prayer that he began to give advice on how to deal with religious dialogue. The love of God, which we noted above, is always his starting point and this flows forth in charity to others. In a letter he wrote to Diego Lainez in 1546, not long before his death, he asserts: "anyone wanting to help the heretics of this age must be careful to have great charity for them and to love them in truth, banishing from his soul all considerations which would tend to chill

---

[82] The pure love which Favre himself feels for these significant figures also echoes the eighteenth of the Rules for Thinking, Judging, and Feeling with the Church: "It is granted that we should value above everything else the great service which is given to God because of pure love." Eighteenth Rule, *Spiritual Exercises* 370.

[83] See Chapter 3.

[84] "That same year in Ratisbon I was given other favors. In the first place, our Lord granted me grace to accomplish some remarkable things in his service, especially in the confessions of many noblemen of the imperial court or at the court of my prince, the duke of Savoy, who had chosen me as his personal confessor. Much good was done in these confessions, and much seed was sown for the still greater good which resulted from them. And the same is true of the Exercises made by important persons, Spaniards and Italians as well as Germans, all very influential." *Memoriale* [22], *Spiritual Writings* 76.

[85] Favre continues, "since the other time in Regensburg he only heard and wrote down the First Week. There is another doctor of canon and civil law who wants to make them; he met spontaneously with me to agree on an hour and a half of work. He still has not begun, nor would I be able to manage that much. The bishop of Speyer would be willing to give an hour a day for exercises if I could visit him in his castle a German league from here; but with all my other occupations I am not taking him up on it. So thanks be to God, I have no lack of harvest to keep me busy." Pierre Favre, Letters, in *Spiritual Writings*, 335.

his esteem for them."[86] Favre was also aware that learning of itself would not convert anyone. He recommended to others the offering of prayers and penances as more successful than arguments.[87] Indeed when we consider Favre's pastoral practice we can see that he gradually shifts over time to concentrate more on the reform of the clergy seeing them as the natural leaders to assist the renewal of the Church. [88]

Obedience

Finally, we might note Favre's profound understanding of the meaning of obedience. During the course of his time in Germany at the various meetings to which he was sent by the Pope, he had come to see that by the judgment of normal criteria, many ecclesiastical and religious superiors were not worthy of obedience. Nevertheless, he was convinced that the will of God could still be made known through such unworthy superiors. The manner in which he suggested people should proceed with an unworthy superior is to trust that the will of God could still be made known and to actively look to the good qualities of the superior.[89]

---

[86] Letter to Diego Lainez, On Dealing with Heretics, Madrid, March 7, 1546, *Mon Fabri*, 399–402 [*Epist.* 138] cited in *Spiritual Writings* 379. He continues in the same letter: "We need to win their goodwill, so that they will love us and accord us a good place in their hearts. This can be done by speaking familiarly with them about matters we both share in common and avoiding any debate in which one side tries to put down the other. We must establish communion in what unites us before doing so in what might evince differences of opinion." There is a very helpful discussion of the nature of religious dialogue as advocated by Pierre Favre, in an unpublished paper by Brian O'Leary, S.J., "Encouragement to Religious Dialogue; A Letter of Blessed Pierre Favre, S.J. [1546]."

[87] Cf. Purcell, *The Quiet Companion*, 89.

[88] Cf. *Spiritual Exercises* 359. Cf. also "the only arguments needed are sweat and blood [bodily austerities]." Purcell, *The Quiet Companion*, 89. "It is interesting to note the line of Peter Favre's thinking followed between 1540 when he arrived in Germany, and 1546, when he advised Lainez how to deal with heretics. First he observes for himself, and not without grief, the numbers of Catholics, clerical and lay, living lives at variance with the faith they profess; he notes the defections from the Church, pastors and people going over to the new religion. He sets himself to discover the reasons for the laxity, the reasons for abandoning the faith of their fathers. He finds that the faith is not taught, nor understood, not appreciated, not lived up to; he meets individuals who defend their moral lapses by choosing from Scripture or Tradition some text that conveniently justifies the action taken or contemplated. Experience convinced him that defection began not in the mind but in the heart, not in the intellect but in the will. Experience also convinced him that moral rehabilitation had to precede not follow the recovery of a lost faith, and that it, too, began not in the intellect but in the will. As time moves on we see him concentrating more and more on the clergy, and then on the higher, and better educated clergy, the shepherds of the flock of God. Reformed prelates meant, in his estimation, a reformed clergy; and good priests meant good people." Ibid., 169.

[89] Cf. *Spiritual Exercises* 362. Also "[Favre's] travels brought him face to face with the unpalatable fact that many bishops and religious superiors were unworthy of obedience, judging by

The real focus of his understanding of obedience,[90] however, lies in his sense of the Trinity. For Favre obedience was essentially obedience to the Trinity. Here a passage from his *Memoriale* gives significant insight:

> One day within the octave of the Visitation of the Blessed Virgin Mary, I experienced certain deeply felt longings in which I asked God the Father to be a father to me in a special way (unworthy though I am) and that he might make of me his son to obey and acknowledge him. I asked the Son of God our Lord that he might deign to be my Lord and that by his grace I might serve him in all fear for the future. I begged the Holy Spirit to be my master and to teach me to be his disciple. To obtain these gifts I implored with great devotion the help and the intercession of her who was the chosen daughter of God the Father, the servant and mother of Jesus Christ, and the disciple of the Holy Spirit – I mean the Blessed Virgin Mary, who can with ease obtain all these graces from God. I desired also that she might teach the true way to be a son, and to be a servant, and to be a disciple according to his example, because she knows how Jesus Christ lived as her son and servant and disciple, and thus will know how humble he was and how he fitted into each of those three states of life.[91]

Here there is clear reference to the obedience offered to all three persons of the Trinity which is the essential foundation for all obedience for Favre. In addition, there is a sense in which he sees the obedience of Christ to his mother as exemplary of the kind of obedience due to a human superior. It is

---

purely natural criteria. He began to understand the popular demand for reform in the ranks of church leaders." He gradually develops the idea of the importance of humility "to our superiors and indeed to all creatures. Humility soon becomes synonymous with obedience, and the motive is the fear and love of God. Throughout the reflections in the *Memoriale* the problem of unworthy superiors is clearly in his mind, and he emphasizes how 'regarding and being attracted to only what is good (in them), and not by what is bad' [39]. In fact the worse the superior is, the greater perfection attained by the subject as an obedient, conscientious and faithful servant. Rebellious servants do not deserve good masters, while bad masters do not deserve to have better servants. The general lesson is that reform begins from within the individual; and this does not have to wait until all superiors are perfect. God's will can still be made known, even through an unworthy mouthpiece." O'Leary, S.J., *Pierre Favre and Discernment*, 129.

[90] It is important to recall the Deliberation of the First Fathers of 1539 "which centred on the question of obedience. Favre was fully in accord with the result of that deliberation which was expressed in these words: 'Finally with the help of the Lord, we arrived at this conclusion, expressed as a judgment and unanimously without any dissenting voice: for us it is more opportune, indeed even necessary to give obedience to one of ourselves; in order the better to carry out our original aspiration to fulfil in everything the will of God; to preserve our Company in greater solidarity; finally, to provide in a convenient way and in particular cases for our spiritual activities and temporal affairs." O'Leary, S.J., *Pierre Favre and Discernment*, 127.

[91] *Memoriale* 40, *Spiritual Writings* 90.

clear then that when he obeys a human superior he does so in order to enter into a deeper relationship with the Trinitarian persons. In all of this Mary is the model of humble obedience to the will of God ever at work through every moment and every action. Indeed she might well be seen as exemplar of all the vows. It is noteworthy also that "On the first anniversary of his profession the octave day of the Feast of the Visitation (July 9, 1542), Favre committed the care of his obedience to Jesus Christ, who himself became obedient unto death."[92] And once more we also find an echo of the important Triple Colloquy of the key meditations of the *Spiritual Exercises* where Our Lady is an intercessor for the important graces desired in prayer.

We have explored the life and spiritual writings of Blessed Pierre Favre and traced therein elements of the ecclesial disposition. The seed-ground of his family and early education bore fruit in an apostolic vocation at the service of the Church. Clearly operative is a deep intimacy with Christ which leads him to a Trinitarian perspective. Indeed this is most expressively exemplified in the essential Trinitarian grounding of his understanding of obedience. Distinctive characteristics of his way of living this ecclesial disposition are his focus on the centrality of the sacraments for interior reform and the helpful nature of devotions for maintaining a sense of the presence of God. Finally, in the way in which he related to the heretics of his time we can see a focus on the graced nature of the human person who with love and charity might be assisted to deepen their relationship with God and the Church.

---

[92] O'Leary, S.J., 130, O'Leary continues: "Once more, obedience, as well as poverty and chastity emerge in the context of the Trinity. ... One can say that Favre's constant aim was to seek find and fulfil the will of God. By natural inclination he preferred to have that will expressed through direct and explicit commands from a superior, even when that meant the necessity of practising blind obedience. ... But owing to the nature of the apostolate, he was forced in most cases to discover God's will through experience: that is, through what is techni-cally known as discernment."

5

Mary Ward

A recusant heritage and a disciplined faith formation nurtured a deep encounter with Christ for Mary Ward. This intimacy was the foundation for her progressive discernment and grounded her ecclesial disposition, which was particularly characterized by: courage, faithfulness, generosity and confident freedom in the Lord. It is a passionate love of God that drives her endeavors and is manifest in the manner of her obedience which embraces suffering for the fruitfulness of her mission in the service of the Church.

In a meeting with religious women at World Youth Day in Madrid August 2011, Pope Benedict reminded them that every charism is an evangelical word which the Holy Spirit recalls to the Church's attention.[1] It is not by accident that consecrated life is, as the Apostolic Exhortation *Verbum Domini* in 2010 stated, "born from hearing the word of God and embracing the Gospel as its rule of life. A life devoted to following Christ in his chastity, poverty and obedience becomes a living 'exegesis' of God's word ... Every charism and every rule (all constitutions) springs from it and seeks to be an expression of it, thus opening up new pathways of Christian living marked by the radicalism of the Gospel."[2] This Gospel radicalism is profoundly rooted in an intimate relationship with Christ being "rooted and built up in Christ."[3] It finds expression in the mission that God entrusts to human persons and it flourishes in communion with the Church. Such gospel radicalism is clearly evident in the lives of St. Ignatius and Venerable Mary Ward in the profundity of their individual intimacy with Christ; in the mission which each embraced rooted in their understanding of the integration of contemplation and action; in the *Constitutions* they fashioned and in their deep love for and desire to serve the Church even when they experienced suspicion and hostility within the body of Christ.

---

[1] Cf. Jn 14.26
[2] *Verbum Domini*, Benedict XVI, post-synodal Apostolic Exhortation on the Word of God in the life and mission of the Church, September 30, 2010, [83].
[3] Col. 2.7.

This chapter focuses on the only person under consideration in this book who was not a Jesuit, or a priest, nor a man. She is a woman who lived in dangerous times—the late sixteenth and early seventeenth century—and who truly exemplifies in her life and writings Ignatius' ecclesial disposition. Mary Ward was a pioneer of apostolic religious life for women and, as with most founders of religious congregations, she was ahead of her time in advocating this way of life which seemed inconceivable to her contemporary Church leaders. Her quiet confidence and determined respectful representation of illuminations she believed were from God earned her much suffering and opprobrium. Yet she willingly endured every difficulty convinced of the divine inspiration of what she requested and remained always faithful to the Church she loved.

The Witness of Life

Unlike Ignatius who spent his youth as a nominal cultural Catholic until the time of his conversion in an area of Europe not subject to the persecution of Catholics, Mary Ward's early years saw the fierce persecution of Catholics in England. It was in that northern county of Yorkshire[4] that Mary Ward was born in 1585 at Mulwith, near Ripon, into a Roman Catholic family[5] whose recusant members had already suffered heavy fines and imprisonment for the faith.[6] It is reported that her grandmother was imprisoned for her faith on a number of occasions, in all for fourteen years and continued persecution forced her father in 1597–8 to break up his household sending Mary to live with other Catholic families.[7] Of her

---

[4]"The North of England, that restless border facing Scotland, has always shown individuality." Henrietta Peters, *Mary Ward: A World in Contemplation,* trans. Helen Butterworth, (Leominster: Gracewing, 1994), 4.

[5]"Their status was that of gentry, at the level of well-to-do property owners between nobility and burgher, which sometimes was elevated into the nobility or entered into by marriage." Ibid., 5.

[6]The Earl of Huntingdon had promised Queen Elizabeth that he would stamp out the old faith. Fines were heavy for refusal to go the Protestant Church, forty or fifty times a skilled worker's wages for a month. The recusant rolls of 1591–2 list Mary's mother Ursula Ward as indicted on four counts of recusancy and fined a total of £80.

[7]Henry Garnet wrote of the situation in a letter to the Jesuit General Aquaviva as follows: "Many Catholics change their dwellings [in order to receive the sacraments] and go, as it were into voluntary exile, and live unknown and obscurely in remote parts of the country. If there were some one place where they might be permitted to live in peace, they would consider themselves to be treated fairly enough. But the faithful are not left to themselves anywhere. It is impossible save at the greatest risk to baptize infants, celebrate marriages, give the sacraments or to offer the sacrifice according to the Catholic rite. Expectant mothers have to travel to far-away places for the birth of their offspring in order not to be asked about the christening of their offspring." Letter Henry Garnet to Claude Acquaviva, February 11, 1592, F.G. 651, cited in *A Study of Friendship*, 54.

parents Mary wrote in later years: "Both my parents were virtuous and suffered much for the Catholic cause."[8]

The two early biographies of Mary Ward recount that the first word she spoke was "Jesus,"[9] and the story is symptomatic of that intimacy with Christ that was a feature of her life and that we can trace in terms of her growing development. This concentration on the holy name of Jesus is very important to her through her life—so much so that she desired the name of Jesus to be in the name of the institute that she founded. We know too that in her later years she concluded her letters often with "May Jesus have you in his keeping"—this is indicative of her constant companionship with Christ even to the last word she uttered on her deathbed. It is also clear that this devout Catholic family knew the reality of persecution[10] and this experience was the foundation from which Mary grew to prize her Catholic faith.[11]

What also sustained the faith amidst such persecution bringing inspiration and consolation was the example of martyrs like Edmund Campion martyred in 1581 and another Jesuit priest Robert Southwell martyred in 1595 when Mary Ward was at the impressionable age of 10. Amongst Southwell's prose works, we find a guide to Christian living for laypeople under the title of *Short Rules of a Good Life*.[12] Mary Ward refers specifically to this work as having a significant formative role on her spirituality.[13] Within this short volume, Southwell emphasizes the ability of human

---

[8] From Mary Ward's *Autobiography*, cited in *Mary Ward 1585–1645: 'A Briefe Relation' with Autobiographical Fragments and a Selection of Letters*, ed. Christina Kenworthy-Browne, C.J. (London: Catholic Record Society, Boydell Press, 2008), 105.

[9] "… hearing her Mother forth of a sudden apprehension the child might fall, say JESUS bless my Child, she turned with a sweet smile and sayd distinctly, JESUS: which was the first, and all the words she spoke of many Months after." Mary Poyntz, *A Briefe Relation: Of the Holy Life, and Happy Death, of our Dearest Mother, of Blessed Memory, Mistress Mary Ward*, 1, cited in ibid., 3.

[10] The royal proclamation of 1591 established a commission in every shire, and sub-commissions in parishes for the weekly examination of householders regarding belief and Church attendance. In 1593 the last and most severe parliamentary statute against Catholics prohibited them from approaching within five miles of a corporate town, and in certain cases deprived Catholic parents of the right of educating their children.

[11] This laid the ground for her later acceptance of the Rules for Thinking, Judging, and Feeling with the Church.

[12] We know the popularity of this work as it went through eight publications between 1588 and 1622. See Robert Southwell, S.J., *Two Short letters and Short Rules of a Good Life*, ed. Nancy Pollard Brown (Charlottesville: University Press of Virginia, 1973).

[13] Although her first formal experience of the *Spiritual Exercises* came after 1608, this work was one of the first literary sources from which she received some knowledge of them. Southwell closely follows the plan of the *Exercises*. He grounds the good life on the "First Principle and Foundation"; he advises "continual warfare" against the world, the flesh and the devil.

persons to co-operate with God's grace and throughout he seeks a sound theological basis for spirituality.[14]

It is important to note that the spiritual formation that Mary received was mostly at the hands of members of the Society of Jesus.[15] These men, often remaining resident in the houses where Mary Ward stayed for some considerable time, were her confessors and spiritual directors from an early age. The Jesuits took the formation of the young very seriously and encouraged the practice of an intense reception of the sacraments and a disciplined life of prayer. Fr. James Sharp, writing in 1610, described the religious life of the Babthorpes with whom Mary Ward lived at Osgodby south of York for seven years from 1600–6.[16] "Each day had begun with two masses. Evensong at 4 p.m. was followed by Matins, with the Litanies at 9 p.m. Sermons, catechisms, and spiritual lessons were given every Sunday and holy days. Most of the household also attended meditation and mental prayer and all would confess and receive the Eucharist at least every fourteen days."[17]

It was in this house, through a passing conversation with a servant[18] that Mary first experienced her desire to become a religious. Of particular importance with regard to her vocation, was Father Richard Holtby, S.J.,[19]

---

[14] "He parallels in diagrammatic form the relationship of God's grace and human co-operation: justification as the action of God and its effects in human beings. He indicates the action of grace, with each of the theological virtues bringing about a human response. This response begins with the intellect's consideration of God's justice and mercy and the merits of Christ and culminates in the will's desire to avoid all sin. The theology underlying Mary Ward's later description of the 'estate of justice' (1615) suggests the influence of Southwell's exposition." Jeanne Cover, IBVM, *Love – The Driving Force: Mary Ward's Spirituality: Its Significance for Moral Theology* (Milwaukee: Marquette University Press, 1997), 35.

[15] Mary Ward's confessors and directors included: Fr. Richard Holtby, S.J., Fr. John Mush, S.J., and Fr. James Sharp S.J. in her earlier life, and later Fr. John Gerard, S.J. became her retreat director, friend and supporter.

[16] "Mary would have reached the age of sixteen on January 23, 1601. According to English law, on that day she would come of age in religious matters, which means that she was obliged to live as an Anglican, attend church services and receive the sacraments in the Anglican rite. If she did not comply with these state regulations, she would come under the relentless legal system of fines for recusants. … if she were away from home however, she would be exempt." Peters, *Mary Ward: A World in Contemplation*, 45.

[17] "Father Pollard's Recollections of the Yorkshire Mission," in *The Troubles of Our Catholic Fore-Fathers – Related by Themselves,* ed. John Morris, third series 1877, cited in Cover, IBVM, *Love – the Driving Force*, 30.

[18] The servant was Margaret Garrett who spoke to Mary about religious life. Mary said later of this conversation: "I thought the most perfect thing would be to take the most austere and secluded order." But with maturity she came to realise that mere austerity was not enough. The simple pursuit of God's will could turn out to be more rigorous than any religious rule, and lead to an agony of mind and spirit greater than martyrdom inflicted by rack, rope or knife.

[19] Fr. Richard Holtby (1553–1640) was a Yorkshire man who converted to Roman Catholicism and entered the Society of Jesus in 1583, two years before Mary Ward's birth. He was sent to England by the Jesuit Superior General in 1589.

who worked in the north of England between 1593 and 1606. In the Jesuits she encountered, Mary saw the life of an active apostolate, deeply rooted in prayer and courageous in action. She saw also the practical outworking of the *Constitutions* in Jesuit lives and even the death of the martyrs. The fruitfulness of this way of life and the great service that was being offered to the Church was unambiguous. I would suggest that these things became imprinted on her heart and her ability to recognize the later significant insights was due to the refining fire of persecution; the discipline of prayer; the example of Jesuit lives and the profound intimacy of her relationship with Christ nurtured during these early years.

From her teenage years she resolved to enter religious life. This was problematic at the time, since her parents thought she would do more for the Catholic cause to marry well and provide another safe haven for Catholics within the country. This in itself was a laudable ambition endeavoring to give added strength and support to the English Mission and the Catholic cause in the North of England. Mary's parents suggested various eligible suitors including the Catholic Earl of Westmorland[20] whom her father and her confessor had particularly urged her to marry. Each in turn, however, Mary rejected, she was convinced that a religious vocation was the way God was calling her. Eventually her confessor, Father Holtby, was reconciled to Mary's decision to enter religious life and her father finally gave his consent.

In the early years of the seventeenth century anyone desiring to embrace a religious life had to leave England for the European Continent. The Reformation had ensured closure of all religious houses in Britain. To enter religious life then, was to leave the country of her birth, to enter an enclosed convent and to remain for the rest of her days devoted to praying for the Church and the world behind closed doors—a hidden life. This contemplative life was what Mary deeply desired. In 1606 Mary left England for the Netherlands armed with letters of introduction to the Jesuit Fathers in St Omer.[21]

The Progress of Discernment

As a young teenager Mary had discerned her vocation was not to marriage but to religious life. She initially saw her call to be a Poor Clare—the most austere contemplative order of that time. She entered a convent of

---

[20] Edmund Neville, Earl of Westmoreland, who swore if Mary Ward refused to marry him that he would not marry. In 1606 he entered the English College in Rome and became a Jesuit. He died on the English mission in 1648.

[21] St Omer is now part of France but in the early sixteenth century it was part of the Spanish Netherlands near Calais. The region became part of France in 1677.

Poor Clares at St Omer· but by the misdirection of one of the Jesuits[22] she became an out-sister of the Poor Clares, begging for the community each day in the town. This vocation was one for which she was utterly unsuited by character and education. She embraced it as she had been told by the Jesuit Father, who received her at St Omer, that it was the Will of God she should do so. Here, we see clearly how obedience to the will of God was of central importance in her life even at this early stage of her religious vocation.[23] Though she had a clear interior sense that this way of life of an out-sister was not what she had been called to, because a Jesuit priest, representative of the Church, had told her it was God's will she was obedient. Here, it is important to stress that Mary Ward's obedience was focused on "the will of God" which she so revered. She was well aware that this Jesuit was not her religious superior to whom she was bound by obedience. Rather it was her great desire to accomplish the will of God that led her to follow the direction indicated by this priest who insisted that it was the will of God that she should become an extern sister for the community of Poor Clares.[24]

---

[22] Fr. George Keynes, S.J., who from 1595 was professor of moral theology in the English seminary in St Omer. He died there in 1611.

[23] We might perceive that the characteristics of the thirteenth rule of the Rules for Thinking, Judging, and Feeling with the Church were already operative in her life here.

[24] "The Jesuits had undoubtedly been informed of Mary Ward's desire to enter and of the approximate time of her arrival in St Omer. First of all Fr. Keynes said that Mary Ward had long been expected in the Convent of the Poor Clares in St Omer. Some young Englishwomen had already been living there for some years. The spirit of the community and above all of these English women, was excellent. However, she could not be admitted as a choir sister, as the convent was more than full. The nuns had decided not to accept any more Englishwomen as choir sisters but one of Lord Lumley's nieces, Anne Campian, who had recently been refused for the choir, lived there happily as a lay sister. The Abbess had even postponed Anne's clothing until Mary Ward's admission. Fr. Keynes informed her that the sisters had a place for her outside the enclosure: 'those without added an act of charity in maintaining the others by their religious labours and an act of humility in begging for the rest. The priest added that those within the enclosure and those without were one and the same order and rule, only that to those without were added an act of charity in maintaining the others'. Whether or not Fr. Keynes' information was due to a misunderstanding, his statement that the out-sisters had the same life-style and Rule as the choir sisters was completely untrue. The lay sisters followed the Third Order of St Francis. They were Tertiaries. The choir sisters had the strict Rule of St Clare. In conclusion [Fr. Keynes] expressed his admiration for the Providence of God in the circumstances, coinciding with the great desire of the nuns to accept me so quickly, never having seen me, affirming that it certainly was the will of God and my true vocation.' With hindsight we can say that she should have recognised her instinctive impulse to refuse as a warning. But, convinced that the Rule of the Order was the same for both, that the out-sisters had more opportunity to practice humility, and that her repugnance was the reaction of pride, she ignored the danger signals given by her very sound instinct. One must not forget either, that Mary Ward was talking to a religious thirty years older than herself, whom she regarded as a person of mature judgment. At the moment of decision, she was struck by the words 'the Will of God.'" Peters, *Mary Ward: A World in Contemplation*, 75–6.

By another dispensation of Providence she became a choir sister in the Poor Clares at St Omer, and then was inspired to found a new convent of Poor Clares for English women, nearby at Gravelines. As a member of this latter community, in this quiet life of prayer, with austerity and in seclusion, Mary Ward was happy. Here at last was the contemplative life she had long desired. The Lord, however, had other plans. After only a few months in this new foundation on the Feast of St. Athanasius 1607, while prayerfully sewing, Mary experienced a divine illumination and she realized: "that I was not to be of the Order of St. Clare; some other thing I was to do, what or of what nature I did not see, nor could I guess, only that it was to be a good thing, and what God willed."[25] There was at that time no possibility for women of bringing together an ascetic ideal [associated with monasticism] and an active life. The conception of women living an active life in union with God was entirely alien.

This illumination on the Feast of St. Athanasius disrupted her plans for the Poor Clare form of contemplative life. She left the convent and returned to London, in order to assist her fellow Catholics in that city. She also pondered whether she should take another rule such as the Carmelites. Accordingly, in 1609, Mary Ward was in London undertaking what we might see as the spiritual and corporal works of mercy with a clear emphasis on spiritual conversation which is a primary ministry mentioned in the *Constitutions*. Spiritual conversation involves human encounters in the immediate circumstances of ordinary life, seeking the presence of God in them. At times, Ignatius suggested a complementary relationship between this practice and preaching for Jesuits.[26] Mary was encouraging people in

---

[25] M. C. E. Chambers, *The Life of Mary Ward [1585–1645]*, Vol. 1 (London: Burns & Oates, 1882), 180.

[26] In the *Constitutions* he wrote: "And if two set out, it seems that with a preacher or lecturer there could well go another [who] could gather in the harvest which the speaker prepares for him, and who could aid the speaker by conversations and the other means used in dealing with our fellowmen." [624]. Ignatius also used spiritual conversation to reach individuals who would never hear God's word if it meant entering a church. These included prostitutes and society's outcasts. At inns and in the streets, Ignatius and other Jesuits took advantage of chance encounters to minister to spiritual concerns. Some of their conversations gave guidance in prayer. Others focused on the interpretation of the spiritual life as manifested to the will, the senses, or the emotions. Interpretive conversations were expected to identify the Spirit's leading of this person, to God and to the Church. Although it could serve various purposes, as an apostolic ministry one constant remained: Spiritual conversation extended the reach of the Word into settings at some remove from the congregational worship and to persons in walks of life incompatible with the faith of the Church. Ignatius' apostolic work with prostitutes in the Casa Santa Martha, a home that he had opened for their social and spiritual renewal, gives one concrete indication. It is mentioned in many sources. Apostolic work with persons who would be described as un-churched is a prominent feature of the Jesuit historical narrative. In our contemporary time, Jesuits are being encouraged to re-appropriate the apostolate of spiritual conversation. This is an activity that was both esteemed by Mary Ward and has proliferated within the congregation she founded. We know that Mary Ward encouraged superiors to give the Exercises if a priest could not be found. We know also that she highly prized spiritual

their faith; preparing them to receive the sacraments; arranging for priests to meet with groups of Catholics; and visiting those in prison on account of their faith.

This was a dangerous apostolate and she often traveled in disguise.[27] "She labored day and night in seeking to gain lost souls, despising danger either to life or honor, for she was accustomed to say that: 'God is not wanting to good wills, and that it gives Him pleasure that we should trust Him, when He gives us light to know that He trusts us.'"[28] Mary mixed in the society to which her birth gave access but with a missionary spirit that sought, through the ministry of spiritual conversation, to attract others to a deeper interior life. She devoted herself particularly to the sick and to the Catholics in prison. The fruit of her efforts also included a substantial number of religious vocations.

It was at this point, while she was helping other Catholics to develop their interior life, that she experienced what became known later as the *glory vision* or illumination. Mary was sitting brushing her hair when:

> I was abstracted out of my whole being and it was shown to me with clearness and inexpressible certainty that I was not to be of the Order of St. Teresa, but that some other thing was determined for me, without all comparison more to the glory of God than my entrance into that holy religion would be. I did not see what the assured good thing would be, but the glory of God which was to come through it, showed itself inexplicably and so abundantly as to fill my soul in such a way that I remained for a good space without feeling or hearing anything but the sound, "Glory, Glory, Glory."[29]

Mary was totally transported by this intellectual understanding—coming as it did after what she had considered a 'cold' meditation, with a resolution to give financial assistance to a young woman wanting to enter a convent.

---

conversation both amongst the sisters and with others. Today we find it evident in work amongst those on the margins of society. It is also an apostolate that informs ecumenical and inter-faith dialogue. More than this it is an everyday activity amongst communities and in the many diverse areas of the apostolate. It may well be that there is a particular feminine genius and grace at work here focused in the "ordinary" which of course means that it then becomes the extraordinary.

[27] "The success with which God rewarded her daring attempts only urged her on to further enterprises, and gave her greater confidence in [God]. ... She led back into the fold of the Catholic Church, not a few of those who had wandered from the path of the true faith. ... her prayers and her holiness of life made as many conversions as her powers of controversy. Her courage and perseverance were indomitable." Chambers, *The Life of Mary Ward [1585–1645]*, 223–4.

[28] Ibid.

[29] Mary Ward, *Italian Autobiography*, 1629, cited in Chambers, *The Life of Mary Ward [1585–1645]*, 227.

It was precisely in this concrete consideration when Mary was pondering an action, while brushing her hair that this spiritual illumination came with great clarity. In the midst of her active concern with another matter Mary recognized the revealing touch of God.

Such recognition also indicates that she had already been granted a contemplative disposition—resulting from her disciplined practice of prayer. This was the foundation of her activity and had refined her sensitivity to the presence of God at work in her life. Her previous illumination had brought clarity amidst her uncertainty. She knew she was not to be a Poor Clare. Now, in 1609, it was clear she was not to become a Carmelite, and she had finally to abandon the possibility of a purely contemplative life. Here, we can also see illustrated that sensitive attunement to the working of God and the discernment of the spirit of God that characterized the life of Ignatius. There is a clear sense of a progress of discernment here. There is a deep sensitivity to the movement of the Spirit of God within her. Each time she articulates what she heard, there is no sense of confusion. At each stage she builds on previous discernment. This is a very Ignatian way of proceeding.

Sensitivity to the Spirit of God and a discerning love for the will of God was the foundation for her activity. There was "something more" that God was calling her to do, and it is clear that this, as yet unspecified, task became the object of Mary's desire capturing both her imagination and her heart—the seat of all desire. What we observe here is the dynamic of the *Spiritual Exercises*. The *Exercises* work with the raw material of our desires and build on those desires to strengthen deeper desires which then become the matter for further prayer. Mary Ward had developed a contemplative spirit that was able to recognise on St. Athanasius' day that she was not to be a Poor Clare—but some other good the Lord desires for her. So she begins to desire and pray for that good. In London she has this other illumination of glory. Now she knows that this good, whatever it is, will be more to the glory of God. So this then becomes her desire—she prays on this good that is more to the glory of God. It was from this time that she began to attract other companions. In 1611 she receives a further illumination: this good that is something more to the glory of God is to found an order of women who will have an active apostolate. In a further illumination following a bout of sickness she was convinced that God was calling her to "*Take the same of the Society.*"[30] She was to found an Institute that would

---

[30] Mary Ward wrote to the Nuncio Albergati concerning this illumination as follows: "Being alone, in some extraordinary repose of mind, I heard distinctly, not by sound of voice, but intellectually understood, these words, '*Take the same of the Society*'. So understood as that we were to take the same both in matter and manner that only excepted which God by diversity of sex hath prohibited. These few words gave so great measure of light in that particular Institute, comfort, and strength, and changed so the whole soul, as that it was impossible for me to doubt but that they came from Him, Whose words are works." Some years later in an

have the same Constitutions as the Society of Jesus—to engage in an active apostolate at the service of the Church.[31]

The key principle underlying Mary Ward's practice of discernment consisted of a deep trust in God's providential care. While she understood that discernment concerns the free sincere and loving human response to God, with Ignatius she believed that it is God's faithfulness which gives discernment its truth. The aim of discernment is to distinguish the true good—the doing of God's will—from all illusory forms of good. The true good is always in conformity with the teaching and example of Christ in whom we find the expression of the most perfect choice of the true good. Discernment requires a harmony of will, understanding and affectivity with the will of God. And discernment is related to action—what is to be done or not done.

The Fundamental Importance of "Glory"

It is the *glory vision* of 1609 that marks the beginning of Mary Ward's Institute.[32] Mary Ward's *glory vision* points not only to the heart of her individual existential situation but also to the "proper center of theology." Her apprehension of glory in this illumination is firmly rooted in the Christian theological tradition. For God's splendor reveals and authenticates itself precisely in its own antithesis, as love selflessly serving out of love. We see this definitively in the salvific action of God on behalf of human beings in the Incarnation, Passion, Death and Resurrection of Christ.

There are two theological realities operational here: the glory of God and the covenant to which God's glory invites the human person. God is not only glorious in the very reality of the Trinity one God in three persons, but God is also glorious-for-us. God is not only Love in the eternal act of indwelling between the Father and the Son and the Spirit who is Love, but God also loves human persons to whom God freely chooses to disclose divine love in their very creation. The Trinity is love ad-intra and ad-extra. Accordingly, God's love is a mutual revelation of the divine Persons in whom they are Lover, Beloved and Love and an external revelation of

---

account in a letter she wrote to Fr John Gerard, S.J. in 1619 she stated: "What I had from God touching this, was as follows [understood as it is writ, without adding or altering one syllable], 'Take the same of the Society. Father General will never permit it. Go to him.' These are the words whose worth cannot be valued, nor the good they contain too dearly bought; these gave sight where there was none, made known what God would have done, gave strength to suffer, what since hath happened, assurance of what is wished for in time to come." Cf. Chambers, 283–4.

[31] In early seventeenth century Europe this was a scandalous suggestion.

[32] In 1978 the original branch of Mary Ward's Order asked for, and was finally granted, the Constitutions of the Society of Jesus.

love as God's nature to each human person. Clearly the Trinitarian understanding that underlay Ignatius' ecclesial disposition was an ingredient in Mary Ward's own understanding of her glory vision.

Human beings always stand in awe of God who is always greater, always mightier, always transcendent, always completely and irrevocably Other. The love between Creator and creature is always of the powerful Lord who graciously and mercifully bestows kindness and delight on his servant. This understanding gives coherence to Mary Ward's existential experience of the inexplicable nature of the glory of God that in abundance filled her soul.

The foundation of the God-human covenant is the paradox of God's glory as love—the divine desire to exchange love with human beings and for them to bear fruit.[33] Mary Ward understood this reality in her awareness that God was calling her through the *glory vision* to something new that would not only fulfill her religious vocation but that would also be fruitful in the life of the Church. She recognized this illumination as an echo of God's glory, and, as a woman who had been formed by Jesuits—who focused their mission "to the greater glory of God"[34]—she was sensitive to what might rebound to the glory of God.

We can glimpse in Mary Ward's *glory vision* traces of a Trinitarian understanding that characterized the life and work of Ignatius. For both, Christ was the center of their lives and it was Christ who revealed for them the reality of the Trinity. In Christ the Word-made-flesh is the "form" of the Father, his very divinity hidden in his humanity was revealed in the glory of the paschal mystery. The Cross is the entry point through which humanity encounters a new truth, a new goodness and the awareness of beauty. The free self-emptying of the Son reveals the truth about God as light and love. God has made known the reality of the Trinity and now desires a human response. The pattern of divine love is the Cross—a pattern of life for Mary Ward and those who followed her who are drawn into the divine trajectory. This is not a destructive burden but rather a source of empowerment enabling a deeper refining of interior dispositions, a more refined *sensus Christi*.[35]

For Mary Ward, contemplation and action were intertwined. It is not a form of contemplation that leads to epistemological issues—our activity of gaining knowledge—rather it is a contemplation that leads to action and an action that leads to the discovery of truth. The theological task, which is always a scriptural exegesis attentive to the signs of the times, continues in the Church through the prayerful reflection on the word of God and the celebration of the Eucharist. It is from this place of prayer and sacraments

---

[33] Cf. Jn 15.

[34] *Ad Maijorem Dei Gloriam.*

[35] *Sensus Christi* really the sensitivity of Christ, cf. St. Paul speaking of putting on the mind of Christ that we might feel with Christ's feelings, with the sentiments of his heart which are basically love for the Father and for all human persons.

within the Church that the individual members live their vocation as part of the reconciling mission given to the Church by Christ. For Mary Ward the primary embodiment of this work of reconciliation lay in the Church as the body of Christ.

For Mary as for Ignatius the institutional structure of the Church was vital since Christ had guaranteed the presence of his Spirit within the Church. They could not see any definitive conflict between the freedom of the individual conscience and the teaching of the institutional Church.[36] This was despite the fact that both found their lives and work called into question by Church authorities. Rather, they saw a creative tension between the action of the Holy Spirit operative in the Church and in the individual— a creative tension that was fruitful for the life of the Church.

The Driving Force of Love[37] which Promotes Union with God and Mission

Both Ignatius and Mary Ward believed that the institutes they founded were of divine origin and at the service of Jesus. The first paragraph of the Preamble in the *Constitutions* begins with God's action over the whole Society then moves to the Holy Spirit's action in each member, and ends in the member's own actions: "God our Creator and Lord is the one who in his Supreme Wisdom and Goodness must preserve, direct and carry forward in his divine service this least Society of Jesus, just as he deigned to begin it."[38] The foundation of the Society and Mary Ward's Institute can thus be understood as totally dependent upon the wisdom and goodness of God in whom we hope and from whom all that we do proceeds as from its primary source. Recognition of this reality is a first step towards union with God: "on our own part what helps most toward this end must be, more than any exterior constitution, the interior law of charity and love which the Holy Spirit writes and imprints upon hearts."[39]

This emphasis on the love that the Holy Spirit imprints on the heart was seen by Nadal as a special grace of the Society. It finds expression also in Mary Ward's maxim that "the true children of this company shall accustom themselves to act not out of fear but solely from love, because they are called by God to a vocation of love." This providential love is given its

---

[36] Ben Quash makes a similar point when he states: "Ignatius was committed to the view that there could be no absolute conflict between the nearness of the God of his conscience and experience [the grace from within] and the institutional direction of the official Church [the God from without]." "Ignatian Dramatics" 85, *The Way* 38 (January 1998): 77–86.

[37] Cf. Cover, IBVM, *Love – The Driving Force.*

[38] *Constitutions of the Society of Jesus* [134].

[39] Ibid.

most concrete divine expression in the Incarnation.[40] The contemplation of the Incarnation as we have recalled begins the second week of the *Spiritual Exercises*. It encapsulates the Ignatian understanding of the universe, the Trinity and Christ himself. It is a microcosm of Ignatius' theological understanding.

Essential intimacy with Christ

The grace Ignatius looks to is an intimate knowledge of God. It is fundamentally an apprehension enabled by the Holy Spirit at the level of our very being—an ontological knowledge—of God's passionate commitment to each one of us. This is the primordial reality that Ignatius is concerned that we should understand. This is the reality that Mary Ward understood and in which she trained her sisters. It is this intimate knowledge of divine love which impels towards union with God and a participation in Christ's redemptive mission which flows from such contemplative union. Brian O'Leary has termed the Ignatian tradition of union as conative mysticism[41] focused particularly on the union of will. I would move further and suggest that the union involves an integration of will, intellect and affect at such a depth of being (ontological) that to attempt to make a primary focus is to some extent to undermine the very nature of the union.[42] The Incarnation has a Trinitarian scope and we need also to come to terms with its ontological proportions which also affect our understanding of vocation and mission.

It is clear from what has already been indicated that for Mary Ward the possibility of living in such an ecclesial way, so that the mission of Christ may be promoted, involved a deeper contemplative living that found expression in an active apostolate. The *glory vision* reveals that she already had a well-developed contemplative prayer life. It was this integration of

---

[40] It is also the impetus for the formulation of the *Constitutions* to assist apostolic endeavors. "Nevertheless, since the gentle disposition of Divine Providence requires cooperation from his creatures, and since too the vicar of Christ our Lord has ordered this, and since the examples given by the saints and reason itself teach us so in our Lord, we think it necessary that constitutions should be written to aid us to proceed better, in conformity with our Institute, along the path of divine service on which we have entered." Ibid.

[41] "The word is unfamiliar to most people and does not appear in many reputable dictionaries, even dictionaries of spirituality. However Encarta English Dictionary defines this word as 'a mental process involving the will, e.g. impulses, desire or resolve'. We are certainly familiar with the terms 'desire' and 'resolve' from the *Spiritual Exercises* and impulse corresponds to certain kinds of movement. ... A conative mysticism will not be so much a union of minds or of affectivity as a union of wills. We will what God wills; we want what God wants." Brian O'Leary, S.J., "'Hither I must come to draw' Mary Ward and the Ignatian Constitutions," *The Way* 51/3 (July 2012): 29–41.

[42] Perhaps a helpful analogy might be the *perichoresis* of Trinitarian relations.

contemplative prayer and action that enabled her to be extraordinarily effective in her apostolic efforts and to endure the suffering that marked her vocation seeing this as part of her sharing in the redemptive mission of Christ.

The prevailing seventeenth century understanding of religious life for women exacerbated the interior struggle and search Mary Ward experienced. Canon law at this period of history insisted on any new Order adopting the rule of an already approved existing order.[43] For women, however, the only existent orders were enclosed religious. Mary Ward's conviction was that she was to take a rule that would enable the possibility of secret apostolic work amongst the persecuted Catholics in England in the manner in which she had already been working. This required the freedom of non-enclosure, and to be able to assume differing modes of dress if necessary both to avoid detection and to be able to mix with all classes of society.

In addition Mary and her companions would need permission to live amongst heretics and schismatics as and when necessary. With regard to observance of the Divine Office, Mary asked for the same dispensation as that granted to the Jesuits. If women were to lead an active apostolic life, they would not be able to sing the regular hours of the Office in choir. Only the *Constitutions* of St. Ignatius would enable this manner of life. It is important to note that in the years following her illumination of 1611 with its decisive "Take the Same of the Society," no matter what pressure was brought to bear upon her, Mary Ward continued to insist that this is what God was asking of her. Moreover, she also requested that the governance of the order should be by a woman superior general. Again, such a suggestion was unheard of in the first half of the seventeenth century. It was another hundred years before Pope Clement XI would give permission for women to govern women.[44]

An irruption of protest was forthcoming from many quarters within the Church.[45] Women could not govern themselves; they could not be trusted without enclosure; what would they be doing "gadding about"? Were they trying to be "Jesuitesses"?[46] It could not have been a less favorable time

---

[43] The Council of Trent 1545–63 had declared that all religious communities of women must take solemn vows and be subject to enclosure. Session XXV, Decree on regulars and nuns, Chapter 5, in *Decrees of the Ecumenical Councils,* Vol. 2, ed. Norman Tanner, 777–8, cited in Mary Wright, *Mary Ward's Institute: The Struggle for Identity* (Sydney: Crossing Press, 1997), 36 fn. 26.

[44] This permission was granted in 1703.

[45] "My confessor resisted, all the Society opposed" Mary Ward, Letter from Mary Ward to Nuncio Antonio Albergati, May/June, 1621, *Till God Will: Mary Ward through her Writings,* ed. Gillian Orchard (London: Darton Longman & Todd, 1985). Fr. Lee, Mary Ward's confessor, began by being opposed and later came to support her efforts. When he died in 1615, Fr. John Gerard, S.J. became both her confessor and the firm supporter of the Institute.

[46] This was a derogatory term applied to Mary Ward and her companions.

to be requesting such a novel form of life for women. At a period when the focus of attention in Rome was on combating Protestant Reformers while at the same time renewing the Church, Mary Ward's request was an unwelcome distraction.

In England, where Mary wished to practice an apostolic ministry, the relations between the secular clergy and the Jesuits were very difficult. Some of the former resented the mobility and apparent freedom of the latter. Mary Ward had always been closely associated with the Jesuits since her youth and thus also faced hostility from the secular clergy.[47] The Jesuits, however, apart from significant individuals who were convinced of the truth of Mary Ward's divine illuminations, were highly suspicious of Mary's intentions. They were determined not to be even loosely associated with this new project. The two Jesuit Generals who spanned Mary Ward's lifetime, Claudio Aquaviva (1581–1615) and Muzio Vitelleschi (1615–45), both warned their men against supporting Mary Ward and her fledgling Institute. Alongside this suspicion there were also the moves that were being made to forward Ignatius' cause for canonization, which might be impeded, if it was thought the Society was lending its support to such a "revolutionary" plan as that proposed by Mary Ward.

From the time of her illumination of "Take the Same of the Society" Mary worked on a possible rule for her Institute. In 1612 an initial plan[48] was drawn up. This was revised and in 1616 a memorial plan was presented to Pope Paul V seeking approval for this mixed life of contemplation and action. In this plan there are clear links to the Ignatian *Constitutions*. The aim of her Institute was stated as: "To work at the perfection of our own souls and to devote ourselves to the salvation of our neighbor by the education of girls, or any means that are congruous to the times, or in which is judged that we can by our labors promote the greater glory of God and in any place further the propagation of our Holy Mother, the Catholic Church."[49] Here we see an echo of the first rule for Thinking, Judging, and Feeling with the Church. There is a clear sense of a desire to be at the service of the Church and yet, at the same time, there is a sense of pushing

---

[47] "Mary's proposal encountered fierce opposition from the English secular clergy who were vehemently opposed to the Jesuits. They suspected in Mary Ward's activities a covert Jesuit plot." See "Memorial from the superior of the clergy and his assistants, against the Jesuitesses, 1622," in *Dodd's Church History of England*, Vol. 4, ed. M. Tierney, "Introduction," A. F. Allison, "bibliographical index," R. E. Scantlebury (Farnborough: Gregg, 1971), n. XLV, ccxxvii–ccxxx. This document, called "Harrison's Memorial," was sent to the Holy See in 1622 by a group of ten English secular clergy. Its charges appear to have been referred to by Pope Urban VIII in his bull suppressing the Institute. For a full exposition of this topic, see J. Grisar, *Die ersten Anklagen*, cited in Mary Wright, *Mary Ward's Institute*), 11, 37 fn. 39.

[48] This plan was known as the *Schola Beatae Mariae*.

[49] This plan was known as the Ratio *Instituti*.

boundaries as the Church at the time seemed unable to countenance what Mary Ward requested.

Over a number of years there was prevarication amongst the authorities in Rome. Good reports were received from local bishops and princes about the work undertaken by the 'English Ladies'. At the same time their enemies also sent in disquieting reports about this novel way of life. In 1621, Mary Ward decided to travel to Rome herself to see the Holy Father with the final version of her rule in hand. This third plan of the Institute was almost exactly the same as the *Formula Instituti* of the Society of Jesus,[50] the foundational document which had established the Jesuits. The journey to Rome was undertaken on foot, taking two months, with the small group arriving in Rome on Christmas Eve 1621. Mary Ward, along with her companions, were received with great courtesy by Pope Gregory XV. He promised that a committee of Cardinals should be appointed to look into the matter of this new Institute. Mary was given permission to start schools in Rome and various other European cities.

Opposition to this new Institute continued to grow through that decade. In 1625[51] the schools in Rome, Naples and Perugia were closed and Mary Ward returned to England, stopping in Munich where she was asked by the Elector to found a new house in that city. In 1631 the final blow came. Mary was condemned as a heretic, schismatic, and rebel of Holy Church by the Inquisition. For two months she was imprisoned in the Poor Clare convent at Anger.[52] She was deprived of the sacraments, and became very ill. During this time she wrote secret letters to her companions using lemon juice and urged them to maintain their obedience to the Pope.

The Holy See was petitioned for her release, which was eventually granted. Mary then returned to Rome, again on foot, to plead her innocence. The new Pope, Urban VIII, received her with kindness, but the Institute had been officially suppressed by the Papal Bull of January 1631.[53] She was allowed to live in Rome with her companions in a private capacity. In 1637 she traveled back to England. From London she moved to Yorkshire at the outbreak of the English civil war. Mary Ward died January 30, 1645 at Heworth just outside York.

---

[50] See Part I, Chapter 2.

[51] In July 1624 the newly formed Congregation for the Propagation of the Faith, which had become involved, "since England was under its jurisdiction, issued an edict requiring the 'Jesuitesses' to adopt enclosure. At the same time, the matter remained also in the hands of the Congregation for Bishops and Regulars. When Mary appealed to the new Pope Urban VIII, he set up a particular congregation of four cardinals to examine her case. On April 11, 1625, the Congregation for Bishops and Regulars issued a decree closing the Italian houses of the Institute because the members would not accept enclosure." Wright, *Mary Ward's Institute*, 11.

[52] A suburb of Munich.

[53] *Pastoralis Romani Pontificis* 1631.

The Witness of Mary's Writings

At the instigation of her confessor, Fr. Roger Lee, S.J.,[54] Mary Ward wrote her autobiography; the final introduction to it, written in her own hand, was dated 1617. It covers the years 1585–1609, and consists of: autobiographical fragments written by Mary in English; 28 quarto pages in Italian, probably dictated to her secretary in Rome between 1622 and 1626.[55] Within the narrative there are interspersed a number of prayers as Mary reflects on the working of God in her life. In addition there are a number of extant letters and retreat notes, plus a collection of "maxims," or pithy sayings, attributed to Mary Ward and a number of reports on conferences she gave to the early companions.

From her youth her writings indicate that she frequented the sacraments with great fervor.[56] What is most noticeable here is that she undertakes these practices with great love, and in later life she encouraged this disposition in her companions. "I will do these things with love and freedom or leave them alone."[57] It is with this same loving fervor that she gradually came to embrace the religious life, seeing this as a particular gift from God to her even before she fully appreciated it.[58] This focus on true love and not obligation is reminiscent of the *pure love*[59] cited in the last of the Rules for Thinking, Judging, and Feeling with the Church and certainly is at the heart of the ecclesial disposition we are considering.

Central to Mary Ward's life and writings is that pre-eminent desire both to find the will of God for her and to faithfully live this out whatever the circumstances. In this manner her searching is resonant with the life and work of St. Ignatius as from the time of Manresa he moved towards the founding of the Society of Jesus. For both the will of God was also consonant with a service of the Church. Time and again this desire for the will of God is echoed in Mary's writings.[60] When she left the first Poor Clare convent in 1607 her notes record this thought: "I

---

[54] Fr. Roger Lee, S.J. (1568–1615) was Mary Ward's spiritual director at St Omer from 1608 until his death.

[55] Both manuscripts are preserved in the C.J. Archives.

[56] We might see operative here a resonance with the Second of the Rules for Thinking, Judging, and Feeling with the Church, *Spiritual Exercises* 354.

[57] "Autobiography."

[58] Ibid. The prayer she makes at this point in her autobiography is particularly telling, "O Parent of parents, and Friend of all friends, ... here without entreaty Thou tookest me into Thy care, and by degrees led me from all else that at length I might see and settle my love in Thee. What had I ever done to please thee? Or what was there in me wherewith to serve Thee? Much less could I ever deserve to be chosen by Thee. O happy begun freedom, the beginning of all my good and more worth to me at that time than the whole world besides," cited in Orchard, *Till God Will: Mary Ward through her Writings*, 9.

[59] Eighteenth Rule, *Spiritual Exercises* 370.

[60] All references are to be found in the Institute Archives, Munich.

will embrace with all affection the will of God, which only I desire."[61] In her various retreat notes we find written "I will give Him what I have; and all that I need I will find in Him; and in humble self-surrender I will wish for whatever His providence arranges for me ... In his will only I find quiet rest."[62]

In 1615 she was granted a further illumination that she termed 'the estate of justice.' She perceived the possibility of living contemplation in action. She saw that both were derived from the same source, namely the love of God which then stimulated action in the way of love of neighbor. Key to a living out of this interior state were a particular form of freedom and the quality of sincerity/verity. The freedom she spoke of has a three-fold dimension: freedom from attachment to earthly values and things; freedom for any kind of good works; freedom to refer all to God. Mary Ward saw freedom as a graced gift so integral to human beings that real freedom is a return of oneself and one's choices to God both in a kenotic disposition and a way of life of ongoing self-gift. Freedom for her was a dimension of love, primarily as we have already seen, God's redemptive love through Christ which liberates human beings and enables them to respond in love to God and others and be open to all that is good and true. Referring all to God was akin to Ignatius' finding God in all things. Mary's own lived spirituality embodied the freedom of which she spoke. It was this freedom and availability for whatever God wills that marked her sense of mission. Alongside this there is an emphasis on sincerity and truth as the faithful response of the human person "that we be such as we appear and appear such as we are."[63] Christ was for her the exemplar of all virtue for every human person. Her insights regarding a spirituality which unites contemplation and action enabled her to direct the apostolate of the Institute to the universal good of the Church and the personal good of individuals.

---

[61] Retreat Notes 1607.

[62] Retreat Notes 1612.

[63] In addition "Mary did not consider the virtues of the 'estate of justice' as exclusive to women. Rather, she was quick to refute any artificial dichotomy between the spirituality of men and women. Addressing the 'fathers of the Society' she emphasized the necessity of these virtues and warned them against relying on their natural talents and opportunities for learning [Mary Ward letter to Fr. Roger Lee November 1615]. Christ is the exemplar of all virtue and all are called to follow him. Learning that one of these Fathers had claimed that the fervor of members of her Institute would soon decline because they were 'but women' she replied: 'Fervor is a will to do well, that is, a preventing grace of God and a gift given gratis by God, which we could not merit. It is true fervour doth many times grow cold but what is the cause? It is because we are imperfect women, and love not verity. ... It is not *veritas hominum*, verity of men, nor verity of women, but *veritas Domini*, and this verity women may have as well as men. If we fail, it is for want of this verity and not because we are women." (From Mary Ward's addresses to her companions at St Omer, December 1617 to January 1618) cited in Cover, IBVM, *Love – The Driving Force*, 61–2.

The Fruitfulness of Mission

Whoever desires to serve as a soldier of God beneath the banner of the cross in our Society, which we desire to be designated by the name of Jesus, and to serve the Lord alone and the Church, His spouse, under the Roman pontiff, the vicar of Christ on earth, should, after a solemn vow of perpetual chastity, poverty and obedience, keep what follows in mind. He is a member of a Society founded chiefly for this purpose: to strive especially for the defence and propagation of the faith and for the progress of souls in Christian life and doctrine by the ministry of the word, by spiritual exercises and works of charity and specifically by the education of children and the unlettered.[64]

Thus states the Formula[65] of the Institute in the *Constitutions of the Society of Jesus*.[66] The *Constitutions* presume a graced experience of the *Spiritual Exercises*. Such an experience involves the Holy Spirit of love drawing the individual to a deep appreciation of providential care that can be perceived in and through the whole of life. This graced awareness involves recognizing oneself as a forgiven sinner and as one invited to share in the redemptive work of Christ for the salvation of the world. The specificity of the individual ministry is within the mission of the Congregation for "the defence and propagation of the faith and the progress of souls in Christian life and doctrine." The Contemplation to attain the love of God[67] is the summative expression of such an appreciation of God at work in and through all things, even the smallest and seemingly least important.

---

[64] John Padberg, S.J. (ed.), "The Formula of the Institute" [1], in *The Constitutions of the Society of Jesus and Their Complementary Norms* (St. Louis: Institute of Jesuit Sources 1996), second reading. Constitutions of the Congregatio Jesu.

[65] In Mary Ward's 1619 letter to John Gerard she also adds that through the 1611 illumination she was "brought home," that is to the Society of Jesus and to the "matter and manner" found in the *Exercises* and the Formula. André Ravier, after painstaking work sifting the varied and conflicting views on Jesuit spirituality, asserted that its two fundamental sources are the *Spiritual Exercises* and the Formula. He describes the latter as the means through which one gains access to the experience of Loyola and his first companions. It establishes the point of reference essential for living by the spirit and plan of the first Fathers "through the changes and vicissitudes of history." Mary Ward's lived and formulated spirituality and her plans for her Institute indicate that it was in the *Exercises* and in the Formula that she found the essentials of her spirituality.

[66] And with one change of pronoun thus also states the Institutum of the Institute of the Congregatio Jesu and, with a more detailed outlining of apostolates, so states the Institutum of 1621 of the *Constitutions* Vol. I of the Institute of the Blessed Virgin Mary. It is interesting to note that 85 percent of the *Ratio Instituti* which Mary Ward presented to Gregory XV corresponds word for word with the Formula. The end of the Institute like the Society of Jesus is the glory of God through love of God and of neighbor. Its apostolate is the defence and spread of the faith and mission is universal.

[67] *Spiritual Exercises* 252ff.

Here one of Mary Ward's three speeches at St Omer is helpful in illustrating the practical outworking of God at work in all things as Mary understood this, as Patricia Harriss[68] indicates in her booklet *A First Look at the Mary Ward Documents*. "In the second speech Mary Ward reflects that nothing happens by chance; everything, however small comes from God. Many are converted by some word of the gospel. It is not true that women's words are not to be regarded because they are not to preach: anyone who speaks by virtue of office is to be listened to." Mary's own experience of spiritual conversation in London and elsewhere bore witness to her belief that women had an important contribution to make in the ministry of the word drawing from their experience of union with God.

In a conference she gave to the sisters in St Omer in 1619 she emphasized: "Our way to heaven must be to accept all from His hands and to work for Him alone."[69] In the midst of great poverty she wrote to one of the early companions, Barbara Babthorpe in Naples, September 16, 1623: "To live or to die for God is equal gain when His will is such."[70] To the same recipient on February 16, 1627, when the storm clouds of opposition were increasing Mary Ward wrote: "Pray that I may have but one will with God's and then what happens will always be most welcome." To another of the early companions, Winifred Wigmore, she wrote from Munich in 1627: "All that is not in Him and for Him will pass away with time."[71]

It is clear that Mary Ward saw the reality of opposition to her desire for this new form of life for women as part of God's providence and that if she persevered his will would be made known, whatever that might be. As early as 1618 in her retreat notes of that year she recognizes the ongoing suffering and difficulties that will continue to accrue as she seeks recognition for the Institute. "I offered myself to suffer with love and gladness whatsoever trouble or complexity should happen in my doings of His will, but besought Him that none of those things might hinder what he wished should be done."[72] From the prison of the Anger Convent in Munich in 1631 she wrote to the sisters in a lemon juice letter.[73] "With all this [i.e. the conditions of her imprisonment] and what else God will send, you and I must and will be most contented till our Lord dispose otherwise."[74] She was imprisoned in a small cell where most of the window was covered so there

---

[68] Patricia Harriss C.J., *A First Look at the Mary Ward Documents*, booklet privately printed and not published, 2010.

[69] Conference for sisters 1619.

[70] Letter Mary Ward to Barbara Babthorpe September 16, 1623.

[71] Letter Mary Ward to Winifred Wigmore 1627.

[72] Retreat Notes 1618.

[73] She wrote in lemon juice on the paper that wrapped things sent in to her, in order that the letters should pass undetected and that the sisters might read them by gently warming the paper, at which the writing would then appear.

[74] Cf. fn 30.

was little light. The previous occupant had recently died of a contagious sickness in that same cell.

This focus on the dynamic will of God was complemented by her great trust in God particularly in the most adverse circumstances. Again from the Anger Convent in Munich she wrote to her companions: "You have great cause, in my poor judgment, to have more than ordinary confidence in the goodness and providence of God. Be not troubled at what you cannot mend, but confide in God."[75] Again, in another lemon juice letter, she wrote: "Our Lord and Master is also our Father and gives us no more than what is ladylike, and most easy to be borne."[76] In a letter to another early companion, Winifred Bedingfield, she wrote on October 9, 1634: "Be confident in God and more than ever grateful for His unseen goodness."[77] Finally as she lay dying she consoled and encouraged her sad companions with the words: "What? Still look sad? Come, let us rather sing and praise God joyfully for all his loving-kindness."[78]

The Importance of Devotions

When Mary Ward was first aware of her religious vocation she was much encouraged by listening to an old servant who told her tales of religious life in former times and of those who had been martyred for the faith. At this time she began to set herself exercises of prayer, penance and mortification. She was beginning to distinguish between the ways of God and the ways of other promptings, as Ignatius himself had done and of which he left a legacy in the Rules for Discernment of Spirits in the *Spiritual Exercises*. At one stage she found that she had accumulated so many different little acts of devotion that she could not remember them all and was becoming weary in the effort to do so. She then began to worry that she was not following inspirations from the Lord. Finally she took her anxiety to prayer and had a sense of the Lord's response:

> He gave me courage to reason in this manner with myself: these things are not of obligation but of devotion, and God is not pleased with certain acts made thus by constraint, and to acquire one's own quiet. Therefore, I will do these things with love and freedom, or leave them alone.

This very practical and prayerful attitude Mary was to bring to her devotions throughout her life. She always maintained a keen sense of

---

[75] Lemon juice letter, 1631.
[76] Ibid.
[77] Letter Mary Ward to Winifred Bedingfield, October 9, 1634.
[78] January 30, 1645, Hewarth near York.

the importance of prayer, penance and mortification but undertook these sensibly and with a great love for the Lord.[79]

Mary had a great devotion to the Blessed Virgin Mary and expressed this throughout her life, both in terms of pilgrimages to Marian shrines and in her daily exercise of piety. In 1619 in Liege she wrote: "I never fail of what I ask, or can ask of her absolutely."[80] In the following year in her retreat notes she wrote: "Our Blessed Lady is very helpful and bountiful to those that serve her in any small way."[81] For Mary the observance of particular devotions was a practice that had begun in her childhood and continued throughout her life. She understood that such devotions wisely undertaken are helpful aids to growing in holiness. It was natural to her therefore to "praise relics of saints, by venerating the relics and praying to the saints."[82] Mary Ward was also particularly careful about all things pertaining to the celebration of the liturgy. In 1639 from London she wrote to Barbara Babthorpe that: "things belonging to the service of God must shine. Think out and find whatever can be found to adorn our churches, especially during the Quarant' Ore."[83]

The Practice of Obedience

From her youth Mary had valued the practice of obedience. Though her sense of her religious vocation came to her at an early age, her parents were of the opinion she would do well to marry. Mary was obedient to their wishes until she reached the age of twenty-one when she was free to make her own choice of her way of life. She states in her autobiography:

> This grace [of vocation] by the mercy of God has been so continuous that not for one moment have I thought of embracing a contrary state. My parents, though otherwise extraordinarily pious, would not for any consideration give their consent, for I was the eldest child and much loved especially by my father. I was therefore obliged to remain in England six years and some months longer.[84]

This early practice of the virtue of obedience was clearly enhanced when it came to making a vow of obedience. It is apparent that for Mary Ward, like Ignatius, obedience to superiors was ultimately an obedience offered

---

[79] Cf., *Spiritual Exercises* 358.
[80] Retreat Notes, Liege 1619.
[81] Retreat Notes, Eger Austria 1620.
[82] Sixth Rule, *Spiritual Exercises* 358.
[83] The practice of forty hours' devotion with exposition of the Blessed Sacrament.
[84] *Autobiography of Mary Ward*, Institute Archives, Munich.

to God. Therefore, it should be offered freely and with great love and the desire to serve God ever more perfectly.[85] In this manner Mary wrote to Winifred Wigmore from Rome in 1624: "Your entire resignation and full dependence upon the will of God and Superiors I far more esteem than if you had the grace of working miracles and lacked these qualities."[86]

To the same early companion the following year she wrote of the importance of being united with the superior both in will and in prompt obedience: "Ask sometimes of God that He would give you grace ever to be fully and perfectly united with your Superior in will and work." And she continues: "Who hath this hath a great deal and wants but little."[87]

Perhaps the clearest example of Mary Ward's understanding and practice of obedience is in the face of the opposition and hostility that she faced from authorities within the Church. Here it is helpful to note that while she was always deeply respectful of Church authority at the same time she did not deny or repress the desires that had arisen in her through her experience of God in the various illuminations she had received. Already by 1622, the English clergy had constructed a substantial case against her and sent this to Rome. Although the Holy Father always received her with great courtesy, the ecclesial authorities felt the time had come to curtail the rapid spread of this new Institute. A real concern was the expressed desire for women to govern themselves. It was felt that this would cause division and disruption within a Church that was still struggling to maintain a renewed solidity following the Reformation. The first direct action taken was the closing of the schools in Rome in 1625.

In 1628 the Papal Nuncios in various countries received instructions to suppress houses of the Institute in their own areas. Mary Ward did not know this when in 1629 she met with a committee of Cardinals asking once more for recognition of the new Institute. At the end of 1630 Mary moved to Munich to await the decision of the Pope and Cardinals. In January 1631 Pope Urban VIII signed the Bull of Suppression.[88] He had become increasingly anxious that the Institute might be damaging to the Church.[89]

---

[85] Cf. Mary Ward in a letter to Winifred Bedingfield, Rome, 1634: "Begin to serve Him with abundant love and the greatest perfection." Institute Archives, Munich.

[86] Letter Mary Ward to Winifred Wigmore, January 18, 1624. Institute Archives, Munich.

[87] Letter Mary Ward to Winifred Wigmore, Monte Cassino, 1625. Institute Archives, Munich. Here we have clear sense of the tenth rule of the Rules for Thinking, Judging, and Feeling with the Church affirming that "we ought to be more inclined to approve and praise the decrees, recommendations, and conduct of our superiors." Tenth Rule, *Spiritual Exercises* 362

[88] January 13, 1631, Pastoralis Romani Pontificis.

[89] Political realities were also to the fore in the suppression of the Institute. The fact that the Emperor and the Elector of Bavaria were supporting Mary Ward made Urban VIII uneasy. He had looked to these two Catholic princes to assist him in the Thirty Years War. This meant that the text of the final Bull was very strong—indeed harsh—in its language so that there could be no possibility of these princes supporting the growth of the Institute thereafter.

It is unsurprising that Mary Ward and her companions were deeply hurt by the publication of the Papal Bull. It accused them of presuming authority to found a new religious order in direct contravention of the decrees of the Councils of the Lateran and Lyons.[90] Members were commanded to give up life in community, to close their houses and schools, to lay aside the habit and other distinctive forms of religious life. They were released from their vows and free to marry or to enter an approved Order should they wish, and if they were accepted. To all this Mary Ward and her companions submitted, accepting the public shame, humiliation and loss of honor that accompanied it.

Less than a month later, Mary Ward was imprisoned in the Anger Convent. During her imprisonment she continued to suffer from the poor health, which had been a feature of her life since she first followed her religious vocation. Her health deteriorated to such an extent that she was finally allowed to receive the last sacraments. She wrote what she imagined to be her last "apologia" in which she stated that 'she never had, nor to gain a million lives, would she do, think or say the least that might be contrary to the Catholic Church, but contrary-wise, from her earliest years she had employed her life and labors in the service of Holy Church."[91] Despite what must have appeared to be a near hopeless situation Mary Ward still maintained her confidence in God and her humble obedience to the Holy Father and the Church.

Mary's Ecclesial Disposition

"To serve the Lord alone and His spouse the Church under the Roman Pontiff the vicar of Christ on earth."[92] This as we have seen is the clear aim of the Society of Jesus and the Institute and was the request of Mary Ward. It is really difficult today to imagine the shock and horror that greeted Mary Ward's request for this novel service by women in the church. It is vital to keep in mind the context of her time. She was arrested and imprisoned as a "heretic, schismatic and rebel of Holy Church," though later released by direct intervention of the Pope. She was caught in the hostility that was growing between the secular clergy and the Jesuits in England. She was surrounded by spies and informers and left in ignorance about decisions that were made about her and against her. What is most important though

---

[90] The Fourth Lateran Council [1214] and the Council of Lyons [1274] enacted decrees which required that future founders of religious institutes adopt one of the four established rules [St. Basil, St. Benedict, St. Augustine, St. Francis].

[91] From the "Brief Relation" 25–6, cited in Orchard, *Till God Will: Mary Ward through her Writings*, 110.

[92] Preamble to the *Constitutions*.

is the response of Mary Ward herself. Like Ignatius, Mary Ward contributed to the reform of the Church from within. Through the work of her sisters on the English mission and in schools she helped young women to grow in a relationship of intimacy with Christ. She encouraged the development of their spiritual lives and educated them to be actively involved in the life and mission of the Church. Her disposition towards the Church was fuelled by the profound apprehension of the grace of the second week, mentioned above, that intimate knowledge of God's love at the source of her being. This intimacy with Christ also fuelled her passionate commitment to the Church.

Mary Ward loved the Church because she loved Christ. Like Ignatius she saw a creative tension between the action of the Holy Spirit operative in the Church and in the individual—a creative tension that was fruitful both for the individual and the life of the Church. In the face of severe persecution Mary was enabled to live without bitterness or resentment. Part of the reason for this can be traced to an illumination in 1625 when "she received from our Lord so much light and knowledge regarding the forgiveness of enemies, that henceforth she cherished a tender affection for all who wronged her, and was in the habit of calling them friends."[93] In this ability to forgive Mary clearly evinces the intimacy of her relationship with Christ.[94] And as John Paul II stated,

> Christ did not fail Mary Ward. No matter how great were the diffi-culties which she had to undergo – ill-health; dangerous journeys; imprisonment; above all, being misunderstood even by important people within the Church – in all of this, she never lost her trust and good humor. And look how fruitful her life has been, all because she built her whole life on the friendship of Jesus! [She was a] pilgrim of hope whose abiding treasure was the life of grace within her, from which she drew energies for a task which because of its dynamism and enterprising spirit seemed unusual and inexplicable to many of her contemporaries.[95]

---

[93] Ibid. from the Brief Relation op. cit.

[94] She is also exemplary of Ignatius' own practice when he recommended his brother Jesuits in the *Constitutions* [101] to welcome "contempt, lies and injuries and to be accounted and looked upon as fools because they desire to resemble and imitate in some degree our Lord Jesus Christ who is the true way that leads to life." Those familiar with the *Exercises* may also recognise an echo of the triple colloquy of the Two Standards.

[95] To the members of the Institutes which have as their Foundress this "incomparable woman"—as Pope Pius XII called her—"I wish to express my greetings and appreciation. The whole Church admires the work that you do in the formation of the young and in other forms of apostolate in various parts of the world. As members of the Institute of the Blessed Virgin Mary, of the Institute of the Blessed Virgin Mary of Loreto and of the Institute of the Blessed Virgin Mary of Toronto, you find in the charism of your Foundress the wisdom and insights needed to persevere in the mission which Christ has entrusted to you." John Paul II, Address to the Young People of the Mary Ward Schools, October 5, 1985.

The Same but Different

In Mary Ward we encounter the feminine manner of living out the Ignatian ecclesial disposition honed through a lifetime of persecution. Light years ahead of her own time she endeavored to carry out the task she believed God had called her to undertake. She strove to bring before the church the reasons why this new way of life was both a gift to the church and would be of great service to the church. At all times she conducted herself as a faithful daughter of the church amidst many scurrilous tales about her and her companions. She attracted young women who were prepared like herself to offer obedience and service to the church and to comfort and support Catholics in those lands—notably England—where they suffered persecution.

Forged in the fire of persecution and refined by a growing intimacy with Christ Mary Ward's path of discernment was sure-footed. The transforming power of her relationship with God was a witness to holiness admired by many of those who could not accept her vision. Never daunted by persecution, confident in the spirit at work within the Church that treated her so badly, she left the legacy of a clear foundation for those who became her spiritual daughters. "The same of the Society" was worth the commitment of her whole life to an enterprise she knew to be of divine origin and thus it could not fail.

From her earliest days we have seen that Mary was prepared, by nature and grace. It is clear that her ecclesial disposition was grounded in her relationship to Christ and through Christ she developed her Trinitarian understanding. Of the Father's love she never had any doubt, and she saw the presence of the Spirit at work throughout her life, even in the many 'enemies' she encountered, for whom she always prayed with great compassion. Her manner of dealing with all was with great courtesy and reverence, putting into practice the presupposition of the *Spiritual Exercises* and appealing to the graced nature of the person with whom she was engaged.

It is a mark of the truth of her insight that the Congregation she founded in 1609 still persists within the Church to this day. Like Ignatius, Mary Ward believed *Veritas Domini manet in aeternum*. "The truth of the Lord endures forever. Note that it is not the truth of men, nor the truth of women, but the truth of God, and "that divine truth is shared equally by women and men."[96] In that truth of God Mary Ward stands as a singular feminine exemplar of the Ignatian ecclesial disposition, taking "the same: but differently—a new pathway of Christian living—a "lived exegete of the word of scripture and the Word made flesh."

---

[96] Conference for sisters, November 1617.

PART THREE

Twentieth Century Jesuit Theologians

Introduction

In Part II we explored two exemplars of the Ignatian ecclesial disposition from the sixteenth and seventeenth centuries. In this man and woman it became apparent that significant characteristics of the ecclesial disposition were reflected in their intimate relationship to Christ in the clear Trinitarian foundation of their understanding, and in the compassionate, reverent approach they maintained toward others with whom they related even those who proved themselves to be hostile. There is also evidence of progressive discernment whether it be in Pierre Favre's deeper understanding of the sacrament of reconciliation and his profound trust that God works through other than Christian agents; or Mary Ward's long search for the will of God that resulted in an active apostolic community of women modeled after the Society of Jesus. Such discernment is always seen in conjunction with and not opposed to ecclesial commitment.

Another highly significant feature of the lives of these historical figures—as it was in the life of Ignatius—is the dimension of a willingness to suffer as a result of following what they saw to be the leading of the spirit of God. Such suffering, I suggest, both deepened their individual relationships with God and refined their ecclesial disposition. In the case of Pierre Favre we saw his deep distress at the situation of the Catholic clergy and faithful during the period of the Reformation and Counter Reformation. In Mary Ward we see what we might term a "spiritual martyrdom"[1] as she held firm to the divine inspiration she received and was obedient to the Church even at the expense of what may have seemed like the destruction of her life's work.

In Part III of the book we make a significant move across centuries as we consider the lives and writings of two twentieth-century Jesuit theologians, again seeking to trace something of Ignatius' ecclesial disposition. We shall once more be looking to perceive the importance of an intimate relationship with Christ in each man's life. We shall explore the ground of their understanding to see if it has a Trinitarian base. We shall expect to see expressed within their engagement with others that reverence born of an appreciation of the graced nature of each human person. Finally we shall not be surprised to see the dimension of suffering in the outworking of a progressive discernment as they each endeavor to attune their lives and work to the service of the Church.

---

[1] When Mary was sixteen and read the lives of the holy martyrs, she was seized with such a burning desire to follow their example that she felt only martyrdom itself could satisfy her longing, until our Savior revealed to her interiorly that what He required of her was spiritual rather than bodily martyrdom.

6

Cardinal Henri de Lubac, S.J.

The Witness of Life

Though most of his life was lived in the twentieth century, Henri de Lubac was actually born in Cambrai[1] in Northern France at the end of the nineteenth century on February 20, 1896.[2] His family could trace their antecedents back into the early history of France and maintained their support of the Church even in the difficult anti-clerical and anti-religious periods of the late nineteenth century.[3] In his later life de Lubac spoke of his early age as a time when he was raised according to the restrictions of economy necessary for a family of eight but that the six children were 'bathed' in the tenderness of his parents. He paid a touching tribute to his mother:

> My mother was a simple woman. Her entire education was received in the country and in the cloister of a Visitation monastery, according to the custom of the times. Her entire upbringing rested on the foundation of Christian tradition and piety. I never saw anything in her but self-forgetfulness and goodness. After the death of my father, who had worn

---

[1]Cambrai lies along the Escaut river, south of Roubaix.

[2]He was the third of six children born to Maurice Sonier de Lubac (1860–1936) and Gabrielle de Beaurepaire (1867–1963). "Although de Lubac's father was originally from the region south of Lyons, he worked for the Banque de France, which transferred him to positions in the east and north of France, in particular, to Cambrai during the years 1895–8." Voderholzer, *Meet Henri de Lubac*, 25.

[3]"Pursuant to the law of March 29, 1880 members of religious communities were expelled from their houses and institutions. In Lyons the expulsion of the Capuchin Franciscans led to demonstrations on November 3, 1880, during which one protester was killed. De Lubac's father, together with some friends, was escorting the expelled friars and became involved in a brawl, during which he injured one of the counter-demonstrators slightly in the face with the pommel of a sword. For this he was sentenced to a jail term and fined sixteen francs. The court of appeals in Lyons recognised that he had acted in self-defence, but punished him for carrying an unauthorised weapon and upheld the fine. In the Sonier household, this judgment was regarded as an honor." Ibid.

himself out in daily labor, she said to me one day: "We never had the least disagreement." She remained a widow for a quarter of a century, and the intimacy between us grew.[4]

This intimacy marked de Lubac's life. So profound was the understanding between mother and son that in later years during the time of difficulty and the suspicion that surrounded de Lubac's work when a well-intentioned religious talked to his mother with regard to the concerns about de Lubac's orthodoxy she replied: "I know my son; I know that he will always be a submissive child of Holy Church."[5] Indeed, her only concern was later when De Lubac was rehabilitated and was appointed to Vatican II. "When she learned that ... I had been called to Rome for the Council, disturbed by what seemed to her to be honors, the two letters she addressed to me said each in nearly the same terms: 'I pray Our Lord to keep you in humility.'"[6]

As a boy he was at schools run by religious in Bourg-en-Bresse and Lyons with the Christian brothers, then in 1905 at St Joseph's Preparatory School with the Jesuits and later from 1909–11 at their college Notre Dame de Mongré in Villefranche-sur-Saône.[7] Already then through the example of his parents, and from his childhood education, de Lubac had an appreciation of religious life. This was strengthened through his encounter in his later school years with Fr. Eugène Hains, S.J. who was his spiritual director from 1909 to 1913[8] and through whose assistance he came to discern a call to religious life. In later life de Lubac shared a letter that had been sent to him by Fr. Hains dated January 6, 1962, shortly before the latter's death, indicating the constancy of the relationship over time.

> ... Providence brought us together at the moment when you were searching for your path, and that is not forgotten. I faithfully say, every day, the *Veni sancte Spiritus* for you, as you know; and I am delighted at the good your books and teaching do. Who would have said, a few years ago, that you would be one of the theologians of the Council? ... I hope that you can work for a long time yet for the good of the Church.[9]

De Lubac finished his schooling at the College of Moulins Bellevue and earned his baccalaureate. Thereafter he studied law for two semesters at the *Institut Catholique* in Lyons. In October 1913 de Lubac entered

---

[4]Note made Chantilly, February 23, 1975, in Henri de Lubac, *At the Service of The Church: Henri de Lubac Reflects on the Circumstances that Occasioned His Writings*, trans. Anne Elizabeth Englund (San Francisco: Ignatius Press, 1993), 152.
[5]Ibid.
[6]Ibid.
[7]Twenty-five kilometers north of Lyons. Teilhard de Chardin had completed his school education here some years prior to the arrival of de Lubac.
[8]Fr. Hains was spiritual father and rector of the College Notre Dame de Mongré at that time.
[9]De Lubac, *At the Service of The Church*, 402.

the Jesuit novitiate. Because of French laws that were hostile to religious communities,[10] the Jesuits of Lyon had been forced to relocate their novitiate to the south coast of England from 1901–26. Accordingly, de Lubac entered the Jesuit novitiate at St Leonards-on-Sea in Sussex. It is interesting that Mary Ward three centuries previously had to leave her native land to enter religious life on the continent and in the twentieth century de Lubac had to leave his native land to enter religious life in England.

After his novitiate de Lubac was drafted into the French army in 1914 where he served through the rest of World War One. From 1915–18 he was stationed on the front with the Third Infantry Regiment.[11] During this time, in November 1917 he received a serious head wound in action and suffered continual spells of dizziness and earaches in the years that followed until in 1954 an operation finally resolved the problem. For his courage in action de Lubac received the "Croix de Guerre."[12] On his return to the Jesuits after his demobilization in 1919 he first studied humanities at St Mary's College Canterbury.[13] He then undertook his philosophy studies and his first theological studies at the Maison Saint-Louis in St Helier, Jersey from 1920–1923.

After a period of "regency"[14] when he returned to the Jesuit College of Notre Dame de Mongré as assistant to the Prefect of studies, de Lubac started his advanced theology work in Hastings[15], a time he thoroughly enjoyed as is evidenced from his comments at a celebration of one of the priests who had made an impression on him during the time he studied at Ore Place—Fr. Emile Delaye. "Anyone who did not live at Ore Place did not know in all its fullness the happiness of being a 'scholastic.' There we were really rather far from the world, away for a while from nearly all the responsibilities of the apostolate; alone among ourselves, as if in a big ship

---

[10] "The Jesuits were a particular focus of opprobrium. The Society of Jesus had been suppressed by Pope Clement XIV in 1773 and was not re-established as an order until 1814; as of 1832 the Jesuits were able to gain a firmer footing again in France. The year 1850 brought the law granting full educational freedom and inaugurated a period of consolidation. Toward the end of the nineteenth century, however, tensions worsened again in every respect. As early as 1880, the Jesuits, too, not being a government-approved association, were once more deprived by law of the right to give instruction. Thirty-seven colleges were dissolved. Those who were expelled, some of them forcibly, travelled to England, Belgium or Spain, or else went to the mission." Voderholzer, *Meet Henri de Lubac*, 28.

[11] This regiment was stationed in Antibes, Cagnes-sur-Mer and chiefly in Côte des Huves les Éparges near Verdun.

[12] The Croix de Guerre was a military decoration instituted April 1915 by the French Government to recognize acts of bravery in the face of the enemy specifically mentioned in dispatches.

[13] Though he was meant to be attending to the study of Latin and Greek he also spent his time with the works of Augustine and Irenaeus.

[14] Within Jesuit formation a period of regency involves some practical activity in one of the apostolates of the Order.

[15] Ore Place, Hastings, was on a hill overlooking the town.

sailing, without a radio, in the middle of the ocean. But what an intense life within that ship, and what a marvelous crossing."[16] During the time at Ore Place de Lubac was a member of a group of about ten students who regularly met with Fr. Huby to discuss a selected topic. This group gave de Lubac the opportunity to further pursue an area of study that had emerged as important for him during his philosophical studies, namely the question of the supernatural. Indeed, the first draft of the book that he would later publish in 1946 was written during this time.[17]

De Lubac completed his theological studies at Lyons Fourvière[18] after the relocation of the Jesuit theologate back to Lyons from Hastings in 1926. Here he was ordained to the priesthood on August 22, 1927. It seems remarkable that he was assigned to teach fundamental theology in the Catholic faculty[19] at Lyon in 1929 without having a doctoral degree. In addition he was asked to take on a course in the history of religions. Of that time he recounted later:

> I had scarcely begun my teaching of fundamental theology some six months before (a doctoral course, the particular subject of which was normally to change every year): then one fine day in the spring of 1930, our dean said something like this to me: 'My father … there is a serious lack in our Faculty. The history of religions is taught everywhere in the universities; … But we see no specialist to hire, and besides, our Faculties do not have the means to found a new chair. The discipline closest to

---

[16] He continues: "At the helm, under the very good and peaceful direction of Father Riondel, a prefect who was still young and as welcoming and encouraging as he could be. And not lacking in bold wisdom! What a joy it was to plough the waters of the high sea with him, to explore in every sense the infinite spaces of dogmatics, to lose oneself, without getting lost, in the depths of mystery! Two names will for me always remain associated with the memory of those happy years. Father Joseph Huby, whom we still mourn; and Father Emile Delaye, whom we are celebrating." De Lubac, *At the Service of The Church*, 15–16.

[17] The subject of the supernatural "was at the center of the reflections of the masters about whom I have spoken: Rousselot, Blondel, Maréchal; we discovered it at the heart of all great Christian thought, whether that of Saint Augustine, Saint Thomas or Saint Bonaventure (for these were our classics par excellence); we noted that it was likewise at the bottom of the discussions with modern unbelief, that it formed the crux of the problem with Christian humanism. Father Huby, following the line of reflection inaugurated for us by Rousselot, had warmly urged me to verify whether the doctrine of Saint Thomas on this important point was indeed what was claimed by the Thomist school around the sixteenth century, codified in the seventeenth and asserted with greater emphasis than ever in the twentieth." Ibid., 35.

[18] "Fourvière (from Latin *forum vetus*, 'old forum') is the most ancient settlement of Lyons, site of Notre Dame Basilica (1872–96), a landmark of the city and the destination of one of the most important Marian pilgrimages in France." Voderholzer, *Meet Henri de Lubac*, 42 fn. 20.

[19] The Catholic Theological Faculty was situated on the central Presqu'île peninsula surrounded by the River Saône on the western side and the Rhône on the east. The Jesuit scholasticate at Fourvière was on a hill overlooking the modern city center from the west. The Jesuit scholasticate was closed in 1974 when it became part of the Centre Sèvres in Paris.

the history of religions is yours; would you agree to undertake a supplementary course beginning this next October?' I had the weakness to accept. Without preparation, without books, without knowledge of any language, European or Asiatic, without any spare time beforehand, and with the prospect of another supplementary course to provide in the transformed program of the Faculty, it was an impossibility; especially since it would be necessary for me to change the subject matter every year, for I would have the same students several days in a row. Finally, it had to go well.

The example of obedience offered here is compelling.

He taught in Lyon with some interruptions until 1961.[20] He did not initially teach in the Jesuit theologate at Fourvière, but between 1935 and 1940 he did direct some courses there. At the Catholic Theological Faculty he had significant contact with doctoral students including Hans Urs von Balthasar who records the impact of his meeting with de Lubac in 1933 and the influence that the latter exerted in helping him to develop the direction of his studies.[21] For his part, de Lubac appreciated the promise of von Balthasar and others in the new generation of theologians. "A new generation full of life ... and the very dear and faithful Hans Urs von Balthasar, whose brilliance was already shining forth." It was at that time, during fifteen days of rest at Annecy during the Easter season, that Balthasar "read the entire works of Gregory of Nyssa."[22]

In 1942 de Lubac with Jean Danielou, S.J.,[23] founded the series *Sources Chrétiennes*.[24] This was designed to make medieval and patristic texts more

---

[20] "My years of teaching in Lyons can be divided into three very different periods: first of all, before the Second World War, then during the years of the war and occupation, and finally the years that followed, from 1945 to 1950. A fourth period should be added to these, that of my nearly total professorial unemployment, from 1950 to 1960." De Lubac, *At the Service of The Church*, 44.

[21] "In Lyons during my theological studies, it was the encounter with Henri de Lubac that decided the direction of my studies. Because exegesis was weak, the Fathers easily won the upper hand. Origen (who was for me, as once for Erasmus, more important than Augustine) became the key to the entire Greek patristics, the early Middle Ages and, indeed, even to Hegel and Karl Barth." Hans Urs von Balthasar, *My Work: In Retrospect* (San Francisco: Ignatius Press, 1993), 89. See also Chapter 8.

[22] De Lubac, *At the Service of The Church*, 47.

[23] Jean Daniélou, S.J. (1905–74), Jesuit theologian, patristic scholar, spiritual writer, Bishop and Cardinal. He entered the Society of Jesus in 1929. He studied under Henri de Lubac in Lyons and received his doctorate in theology in 1942. At the invitation of Pope John XXIII he served as an expert advisor at Vatican II (1962–65). He was made a Cardinal by Pope Paul VI in 1969 and in the same year was elected to the Académie Française.

[24] Founded in 1942 by the Jesuits: Jean Daniélou, Henri de Lubac, and Claude Mondésert. Today *Sources Chrétiennes* sees its basic purpose in three-fold terms: 1) to edit the most important texts from the first 1400 years of the Church, most them written by the Church Fathers. These writings include: apologetics, biblical commentary, sermons, treatises, letters, liturgies, poems, hymns, dialogues, ascetic writings, Church canons and history; 2) to teach the reading of these texts and the interpretative and editing methods; and 3) to organize some

widely available. It was a collection of bilingual, critical editions of early Christian texts and of the Fathers of the Church that has been of inestimable value for both the study of Patristics and the doctrine of Sacred Tradition.[25] From 1941 during the Nazi occupation of France, he became co-editor of a clandestine journal of the resistance *Cahiers du Témoignage Chrétien.*[26] Here he endeavored to show the incompatibility between Christianity and the anti-Semitism that was being propagated by the Nazi regime. On a number of occasions he had to hide to prevent being captured and executed by the Gestapo. He wrote later: "The *Cahiers* enterprise gave rise to many instances of heroic self-sacrifice, much of which will always remain hidden."[27]

For five years from 1945 de Lubac was editor of the *Recherches de Science Religieuse.*[28] From the 1940s he actively collaborated in the collection *Théologie.* This was a project that had developed at Fourviére and involved the Jesuits: Victor Fontoynont, Henri Rondet, Pierre Chaillet, and Henri Bouillard. The idea was to found a series that would be the outlet for writing by the various academics at Fourviére. "It was known by the title 'Théologie,' and Father Bouillard, professor of fundamental theology, had written the prospectus."[29]

---

and participate in numerous seminars, conferences and international symposiums with the aim of contributing to the advancement of Patristics, i.e. the knowledge of the Church Fathers.
[25] Cf. *Spiritual Exercises* 363.
[26] This underground journal was intended to convince French Catholics of the complete incompatibility of Nazi ideology and activities with Christian beliefs. Along with Pierre Chaillet and Gaston Fessard, Henri de Lubac was one of the founders and a key source of inspiration for the journal. Jean Watelet wrote of the journal: "*Les Cahiers et Courriers du Témoignage chrétien ont été parmi les textes les plus importants de la presse clandestine; ils ont été aussi parmi les premiers titres de la presse de la Résistance, et le P. Chaillet, leur fondateur, a dirigé simultanément deux publications, les Cahiers, brochures de plusieurs dizaines de pages traitant, du point de vue chrétien, de tous les grands sujets de l'époque, et le Courrier, plus facile à transporter et à diffuser, ce dernier atteignant jusqu'à des tirages de 100,000 exemplaires. Un an après leur première parution à Lyon en 1941, ces deux périodiques rayonnaient vers la zone occupée mais aussi vers l'étranger, et parvenaient même au Canada. Ils faisaient connaître la morale chrétienne de la Résistance, les textes pontificaux, et assuraient de leur fidélité la hiérarchie de l'Église de France.* "Ainsi, écrit le P. Chaillet dans sa préface, aux heures où semblait régner la puissance des ténèbres, le Témoignage chrétien a empêché que la vérité fût étouffée, la justice bafouée avec la complicité du silence [...]. Cette action ne fut possible que grâce au dévouement ardent d'innombrables militants; plusieurs sont morts en portant témoignage, le martyre était dans la logique de leur engagement.*" R. Bédarida, *Cahier and Courrieur Clandestin du Témoignage chrétien 1941–1944,* 1980. 2 vols, 279+285 pp.; 22 cm. Rééd. intégrale en fac-similé. Bulletin des Bibliothèques de France, http://bbf.enssib.fr/consulter/bbf-1981-05-0310-009 (accessed March 9, 2013).
[27] De Lubac, *At the Service of The Church,* 53.
[28] Research of Religious Science was founded in 1910 in Paris by the Jesuit theologican Léonce de Grandmaison. The editorial line of the journal was that beyond the modernist crisis, it was right to do historical research in theology in the understanding of Christian dogma.
[29] De Lubac, *At the Service of The Church,* 30. He continues: "Before the end of the Second World War, the 'Théologie' series was launched, under the official direction of the rector of Fourviére and with Fr. Bouillard as the first and very diligent secretary."

On the occasion of the fiftieth volume to be published Fr. Bouillard stated that the twofold aspiration that had been at the heart of the project was: "to go to the sources of Christian doctrine, to find in it the truth of our life."[30] In the foreword to the fiftieth volume there is an inspiring synthesis of how theology, scripture, prayer, the Church and tradition are related. "Theology, which is a work of the reason, cannot without danger ignore the very movement of human thought; but its true refreshment comes from submersion in the Word of God, such as it is taught in the Church, ripened in a time-honored spiritual experience, developed by those great Doctors who were at once geniuses and saints. When a theologian works, it is to this school that he returns."[31] In 1953 he became a member of the *Institut de France* [*Académie des Sciences Morales*].

De Lubac's first work *Catholicisme* [1938] contains many of the major themes of his theological work for the years that followed. It was subtitled "A Study of Dogma in Relation to the Corporate Destiny of Mankind." De Lubac said of this work that it was made up of "bits and pieces that were first written independently, then stitched together, so to speak, into three parts, without any preconceived plan."[32] It seemed intended to show the unitive power of Catholic Christianity which was able to overcome all division. It emphasized the communal nature of salvation. It asserted that humanity has a common destiny, just as it has a common vocation within salvation history.

De Lubac said of this work that, "In general, one might say that the work tries to show the simultaneously social, historical and interior character of Christianity, this threefold mark conferring on it that character of universality and totality best expressed by the word 'Catholicism.'"[33] This communal emphasis was reiterated in *Corpus Mysticum* which de Lubac completed in 1938, though it was not published until 1944.[34] Here he stressed the indissoluble link between the Church and the Eucharist from earliest times in contradistinction to the rapid growth of individualism which was taking place in society. It was important, he stressed, to re-appropriate: "the beautiful considerations of the past, the symbols flowing with doctrinal richness."[35]

---

[30] Ibid.

[31] Ibid. 31.

[32] De Lubac, *At the Service of The Church*, 27.

[33] Ibid. De Lubac also owns his indebtedness for the publication of the book to Fr. Yves Congar, O.P., who had just begun the ecclesiological series "*Unam sanctam*" at Editions du Cerf.

[34] Though it was published in some sections in the journal *Recherches de science religieuse* 1939 and 1940.

[35] Henri de Lubac, *Corpus Mysticum: The Eucharist and the Church in the Middle Ages*, trans. Laurence Paul Hemming and Susan Frank Parsons (Notre Dame, IN: University of Notre Dame Press, 2007), 229. Within this work de Lubac assists a more profound understanding of the nature and development of the doctrine of transubstantiation. "The dialectic of substance and accidents ... would correspond to the dialectic of the sign and the reality.

He also composed a number of short works during the late 1930s and early 1940s on the possibility of knowing God and the very nature of belief.[36] Amongst these, the small work *Paradoxes* caused considerable difficulty for de Lubac. He wrote of this later

How, when the little book appeared, serious men could think they caught the scent in it of a weapon against the faith of Holy Church, an attempt by neo-modernism, a desire to combat underhandedly the teaching of Saint Thomas, I still do not know. Without pretending to systematize anything I took my material from the purest Catholic tradition, which I loved more and more every day, with no end but to open the treasure of it to a few brothers, both known and unknown, without any intention of laying the foundations of a learned treatise, and even less, if possible, of trying to pick a quarrel with anyone.[37]

In the 1940s in France a theological movement was identified known as the 'nouvelle théologie' or new theology,[38] though de Lubac maintained that the actual existence of such a group was mythical. In his classes on the history of religions he spoke about "Christian Newness" (*La Nouveauté chrétienne*) but this was not to be equated with any new theology. Nevertheless, the perception of this movement was that it proposed modernist views antithetical to the doctrines of the Catholic Church.

In 1946 de Lubac's work *Surnaturel* was published[39] which focused on the supernatural destiny of the human person and challenged the contemporary interpretations of St. Thomas Aquinas. De Lubac's contemporaries, who felt their methodology and doctrine were being attacked, complained about him to the Holy See. In 1950 when Pius XII published the encyclical *Humani Generis*[40]—an attempt to counteract what was thought to be a series of modernist ideas which were believed to be endangering Catholic

---

Sacramental realism would no longer be anything but that which symbolism augmented, and persistent faith in a real presence of Christ in the sacrament would be protected, for further centuries, by a sacramental theology with quite other appearances and implications." Ibid.

[36] These included: *Le Drame de l'humanisme athée* (1944); *Proudhom et le christianisme* (1945); *De la connaissance de Dieu* (1945); and *Paradoxes* (1946)

[37] *At the Service of The Church*, 35.

[38] Membership of this group was first used as a criticism against de Lubac in 1941 by Fr. Garrigou-Lagrange, O.P.

[39] "[It] was printed in Lyons in 1945–6. Paper was lacking. One part of the edition was done on big bulking paper, another on smooth paper, so that the first lot of copies were twice as thick as the second." De Lubac, *At the Service of The Church*, 37.

[40] Pius XII, "Encyclical Concerning Some False Opinions Which Threaten to Undermine the Foundations of Catholic Doctrine," *Humani Generis*, August 1950.

doctrine—many believed that it contained a condemnation of de Lubac's position.[41] This was, however, not de Lubac's opinion as he wrote later:

It seems to me to be, like many ecclesiastical documents, unilateral: that is almost the law of the genre; but I have read nothing in it, doctrinally, that affects me. The only passage where I recognize an implicit reference to me is a phrase bearing on the question of the supernatural; now it is rather curious to note that this phrase, intending to recall the true doctrine on this subject, reproduces exactly what I said about it two years earlier in an article in *Recherches de science religieuse*. (So I could presume with some probability that the expression had been substituted, perhaps at the last moment, for another one by someone who was familiar with my article and favorably disposed toward me.)[42]

Nevertheless, public perception was that de Lubac was somehow "suspect" in his theological work.

Certainly de Lubac's work appeared original and manifested a fresh appreciation of the tradition in a way that spoke to contemporary circumstances. After the publication of *Humani Generis*, however, he left his post at Lyon and moved to Paris. Here he spoke of leading the existence of a recluse. At first the Jesuit Superior General Jean-Baptiste Janssens had firmly supported de Lubac, but the more the attacks on the latter increased the more reserved the former became. The General sought to deflect accusations against the Society as a whole by removing de Lubac from his teaching position and requiring him to submit his writings to a more stringent form of censorship. "His books were banned, removed from the libraries of the Society of Jesus and impounded from the market."[43]

In 1953 by a conjunction of favorable circumstances[44] *Méditation sur L'Eglise* was published. Throughout this period Henri de Lubac had experienced a form of silent ostracism. He later wrote of this time, which he saw as his "exile," that he was never questioned by the authorities in Rome, or by his own Jesuit Curia, about his views or the issues that were causing concern. He never knew of what exactly he had been accused. "No

---

[41] "The quite objective and, so to speak, non-temporal sense of a document of this genre is one thing, the meaning given to it by circumstances and passions is another." Ibid.

[42] De Lubac, *At the Service of The Church*, 71.

[43] Hans Urs von Balthasar, *The Theology of Henri de Lubac* (San Francisco: Ignatius Press, 1983), 17. "The order was given to withdraw from our libraries and from the trade, among other publications, three of my books: *Surnaturel*, *Corpus Mysticum* and *Connaissance de Dieu*—as well as (from our libraries) the volume of *Recherches* containing my article 'Mystère du surnaturel.'" De Lubac, *At the Service of The Church*, 74.

[44] Father General was on holiday and the censorship official was also absent when the book was sent to Rome, so two other French Jesuits were asked to read the work and commented most favorably on the text which was then sent for publication. It became a favorite work of the Archbishop of Milan, Monsignor Martini who later became Paul VI.

one ever communicated to me any precise charge. ... No one ever asked me for anything that would resemble a 'retraction,' explanation or particular submission."[45]

De Lubac's rehabilitation was slow in coming.[46] Some prominent people[47] continued to support him during this time. His Provincial[48] insisted that he keep writing and Cardinal Gerlier who had oversight in Lyons insisted on keeping his chair of theology vacant. De Lubac even had friends at the heart of the Vatican. The papal confessor Fr. Augustin Bea gave four of de Lubac's books to Pope Pius XII to read. These were two books on Buddhism,[49] *Sur les chemins de Dieu*[50] and *Méditation sur L'Eglise*. The response from the Pope was very positive, and a letter dated March 29, 1958 conveying encouraging sentiments was written to de Lubac by Fr. Bea.

The terms of the letter give clear indications of the appreciation of both de Lubac's work and his disposition of loving obedience towards the Pope. It is worth quoting substantively:

> I am happy to be able to communicate to you that the Holy Father has accepted with truly paternal kindness and with great joy the homage of your four volumes, which you presented to him through my hands, along with your beautiful declaration of dispositions of faith, obedience and affection toward the Vicar of Jesus Christ on earth. The Holy Father had a lively interest in the topics of your books and particularly of the fine work *Méditation sur L'Eglise*. He was delighted to see the scientific soundness attested to by the numerous notes and quotations. The Holy Father asked me to communicate his great gratitude and to tell you that he expects much more from the talents the Lord has given you for the good of the Church. He sends you wholeheartedly his blessing for your person, particularly for your health, and for all your works, and he encourages you to continue with much confidence your scientific activity from which much fruit is promised for the Church. You can be sure, my Reverend Father, that you have given great consolation to the Holy Father by your homage and your very devoted declaration.[51]

---

[45] De Lubac, *At the Service of The Church*, 78.

[46] De Lubac noted a certain lessening of the severe policy adopted towards him in the years 1955–6.

[47] Including the General Superior of the Ursulines of the "Roman Union" Mother St. John who invited de Lubac to Rome in 1953 to give some classes to the young religious and provided accommodation since the Jesuit houses in Rome were closed to him.

[48] Fr. André Ravier.

[49] It had been suggested that de Lubac write on Buddhism while he was unable to write on any Catholic doctrinal matters.

[50] This was a new and enlarged edition of *Connaissance de Dieu*.

[51] De Lubac, *At the Service of The Church*, 89–90.

For our purposes, in understanding the ecclesial disposition as manifested in de Lubac's life what is most significant during this time is that he never once publicly criticized his superiors. He did not understand why he was being ostracized but he maintained his sense of the presupposition of the *Spiritual Exercises,* namely, that his superiors were seeking what was good.[52] Finally in 1958 he received a letter from Fr. General Janssens indicating an awareness of the difficulties he had suffered: "It is clear that there have been misunderstandings on all sides. History teaches that men guided by the most honest intentions manage to have difficulties in being understood. What is important is to recognize at least the loyalty of those who make you suffer and whom one has made suffer. *'Diligentibus Deum, Omnia cooperantur in bonum.'*"[53]

It is particularly noteworthy that de Lubac never allowed himself to become bitter despite the difficult circumstances that he faced. He always seemed to find some excuse or attenuating circumstances for the actions of those at whose hands he suffered, and he always endorsed Church authority. Hans Urs von Balthasar said of him, "He expressly stated that his true opponents were not the Roman authorities but a group of integralist professors both inside and outside the Society of Jesus. His unequivocal stance in favor of ecclesiastical authority, especially the papacy, shows that there was not a trace of anti-Roman sentiment in him."[54] In addition de Lubac did not fail in his love for the Church which appeared to treat him so unkindly. Clearly operative is the First Rule of the Rules for Thinking, Judging and Feeling with the Church.[55] Though he was never formally criticized, and despite a silent campaign which ostracized him, de Lubac maintained a loving obedience to the Church and those in authority within the Church.

Indeed, de Lubac's faithfulness and love of the Church all during this time was revealed in a short work in 1953, *Méditation sur L'Église.*[56] Within this book he draws a picture of what the true "man of the Church" is like. As with a self-portrait by an artist, for example Rembrandt, so we may trace the lines of de Lubac's own spirit and characteristics in this depiction:

> In a true man of the Church the uncompromisingness of the faith and attachment to Tradition will not turn into hardness, contempt or lack of feeling. They will not destroy his friendliness, nor will they

---

[52] In this way he is evidently in accord with the tenth rule of the Rules for Thinking, Judging, and Feeling with the Church, *Spiritual Exercises* 362.

[53] De Lubac, *At the Service of The Church,* 91.

[54] Urs von Balthasar, S.J., *The Theology of Henri de Lubac,* 19.

[55] *Spiritual Exercises* 353.

[56] The English translation was given the title, *The Splendour of the Church,* a title that embarrassed de Lubac as it had a triumphal sound to his ears.

shut him up in a stronghold of purely negative attitudes. ... He will not give way to the spirit of compromise ... He will take great care that some generalized idea does not gradually come to take the place of the Person of Christ. ... His total and unconditional faith will not come down to the level of a sort of ecclesial nationalism ... He will hold himself apart from all coteries and all intrigue, maintaining a firm resistance against those passionate reactions from which theological circles are not always free, and his vigilance will not be a mania of suspicion ... He will not show himself hostile on principle to legitimate diversity.[57]

In 1958, de Lubac was permitted to return to Lyons. In 1960, Pope John XXIII, having come to admire de Lubac during his time as Papal Nuncio in France, invited him along, with Yves Congar, O.P., to be a consultant for the preparatory Theological Commission of the Second Vatican Council. De Lubac noted later that: "John XXIII had undoubtedly wanted to make everyone understand that the difficulties that had occurred under the previous pontificate between Rome and the Jesuit and Dominican Orders in France were forgotten."[58] At the Council, de Lubac served as a theological expert [peritus] and particularly influenced a number of the documents: The Constitution on Divine Revelation (Dei Verbum) and the Pastoral Constitution on the Church in the Modern World (Gaudium et Spes). Some of his ideas were also reflected in the Decree on the Church's Missionary Activity (Ad Gentes). Pope Paul VI, as we have already noted, prior to his election had come to have a great appreciation for de Lubac and this was also evident during the course of the meetings of Vatican II.

During the Council, de Lubac also established a good working relationship with Cardinal Karol Wojtyla, later Pope John Paul II. He was appointed by Paul VI to be a consultor for the Secretariat for Non-Christians instituted in 1964 as well as for the Secretariat for Non-Believers instituted in 1965. With regard to the latter body de Lubac became increasingly concerned about the drift away from Catholic theology[59] and as he saw it, the uncritical adoption of a sociological way of viewing the Church

---

[57] Henri de Lubac, S.J., The Splendour of the Church, trans. by Michael Mason, (London: Sheed and Ward, 1956), 184–5.

[58] De Lubac, At the Service of The Church, 116. De Lubac indicates here also that he only received the news when he saw the names of the appointees in an issue of the French newspaper La Croix. During the time of the preparatory commission de Lubac also made a spirited defence, both oral and written, of Father Teilhard de Chardin as a faction of the commission was demanding an explicit condemnation of him and "was making some outrageous misinterpretations of his thought." Ibid., 117.

[59] "It became clear to me that the most influential organizers, under the pretext of a historico-sociological analysis, were pursuing a practical end; I myself saw in it the pursuit of an illusion and the seed of a denaturation of the Church." Ibid., 119.

and the increasing trends towards secularization.[60] After the Council, de Lubac made many foreign trips explaining the documents of the Council. He was appointed as one of the original members of the International Theological Commission set up in 1969 and it was here that he developed a close working relationship with Hans Urs von Balthasar and Joseph Ratzinger—later Pope Benedict XVI. He continued to write on the Church in particular about the differing crises she faced. In 1969 he published *La Foi Chrétienne* and *L'Église dans la Crise Actuelle*. He was concerned about a certain uncritical disorder that he believed to have settled over theology. He also found time to continue his work on the history of theology after the Council.

In 1983 John Paul II elevated him to the rank of Cardinal. At this point, de Lubac requested and was granted a dispensation from becoming a bishop before becoming a Cardinal. He argued that he could not fulfill the duties of a bishop because of his age and therefore he should not be appointed to the episcopate. At eighty-seven he became the first Cardinal after Vatican II who was not a bishop, and just before his death he was the oldest living Cardinal. His last published work was an autobiographical reflection published in 1989.[61] De Lubac died in Paris on September 4, 1991.

The Witness of de Lubac's Writings

Henri de Lubac wrote over forty books and, in addition, numerous articles and smaller works. Even so, de Lubac was not a systematic writer or thinker. Many of his books seem to be composed of historical studies loosely linked together. At the same time, von Balthasar described de Lubac's work as an organic whole: "that unfolds an eminently successful attempt to present the spirit of Catholic Christianity to contemporary man in such a way that he appears credible in himself and his historical development as well as in dialogue with the major forms of other interpretations of the world—and even feels confident in proposing the unique complete ['Catholic'] solution

---

[60] "As the Council continued it was possible to perceive as early as 1964 signs of a growing para-conciliar agitation, often far removed from the will of the [Conciliar] Fathers, I remember having said to a certain number of them with whom I could speak frankly: 'After the Council closes, as soon as you return to your diocese, do not fail to explain at length and at large the results obtained, to take the initiative in the orientations to be promoted; otherwise you could have difficulties.' One of them said to his secretary: 'Father de L. is a wise man.' This was, I do believe the only fruit of my interventions. The difficulties were not lacking. The Yes said wholeheartedly to the Council and to all its legitimate consequences must, in order to remain consistent and sincere, be coupled with a No that is just as resolute to a certain type of exploitation that is in fact a perversion of it." Ibid., 118.

[61] *Memoire sur l'occasion de mes écrits* (Namur Belgium: Culture et Verité, 1989) later published as Henri de Lubac, *At the Service of The Church*.

to the riddle of existence."[62] De Lubac's work gave credibility to contemporary Catholicism.

The inner coherence that von Balthasar points to in this citation can be traced from the very first book which de Lubac published—*Catholicisme*. Avery Dulles, S.J.[63] compared this work to the trunk of a tree in which the various chapters are the branches. These branches produce further foliage and fruit through their development throughout his other works. In this way this first work is—as it were—programmatic for all his later works. The central tenet is that to be Catholic is to be comprehensive and universal and to exclude nothing. In this way he echoes Ignatius' understanding in the *Contemplatio* of the *Spiritual Exercises* of seeing God in all things and responding to God in and through all circumstances. De Lubac sees the redemptive work of God permeating humanity and indeed the entire cosmos.[64]

The Centrality of Christ

This is not, however, a vague pantheistic understanding. It is rather more in line with Paul's assertion that God in Christ reconciles all things to Himself.[65] For the central mystery of faith is Christ. De Lubac did not write a specific book on Christ—just as he did not write a book on Christian mysticism though he owned that mysticism had been his inspiration throughout his work—but his work is Christocentric and Christ is the primary focus for Christian mysticism. And the mission of the Church to the whole world rests on the reality that the Church is the body of Christ.[66] There is therefore an interior, intensive reality of the very nature of the Church as conjoined to Christ. There is also an exterior, extensive reality of the universality of the Church. This assertion of the intimate union of Christ and the Church echoes the veracity of the First Rule of the Rules for Thinking with the Church.[67] At the same time the word "Catholic" can only be fully understood in its universality by the way it is expounded in the

---

[62] Hans Urs von Balthasar, S.J., *The Theology of Henri de Lubac*, 24–5.

[63] Avery Dulles, S.J., "Henri de Lubac: In Appreciation," *America*, September 28, 1991.

[64] We see an echo of this understanding in the ministry of Pope Francis: see the last section of this book.

[65] Cf. Col. 1.

[66] "*Catholicisme* placed Christ's Church in a coordinate system: first, [vertical] transcendence of Christianity [as an individual historical form among others] to the totality of the world-redemption contained in it; then, [horizontal, temporal] transcendence of the time of promise to the time of fulfillment, of the Old Covenant to the New Covenant." Hans Urs von Balthasar, S.J., *The Theology of Henri de Lubac*, 61.

[67] *Spiritual Exercises* 353.

life of Christ. From the life of Christ developed the fullness of Christianity in the early Church.

Accordingly, the theology of de Lubac aimed to "recover Christianity in its fullness and purity" by "returning to its sources, attempting once more to seize it within its periods of explosive vitality."[68] Thus it was that De Lubac returned to patristic and early medieval writers where he found what he considered an authentic sense of Catholicism. He saw this as particularly focused in a personal understanding of the revelation of Jesus Christ, the word of God, the one in whom the very character, form and purpose of revelation are revealed.[69] Thus divine revelation is God's self-revelation and Christ stands at the center as the living word of the Father; this is what the Fathers taught and this is what de Lubac endeavored to convey. As Avery Dulles stated, "He labored to retrieve for our day the insights of Irenaeus and Origen, Augustine and Anselm, Bernard and Bonaventure.[70] He remained a devoted disciple of Thomas Aquinas, whom he preferred to contemplate in continuity with his predecessors rather than as interpreted by his successors."[71] So he saw the faith of the Church as primarily concerned with assisting a personal relationship with Christ who with the Holy Spirit enables reconciliation with the Father and amongst human persons.[72]

Another major work that caused considerable consternation on its publication was *Surnaturel*.[73] De Lubac considered that there had been a serious rift in Catholic understanding in the period of the later middle ages and early modern times. This rift consisted of a breaking down of the understanding of Catholicism into a series of component parts that were autonomous from one another. Thus scripture, moral theology, dogmatic theology and mystical theology, were all seen as discrete entities. Worse still, reason became separated from faith such that the latter was associated with feeling as opposed to intelligence.

> I believe I showed, particularly in the second part, the composition of which is rather strict, that since the various schools of modern

---

[68] Henri de Lubac, *Paradoxes* (Paris: Livre Francais, 1946), 67–9.

[69] Cf. *Dei Verbum* para. 2. "Jesus Christ ... is himself both the mediator and the sum total of Revelation."

[70] Cf. *Spiritual Exercises* 363.

[71] Dulles, S.J., "Henri de Lubac: In Appreciation."

[72] Illustrative of this truth is an intervention that de Lubac recalled from the Vatican Council when an African Archbishop speaking on behalf of his fellow sixty-seven African bishops stated: "Fundamentally, Christ himself is the Revelation that he brings ... The truths that we are to believe and the duties that we are to perform should be seen above all as they are related to a living person. Tell the world that divine revelation is Christ. The beautiful face of Christ must shine more clearly in the Church. In that way you will renew the miraculous signs of love and fidelity that were resplendent in the early Church." Cited in Henri de Lubac, *Entretien autour de Vatican II: Souvenirs et Réflexions* (Paris: Catholique-Cerf, 1985), 51.

[73] *Surnaturel* 1946.

Scholasticism had abandoned the traditional systematic (and already a bit compromised) synthesis in the work of Saint Thomas, they could only wear themselves out in sterile combats, each being both right and wrong, against the others, while withdrawing from living thought into an artificial world, leaving the field open to all the ups and downs of a "separated philosophy"...[74]

It was this understanding that his work *Surnaturel* challenged. It is clear within this book that Christ is the one who illumines the problematic that human beings are to themselves. It is also by the grace of Christ that humanity comes to recognize that the final goal of human life is communion with the Triune God.

In particular, de Lubac emphasized that the desire for the supernatural was at the very heart of what it means to be a human person. Thus, as English theologian John Milbank states, "The grammar of Christian life was re-envisaged; [it is—as it were—as though the whole way in which we understand the language of our faith was re-assembled] so too was ontology itself."[75] The very understanding of being itself was also revitalized. This was a reclaiming from the tradition of the understanding that God in himself is the coherent whole upon whom the universe depends. In creation that coherence is also mirrored particularly in the creation of the very being of human persons who are made in the image and likeness of God. Human persons, therefore, have a clear coherence in their very being since they reflect something of the reality of their Creator.

In Christ, de Lubac recognized the fullness from which, as human persons, we draw our life. In our human creation there is a dynamic drive of the spirit towards God. Fundamental to de Lubac's understanding of the human person is an acceptance of paradox and mystery. This focus on the mystery of the human person was in stark contrast to the rationalistic tendencies of modern scholastic theology. "The work thus constituted a sort of attempt to reestablish contact between Catholic theology and contemporary thought, or at least to eliminate one basic obstacle to that contact—not with a view to any 'adaptation' whatsoever to that thought, but rather with a view to engaging in dialogue with it."[76]

In Christ, de Lubac saw both the gift of God and the fulfillment of Old Testament prophecy. Nature, the gift of God in creation, can be seen to be a preparation for grace, while at the same time grace is always an unmerited

---

[74] De Lubac, *At the Service of The Church*, 36.

[75] John Milbank, *The Suspended Middle: Henri de Lubac and the Debate Concerning the Supernatural* (Grand Rapids, MI and Cambridge: Wm B. Eerdmans, 2005), 4.

[76] De Lubac, *At the Service of The Church*, 36. Within the *Spiritual Exercises* Ignatius Loyola advocated, as we have seen, the principle of finding God in all things; applied to the practice of dialogue this would be a consistent openness to engagement, which is not the same as either adaptation or false compromise or conformity.

divine gift of God to human persons. In a somewhat similar manner, the Old Testament foreshadowed the New Testament without necessitating the Incarnation. The Word became Flesh in Christ Jesus through the gratuitous gift of God. So, always de Lubac sought to emphasize how the New Testament gives, as it were, the "network key" for interpreting the Old Testament, which is fulfilled in the person and work of Christ, in his Passion, Death and Resurrection and in the Church which Christ brings into being. De Lubac often spoke of the Christ event (using *fait du Christ* and *l'acte du Christ* which we might conceivably translate as "Christ event"), "Christianity is based on an event, the Christ-event, the earthly life of Jesus, and Christians are those who believe today that he lives."[77] This emphasis on the personal understanding of revelation in line with patristic thought is one of de Lubac's most important contributions in the area of Christology and it is clearly evident in the conciliar document on Divine Revelation, *Dei Verbum*.

De Lubac's ongoing hope, in his work, was to make known and to make accessible some of the riches of the Catholic tradition. He was very concerned that many following the Council were cynical about tradition. "I see with sadness the spread of an indifference, when it is not a flaunted scorn or a resentment full of bitter hatred with respect to the tradition, which alone has the promise of life and of renewal because it is the bearer of eternity. At the same time I see a harsh demand for 'pluralism' which, in its worship of differences, shatters the harmony of the great Catholic concert and tends not to enrichment, but to the dislocation of Unity."[78] He also desired to help those who read his work to appreciate the centrality of Christ, and how it is only in and through Christ that we come to appreciate the loving desire of the Trinity for all humankind. Once more we recall the way in which he echoes his spiritual father, Ignatius, here in understanding that there is a Trinitarian mystical horizon against which all is seen. This Trinitarian appreciation roots also his understanding of the Church and his relationship to the Church.

We can see then, that de Lubac was not interested in innovative views *per se*, rather drawing from scripture and tradition he endeavored to reclaim for his contemporaries the riches of the gospel understanding

---

[77] Henri de Lubac, *La Révélation Divine*, 45.

[78] De Lubac, *At the Service of The Church*, 146. He continues: "How I would like to be able to cry out with the same persuasive tone to those of my brothers who are letting themselves be seduced by this music of perdition what in the last century Newman declared to his contemporaries: 'There is [he said] a depth and a power in the Catholic Religion, a fullness of satisfaction in its creed, its theology, its rites, its sacraments, its discipline, a freedom yet a support also, before which the neglect or the misapprehension about oneself on the part of individual living persons, however exalted, is as so much dust when weighed in the balance. This is the true secret of the Church's strength, the principle of its indefectibility, and the bond of its indissoluble unity. It is the earnest and the beginning of the repose of heaven.'" Cited in ibid.

centered on Christ. He believed that the work of Vatican II had finally overcome the bane of rationalism at the heart of a narrow neo-scholasticism and opened the way for a re-appropriation of the tradition. Unfortunately, in his own native land of France, and to an extent in the wider Church, the demise of neo-scholasticism was seen as also the collapse of the tradition. The rigors of a narrow theological approach were conflated with a sense of Catholic tradition as a whole. This was the reason for de Lubac's many international trips to explain the work and documents of Vatican II. This was also the stimulus for his later post-conciliar publications. He was concerned to address what he saw as a self-destructive tendency amongst some contemporary Catholic theologians who tried to separate a "spirit" of the Council from the documents of the Council.[79] This tendency led to attempts to move beyond the Council in practical terms even before there was a real comprehension and assimilation of the teaching of the Council. De Lubac was well aware that, as the Fourteenth Rule of the Rules for Thinking, Judging, and Feeling with the Church indicates, *great caution is necessary in our manner of speaking and teaching about all these matters.*[80] The dissension and turmoil that emerged after the Council appeared to de Lubac, who was well versed in Ignatius' *Rules for Discernment*, to be the sign of the spirit opposed to the gospel.[81]

The Vitality of the Church

As we have seen, Christ was central to the understanding and work of de Lubac. Since Christ is conjoined to the Church as Ignatius and de Lubac both remind us, then there is an unceasing dynamic of Christ's work within the Church on which the latter is always dependent.

> The divine call that summons her into reality and the divine principle that animates her make her always anterior and superior to anything that can be enumerated and distinguished in her; you can say that she was born of the apostles, yet they themselves were first conceived by her. And it is this Church in her entirety who is, in her unicity and her unity,

---

[79] One might argue that this itself is a somewhat perverted form of neo-scholasticism. Also "De Lubac observed a break with Tradition, as if theology had come into its own only with the Second Vatican Council. In *Entretien autour de Vatican II,* he talks about an 'underground council' [*para-concile*] that was active as early as 1962 and went public in 1968, resolutely determined to distance itself from the preceding Councils of Trent and Vatican I." De Lubac, *Entretien autour de Vatican II*, 33–57; abridged English translation cited in Rudolf Voderholzer, *Meet Henri de Lubac: His Life and Work,* trans. Michael J. Miller (San Francisco: Ignatius Press, 2008), 94.

[80] Fourteenth Rule, *Spiritual Exercises* 366.

[81] See Part I, Chapter 2.

indissolubly a hierarchical society and a community of grace, under two different aspects respectively.[82]

Therefore it comes as no surprise to find the Church is at the heart of de Lubac's work, particularly his later work. The distortions, oversimplifications, and misinterpretations of the Council led to a great deal of confusion in the Church. De Lubac was both dismayed by this and challenged to respond in a way that might prove helpful for the life and vitality of the Church. In 1969 in *L'Église dans la Crise Actuelle*[83] de Lubac attempted to show the continuity between Vatican II and the Church's tradition. He emphasized that two conditions were essential for genuine renewal in the Church. First, there must be a real and deep love of Jesus Christ. Secondly, there must be a real and deep love for the unity of the Church. This leads also to the underlying relationship between the Eucharist and the Church. Here we see once more how de Lubac expresses the conjoining of the love for Christ, love for the Church and love for the Eucharist that were at the heart of Ignatius' own experience and ecclesial disposition.

Private Christianity is not an option De Lubac asserts.[84] Membership of the Church and participation in her institutions are vital for growth in faith and daily living and lie at the heart of the Christian vocation. The Christian faith is expressed and preserved and transmitted through the liturgy, the creed, the missionary, and reconciliatory activity of the Church seen as part of the redemptive work of Christ.

> It is the Church that believes. It is she who confesses the Trinity, she who offers praise and thanksgiving; it is she who hopes and awaits the return of her Lord, she who bears witness to him by her unfailing faith which bears fruit throughout the world. It is she who, advancing in faith, prays and works, seeking in all things to fulfill the divine will. It is she whom

---

[82] Henri de Lubac, *The Splendour of the Church*, 111.

[83] Henri de Lubac, *L'Église Dans La Crise Actuelle*, (Paris: Cerf, 1969). This had first appeared as an article in the *Nouvelle revue théologique* and was the amplified text of a conference given at the University of St. Louis. De Lubac said of this work: "Given the advanced state of the crisis, perhaps I made an error in publishing so brief and summary a text, which rather assumed the tone of a manifesto instead of patiently examining a single, well-chosen point in order to throw light on it. Yet how can one react effectively to a state of mind that penetrates all sectors of thought that brings everything into question at once, on principle and on every level, without anything being really studied and discussed. In this same booklet, I was imprudent through omission, by recalling the necessary love of Jesus Christ without specifying that Jesus was the Way to the Father; I was still so little aware of the 'Christian atheists' and 'Jesusism' that were beginning to flourish. It has since then been necessary to specify that 'Christological concentration' was in no way 'Christological reduction' leading to 'anthropological reduction'! Later I would have to specify still further, in the opposite sense, that 'Christocentricity' is not necessarily an exclusion of the Holy Spirit." De Lubac, *At the Service of The Church*, 132.

[84] See in particular de Lubac, *The Splendour of the Church*, 302–9.

the Spirit of Christ gathers into one and unifies; she whom he enlightens and guides throughout her long earthly pilgrimage. It is she who, while awaiting the face-to-face vision, faithful amidst trials and darkness, resisting all scandal, jealously preserves the deposit entrusted to her.[85]

Indeed, so great was the unity between de Lubac's love for Christ and for the Church that it was clearly evinced in his life. As he had previously suffered alone in his time of being ostracized, now he suffered with the Church in this time of confusion. He expressed his understanding of this experience in a way that linked it with the passion of Christ. He asserted that all that the Church suffers may be fruitful if it is united in truth with the sufferings of Christ, since he is the head of his body—the Church. This one great truth unites all members of the Church, and nowhere more profoundly than in the liturgy of Good Friday:

> It is possible that many things, in the human aspect of the Church, disappoint us. It can also happen that we can be profoundly misunderstood without being at fault ourselves. It is possible that, even within her, we have to suffer persecution ... Patience and loving silence will be of more value than all else; we need not fear the judgment of those who do not see the heart, and we will think that the Church never gives us Jesus Christ in a better way than in the opportunities she offers us to be conformed to his Passion. ... The trial will perhaps be heavier if it comes, not from the malice of a few men, but from a situation that might appear inextricable: for then neither a generous forgiveness nor the forgetting of one's own person is sufficient to overcome it. Let us nevertheless be happy, before 'the Father who sees in secret', to participate in this way in that *Veritatis unitas* that we implore for all on Good Friday.[86]

Though this book was written before the Council under the title *Méditation sur L'Église,* the theology is very much the theology of the Council itself. The mystery of the Church is set in the context of the entire mystery of salvation. The themes of the work seem to be laying out guidelines for *Lumen Gentium,* the Vatican II document, on the Church. The Church as a mystery prefigures the first chapter of that document. The dimensions of that mystery are spelled out in Chapter 2 of the document. Central to the whole document is the understanding that the Church is both divine in Christ and also rooted in human beings. The Church is both visible and invisible.

At the heart of the Church is the Eucharist. The Church makes the Eucharist through her hierarchical body in the very sacramental celebration

---

[85] Henri de Lubac, *The Christian Faith: An Essay on the Structure of the Apostles' Creed,* trans. Richard Arnandez (San Francisco: Ignatius Press, 1986), 187–8.
[86] Ibid., 164.

of Eucharist. At the same time for de Lubac the Eucharist is central to the life of the Church as incorporating her into Christ's body.[87] For de Lubac, the reality of communion is not primarily about what is received, namely the body of Christ, nor about an action between Christ and an individual, rather communion has primarily a communal focus, the incorporation of human persons into Christ's ecclesial body.[88] Indeed, the Eucharist is the sacramental presence of Christ within history. The Eucharist continues his life-giving presence within the Church which he revitalizes by his very real presence.

> Eucharistic realism and ecclesial realism: these two realisms support one another, each is the guarantee of the other. Ecclesial realism safeguards Eucharistic realism and the latter confirms the former. The same unity of the Word is reflected in both. Today it is above all our faith in the 'real presence', made explicit thanks to centuries of controversy and analysis that introduces us to faith in the ecclesial body: effectively signified by the mystery of the altar, the mystery of the Church has to share the same nature and the same depth.[89]

In a world hostile to Christianity, the Church, in and through her leaders and preeminently through the papacy, guards human persons from any attempt to make absolute either state or culture. The Church stands as a guarantor of the dignity of the human person endowed with God-given freedom. Indeed, de Lubac directs attention to the ministry of the papacy for the unity and freedom of the Church.[90] Pre-eminently the Church is the sacrament of Christ both leading members to Christ and by the very manner of her configuration to Christ, the Church may also be said to "contain" Christ. This is the mystery of the Church that cannot be reduced to either anthropology or sociology. The mystery of the Church is more profound, de Lubac asserts, than the thought and understanding of any individual believer.

The Church nurtures the life of the individual believer and the natural response to that is gratitude. In this nurturing role the Church is seen to

---

[87] Ibid., 86.

[88] Susan Woods gives a timely caution in relation to this understanding. Although it may appear that "distinctions between Christ and his Church seem blurred, with the result that the Church can seem to be accorded a dignity proper to Christ alone, there are distinctions which maintain the difference" within de Lubac's work, Susan K.Woods, *Spiritual Exegesis and the Church in the Theology of Henri de Lubac* (Grand Rapids, MI: Wm B. Eerdmans and Edinburgh: T&T Clark, 1998), 59. Also, "The Eucharist/Church correlation is most closely associated with the anagogical sense when the Eucharist is considered as equivalent to the allegorical sense of Scripture and the Church is seen as the fulfillment of the union of Head and body in the *totus Christus*." Ibid., 68.

[89] De Lubac, *Corpus Mysticum*, 231–2.

[90] See particularly Chapters 6 and 7 in *Les Églises Particulières dans L'Église Universelle* (Paris: Cerf, 1971).

act as a mother to whom the natural response is one of gratitude and obedience.[91] De Lubac links the authority structure of the Church with the understanding of the motherhood of the Church. He argues that it is only when this motherhood is recognized and affirmed as the primary and indeed all-encompassing medium, that ecclesial authority can have the quality and character of fatherhood. So the motherhood of the Church guarantees the fatherhood of the hierarchical office. All authority in the Church flows from this reality. Such an understanding also gives a revivifying understanding of tradition.

> Tradition, according to the Fathers of the Church, is in fact just the opposite of a burden of the past: it is a vital energy, a propulsive as much as a protective force, acting within an entire community as at the heart of each of the faithful because it is none other than the very Word of God both perpetuating and renewing itself under the action of the Spirit of God; not a biblical letter in the individual hands of critics or thinkers, but the living Word entrusted to the Church and to those to whom the Church never ceases to give birth; not, moreover, a mere objective doctrine, but the whole mystery of Christ. Through this tradition, as the Second Vatican Council reminded us, the Church passes on to each generation 'all that she herself is,' all that gives her life (*Dei Verbum* c.2, n.8). In that very continuity, tradition is thus a perpetual principle of renewal; it ensures for the body of the Church, under the vigilance of her pastors, that perpetual youth.[92]

In considering the Church as mother, the figure of Mary is of importance also as we consider the sanctifying maternity of the Church. In Mary, de Lubac saw that openness to her Lord that enabled her initial "fiat" of obedience to God's ways, so that the Word might become flesh within her and be born as Jesus Christ. The Church was founded on faith in her Lord. Yet in Mary alone—*in sola Virgine stetit Ecclesia*[93]—was the Church constituted on Holy Saturday when all the disciples had fled in confusion. This close link between the Mother of God and the Church is the reason why in the Vatican II document on the Church—*Lumen Gentium*—there is a final chapter on the Virgin Mary. De Lubac asserts that: "the links

---

[91] Thus, we recognize once more in the work of de Lubac the intimate terms of the first rule of the Rules for Thinking, Judging, and Feeling with the Church. *Spiritual Exercises* 353.

[92] Henri de Lubac, *The Motherhood of the Church*, trans. Sr. Sergia Englund, OCD (San Francisco: Ignatius Press, 1982), 91.

[93] Philip the Chancellor [d. 1236] and Caesariou of Heisterbach [d. 1240] stated that in Mary alone stood the Church. Philip in his *Summa de bono*, wrote: "thus they say that the Church existed solely in the Virgin whose faith endured during the Passion: and it is for this reason they say that she is commemorated on a Saturday." Gerald Christianson, Thomas M. Izbicki, and Christopher M. Bellitto, *The Church, The Councils, and Reform: The Legacy of the Fifteenth Century* (Washington, DC: Catholic University of America Press, 2008), 214.

between Our Lady and the Church are not only numerous and close; they are essential and woven from within. ... more contemplation of the one is indispensable if the other is to be understood."[94]

The intimate connection between the Church and Mary is found both within scripture and in the tradition. Ignatius himself had a tender devotion to the Mother of God and a clear sense of the importance of her intercession as exemplified in the *Spiritual Exercises*. She also is the one who intercedes with her Son for the Church both as individuals and as a united body. De Lubac says of her that Our Lady "comprises in an eminent degree all the graces and all the perfections of the Church; [...] in her the whole Church is outlined and at the same time already completed ... she is the perfect form of the Church."[95] For de Lubac the mystery of the Church is the continuation of the mystery of Mary and her response to God. It is the same mystery unfolding to ever more profound depths in the midst of Christ's body, the Church.[96] In the twentieth century we can trace more developed expressions of the intimate link between Mary and the Church in the work of Catholic theologians: Henri de Lubac, Hans Urs von Balthasar and Avery Dulles who all exemplify this understanding. Pope John Paul II, Pope Benedict XVI and Pope Francis have also promoted a revitalized recognition of the place of Mary in the life of the Church.

For de Lubac, God made the persons of the Trinity accessible through the life, suffering, death and resurrection of Christ. This is at the heart of Christian faith. Christ has guaranteed that his Spirit is at work within the Church and that he is at work through the ministry of word and sacrament within the Church. In the reading of and reflection on scripture within the community and in the celebration of the sacraments, Christ makes himself known. Indeed, de Lubac holds that only in and through his body the Church does Christ make himself known.[97] It is the seed of this genuine attitude that prompts the desire to develop an ecclesial disposition along the lines of that indicated by Ignatius. It is the humility of such a desire that it can contemplate the possibility of setting aside *all judgment of our own*[98] as the First Rule indicates. For de Lubac, the starting point, the subject of the Church's faith, was not the individual but Christ and the Church as his body. As this is the case, a process of education in the faith is necessary to

---

[94] De Lubac, *The Splendour of the Church*, 255.

[95] Ibid. 259. Also, "In the total and incessant victory of the grace of Mary [the Church] sees the heralding of her own victory—a victory now already won at her own apex of purity." Ibid., 262.

[96] De Lubac's recognition of the importance of Mary, and indeed of the saints, clearly echoes the praise of devotions that we find in Ignatius' Rules for Thinking, Judging, and Feeling with the Church.

[97] This belief accords with the first statement in the Rules for Thinking, Judging, and Feeling with the Church, *Exercises* 352.

[98] First Rule, *Spiritual Exercises* 353.

bring the individual to an ecclesial faith, whereby one might believe in and with the Church what the Church believes.

In this way obedience to the Church becomes obedience to her Lord. The unity of faith then rests on the belief in the Triune God who in Christ made known his loving and redeeming grace and continues to work in and through the Church. It is in and through that very Church that the individual believer is brought to a deep interior union with the one who is head of the Church, Christ himself, and through him into the very life of the Trinity. In this way each individual is drawn also into the holiness of the Church in the Church's act of faith, made known in the subjective holiness of Mary and the saints. Also, as Christ gave his spirit as a gift to the Church, this gift imbues all authority in the Church, which is meant to be exercised in a spirit of service. All such authority de Lubac emphasizes is focused by a singular prerogative through the Pope as the center of unity for the Church[99]—*Sub Petro cum Petro*.

In his love for the Church, de Lubac endeavored to reclaim some of the riches of the Catholic tradition. "Without pretending to open up new avenues of thought," he wrote, "I have rather sought without any archaism, to make known some of the great common sources of Catholic tradition. I wanted to make it loved and to show its ever-abiding fruitfulness."[100] This was far removed from constructing a new form of theology. Indeed de Lubac said of himself: "I do not have the temperament of a reformer, still less of an innovator ... I have neither plan nor purpose to propose, all the more reason for my not being the head of any school."[101]

Throughout his life and his writings de Lubac remained steadfastly committed to the Catholic tradition and to a deep love for Christ and his Church that he desired to share with his readers. The years of his suffering from misunderstanding, ostracism and misinterpretation refined his spirit and with an authentic humility he emerged from this period of life with even greater desire to serve the Church. The Ignatian ecclesial disposition clearly illuminates his work and we have traced the resonance of a number of the Rules for Thinking, Judging, and Feeling with the Church. The centrality of Christ radiates from his work and the life of the Trinity underpins his exploration of the faith and the tradition.

His keen sense of the reverence due to human persons made in the image of God infuses his attempts to deal with the confusion of the post-conciliar

---

[99] "We will therefore say that for Peter and the one who succeeds him, what is concerned, according to the Gospel, is a singular prerogative, and that the failure to recognize this singular prerogative, in whatever century or circumstances one lives, would be in principle the negation of the Church such as Jesus Christ wished her to be." De Lubac, *The Motherhood of the Church*, 278.

[100] Henri de Lubac, "*Memorie sur L'occasion de Mes Écrits*," cited in Dulles, S.J., "Henri de Lubac: In Appreciation."

[101] Henri de Lubac, *At the Service of The Church*, 268.

period with sensitivity and theological clarity. In exploring the life and work of de Lubac we have encountered a distinctively different expression of Ignatius' ecclesial disposition and one that is linked to an understanding of ecclesial faith. Yet the essential tenets of that disposition, which we outlined in Chapter 3, still remain present, even when the expression of those tenets has crossed four centuries. As we move to consider the life and work of another twentieth-century theologian we shall encounter more diversity. Our focus, however, will be on the essential profound characteristics that are not bound to time and are gifts of grace ever building on the initial grace-gift, which is the life of unique human persons. We shall continue to see operative those essential ingredients of the ecclesial disposition of Ignatius made known in his twentieth-century sons.

7

Cardinal Avery Dulles, S.J.

The previous chapter considered a European theologian, the French Cardinal Henri de Lubac, who exemplified the ecclesial disposition of Ignatius in his life and work. This snapshot of Ignatian-centric theologians, however, would lack balance without reference to a theologian from across the Atlantic, in particular one from the United States of America. The vibrancy of intellectual life within the United States, and particularly in the area of academic theology, has been of enormous significance. In the twentieth and into the twenty-first century, One of the foremost Catholic exponents of academic theology during this time has been Avery Cardinal Dulles.

The Witness of Life

Auburn, New York was the birthplace of Avery Dulles on August 24, 1918. He was baptized Charles Avery Dulles but was never called Charles. As a young adult he legally changed his name to Avery Dulles. He was the son of John Foster Dulles and later Secretary Avery Dulles. His

7

Cardinal Avery Dulles, S.J.

The previous chapter considered a European theologian, the French Cardinal Henri de Lubac, who exemplified the ecclesial disposition of Ignatius in his life and work. This snapshot of twentieth century theologians, however, would lack balance without reference to a theologian from across the Atlantic, in particular one from the United States of America. The vibrancy of intellectual life within the United States and particularly in the area of academic theology has been of enormous significance in the twentieth and into the twenty first century. One of the foremost Catholic exponents of academic theology during this time has been Avery Cardinal Dulles.

The Witness of Life

Auburn, New York was the birthplace of Avery Dulles on August 24, 1918. He was baptized Charles Avery Dulles but was never called Charles. As a young adult he legally changed his name to Avery Dulles.[1] He was the son of John Foster Dulles[2] and Janet Pomeroy Avery Dulles.[3] "By

---

[1] Anne-Marie Kirmse, O.P. and Michael M. Canaris (eds), *The Legacy of Avery Cardinal Dulles SJ: His Words and Witness* (New York: Fordham University Press, 2011), 3.

[2] John Foster Dulles (1888–1959). "The Dulles family came from Ireland to the United States in the late eighteenth century. ... The Irish origin of the clan stems from William Dulles (whose original surname may have been Douglas) a military man from Scotland who fought in the Battle of the Boyne in 1690. After the battle he settled in Ireland." Patrick W. Carey, *Avery Cardinal Dulles SJ: A Model Theologian, 1918–2008* (New York and Mahwah, NJ: Paulist Press, 2010), 1–2.

[3] Jane Pomeroy Avery Dulles (1891–1969) came from a prominent Auburn family. She was particularly interested in art and European culture to which she introduced her children on European visits to Italy and Paris. "Avery recalled with fond memories early experiences with medieval and modern art and architecture and the sensitivity and knowledge his mother brought to this part of his early education. This initial introduction to art and medieval culture would have a long-lasting influence upon his sensitivities to sign and symbol. In 2001, he recalled that the 1932 spring vacation in Italy had impressed him with the "inner coherence

the time of his son Avery's birth, the young John Foster had already been recognized for his legal abilities in international affairs, had absorbed some of the moral idealism of the age of Wilson and had well-placed friends and acquaintances and business associates in government as well as on Wall Street. He was also very much a family man involved in the lives of his children."[4] Unlike Henri de Lubac, the Dulles family was firmly entrenched in the American Protestant establishment. Avery Dulles thus had no family context that oriented him naturally towards religious life or magisterial authority in the Catholic Church. As a convert though he truly valued the faith he had chosen.

There was, however, a strong family tradition of involvement in politics and a deep commitment to American democracy and the wellbeing of the nation and this stood Dulles in good stead as a precondition for his life of commitment within the Society of Jesus. Service within the political life of the nation was the family tradition. Dulles' father, John Foster Dulles, served as Secretary of State in the Eisenhower administration from 1953 to 1959; his great grandfather, John Watson Foster was Secretary of State in the administration of President Benjamin Harrison; and his great-uncle, Robert Lansing served as Secretary of State for President Woodrow Wilson. Dulles' uncle, Allen Dulles was the first civilian director of the CIA for President Eisenhower in the years between 1953 and 1961. Alongside all this political involvement at the highest levels of US government, Dulles' grandfather Allen Macy Dulles was a Presbyterian pastor and a co-founder of the American Theological Society.[5]

Avery Dulles, however, did not receive a strict Presbyterian upbringing.[6] He attended primary school in the city of New York at St. Bernard's School a private school in Manhattan. Thereafter,[7] he attended private secondary schools in Switzerland in 1930 at the Institut Le Rosey, a prestigious inter-national boarding school, and from 1932 to 1936 at the Choate School in

---

between the religious themes and the aesthetic quality of the masterpieces of the high Middle Ages and the Renaissance. His increasing love of the beautiful he accredited to his mother." Ibid., 17.

[4] Carey, *Avery Cardinal Dulles SJ*, 11.

[5] Avery Dulles was elected president of the American Theological Society 1978. One might speculate that theology was in the family genes!

[6] "In the midst of the Roaring Twenties, as John Foster Dulles' wealth increased, the Puritan Sunday gave way to the recreational Sunday. ... [Holiday] homes outside of New York City were places of retreat and relaxation on weekends and during the summers. Once they began going to [these] on weekends, the Dulleses abandoned their regular Sunday religious practices and replaced them with dinner parties for family and acquaintances, sailing, golf, tennis, bridge, ping-pong, and backgammon. ... By the time Avery was ten years old, religion or religious practice was no longer a matter of great moment in his life." Carey, *Avery Cardinal Dulles SJ*, 14.

[7] "In 1930, when he was twelve years old, his parents decided that he should have the benefit of education abroad as his father and mother, grandfather and grandmother had had before him." Ibid., 15.

Wallingford, Connecticut, a preparatory school. During this time he began to shape his literary skills by publishing in the student paper poems and articles.[8] By the time he began his tertiary education at Harvard[9] in 1936 Dulles had abandoned his Presbyterian faith and was an agnostic scientific rationalist. At Harvard, however, he was very influenced by his second year tutor—a Catholic professor named Paul Doolin[10]—and he began to consider the question of religion more seriously.

The lively nature of Doolin's faith, who was himself a convert, won the admiration of Dulles.[11] It was nearly three years later that Dulles finally entered the Catholic Church but "throughout that period the teaching of Paul Doolin was to serve me as a guide and reference point."[12]His religious doubts were finally challenged during a profound personal experience while he was at Harvard. On a rainy day in February 1939 he was in the Widener Library studying Agustine's *De Civitate Dei*—The City of God—when something prompted him to go outside. He walked down to the Charles River in Cambridge and he caught sight of a tree in bud and beginning to flower. As he wrote of this moment years later it is clear that he experienced a profound moment of grace.

---

[8] For a list of these publications see, Kirmse, O.P. and Canaris (eds), *The Legacy of Avery Cardinal Dulles SJ*, 3–4.

[9] Dulles considered Princeton where his grandfather, father and uncle Allen had studied; Yale where many of his peers were going but he chose Harvard because "he felt that his interests in medieval and Renaissance art and history would be best served by the Harvard faculty." Carey, *Avery Cardinal Dulles SJ*, 21.

[10] Paul Doolin was about to leave the Harvard faculty for that of Georgetown when Dulles first met him, but this move was delayed and he was assigned as Dulles' teacher for eight months. "Doolin's impact extended well beyond his expertise as a historian. Dulles spent many an hour in Doolin's room discussing literature, philosophy, politics as well as history. This one-on-one contact with a Harvard tutor who had a deep sense of spiritual values and a vigorous critique of the materialism and subjectivism of modern liberal culture awakened Dulles' first substantial contact with a committed Catholic intellectual, and he drank deeply from Doolin's well of wisdom. ... It was not just Doolin's philosophy that appealed to the nineteen year old Dulles; it was the fact that Doolin had incorporated that philosophy into his own character, making him a powerful and credible presence." Ibid., 27.

[11] "Always dramatic, forceful, and sudden in his speech, his technique was to persuade not so much by arguing as by amazing. He could always find a single phrase or observation, which went to the absolute root of the matter at hand. He had a marvelous gift for presenting his ideas in concrete terms, without becoming involved in vaporous abstractions, and every word which he spoke was a living expression of his own rich philosophy. His statements were not impartial observations, they were intense personal convictions." Avery Dulles, S.J., *A Testimonial to Grace and Reflections on a Theological Journey* (Kansas City: Sheed & Ward, 1996), 22.

[12] He continues: "At the time of hearing it, I was not yet ready to receive Doolin's doctrine, but I treasured it up in the garners of my memory and drew abundantly therefrom in the years that followed. The reasoning behind some of his sudden and abrupt sentences did not become clear to me until long afterward, but their very obscurity served to make one think, for everything that Doolin said fell into an ultimate pattern. None of his remarks was casual or flippant." Ibid., 28.

As I wandered aimlessly, something impelled me to look contemplatively at a young tree. On its frail, supple branches were young buds attending eagerly the Spring which was at hand. While my eye rested on them the thought came to me suddenly, with all the strength and novelty of a revelation, that these little buds in their innocence and meekness followed a rule, a law of which I as yet knew nothing.[13]

"How could it be," he remembered asking himself, "that this delicate tree sprang up and developed and that all the enormous complexity of its cellular operations combined together to make it grow erectly and bring forth leaves and blossoms?" It was as if Dulles had suddenly realized that the beauty inherent in nature is a created beauty reflective of the ordered beauty that lies at the heart of the universe.[14] He wrote, "That night, for the first time in years, I prayed."[15] After that moment, he recorded that he "never again doubted the existence of an all-good and omnipotent God."[16]

From this point on, Dulles began his gradual conversion journey on the path to Catholicism.[17] It took him two years to make his way to the Catholic Church. Since his family background was entirely Protestant and Presbyterian for some generations, Dulles first thought of religion in Protestant terms exploring the different denominations, but in none of these did he find that for which he was seeking. He became an intellectual convert to Catholicism as he was convinced that Roman Catholic philosophy and theology offered a more compelling account of reality as it truly was. Dulles spoke of his conversion in the following terms: "the more I examined, the more I was impressed with the consistency and sublimity of Catholic doctrine."[18]

---

[13] Dulles, S.J., *A Testimonial to Grace and Reflections on a Theological Journey*, 36.

[14] He continued: "The answer, the trite answer of the schools, was new to me: that its actions were ordered to an end by the only power capable of adapting means to ends—intelligence—and that the very fact that this intelligence worked toward an end implied purposiveness—in other words a will ... the same as Him Who moved the stars and made the lilacs bloom." Ibid., 36, 37.

[15] "I knelt down in the chill blackness at my bedside, as my mother had taught me to do when I was a little boy, and attempted to raise my heart and mind toward Him of Whose presence and power I had become so unexpectedly aware." Ibid., 38.

[16] Ibid 47.

[17] It might not be too fanciful to recall the important illumination that Ignatius had beside the river Cardoner.

[18] Dulles, *A Testimonial to Grace*, 84. Also "the power of the ancient faith over ordinary, working-class Catholics in Cambridge served as a witness to Dulles of the potent attractiveness of Catholic worship ... The 'Catholic Faith' he told a Polish audience in 2001, 'had an extraordinary hold on the minds and hearts of the common people ... They were remarkably faithful in their religious observance. Their piety was governed by the same revelation that had inspired the great artists and poets of earlier centuries.' The witness of popular Catholicism was another contributing factor in his process of conversion, and he repeatedly reflected upon

He called his conversion the best and most important decision of his life. He had been attending High Mass regularly on Sundays in his senior year at Harvard. He found himself deeply moved by the ceremonies of Holy Week and particularly the Easter Vigil Mass. It was only after he became a Catholic that he began to appreciate devotional art, initially he had been repulsed by popular devotional practices and art.[19] Dulles came to realize, however, that: "Nothing serves better than visual representation to make us aware of the presence of God and of our communion with the saints, who ever lovingly intercede for us."[20]

After graduating from Harvard in 1940, Dulles spent a year and a half at Harvard Law School before serving in the United States Navy as a World War Two intelligence officer. He had enlisted in 1941 and applied for a commission as an ensign. Though he was personally and morally opposed to war, he saw it as a necessary evil under certain conditions.[21] He was decorated for his service of liaison work with the French Navy and he received the "Croix de Guerre,"[22] and emerged from the Navy with the rank of lieutenant. These war years were a time in which Dulles grew in his faith. His understanding of his relationship with Christ and also his relationship with the Church deepened.

Over these years he was able to make three trips to Rome and on two occasions he attended general papal audiences with Pope Pius XII.[23] On another occasion he was involved in a special audience with the Pope.[24] His disposition was already being formed towards the fourth vow that he

---

this sense of the faith that he found in the churches in his later theological writing. (e.g. Faith of a Theologian)." Carey, *Avery Cardinal Dulles SJ*, 46.

[19] This appreciation is more in tune with the eighth rule of Rules for Thinking, Judging, and Feeling with the Church, *Spiritual Exercises* 360.

[20] Dulles, *A Testimonial to Grace*, 65. Also, "My saints, I could call upon them at will and receive their personal attention. It was as though they had lived and labored but for me." Ibid., 91. The sixth rule of the Rules for Thinking, Judging, and Feeling with the Church became part of his own committed Catholic identity. *Spiritual Exercises* 358.

[21] In April 1942 he wrote a paper "Modern War and the Christian Conscience." "[t]hat considered the injustices of most modern wars, the possibility and conditions of a just war, the just powers of the state in a time of war, and the obligations of a citizen in a time of war." Carey, *Avery Cardinal Dulles SJ*, 67.

[22] A French military decoration for bravery in combat.

[23] The pontificate of Pope Pius XII was from 1939 to 1958.

[24] December 1944, "While touring the Vatican with two other naval officers, he asked a Swiss guard 'if it would be possible to see the pope. He said wait a few minutes and I'll see. He came back in five or ten minutes and said, 'I just talked to the papal chamberlain who told me that the pope is holding an audience for Italian doctors.' I told him that we had two doctors from the American Navy and could they get into the audience to see the pope. And the papal chamberlain said 'yes.' The three of them got into the special audience, but Dulles 'was so nervous that the pope might ask me something about where I had gone to medical school and something about practising medicine in the American Navy' that he worried through the entire affair. Years later he told a group of students in jest, "I was worried that if I lied to the Pope I would spend a thousand years in Purgatory." Carey, *Avery Cardinal Dulles SJ*, 84.

would take as part of his Jesuit commitment. Dulles said of these meetings with the Pope: "I looked up to this pope as a faithful bearer of the Petrine office in troubled times."[25] Dulles himself at this time was a self-deprecating and soft-spoken man, a serious and compassionate officer with real concern for the men under his command.

While he was serving in the Navy he contracted polio. Initially he was left unable to walk for a time, but the symptoms disappeared though they would in later life recur, in a manner permanently detrimental to his health. Upon his discharge from the Navy in 1946, Dulles lived for several months in a Catholic student center[26] in Cambridge, Massachusetts. Here he was influenced by the Jesuit chaplain, Father Leonard Feeney, S.J.,[27] and his devotion to the doctors of the Church.[28]

In August 1946, Dulles with thirty-eight companions[29] entered the Jesuit noviceship of the New York Province, at St. Andrew-on-Hudson.[30] For his family, the conversion to Roman Catholicism had caused great consternation. Roman Catholicism in the United States at that time was a denomination primarily associated with the working class and recent immigrants from Ireland, Poland, Italy, Lithuania and Germany. Dulles was from a family of descendants from Puritan migrants and they wondered how an intellectual young man such as Avery Dulles was could find his truth in what seemed to them such a backward form of Christianity. Dulles further confounded his family with his entry into religious life, which they considered to be a complete waste of his potential. He wrote a compassionate letter to his mother saying: "I am sorry that you will inevitably regret this step, and I know that all I can ask of you for the present is your patient acceptance of my action, since you know that I would not do it

---

[25] He continued "with the passage of years I came to appreciate his teaching on biblical studies, on the Church as mystical body, on the liturgy and on the active participation of the laity in the life of the Church." Dulles, *A Testimonial to Grace*, 98.

[26] St. Benedict's student center.

[27] Fr. Leonard Feeney, S.J. 1897–1978. In 1949 he was dismissed from the Society of Jesus for disobedience. He had refused to accept an official declaration from the Holy See concerning "*extra Ecclesiam nulla salus*" (no salvation outside the Catholic Church) Feeney advocated a very rigid interpretation. In 1953 having refused on a number of occasions to go to Rome to explain his position he was excommunicated. In 1972 he was reconciled to the Church.

[28] In this way we see a resonance with the eleventh rule for thinking with the Church. *Spiritual Exercises* 363.

[29] "Of the thirty-eight young men who entered the Jesuit novitiate at St Andrew in 1946, twelve left before the end of the novitiate, and four others left the Jesuits before ordination. Twenty-six of the thirty-eight who entered were in their teens and were primarily graduates of high schools. ... Ten of the novices were in their twenties, some of whom were college men or had already graduated from college. Four of these men were in their mid-twenties and, like Dulles were veterans of World War II." Patrick W. Carey, *Avery Cardinal Dulles SJ: A Model Theologian, 1918–2008* (New York and Mahwah, NJ: Paulist Press, 2010), 98.

[30] Located about eighty miles north of New York City in Poughkeepsie.

unless I were convinced that it is best for my own sanctification and for the service of God."[31]

Dulles' formation as a Jesuit followed the pattern consistent with the time[32] and molded and developed his ecclesiological vision. By his own account, he came to love the *Spiritual Exercises* which concretized his sense of being called to labor with Christ in the world. Through the *Exercises* he continued to deepen his relationship with Christ. The Ignatian Rules for Discernment of Spirits and The Rules for Thinking, Judging, and Feeling with the Church seemed to him: "to epitomize the mystical and ecclesial dimensions of the Jesuit vocation."[33] This fundamental commitment to Christ and the Church is, of course, key to the ecclesial disposition of Ignatius. "What stands out in [Dulles'] later life is his fundamental commitment to the lordship of Christ, the Ignatian rules for thinking with the Church and the presupposition [of the *Exercises*]."[34] As a mature Jesuit, Dulles applied these principles not only to his own interior life but also to the life of the Church. He expanded the understanding of the *agere contra*[35] to include not just working against interior desolation of the spirit but also "the temptations of the culture that weakened the church's commitment to Christ as Lord."[36]

After the noviceship, Dulles spent three years studying philosophy at the Jesuit scholasticate in Woodstock, Maryland.[37] Here he grew in understanding of the scholastic doctors[38] and completed a licentiate in philosophy. In 1951 he was assigned to teach philosophy at Fordham University in New York for two years, during which time his father John

---

[31] He continued: 'It will mean some degree of separation from you and from my friends in the world. It will mean leaving our Center here, which has surpassed all my expectations as a place where God is genuinely loved and where we love another very dearly in Christ. But the step will be essentially a joyous one, for the priesthood is a tremendous privilege—the greatest that man can enjoy in this life. And I trust that God will find a way of overcoming my personal defects which would otherwise render me totally unworthy." Letter from Dulles to Mother, June 15, 1946, cited in Carey, *Avery Cardinal Dulles SJ*, 95, 597.

[32] This included: two years in the novitiate after which he made permanent vows; two years studying humanities; three years studying philosophy; three years regency (pastoral activity often teaching high school); and four years studying theology; generally ordination followed the third year of theology; after finishing theology there would be a third formative year—tertianship—to reinvigorate the spiritual life and this was followed by final vows.

[33] Dulles, *A Testimonial to Grace*, 101.

[34] Carey, *Avery Cardinal Dulles SJ*, 100..

[35] Working against a temptation, for example while making the *Spiritual Exercises* the temptation to cut short an hour of prayer, Ignatius suggests that to work against this one would be well advised to lengthen by a little the time. *Spiritual Exercises* 157.

[36] Carey, *Avery Cardinal Dulles SJ: A Model Theologian, 1918–2008*, 100. He continues: "At times the cultural temptations were not just external but matched the interior tendencies of the mind and heart and Dulles tried repeatedly to discern how best to work against them in his own soul as well as in the Church and the culture."

[37] Woodstock College was established in 1869 in the Patapsco River Valley twenty-five miles west of Baltimore.

[38] Cf. *Spiritual Exercises* 363.

Foster Dulles received an honorary doctoral degree in 1952. Throughout this time also he was involved in giving spiritual direction to students. The following year Dulles began his theological studies at Woodstock where he took a particular interest in the area of ecclesiology. Gustave Weigel, S.J.[39] was highly influential in encouraging him to a systematic study of ecclesiology, and ecumenism, which became life-long interests for him. He began to write in these areas. "Like his theological mentor Dulles' writing centered on ecclesiology and particularly on the unity of the Church. ... Dulles' commitment to the church's unity and to the Roman primacy as means of preserving unity of doctrine and ecclesial life, reflected his own conversion experience."[40]

Dulles was ordained to the priesthood in 1956 by Cardinal Spellman of New York at Fordham University in the Bronx along with thirty-six other Jesuits. It was something of a publicized affair as his father was Secretary of State. After a year in Münster, Germany for tertianship,[41] during which time he took the opportunity to visit centers of ecumenical activity, Dulles was sent to study at the Gregorian University in Rome.[42] He had been very impressed by the ecumenical activity he saw in Europe and ecumenism was to become the focus of his doctoral work. His dissertation focused on "the participation of Protestant churches in the prophetic office of the one Church of Christ."[43] He was awarded the doctorate in Sacred Theology in

---

[39] Gustave Weigel, S.J. along with John Courtney Murray, S.J. eventually became *periti* at the Second Vatican Council.

[40] Carey, *Avery Cardinal Dulles SJ: A Model Theologian, 1918–2008*, 123, 124. "That fundamental commitment, although nuanced in later years, remained a part of his core ecclesial experience." Ibid. Such a commitment can be seen as clearly linked to the Rules for Thinking, Judging, and Feeling with the Church.

[41] Tertianship is the third year of probation for Jesuits undertaken after ordination, but before final vows.

[42] Avery Dulles was in Rome for the death of Pope Pius XII and the election of his successor Pope John XXIII. November 9, 1958 he preached at Sunday Mass in the following terms: "It was particularly 'thrilling' to be in Rome in the past month, when great numbers had witnessed the impressive funeral of one pope and the election and coronation of another. These 'events' have made us all feel proud to call ourselves spiritual subjects of our Holy Father, the Pope." Carey, *Avery Cardinal Dulles SJ*, 139.

[43] Dulles, *A Testimonial to Grace*, 106. "The topic was narrowed to the ground and role of the prophetic mission in the classic Lutheran and Calvinist traditions ... with the ecclesial status of the Protestant churches. ... It was limited to the prophetic (that is, preaching and teaching) office. The dissertation was primarily an exercise in speculative, not positive or historical, theology, meaning that he was raising a theological problem that he believed Catholic theologians needed to address: Was there a truly prophetic office or mission within these Protestant traditions?" Carey, *Avery Cardinal Dulles SJ: A Model Theologian*, 145. "On the basis of Catholic theological principles and Catholic sources, Dulles argued that Protestant churches did not possess the prophetic office (because they did not belong to the unity and visibility of the Catholic Church), but they exercised a certain prophetic function, and their members who adhered to that preaching of the Christian revelation could make acts of theological faith. Protestant churches had the assistance of the Holy Spirit in carrying out their prophetic

1960. Thereafter he was assigned to be a professor of theology. Ecumenism became a life-long committed interest for him.

Dulles served on the faculty of Woodstock College from 1960 to 1974. It was during this time that the Second Vatican Council[44] met and two of the Woodstock Faculty, Gustave Weigel, S.J. and John Courtney Murray, S.J., served as *periti*.[45] Dulles listened eagerly to the reports of the Council from his two fellow Jesuits—he was particularly interested in the Dogmatic Constitution on Divine Revelation; The Decree on Ecumenism; The Declaration on Religious Freedom, and the Dogmatic Constitution on the Church. He was full of praise for the achievements of Vatican II, but at the same time, he desired to hold these documents in conjunction with the heritage from St. Thomas Aquinas, St. Ignatius of Loyola and the medieval and baroque legacy in theology and philosophy. Already in his work as a theologian he was incorporating in a healthy tension the tradition and the contemporary achievements of Vatican II. He saw no lasting division between these two, nor did he separate theology and spirituality in his work. And in contrast to the focus on individual religious experience which emerged during the early 1960s, "Dulles emphasized the simultaneity of the personal, the sacramental and the ecclesial in all religious experience."[46] This paradigm he derived from the Ignatian practice of "finding God in all things" which "required daily prayer and reflection, sacramental grace, the constant exercise of the theological and moral virtues, [and] a high degree of humility, ... Finding God's will was the goal of the Christian life and the continual aim of a Jesuit theologian's work."[47]

Dulles' personal devotional practice, as noted above, led him to mourn the post-conciliar depreciation of devotion to the saints and the removal of statues and shrines from Churches. He thought "it might be necessary ... to live through a barren season of slovenly improvisation until the Church could experience some kind of cultural revival." [48] In 1964 he was asked by his provincial to become an interpreter of the Vatican Council for Catholics in the United States. He undertook the task gladly, wanting to show why changes introduced by the Council were justified. At the same time he was careful to caution against moving beyond the limits of the Council. This work was to be his major task for the next few decades. Also at a time when authority in society, whether in government, business, education or

---

function, but that function was actually and ultimately dependent on the prophetic office in the true church." Ibid., 146.

[44] Vatican II was announced by Pope John XXIII on January 25, 1959. After four years of preparatory work it opened on October 11, 1962. There were four sessions over the next three years. Pope John died June 3, 1963 and the last three sessions 1963–5 were presided over by Pope Paul VI. The Council ended on December 8, 1965.

[45] Theological consultants.

[46] Carey, *Avery Cardinal Dulles SJ*, 160.

[47] Ibid. 161.

[48] Dulles, S.J., *A Testimonial to Grace*, 109.

Church, was becoming increasingly suspect, Dulles sought "to preserve a role for authority and an official magisterium in the Church."[49]

The years following the Council were difficult for Church and society in the United States. There were violent protests against the Vietnam War beginning in 1964 and continuing into the early 1970s; and there were in 1968 two major political assassinations of Robert Kennedy who had announced his anti-war proclivity and Martin Luther King, the great civil rights activist.[50] There was also significant reaction against Pope Paul VI's encyclical 1968 *Humanae Vitae* on the regulation of birth. Dulles' own response to this encyclical has resonance with Ignatius' ecclesial disposition. Dulles came under considerable pressure to ally himself with other Catholic theologians[51] who were convinced Pope Paul VI was wrong in the decision he had come to against the use of artificial means of birth control and wished him to sign statements to that effect. Dulles' reaction was that he was not a moral theologian and did not feel competent to pronounce on the arguments. "Having been trained to believe exactly what the Pope was now teaching, I had no personal reasons for dissent, and I considered that the burden of proof must be borne by those who wanted the doctrine changed. I saw no reason why the Pope, with his special charism of office, should be obliged to follow the majority of a purely advisory committee."[52] Clearly here, we see evidence of Dulles quietly displaying his faithfulness to the Church at a moment which had such profound significance in the life of the Catholic community. In later years he wrote: "Within the passage of years I came to appreciate the prophetic significance of *Humanae Vitae*,[53] in which the consequences of the new sexual revolution were accurately predicted."[54]

In the decades following Vatican II, Dulles' main concern was focused in the area of theological writing rather than social or pastoral involvements. He had a career as a major Catholic thinker that spanned five decades. In this capacity also he was often asked to review the works of other Catholic theologians, and in doing so he was very honest in his evaluation. He was particularly concerned about the growing polarization that he saw emerging within the Church following the Council. An example of this expressed concern is his review of Richard McBrien's *The Remaking of the Church* published in 1973. McBrien was a friend whom Dulles respected. In a letter to him he wrote: "I may be wrong, and you have every right to

---

[49] Carey, *Avery Cardinal Dulles SJ*, 240.

[50] President John F. Kennedy had been assassinated in 1963.

[51] "Moral theologians at the Catholic University of America, joined by those at Woodstock and other seminaries and colleges, along with a host of priests and laypeople, protested openly against the pope's prohibition of unnatural means of contraception. Moral theologians in particular organized mass meetings and signed letters dissenting from official papal teachings, a first in the history of American Catholicism." Carey, *Avery Cardinal Dulles SJ*, 238.

[52] Dulles, S.J., *A Testamonial to Grace*, 111.

[53] Humanae Vitae, Encyclical Letter of Pope Paul VI on the regulation of birth, July 25, 1968.

[54] Dulles, S.J., *A Testamonial to Grace*, 111–12.

think that I am wrong, but I have to say what I think I see. I think the book, while it makes a good and important contribution, does not help us as much as it might to get beyond the present polarization in the Church…"[55] He then goes on to indicate that it was important to reach out across the divide between so-called progressives and what he calls "traditionalists" and to try to address real concerns. "If there is to be any dialogue with the traditionalists (as they may be called) one must speak to their real, and partly justified, anxieties. The task that your present book leaves undone, in my opinion, is to show that the kind of reforms you ask for are consonant with the Church at the deepest level of her being."[56]

Dulles taught at the Woodstock seminary from 1960 until its closure in 1974, and then at the Catholic University of America in Washington DC until 1988. During this time also Dulles was instrumental in the formation of the Woodstock Theological Center at Georgetown University. In 1988 he returned to Fordham University where he remained until his death as the Laurence J. McGinley Professor of Religion and Society. His primary mission was as a teacher, giving clear well-crafted and intellectually challenging lectures which were informed by his deep faith and wide scholarship but also lightened by a certain self-deprecating humor. Many of his books and articles started as lectures. Dulles was also a visiting professor at a number of universities: The Gregorian University in Rome; Weston School of Theology; Union Theological Seminary in New York; Princeton Theological Seminary; Episcopal Seminary, Alexandria, Virginia; Lutheran Theological Seminary, Gettysburg, Pa; Boston College; Campion Hall, Oxford University; University of Notre Dame; the Catholic University Leuven; Yale University; and St. Joseph's Seminary, Dunwoodie.

Dulles served as president of the Catholic Theological Society of America for the year 1975–6. In June 1976 he gave his presidential address under the title "The Theologian and the Magisterium" developing his theory of the dual magisterium in the Church. "Dulles outlined the relationship between the theologians ('the competent experts') and the hierarchy. He argued for a qualitative difference between the 'authentic magisterium of the hierarchy and the doctrinal magisterium of the scholar.' They had different functions to play in the church."[57] He was concerned to assert that while theologians had the freedom of inquiry the bishops had the authority of office to

---

[55] Carey, *Avery Cardinal Dulles SJ*, 248.
[56] Ibid.
[57] "The hierarchical magisterium's task was to give public expression to teaching and provide juridical definitions. The theologian's magisterium was to investigate the wisdom of the past, analyze the present situation, and open new channels for what John Courtney Murray had called the 'growing edge of the tradition.'" Carey, *Avery Cardinal Dulles SJ*, 337. Also, "Dulles acknowledges that in spite of signs of cooperation between some theologians and some bishops, "the mutual relationship between theology and the hierarchical magisterium is still fraught with misunderstanding, tension, distrust, and occasional bitterness."

protect fidelity to Christian revelation. "The two tasks in the church were not equal. They had different aims and different authority. ... The bishops or the hierarchical magisterium had the authority to protect the integrity of the faith for the entire Christian community, and the theologian had a personal authority that flowed from his or her competence to investigate and speculate on the intelligibility and meaning of that faith."[58]

Two years later, Dulles became president of the American Theological Society 1978–9. His work as an academic theologian coincided with certain paradigm shifts within the discipline of theology as well as significant changes that were brought about by the Second Vatican Council in the 1960s. Dulles tackled many of the issues facing the Catholic Church, which was undergoing what was seen by many to be a profound social transformation. He addressed the changes that had taken place in theology, liturgy and practice in the wake of the Second Vatican Council 1962–5, seeking to explain them to intelligent listeners and readers and to link new thinking to its roots in Catholic tradition.[59] In addition many bishops saw him as a supporter of Vatican II and a voice of moderation within an increasingly polarized Church, and so he was appointed to many ecclesial, ecumenical and advisory committees during the late 1960s and into the 1970s.[60]

From his widespread scholarship in Christian Church history, Dulles was able to articulate certain areas where he felt change was important.[61] This was a contribution to the new understanding of how the Church, after some centuries of isolation from modern thought, might now relate to other Christian denominations and other religious faiths. This was of even greater importance in a time when the Church was gaining millions

---

[58] Ibid., 340.

[59] We see once more a link with rule eleven of Rules for Thinking, Judging, and Feeling with the Church. Eleventh Rule, *Spiritual Exercises* 363.

[60] "He became a theological advisor to a number of bishops and episcopal projects and in 1975 was sought out to provide theological advice on the *National Catechetical Directory*, critiquing drafts and providing detailed suggestions for improvement. In 1969, the United States Catholic Conference (USCC) the public policy arm of the National Conference of Catholic Bishops (NCCB) appointed Dulles to its newly constituted Advisory Council." Carey, *Avery Cardinal Dulles SJ*, 249. Also he periodically attended meetings of the Faith and Order Commission of the World Council of Churches (WCC). In addition from 1966–73 he was appointed consulter to the Papal Secretariat for Dialogue with Non-Believers.

[61] In his later years, Dulles revisited some issues that he had espoused more emphatically and provocatively in the late 1960s and early 1970s and modified his emphases. "Dulles' views on revelation, ecclesiology and ecumenism did not go uncontested during these immediate post-Vatican II years. The ultra-conservative journals periodically criticized him as a liberal reformer who was hypercritical of the past heritage of the church and excessively optimistic and uncritical in his acceptance of modern developments in thought. Some others, who found his theology generally acceptable, criticized his interpretations of the intentions of Vatican II and his ready willingness to minimize the conservative contributions at the council and the continuing relevance of some traditional positions that were included in the council documents." Ibid., 267.

of new followers in diverse cultures. His decisive contribution to theology was not one particular insight that began a school of thought or a particular line of argument, rather it was a distinctive manner of dealing with theological issues. Dulles had a particular style of response to questions that endeavored to listen to all perspectives and then to weigh what he heard against the standard of Catholic tradition.

During the 1970s and 1980s theology became an arena for both strident dissent and conservative polemics, both of which overflowed into Church life. The subsequent doctrinal confusion that followed was a source of deep concern for Dulles. Throughout this time his patient, careful, courteous, charitable and faithful research was—as it were—a bastion of calm amidst the confusion. He believed that it was important for theology to face the new questions put to the Church by the circumstances of life in the world. In doing so, Dulles considered that ongoing creativity was necessary to implant the faith in new cultures and to keep the teaching of the Church abreast of the growth of secular knowledge. It was clear to him that new questions demanded new answers, but he asserted that these must always be sought within the Church's heritage of faith. His own optimism became somewhat subdued by what he saw as violations of the Council's documents and indeed the spirit and directives of Vatican II. "The post-conciliar reformist mentality, he believed needed to be assessed in the light of the council's statements."[62]

Dulles devoted much of his research to interpretations of the Vatican Council's changes, which he said had been misinterpreted by some theologians as a license to try to push the Church into a process of democratization. He was insistent that the Church should safeguard its sacred teachings against both secularization and modernization. As he came towards the end of his time at the Catholic University of America (1974–88) he published *Toward a Theology of Christian Faith: Readings in Theology*, within which he stated that: "Vatican II embodies greater corporate wisdom and theological maturity than the work of most private theologians since the council."[63] He was very concerned to see what he saw as a trend towards extremism amongst some reformist theologians and the debilitating effect this was having on American Catholicism. He wrote, "Chastened by the experience of their own fragility, Catholics are groping for a new identity."[64]

One of Dulles' most important achievements was the careful exami-nation of difficult questions in a public forum. He undertook this twice a year in his later life in the McGinley Lectures at Fordham. This careful exploration and analysis formed a key task during the last twenty years of his life. Topics included: The Travails of Dialogue (Fall 1996); How Real

---

[62] Carey, *Avery Cardinal Dulles SJ*, 275.

[63] Avery Dulles, S.J., *The Reshaping of Catholicism: Current Challenges in the Theology of Church* (San Francisco: Harper & Row, 1988), 153.

[64] Carey, *Avery Cardinal Dulles SJ*, 275.

is the Real Presence in the Eucharist? (Spring 2005); Should the Church repent? (Spring 1998); Religious Freedom: A Developing Doctrine (Spring 2001); Evolution, Atheism, and Religious Belief (Spring 2007); and Who can be Saved? (Fall 2007). In addition, ecumenism, human rights, and faith and politics were all areas he explored.

Other theologians and academics, including those who disagreed with his views, respected Dulles for the high standards of his research and his intellectual integrity. He was also esteemed for being fair in his judgments and clear and lucid in his work. He was acknowledged by all to be a voice of mediation between the Church and American Catholics who challenged the Church. This work of bridge building was a vital contribution to the Church in the United States in the years following Vatican II.

He always tackled opposing viewpoints by utilizing the presupposition of the *Spiritual Exercises*, putting the most generous construction possible on views which might be antithetical to his own.[65] He took new insights into account and responded with answers consistent with the "heritage of faith." Dulles lived long enough to meet doctoral students who chose to write their dissertations on his work. Since he was a humble man, he found this somewhat surprising. He did not regard his work as of particular significance, but saw it rather as the simple task of a theologian well versed in the tradition who used this standard to assess the contemporary questions with which theology was faced.

Dulles loved the Jesuits and loved being a Jesuit. This deep love for the Society fuelled his vocation as a theologian. Ignatius' *sentire cum ecclesiae* is an apt description of his life and work. He never tired of asserting in different ways how faith and reason needed one another. Catholic commentators differed on their assessment of Dulles, some calling him a "conservative," others a "moderate." He had an aptitude for exploring and explaining theological currents in the Vatican. For example when Pope John Paul II asserted as the 'deposit of faith' that women could not become priests, but chose not to declare that this was infallible doctrine, Dulles defended this teaching by saying that: "the Pope did not engage his infallible magisterium in the declaration, rather by his ordinary and non-infallible teaching authority he vouched for the infallibility of the teaching." Indeed Dulles became in the 1990s one of the foremost interpreters of the teaching of John Paul II.

Dulles' faithful rendition of the tradition brought him to the attention of successive Popes. In 2001 he received what might be seen as the ultimate papal endorsement of his work. John Paul II designated a number of new Cardinals early in 2001 and three were from the United States. Archbishop Edward M. Egan of New York and Archbishop Theodore E. McCarrick of Washington—whom Dulles had known for nearly fifty-years[66]—were

---

[65] *Spiritual Exercises* 22.
[66] "Dulles had directed McCarrick in a Fordham devotional group in the early 1950s when the

unsurprising choices. The selection of Avery Dulles was extraordinary particularly since he was not even a bishop.[67] The Pope agreed to Dulles' request[68] not to be made a bishop. Dulles considered being made a Cardinal was more of an honorary appointment. He was eighty-two years of age and thus past the age of voting with other cardinals in electing a new Pope. He said of the honor, "It is very gratifying to think that my theology is considered somewhat important, not only in the United States but for the world's church." In addition he wished to acknowledge his own heritage: "In a wider perspective, I would see it [the nomination] as a gesture of encouragement for American theologians and for my order, the Society of Jesus."[69] A colleague at the Catholic University of America, Joseph Komonchak, said of him, "Dulles' work has been marked largely by a commitment to conversation, which, of course, involves listening as much as it does speaking. And he has been a good listener, first, in the sense that he has attended to the voices of the past in large works on the history of theology, to separated Christians in several ecumenical dialogues, and to fellow Catholics in analyses of post-conciliar church life and theology."[70]

At his investiture in Rome on February 21, 2001, he was carrying a cane due to a recurrence of the polio he had contracted in the Navy. In the last year of his life he suffered increasing incapacity due to this post-polio syndrome. It finally left him paralyzed and mute.[71] During Pope Benedict XVI's visit to the United States in April 2008, Dulles was granted a personal audience although by this time he was unable to speak. It was the Pope himself who requested the meeting.[72] In that same month he was present for his final McGinley lecture which summarized his life as a theologian, but it had to be read for him by Fordham's ex-president Joseph O'Hare, S.J.

---

latter was an undergraduate there. As a seminarian in 1956, moreover, McCarrick had served at Dulles' first Mass." Carey, *Avery Cardinal Dulles SJ*, 515.

[67] "The president of Fordham, beaming with pride, [at a press conference when the announcement was made] tried to summarize the meaning of Dulles' career as a theologian rewarded with the red hat: "Faith seeking understanding defines the mission of the theologian, even as it has consistently defined the life of Avery Dulles, whose intellectual integrity, fairness of judgment and lucidity of style set a high standard for all theologians." Ibid., 516.

[68] This had also been the request of Henri de Lubac when he was nominated a Cardinal.

[69] Carey, *Avery Cardinal Dulles SJ*, 516

[70] Joseph Komonchak, "All Dressed in Scarlet: Avery Dulles Goes to College," *Commonweal* 128 (February 23, 2001): 9. Also "He had critiqued the conservative neo-scholastics when he thought their theological paradigm needed revision, and in most recent years he had come to criticize the liberal paradigm because he believed that it most needed to be challenged." Carey, *Avery Cardinal Dulles SJ*, 521.

[71] A condition he shared with Pope John Paul II for the period prior to his death.

[72] "Sr. Anne-Marie Kirmse [his research associate] was present at the meeting and recorded that the Pope 'literally bounded into the room with a big smile on his face. He went directly to where Cardinal Dulles was sitting, saying 'Eminenza, Eminenza, I recall the work you did for the International Theological Committee in the 1990s.' Unable to speak, Dulles smiled back and kissed the papal ring." Ibid., 573.

In the lecture he concluded a review of his life in theology with an affirmation of faith sustained by the Lord in whom he had believed: "Suffering and diminishment are not the greatest of evils but are normal ingredients in life especially in old age. They are to be accepted as elements of a full human existence. Well into my ninetieth year I have been able to work productively. As I become increasingly paralyzed and unable to speak, I can identify with the many paralytics and mute persons in the Gospels, grateful for the loving and skillful care I receive and for the hope of everlasting life in Christ. If the Lord now calls me to a period of weakness, I know well that his power can be made perfect in infirmity. 'Blessed be the name of the Lord.'"[73] Such an assessment of his situation is surely the mark of a man of courage and humility, and one who had offered to the Lord over many years a service of love.[74] His paralysis increased despite the fact that his mind seemed to remain sharp to the end. He died on December 12, 2008, the feast of Our Lady of Guadalupe, patron of the Americas. Pope Benedict sent a telegram to Cardinal Egan of New York when he heard the news, stating the church's "immense gratitude for the deep learning, serene judgment, and unfailing love of the Lord and his Church which marked his entire priestly ministry and his long years of teaching and theological research."[75]

The Witness of His Writings

"As a theologian, I have found the Ignatian rules [for Thinking, Judging, and Feeling with the Church] applicable to the process by which individual theologians, and the Church in its corporate actions, reach decisions about matters of doctrine."[76] This citation both indicates how Dulles valued these rules and confirms the essential orientation of Dulles' writing. At the same time it locates within his work that ecclesial disposition that we identified as being so essential to the life and work of Ignatius Loyola. Dulles' comment also points to the essential conjunction of Christ and the Church which is the foundation from which decisions about doctrine are made. For Dulles "the theologian who is most prayerfully open to the impulses of the Spirit is best able to enter into the mind of the Church and by this means to

---

[73] Avery Dulles, McGinley Lecture April 2008, Fordham University.
[74] In this way Dulles mirrored the Eighteenth Rule of the Rules for Thinking, Judging, and Feeling with the Church, *Spiritual Exercises* 370.
[75] Telegraph and obituary in "Unfailing Love for the Lord Marks Cardinal Dulles' Life," in *L'Osservatore Romano* (Eng. edn) December 17, 2008, 20. Cited in Carey, *Avery Cardinal Dulles SJ*, 671 fn. 21.
[76] Dulles, *A Testimonial to Grace*, 101.

interpret the Christian faith in fullest conformity with the intentions of the Lord himself."[77]

There was a practical realism in Dulles' understanding of Ignatius' ecclesial disposition. "St. Ignatius's allegiance is not to some abstract idea of the Church but to the Church as it concretely exists on earth, with the Roman pontiff at its summit."[78] This disposition was one of three central foci that he identified as being highly significant for the Ignatian vision and that was clearly identified in the "Formula of the Institute."[79] These also included: the greater glory of God which is the reason for the existence of the Society of Jesus and therefore Jesuits are called always to the *magis*; and the call to a life centered on Christ under the banner of the cross. Finally totally and unequivocally Ignatius was a man of the Church.

By contrast, in the period after Vatican II in North America, Dulles was faced by widespread dissent amongst academic theologians. This focused on some key questions. One was whether theologians had any teaching authority, or whether the magisterium was the only teaching authority in the Church. As we saw above Dulles developed an interpretation which valued the contribution of theologians and the magisterium but which did not give equal authority to both. Another important question raised was the nature of papal teaching authority when it did not claim to be speaking from the position of infallibility. Dulles attempted to respond to these concerns in a series of books and articles. These works included: *The Dimensions of the Church* in 1967;[80] *The Survival of Dogma* in 1971;[81]

---

[77] Avery Dulles, S.J., The McGinley Lecture: "Ignatian Tradition and Contemporary Theology," April 10, 1997. Cited in Avery Dulles, S.J., *Church and Society: The Laurence J. McGinley Lectures 1988–2007*, (New York: Fordham University Press, 2008), 245.

[78] Avery Dulles, S.J., The McGinley Lecture: "The Ignatian Charism at the Dawn of the Twenty First Century," November 29, 2006. Cited in Ibid., 499.

[79] Cited extensively in Part I of this book. For our purposes here, the paragraph most relevant is: "Whoever desires to serve as a soldier of God beneath the banner of the cross in our Society, which we desire to be designated by the name of Jesus, and to serve the Lord alone and the Church his Spouse, under the Roman pontiff, the vicar of Christ on earth, should, after a vow of perpetual chastity, poverty and obedience, keep the following in mind."

[80] This was a revised collection of previous lectures on the Church and was his first attempt to interpret the documents of Vatican II and the consequences pertaining. A major theme was the relationship of the Church to the whole of humanity.

[81] "More than twenty years after *Survival*, Dulles indicated to a correspondent that his main concern in that book 'was to get Catholic readers to accept the possibility of development of doctrine and to take personal responsibility for their faith ... Since authoritarianism and blind conservatism are always a danger, the book may still have some relevance ... I am still opposed to authoritarianism, but I dislike the current tendency to label any exercise of authority as authoritarian. Christian doctrine is normally accepted on authority—that of Christ, the Scriptures, or the teaching Church.' Dulles to Jim Roth, June 8, 1999. In a letter to Gil Costello, October 13, 2002, Dulles wrote that his *Survival* reflected the times in which it was written, 'when many of us were uncertain about how far the changes introduced by Vatican II were going to go. In arguing for the changeability of dogmas, I had in mind the formulated statements, not the truths that these statements convey.' Since the publication of that book 'I

The Resilient Church: The Necessity and Limits of Adaptation in 1977;[82]
A Church to Believe In: Discipleship and the Dynamics of Freedom in
1982;[83] *The Reshaping of Catholicism: Current Challenges in the Theology
of Church* in 1988[84] and *The Assurance of Things Hoped For: A Theology
of Christian Faith* in 1994.[85]

In all of these books Dulles approached the questions both with
openness to engaging with the complexities presented by theologians from
different interpretive positions and from the standpoint of the Rules for
Thinking with the Church.[86] With this practice, he exemplified the tensions
at the heart of the Ignatian ecclesial disposition. In *The Resilient Church*
he stated: "Unlike many ecclesiastical conservatives, I hold that adaptation
need not be a form of capitulation to the world, but that an adapting
church should be able to herald the Christian message with greater power
and impact." On the other hand he indicated: "Unlike certain liberals, I am
deeply concerned that the church, in its efforts at adaptation, should avoid
imitating the fashions of the non-believing world and should have the
courage to be different. Difference is not to be cultivated for its own sake
but is to be fearlessly accepted when Christ and the Gospel so require."[87]

Dulles was consistently opposed to polarization which he saw as
destructive for the Church. In his later volume *A Church to Believe In:
Discipleship and the Dynamics of Freedom*, Dulles explored polarities
which are built into the very nature of the Church such as "personal charism
and the authority of office; religious freedom and submission to God's law;

---

have become more cautious in my statements, emphasizing the continuity of church teachings.
There might be statements, he continued, in *Survival*, 'that I would want to retract today.'"
Cited in Carey, *Avery Cardinal Dulles SJ*, 613 fn. 22.

[82] This was an attempt by Dulles "to appraise and carry forward the theological work of
Catholic ecclesiology in the decade since the Council."

[83] "In the normal, naïve condition of faith, no distinction is made between the Church as
subject and object of faith. This is what I mean to imply by the title *A Church to Believe
In*. I intend a further implication. In many quarters today the question asked is, can we and
ought we to believe in the Church? Is the Church really credible? ... I address the problem of
credibility. How can the Church be recognized as the (or a) true Church? How can it teach
more credibly than it does? If it does not take pains to keep itself credible, the Church can
become a countersign of Christ. It can become an obstacle rather than a help to faith." Avery
Dulles, S.J., *A Church to Believe In: Discipleship and the Dynamics of Freedom* (New York:
Crossroad, 1982), ix.

[84] In which he pointedly stated "Vatican II embodies greater corporate wisdom and theological
maturity than the work of most private theologians since the council." Dulles, S.J., *The
Reshaping of Catholicism*, 153 (see fn. 63).

[85] In this work Dulles "presented the biblical and traditional notions of faith, compared
and contrasted various models of faith, and offered his own constructive theology of faith
in dialogue with the tradition and other contemporary theologies of faith." Carey, *Avery
Cardinal Dulles SJ*, 477.

[86] Cf. *Spiritual Exercises* 353.

[87] Avery Dulles, S.J., *The Resilient Church: The Necessity and Limits of Adaptation* (Garden
City, NY: Doubleday, 1977), 15.

creative theology and mandatory teaching."[88] It was Dulles' consistent assertion that these tensions built into the very life of the Church need not become destructive. "Through faithful discipleship, the Church can use these tensions to build itself up as a society of truth and freedom, thus becoming a more credible sign of Christ in the world. Only a believing Church can be truly credible and only a credible Church can be a matrix of belief."[89]

Dulles' most successful book was *Models of the Church* first published in 1974. He had been asked by the publisher Doubleday to write a book addressing some of the major ecclesiological issues of the day. The book was not intended as a systematic ecclesiology but rather an indication of the different schools of thought about the Church under the titles of "models" synthesizing various biblical images and historical theological paradigms. From the early 1970s he was sure the mystery of the Church could not be contained under any one of the particular models. He spoke of it as "an introduction that might be called a 'dialectics.'"[90] Although some readers of this work thought Dulles was calling them to make a choice of a particular model this was very far from his intention. Rather, he was endeavoring to indicate that all the models had both strengths and weaknesses and that it would be a mistake to opt exclusively for one. In later revisions of this book Dulles tried to bring greater clarity to his earlier work. Certainly, in later years there is no ambiguity in his work. Dulles himself was able to hold different models in a creative tension and allow the experiences of the Church to inform—in different ways—the actions of the people of God. Such a position involved a very dynamic understanding of the Church and continued to allow for the movement of the Holy Spirit ever at work within the Church.

The Centrality of Christ

A life centered on Christ was, as we have seen, crucial to Dulles' understanding of himself both as a Jesuit and as a theologian. He considered the theologian's task was to listen to the wisdom of scripture and tradition and from these two sources to seek further understanding, and possibly formulate a new paradigm. "In my theological explorations I have attempted to retrieve what is best in the tradition, to reject one-sided opinions, and contribute to the formation of a fruitful consensus."[91] The

---

[88] Dulles, S.J., *A Church to Believe In*, x.
[89] Ibid.
[90] Letter, Dulles to John M. McDermott, July 21, 1987, Dulles Papers Fordham University. Cited in Patrick W. Carey, *Avery Cardinal Dulles SJ: A Model Theologian, 19182008*, (New York and Mahwah, NJ: Paulist Press, 2010), 253.
[91] Avery Dulles, S.J., *A Testimonial to Grace*, 119.

essential reality of the Church was for him a matter of revealed truth as a body conjoined to Christ and therefore he considered it needed constantly to be correcting its vision by reference to scripture and the tradition. But the Church is also a dynamic reality as it changes its manner of being and acting from place to place and from age to age.[92]

Dulles considered that the vision of the Church as a community of disciples was very congruent with the ordinary experience of most Catholics. In this focus on discipleship, Dulles recalled the importance of the disciples learning from the Lord in their daily encounters with him. Thus, a growing intimacy with Christ was for Dulles an essential ingredient in being a member of the Church. For him it was the response to the call of Christ. Discipleship he saw as being both a personal response and a costly response moving individuals away from being self-referential to becoming true followers of the risen Christ. Since Christ's body is the Church then disciples are, by their very calling, integral members of the Church. To be a disciple then is to be under authority, to become aware of the Church as both *Spouse of Christ and Mother*, and to respond with the intimacy of affection and the obedience of a disciple.[93] Alongside this understanding of discipleship, Dulles also understood the Church as a communion (*koinonia, communion*). He saw this as an ecumenically fruitful category, and one which had been endorsed by the conciliar fathers at Vatican II.[94]

In addition to his own published work, as we have seen, Dulles served as a theologian on a number of committees for the US National Conference of Catholic Bishops in the areas of doctrine and ecumenism. This was all in accord with his understanding that theology and the work of a theologian always has an ecclesial character. It is within the Church that the work of theology takes place, and it is for the Church that it is undertaken. Thus he was able to state: "I have always tried to make myself available to the

---

[92] In a lecture given in 1992 Dulles stated: "The Church, in its doctrinal heritage and sacraments, has unique resources for raising its members above the sordid quest for pleasure, wealth, and power, and for restraining the drives of hedonism, ambition, and pride that everywhere threaten civil peace and order. Among sincere practicing Christians, God's grace can work wonders, as we know from the example of saints who have heroically sacrificed themselves for the sake of others." "Religion and the Transformation of Politics," McGinley Lecture, October 6, 1992. Cited in Avery Dulles, S.J., *Church and Society: The Laurence J. McGinley Lectures 1988–2007* (New York: Fordham University Press, 2008), 126.

[93] Dulles explores these ideas in much more fulsome detail in Dulles, S.J., *A Church to Believe In*.

[94] "The Extraordinary Synod of Bishops, which was convened at Rome in 1985 to reflect on the significance of Vatican II, asserted in its Final Report: 'The ecclesiology of communion is the central and fundamental idea in the Council's documents.' The Congregation for the Doctrine of the Faith, in a letter of May 28, 1992, added that the concept of communion 'is very suitable for expressing the core of the mystery of the Church and can certainly be a key for the renewal of Catholic ecclesiology.'" "The Church as Communion," McGinley Lecture, March 31, 1993. Cited in Dulles, S.J., *Church and Society*, 129–30.

hierarchical leadership when it has sought assistance from theologians."[95] In this way we can see exemplified in Dulles' writings and his consistent availability to serve the magisterium an extrinsic practice of the Ignatian ecclesial disposition and at times this was clearly indicative of his own interiorizing of the Rules for Thinking, Judging, and Feeling with the Church.

He saw the need in the 1980s to refocus on the nature and function of the magisterium without denying what he had previously written about the teaching role of theologians. Dulles felt that particularly in the United States Catholics "had serious misgivings about the very idea of an authoritative Magisterium."[96] Although Francis A. Sullivan, S.J. had written a standard work on this subject published in 1983,[97] Dulles was invited to make his own contribution and he wrote *Magisterium,* published in 2007 for Catholics who wanted to understand more about the authoritative trans-mission of the faith within the Catholic Church. For Dulles it was obvious that there was a need for "an official or hierarchical magisterium."[98] He asserted that in their prophetic role, hierarchical authorities "speak not in their own name but on behalf of God, whose word they transmit with whatever explanations may be necessary."[99] He also emphasized that "although the teaching function in the church is shared by others—parents, religious educators, and professional theologians—it is authoritative only in the hierarchical magisterium, which possesses the charism of the teaching office."[100]

A very significant publication while Dulles was at the Catholic University of America in Washington DC was his *Models of Revelation.*[101] Within this work Dulles clearly affirmed the predominantly symbolic character of revelation without minimizing the historical and doctrinal aspects that have such prominence in Catholic teaching. In this way Dulles managed to give fresh insight into the understanding of revelation, while clearly maintaining Catholic understanding of doctrine and tradition. This stood in stark contrast to those theologians who emphasized a subjectivist view of symbol rooted in a contemporary understanding of the importance of subjective experience. Dulles understood that experience can be very ambiguous and

---

[95] Dulles, S.J., *A Testimonial to Grace,* 121.

[96] Carey, *Avery Cardinal Dulles SJ,* 550. He continues: "Popular and theological dissent to magisterial statements, furthermore, and a lack of knowledge of the degrees of authority within the magisterial statements made it opportune to clarify the Catholic understanding of magisterium." Ibid.

[97] Francis A. Sullivan, S.J., *Magisterium: Teaching Authority in the Catholic Church* (New York: Paulist Press, 1983)

[98] Carey, *Avery Cardinal Dulles SJ,* 550.

[99] Avery Dulles, S.J., *Magisterium: Teacher and Guardian of the Faith* (Naples, FL: Ave Maria University, 2007), 2, 4, 5.

[100] Carey, *Avery Cardinal Dulles SJ,* 551.

[101] Avery Dulles, S.J., *Models of Revelation* (Garden City, NY: Doubleday, 1983).

dependent on the prevalent mentality within any historical period. Indeed, he emphasized that, "one of the most persistent temptations of theology is excessive accommodation to the tastes and fashions of the day."[102] In his later work *The Assurance of Things Hoped For: A Theology of Christian Faith Assurance,* published in 1994, he took up precisely in this area Hans Urs von Balthasar's criticism of Karl Rahner's transcendental theology, "for being too anthropocentric, too much focused on the subjective component of faith."[103]

This stance of a critical—though not negative—attitude toward the dominant secular culture, Dulles based on his understanding of Ignatius Loyola's principle of *agere contra.* This was a principle of acting against whatever may seem to be drawing one away from faithfulness to Christ or Christ's body the hierarchical Church. In the face of such temptation Ignatius asserted that the individual should do the exact opposite of what a worldly spirit might be suggesting. Again the all-important understanding of how Christ is intimately conjoined to the Church is of fundamental importance. In *The Catholicity of The Church*[104] Dulles built on his earlier work on the Church and surveyed how the dimensions of 'catholicity' came together in the Roman Catholic Church. He contended that: "the structures of Catholicism are providentially instituted to promote and safeguard the catholicity of the Church and of the Christian faith."[105]

In the following decade Dulles published *The Craft of Theology*[106] which involved a series of essays on theological methods. He endeavored to show how his work on revelation and on the Church could establish a theological method that was both faithfully Catholic and at the same time open to development. This was an endeavor to address once more the vexed question of the relationship between theological dissent as he interpreted it and the magisterium as a methodological issue. One consistent principle throughout the work is that the theologian belongs to a living community of faith which is the Church. It is within this living community that the theologian works, and it is to the Church that the theologian submits the conclusions of any work undertaken. It is both the privilege and responsibility of the theologian, to be accountable to the Church. It is also the way in which the theologian may experience that intimacy with Christ and

---

[102] Dulles, *A Testimonial to Grace,* 127.

[103] Carey, *Avery Cardinal Dulles SJ,* 478. He continues: "By 1994, Dulles no longer spoke, as he had in 1983 in *Models of Revelation,* of the 'dialectical balance' in Rahner's notions of transcendental and categorical revelation. ... Dulles remarked to a fellow theologian in 1997 that 'my emphasis falls less on the religious question of how we get to God [as with Karl Rahner and David Tracy] than on the relational question of how God gets to us.'" Ibid., 479.

[104] Avery Dulles, S.J., *The Catholicity of the Church* (Oxford: Clarendon, 1985).

[105] Indeed it was Dulles' assertion that "Without these structures neither the purity nor the fullness of Christianity could be assured." Ibid., 179.

[106] Avery Dulles, S.J., *The Craft of Theology: From Symbol to System* (New York: Crossroad, 1992).

the Church that Ignatius depicts in terms of the Church as both *Spouse of Christ* and *Mother*. "In his later years, he advised theologians that docility and obedience brought one closer to Christ and that dissent, though periodically justifiable, should be "rare, reluctant and respectful."[107]

The Local and Universal Church

In July 2000, Dulles wrote an article for *America*—the Jesuit magazine—entitled "The Papacy for a Global Church."[108] This followed a series of published articles outlining a debate between Cardinal Walter Kaspar and Cardinal Joseph Ratzinger where the two discussed whether the local Church or the universal Church has priority, and by implication, which has the greater role and influence. In simplified terms, Cardinal Kasper asserted unequivocally that the diocesan or local Church came first and is of primary importance while Cardinal Ratzinger held that the universal Church was prior both historically and ontologically.[109] Put perhaps even more simply, Cardinal Kasper was seeking a more decentralized authority while Cardinal Ratzinger was seeking to assert a more centralized Roman authority. Eventually Dulles was drawn into the debate. He took the position of Cardinal Ratzinger that the universal Church is primary both historically and ontologically and claimed that it holds responsibility for the particular. Dulles wrote:

> According to Vatican II [*Lumen Gentium*] the bishop receives his office of government directly from Christ through the sacrament of ordination, but ... the bishop cannot govern a particular diocese unless he is duly appointed by canonical mission and remains in hierarchical communion with the college of bishops and its head, the bishop of Rome.[110]

What Dulles stressed in his argument is the delicate tension that holds between a bishop receiving his office from Christ but working within the structures of the Church. The bishop is appointed canonically by the Pope, but remains continually in communion with both other bishops and the bishop of Rome out of a localized situation. In this way, there is both equality and hierarchy insofar as communion with the bishop of Rome is the key term—not subservience. In addition to this Dulles wrote: "Cardinal Kasper ... would certainly agree that the Catholic Church must be on

---

107 Carey, *Avery Cardinal Dulles SJ: A Model Theologian, 1918–2008*, 423.
108 Avery Dulles, S.J., "The Papacy for a Global Church," *America*, July 15, 2000.
109 By the very nature of its being as Catholic Church the universal Church had priority.
110 Avery Dulles, S.J., "The Papacy for a Global Church," *First Things*, March 2001.

guard against degenerating into a loose federation of local or national churches."[111]

Dulles gave added emphasis to the views expressed above when he wrote "The Future of the Papacy"[112] which was published in the magazine *First Things* the following year.

> As the first Pope after the end of Vatican II, Pope Paul VI had a delicate task of faithfully implementing the Council in the face of resistance from obdurate conservatives and radical progressives. While seeking to keep the reactionary Archbishop Marcel Lefebvre from falling into schism, he authorized liturgical reforms in the spirit of Vatican II, including greater use of the vernacular.[113]

What the above citation illustrates is the way in which Pope Paul VI both saw the diverse opposition groups and the needs of the universal Church. It is clear that Dulles recognized the unique perspective of the Pope. Indeed, he claimed that it is the Pope who both sees the picture of the universal Church and must hold it steady amidst the conflicting demands of both conservatives and radical progressives. With a perspective that transcends the individual or local Churches, the Pope's responsibility is to move the mission of the Church forward with a universality of vision. Dulles' view then is very similar to that of Ignatius when he placed himself and the embryonic Society at the service and disposal of the Pope. Both men knew that the Holy Father has a vision of the Church that is altogether more overarching than the vision any other individual can see, and both Ignatius and Dulles trusted in the judgment of the Pope.[114]

---

[111] Ibid.

[112] Dulles, S.J., "The Future of the Papacy," *First Things*. This was the Erasmus Lecture of 2000.

[113] Ibid.

[114] "Since Vatican II the principal drama within the Catholic Church has been the dialectical tension between centralizing and decentralizing tendencies. The decentralizers tend to see themselves as progressives and want to depict their adversaries as restorationists, but the opposite case can equally well be made. Those who want to reinstate the conditions of patristic Christianity tend to be nostalgic and anachronistic. In the end, the question should not be posed as either or. Precisely because of the increased activity of particular churches and conferences, Rome is required to exercise greater vigilance than ever, lest the unity of the Church be jeopardized. The global character of the Catholic Church today, together with the rapidity of modern communications, makes many new demands on the papal office. ... The Petrine office, as it has developed since Vatican II, has a unique capacity to hold all local and regional churches in dialogue while reaching out in loving service to all." Dulles, S.J., "The Papacy for a Global Church," *America*. Again Dulles emphasizes that the role between centralized and decentralized power—or the dialectic between the magisterial and the individual—is not an issue of one or the other; rather, the two, as is the overarching point, must always be held in tension.

Conclusion

Dulles spent most of his time after Vatican II, as we have already seen, trying to give clarity amidst the conflict of interpretations in the decades after the Council. In particular he was concerned about those theologians who emphasized the novelty of the Council without also emphasizing the continuity with the teaching of earlier Popes and Councils. He had seen his task in different ways as reiterating the importance of the Church as a visible society of divine institution subsisting in the Roman Catholic communion. For him the authority of Christ continues in the Church through the Popes and Bishops who teach in Christ's name, govern as Christ's representatives and participate in Christ's priestly office through the celebration of the sacraments.

Within the United States, Dulles perceived an increased polarization as some Catholics saw the Church as more of a human institution that could change its teaching and sacramental worship to adapt to changing circumstances. Others looked to a form of democratization of the Church and would see the Church as a voluntary association of individuals sharing a common project. By contrast other Catholics who adhered to the teachings of the Church were often labeled traditionalist or conservative. In some cases such conservatism can become an ideology. Some traditionalists impugned the teaching of bishops and Popes and rejected the teaching of Vatican II. The growth of polarization between liberals and conservatives in the Church Dulles saw as a diminishment of the life of the body of Christ.

Dulles spent the majority of his later years trying to reach out across this divide. For him the Catholic Church, despite this polarization, continued to be both "a communion of tradition and authority and open to dialogue and progress."[115] It is maintained in this communion of life by the action of the Holy Spirit who makes present within the Church the intimate experience of God in the Church's life of prayer and worship. Like Ignatius, Dulles was convinced that the Church and Christ are conjoined. Christ conferred upon the Church the Spirit of truth and maintains his presence in and through the sacraments. It is this relationship with Christ that is the foundation from which all flows. Indeed we have seen in this consideration of his life and work the way in which key themes of the ecclesial disposition have been revealed: the endeavor to seek God in and through all things, the prayerful rooting in a relationship with God; obedience to the hierarchical Church; and the determined following of the call of Christ the King to glorify God by a loving self-surrender into his hands.

---

[115] Dulles, S.J., *Reflections on a Theological Journey*, 137.

Assessment of Papal Authority

Dulles had a clear appreciation of the firm hierarchical structure of the Church. He likewise had a deep appreciation of Pope John Paul II's leadership of this structure.[116] He saw a very creative leadership adapted to the contemporary world situation. He also had a deep appreciation of the work of Cardinal Joseph Ratzinger who later became Pope Benedict XVI. "Cardinal Ratzinger, one of the ablest living theologians, has shown firmness and moderation in exercising his role of vigilance as prefect of the Congregation for the Doctrine of the Faith."[117] It is to these two pontiffs and to Pope Francis that we now turn to trace the way in which the ecclesial disposition of Ignatius Loyola has resonance within the contemporary papacy.

---

[116] "Pope John Paul II, who understands and encourages democratic institutions in secular society, shows no doubt in his own mind that the Church is a hierarchical society in which the responsible leadership lies inalienably with the Pope and the bishops, who have received their office by apostolic succession." Ibid.

[117] Ibid.

PART FOUR

The Ignatian Ecclesial Disposition and the Contemporary Papacy

Introduction

In this final part we have a change of focus. From considering different exemplars of the Ignatian ecclesial disposition, both historical and of more recent times, we now turn our attention to consider the contemporary papacy. Pope Francis, elected March 2013 as the first Jesuit pope, brought together in his own person a formed Ignatian ecclesial disposition—trained as he was in the *Spiritual Exercises* of St. Ignatius Loyola—and the responsibilities of ecclesiastical leadership both during his time as auxiliary Bishop and later Archbishop of Buenos Aires and then as Bishop of Rome and Holy Father for the universal Church. In a remarkable way we may trace a consistency and continuity of those key elements of the Ignatian ecclesial disposition resonant within the highest authority of the contemporary Roman Catholic Church.

Within the pontificates of St John Paul II and his successor Benedict XVI also we can trace some of the essential components of the ecclesial disposition. The centrality of Christ is paramount within the teaching of all these pontiffs. Christ is the way to the Father, the revelation of the mystery of the Trinity. This Trinitarian relationship also inspires a profound love for the Church. Christ as the head of the Church with whom each believer needs to seek a personal encounter. Grounded on this foundation there is present within the teaching of these three popes a consistent and coherent articulated vision of the dignity, worth and value of the human person, a revitalized theological anthropology. The pontiffs have endeavored to proclaim this dignity also through an emphasis on the distinctly gifted nature of male and female human persons and on the life-giving sanctity of the sacrament of marriage and the gift of family life both for the Church and the world.[1] Each of the popes has also raised the profile of those consecrated to priesthood and religious life and indicated the vital significance of all vocations to the Church. It is not by coincidence that new ecclesial movements have blossomed and flourished within the Church during the years of these three pontificates. At the heart of their teaching on vocation is the call to a personal encounter with Christ in prayer, an encounter that leads to deep and ongoing conversion and that impels those so converted to mission—a share in the redemptive work of Christ. These themes of prayer, conversion, and mission are also central to the promulgation of the New Evangelization, which has been a clarion call sounding through the

---

[1] It is noteworthy that all three Pontiffs have emphasized the importance of the family and both encouraged and sought means to support family. At the 2012 Synod on the New Evangelization for the Transmission of the Christian Faith, Pope Benedict saw it as important to designate the following synod to be a consideration of Family Life. The Extraordinary Synod of Bishops of October 2014 and the Ordinary Synod of Bishops of October 2015 were both focused on this theme.

years even before the election of Pope John Paul II and having a distinctive character in the proclamation of his two successors.

Common to each pope has been the singular experience of suffering: the physical decline towards death of Pope John Paul II was most clearly viewed on the international stage; the less obvious but no less pronounced patient endurance of Pope Benedict XVI in the face of diminishing energies which with extraordinary humility he acknowledged in February 2013 when he announced his resignation from the papacy. Linked with this were the many years of not just constant adverse criticism but on occasion unveiled opprobrium during his time as prefect of the Congregation for the Doctrine of the Faith. Finally the joining of a physical condition of limitation with an ongoing endurance of darkness and humiliation which has refined a deep humility of spirit in Pope Francis and caused him to incline so consistently to understand and empathize with others, particularly those who are poor and suffering.

Humility and compassion, along with a profound faith, are the qualities with which these men confronted the world and the many problems of contemporary life. It is the poor and humble Christ that Pope Francis called all Catholics to follow and this is the Christ of the *Spiritual Exercises*, the Christ of the "Two Standards" and of the "Third Kind of Humility." "In the midst of divisions and attitudes contrary to the Cross of the Lord, our security is rooted in the Word received and internalized."[2] Thinking with the Church under such a standard of discipleship is the challenge of the ecclesial disposition to the Church and the world of the twenty first century.

> The image of the church I like is that of the holy, faithful people of God. This is the definition I often use ... Belonging to a people has a strong theological value. In the history of salvation, God has saved a people. There is no full identity without belonging to a people. No one is saved alone, as an isolated individual, but God attracts us looking at the complex web of relationships that take place in the human community. God enters into this dynamic, this participation in the web of relationships.[3]

In a later address Pope Francis indicated the importance of the Church as the pilgrim people of God as one that "accompanies the journey that knows how to walk as people walk today."[4] In this way there is the possibility of "building the Church as we walk."[5]

According to Pope Francis all parts of the Church, bishops, priests, lay people, religious are together on this great pilgrimage of faith and together

---

[2] Jorge Mario Bergoglio, *In Him Alone is Our Hope: Spiritual Exercises Given to His Brother Bishops in the Manner of Saint Ignatius of Loyola*, trans. Fr. Vincent Capuano, S.J. and Andrew Matt (Canada: Pierre-Marie Dumont, 2013), 102.
[3] Interview with Antonio Spadaro, S.J., editor-in-chief, *La Civiltà Cattolica*, September 2013.
[4] Pope Francis, Address to the participants in the Plenary Assembly of the Pontifical Council for Social Communication, September 21, 2013.
[5] Ibid.

serve the mission of the Church. Facilitating the mission are the various institutional structures of the Church such as the dicasteries of the Roman Curia and the various departments that assist the Pope. In the early days of Pope Francis' pontificate he appointed a new permanent Council of eight Cardinals[6] to assist as an advisory group looking particularly at the way the governance of the Church was functioning. In a decree issued September 2013[7] making the Council permanent, the Pope stated that the function of the group was "the work of assisting me in the governance of the universal Church and drawing up a project for the revision of the apostolic constitution 'Pastor Bonus'[8] on the Roman Curia."[9]

Alongside the reforming of governance procedures for the Church, Pope Francis had a clear desire to see the Church be more actively engaged in the contemporary world and in particular to accompany those who suffer. "I see clearly that the thing the Church needs most today is the ability to heal wounds and to warm the hearts of the faithful; it needs nearness, proximity."[10] He continued by using a graphic image, "I see the Church as a field hospital after battle." For Pope Francis the primary imperative was to share the good news of salvation in Christ and the gift of God's mercy. "The most important thing is the first proclamation: Jesus Christ has saved you. And the ministers of the Church must be ministers of mercy above all."[11] This has been a theme of the early years of his Pontificate and reflected in his travels particularly to the countries of Korea, Albania, Turkey and the Holy Land in 2014, and the Philippines in 2015.

Following from this priority Pope Francis envisaged a Church as both "a mother and shepherdess."[12] He stated: "The church's ministers must be merciful, take responsibility for the people and accompany them like the good Samaritan, who washes, cleans and raises up his neighbor. This is pure Gospel. God is greater than sin. ... The ministers of the Gospel must be people who can warm the hearts of the people, who walk through the dark night with them, who know how to dialogue and to descend themselves into their people's night, into the darkness, but without getting lost."[13]

---

[6] The first members of this Council were: Cardinal Oscar Rodriguez Maradiago of Teguagalpa, Honduras (co-ordinator); Cardinal Guisseppe Bertello, president of Vatican city-state governate; Cardinal Francisco Errazuriz Ossa, retired Archbishop of Santiago, Chile; Cardinal Oswald Gracias of Bombay, India; Cardinal Reinhard Marx of Munich, Germany; Cardinal Laurent Monsengwo Pasinya of Kinshasa, Africa; Cardinal George Pell, Sydney, Australia; Cardinal Sean Patrick O'Malley, O.F.M., Boston, USA.

[7] Decree issued September 30, 2013.

[8] Pope John Paul II, Apostolic Constitution, *Pastor Bonus*, June 28, 1988. This Constitution had instituted the last major changes in the Roman Curia.

[9] Decree of September 30.

[10] Interview with Antonio Spadaro, S.J., editor-in-chief, *La Civiltà Cattolica*.

[11] Ibid.

[12] Again we have an echo of the Ignatian ecclesial disposition and an understanding of the Church as "mother".

[13] Ibid.

8

The Contextual Background to the Contemporary Papacy

John Paul II—The Third Pope of 1978

With the closing months of the reign of Pope Paul VI,[1] 1978 was the year of three Popes. Following his death on August 6, Albino Luciani, Patriarch of Venice,[2] who took the name John Paul I, was elected to succeed him on August 26. Luciano died suddenly thirty-three days later and in the ensuing conclave the Archbishop of Kraków, Karol Cardinal Wojtyla, was elected Pope on October 16. Taking the name John Paul II, his reign proved to be one of the longest in papal history, lasting almost twenty-seven years until his death on April 2, 2005.

The years between the conclusion of Vatican II in 1965 and the commencement of the papacy of Pope John Paul II were troublesome, particularly in the Western hemisphere. As we saw in previous chapters, in the United States, President John F Kennedy was assassinated in Dallas in 1963 while his brother, Senator Robert F Kennedy, was murdered in Los Angeles in 1968. That year also witnessed the assassination of the activist pastor Martin Luther King in Memphis. In Europe, there were student riots in France and Germany, and Pope Paul VI issued his encyclical *Humanae Vitae.*[3]

Countless advances in medical science were also made during these years. With the use of increased technology, the whole area of biotechnology

---

[1]Giovanni Battista Montini 1897–1978. After the death of Pope John XXIII he became Pope Paul VI on June 21, 1963 until his death August 6, 1978.

[2]Albino Luciani October 17, 1912–September 28, 1978. Born in Bellino, eighty miles north of Venice. On being elected Pope he took the name John Paul I. He was believed to have died from a heart attack.

[3]Pope Paul VI, *Humanae Vitae,* Encyclical Letter of His Holiness Pope Paul VI on the regulation of Birth, July 25, 1968. A commission initially appointed by Pope John XXIII in 1963 and expanded by Paul VI had suggested in a 1966 report to the Holy Father that artificial contraception might not be intrinsically evil. When *Humanae Vitae* was released, however, Pope Paul VI reaffirmed the traditional Catholic teaching on birth control and abortion.

flourished. The subsequent growth of bio-ethics caused Christians to begin thinking through the implications of the new developments. There arose a new questioning: about family life; about the distinctive nature of gender and about the interactions between society at both national and international levels. Within Western urban society the pace of life became increasingly frenetic with further ramifications for family and community life. In 1972, there were a series of airliner hijackings around the world. In that same year terrorist activity in Munich during the Olympic Games led to a serious loss of life.[4] In 1973 a major oil crisis was precipitated causing oil prices to rise dramatically, and fuelling increasing costs of most other products requiring transportation. Finally in 1978 Karol Josef Cardinal Wojtyla was elected the 264th Pope and the first non-Italian since Pope Adrian VI[5] in 1522. Amidst a world seemingly in turmoil, a virtually unknown Polish figure became the head of the Roman Catholic Church.

The Witness of Suffering and Death

In 1981, only three years after being elected Pope, John Paul II suffered an assassination attempt. On May 13, a young Turk named Mehmet Ali Agca[6] fired at point-blank range at the Pope who was circling St. Peter's Square.[7] The bullet did considerable damage and the procedures taken to save his life had severe repercussions.[8] Certainly, the Pope returned to work earlier than his doctors would have liked. The Pope was afflicted by Parkinson's disease in his later years and his increased fragility meant that he often saved his energy for his public appearances; in his final years he maintained an increasing silence within the papal apartments.

In one singular dimension his energy always revived and that was in his engagement with young people. From his earliest times as priest and bishop he had sought out young people and they had responded to him.

---

[4]The 1972 Munich Olympic games, where eight Palestinian terrorists killed two members of the Israeli Olympic team and took nine others hostage. In the eventual gun battle all the remaining hostages were killed along with five of the terrorists.

[5]Pope Adrian VI 1459–1523. Pope from August 1522–September 1523.

[6]A Turkish assassin who had previously murdered a journalist in 1979, he escaped from a Turkish prison before attempting the assassination of Pope John Paul II in 1981.

[7]According to his secretary Fr. Stanislaw Dziwisz, "The bullet passed through the Holy Father's body, wounding him in the stomach, the right elbow and the left index finger. The bullet fell between the Pope and me. I heard two more shots, and two people standing near us were wounded." Cited in Edward Stourton, *John Paul II: Man of History* (London and New York: Hodder & Stoughton, 2006), 206.

[8]The Pope had lost more than six pints of blood so a massive transfusion was required. Later it was discovered that one of these transfusions had carried a virus that continued to trouble him in later life.

He inaugurated "World Youth Day" in 1986[9] which attracted thousands from all around the world. The last of these gatherings during his pontif-icate—in Toronto in 2002—found him very fragile, but still drawing his energy from the affection of the young people who gathered to greet him and to be present for his celebration of Mass. They seemed to sense the deep love that this frail elderly man had both for God and for them.[10] It is this loving service, even to his death, that was recognized by so many young, and not so young, people in the last years of Pope John Paul II. It was estimated that tens of thousands of people, amongst whom were great numbers of young people, gathered in Rome on the evening of April 2, 2005 to pray and keep vigil for him as he died. There were also many present on the day of his funeral Mass, swelling the enormous crowd of some three million people who had flocked to Rome to bid farewell to a beloved Pastor.

Cardinal Joseph Ratzinger—Theologian and Papal Aide

In the same year as the assassination attempt on his life, 1981, Pope John Paul II appointed Cardinal Joseph Ratzinger to what the latter described as a most uncomfortable post, namely the Prefect of the Congregation for the Doctrine of the Faith. His new responsibility was that of promul-gating and safeguarding the doctrine of faith and practices throughout the Catholic world. This was how Pope John Paul II redefined the role of the Congregation in 1988. Ratzinger came to this post as a Vatican outsider with a prodigious energy for work, and he oversaw the promulgation of the New Code of Canon Law in 1983. During his time in this office he faced the challenges of dealing with the Anglican Church and the ordination of women.[11] He also dealt with a number of high profile theologians including

---

[9]In 1984 in Rome there was an international youth meeting where the Pope presented and entrusted to the young people the World Youth Day cross (April 22). In 1985 at an interna-tional youth meeting on the occasion of the International Year of Youth the Pope addressed an Apostolic Letter to the Youth of the World (March 31). December of that year the Pope announced the Institution of World Youth Days. The Bishops were invited to schedule an annual youth event on Palm Sunday in the dioceses and an International event took place every two to three years thereafter.

[10]Cf. *Spiritual Exercises* 370.

[11]The ordination of women within the Anglican communion has been a controversial move. By 2012, twenty-eight out of the thirty-eight Provinces of the Communion had agreed to ordain women as priests and seventeen had decided in favor of women bishops. The Church of England authorized the ordination of women in 1992 and began ordaining them in 1994. The first woman Bishop in the Anglican Communion was Barbara Harris, ordained in Massachusetts in 1989.

Hans Kung,[12] Edward Schillebeeckx,[13] Charles Curran,[14] and Leonardo Boff.[15] In 1985 he published a book length interview, *The Ratzinger Report*[16], which became an international bestseller. He introduced the New Catholic Catechism in 1992 and contributed significantly to the document *Dominus Iesus*[17] in August 2000.

The Formation of Cardinal Ratzinger

Joseph Ratzinger had taught theology at the University of Bonn[18] from 1959 until 1963; in the University of Münster from 1963 to 1966; in the University of Tübingen[19] from 1966 to 1969. In 1968 a wave of student

---

[12] Hans Küng, born 1928. Swiss Catholic priest and theologian appointed by Pope John XXIII as a *peritus* at Vatican II. In the late 1960s he publicly rejected the Church's understanding of papal infallibility. Since 1995 he has been President of the Foundation for a Global Ethic.

[13] Edward Cornelis Florentius Alfonsus Schillebeeckx, 1914–2009. He was a Belgian Roman Catholic theologian. He taught at the Catholic University in Nijmegen. He was a member of the Dominican Order. He queried the relevance to the modern age of church teaching on the virgin birth and resurrection.

[14] Charles Curran, born 1934 in the USA, is a Catholic priest and moral theologian. In 1968 he came to be known as a spokesman for theologians who dissented from the teaching of *Humanae Vitae*. The Congregation for the Doctrine of the Faith contested his position on: a right to public dissent from the ordinary Magisterium; the indissolubility of consummated sacramental marriage, abortion, euthanasia, masturbation, artificial contraception; premarital intercourse and homosexual acts. In a letter to Curran dated July 25, 1986 from the Congregation for the Doctrine of the Faith, under the signature of Joseph Cardinal Ratzinger it states: "This Congregation calls attention to the fact that you have taken your dissenting positions as a professor of theology in an ecclesiastical faculty at a pontifical university. In its letter of September 17, 1985, to you, it was noted that 'the authorities of the church cannot allow the present situation to continue in which the inherent contradiction is prolonged that one who is to teach in the name of the church in fact denies her teaching.' In light of your repeated refusal to accept what the church teaches and in light of its mandate to promote and safeguard the church's teaching on faith and morals throughout the Catholic world, this Congregation, in agreement with the Congregation for Catholic education sees no alternative now but to advise the most reverend chancellor that you will no longer be considered suitable nor eligible to exercise the function of a professor of Catholic theology." Curran is currently teaching at the Southern Methodist University in Dallas Texas.

[15] Leonardo Boff was born in Brazil in 1938. He became a Franciscan priest and one of the most outspoken advocates of liberation theology. He was very critical of Church leadership and outspoken in his political opinions. He eventually left the Franciscans and the priesthood.

[16] Cardinal Joseph Ratzinger, *The Ratzinger Report, An Exclusive Interview on the State of the Church with Vitterio Messori* (San Francisco: Ignatius Press, 1985).

[17] Dominus Iesus, Declaration of the Congregation for the Doctrine of the Faith on the Unicity and Salvific Universality of Jesus Christ and the Church. August 2000.

[18] He was Professor of Fundamental Theology.

[19] Here he was Professor of Dogmatic Theology. His appointment was strongly supported by Professor Hans Küng. Ratzinger had originally met Küng at a conference of theologians in Innsbruck in 1957. In his autobiography *Milestones*, Ratzinger states that he reviewed Küng's doctoral work on Karl Barth and "I had many questions to ask of this book, because,

unrest swept through Europe and Marxism became the dominant intellectual system at Tübingen affecting students and faculty. Ratzinger later said of this time: "There was an instrumentalization by ideologies that were tyrannical, brutal, and cruel. That experience made it clear to me that the abuse of faith had to be resisted precisely if one wanted to uphold the will of the Council."[20] In the face of this hostility Ratzinger returned to Bavaria and to the University of Regensburg[21] where he taught from 1969 until 1977 becoming successively Dean and then Vice President.

During this time he also attended the sessions[22] of the Second Vatican Council. Having been selected as a theological advisor by Cardinal Frings of Cologne, he was named a *peritus*—or official theological advisor at the end of the first session of the Council. Highly regarded as a younger brilliant theologian, he contributed to discussions on the Constitution on Divine Revelation—*Dei Verbum*. He stressed that the Church was a necessary aspect of revelation; it was not a separate entity but inseparable from the living God. He saw the Church as a living organism inseparable from Christ.[23] Resonance with the Ignatian ecclesial disposition is clear.

During the time of the Second Vatican Council, Ratzinger produced an alternate text with Karl Rahner, on the issue of the relationship between Scripture and Tradition[24]—this was accepted by the German bishops. In

---

although its theological style was not my own, I had read it with pleasure and gained respect for its author, whose winning openness and straightforwardness I quite liked. A good personal relationship was thus established, even if soon after ... a rather serious argument began between us about the theology of the Council." Joseph Ratzinger, *Milestones: Memoirs 1927–1977* (San Francisco: Ignatius Press, 1998), 135.

[20] Joseph Ratzinger, *Salt of the Earth: Christianity and The Catholic Church at the End of the Millennium: An Interview with Peter Seewald* (San Francisco: Ignatius Press, 1997).

[21] Historically known as Ratisbon.

[22] He was present at all four sessions of the Council.

[23] Cf. *Spiritual Exercises* 353.

[24] "With regard to revelation, Ratzinger agreed that the preliminary schema was unacceptable and should be withdrawn. At the request of Cardinal Frings, he wrote an alternative text, which was then reworked with the help of Rahner. Yves Congar, though generally sympathetic, called the Rahner-Ratzinger paper far too personal to have any chance of being adopted and criticized it for taking too little account of the good work in the preparatory schemas. Gerald Fogarty calls it a barely mitigated synthesis of Rahner's systematic theology. Notwithstanding the rejection of their schema, Rahner and Ratzinger had some input into the new text prepared by the mixed commission named by Pope John XXIII. Both were appointed as consulters to the sub-commission revising the new text. Ratzinger joined with the German bishops and his fellow experts in getting the idea of the Church as sacrament deeply inscribed into the constitution. Ratzinger was also appointed to a team for redrafting the schema on the Church's missionary activity for the last session of the council. He worked closely with Congar in defining the theological foundation of missions, a theme on which the two easily found agreement. Congar in his diary characterizes Ratzinger as "reasonable, modest, disinterested, and very helpful." He credits Ratzinger with coming up with the definition of missionary activity that was accepted and also with proposing the inclusion of a section on ecumenism in the document. At discussions of *Gaudium et Spes* in September 1965, Ratzinger voiced many of the criticisms that would later appear in his books and articles: The schema was too

the course of this work, Ratzinger realized that he and Rahner, despite reaching similar conclusions, were operating from very different premises. Ratzinger had been trained in a historical reading of scripture and the Church Fathers, and always approached questions from a systematic theological stance.[25] Rahner had been trained in speculative and philosophical theology with, perhaps, a lesser role for scripture and the Church Fathers. The division between the two approaches became clear at the Council, "even though it still took a while for our parting of the ways to become outwardly visible."[26]

After the first session of the Vatican Council, Ratzinger became increasingly concerned about what he saw as a perception that everything was open to revision and that the Vatican Council was in some way a "Church parliament." He endeavored to sound a warning signal about this in a talk at the University of Münster exploring true and false renewal within the Church, but few noticed.[27] He raised similar concerns at the Bamberg Catholic Congress in 1966. In a wry comment he noted: "The tabernacle is detached from the High Altar, and there may be good reasons for that. But one should feel uncomfortable by seeing its place taken by the chair of the celebrant, expressing thus in the liturgy a clericalism which is much worse than that of before."[28] He was also concerned to note that "mere

---

naturalistic and unhistorical, took insufficient notice of sin and its consequences, and was too optimistic about human progress." Cardinal Avery Dulles, "From Ratzinger to Benedict," *First Things*, February 2006.

[25] "In 1965, during the final year of the Council's work, Joseph Ratzinger (again, together with Karl Rahner) published volume 25 of the *Quaestiones Disputatae*, under the title of "Offenbarung und Überlieferung" (Revelation and Tradition, QD 17). His own [first] piece is also entitled, "The Question of the Concept of Tradition: A Provisional Response." The question that sets the tone is of "… the way the word of revelation uttered in Christ remains present in history and comes to man." [4] Joseph Ratzinger begins with an analysis of the way the question was put in the Reformation period, then works out fundamental theses regarding the relation between revelation and tradition, and thus interprets the concept of tradition in the documents of Trent. In his concluding reflection, he sums up his findings: "We are faced with a concept according to which revelation does indeed have [its 'once-for-all' character], insofar as it took place in historical facts, but also has its constant 'today,' insofar as what once happened remains forever living and effective in the faith of the Church, and Christian faith never refers merely to what is past; rather, it refers equally to what is present and what is to come." Cardinal Joseph Ratzinger, *God's Word: Scripture, Tradition, Office*, trans. Henry Taylor (San Francisco: Ignatius Press, 2008).

[26] Ratzinger, *Milestones*, 128–9.

[27] At a lecture at the University of Bonn in January 1963 Ratzinger had expressed his joy that the Council Fathers in November 1962 had by an overwhelming vote of 2,162 to 46 voted to adopt Chapter 1 of the schema on the liturgy. He stated: "It was a decision that augured well for the future, and was at the same time a very encouraging sign that the strength of the movement for renewal was greater than anyone had ventured to hope." Joseph Ratzinger, "The First Session," *The Furrow*, May 1963, 267–88. Yet very soon he became deeply disturbed about the various experimentations carried out in the name of the Council particularly in the area of the liturgy.

[28] Joseph Ratzinger, "Catholicism After the Council," *The Furrow*, January 1967, 3–23.

archaism does not help matters along but neither does mere modernism."[29] His health began to suffer as a result of the stress of moving to and from Rome for the Council sessions and also due to the swirling passions on the Council floor. It was in these latter years that he published his *Introduction to Christianity*.[30] This was the first book to make Joseph Ratzinger known outside the world of the academy, and this work has clear resonances with the Ignatian ecclesial disposition, particularly in Chapter 2 of the book entitled *The Ecclesiastical Form of Faith*.

With the support of Hans Küng, whose doctoral dissertation on Karl Barth he had read, Ratzinger was appointed to teach dogma at the University of Tübingen. This move led him closer to his native Bavaria. While Ratzinger enjoyed Tübingen, two growing concerns made his situation very difficult. Firstly, he disagreed with Hans Küng's interpretation of the Vatican Council and then in 1968, Ratzinger faced the student disruption that appeared to infiltrate many universities throughout Europe. In Tübingen, the manifestation of this disaffection was in the ideological paradigm embraced by students and teachers. There was a focusing on the model of radical Marxist revolution that influenced the whole university. It even appeared that the theology department itself was becoming a center of Marxist agitation. Ratzinger, who was Dean of Theology at the time, vigorously resisted this Marxist influence, joining forces with Lutheran theologians in order to form a more effective resistance.

In the wake of this agitation, Ratzinger decided to accept the offer of a position at the University of Regensburg in his native Bavaria. Here the environment was more peaceful, there was less of a Marxist influence and, in addition, he was closer to his brother. Shortly after his arrival at Regensburg, Ratzinger was appointed to the International Theological Commission.[31] He met Hans Urs von Balthasar during this time and

---

[29] In addition he stated: "Among theologians, there is a certain archaism with the wish to restore the classical form of the Roman liturgy as it was before the additions of the Carolingian age and of the Middle Ages. One does not ask oneself, 'What should the liturgy be like?' but, rather, 'What was it like once?' While the past gives us an indispensable aid to solve the problems of our age, it is not the criterion on which one should found the reform purely and simply. Knowing how Gregory the Great proceeded [to do] is good, but it does not force one to do the same. With such archaisms, the road towards legitimacy [in liturgical reform] has often been destroyed. ... Must every Mass be truly celebrated turned towards the people? Is it that important to be able to see the face of the priest? Isn't it often good to think of him as a Christian with the others and that, consequently, he has all reasons to turn with them towards God and by this act say Our Father with them?" Ibid.

[30] Joseph Ratzinger, *Introduction to Christianity* (London: Burns & Oates, 1969).

[31] The International Theological Commission was established by Pope Paul VI on April 11, 1969. It consists of up to thirty theologians from different parts of the world who are appointed by the Pope at the suggestion of the Prefect for the Congregation for the Faith for five-year terms which can be renewed. They meet once a year in Rome for approximately a week and advise the Magisterium and particularly the Congregation for the Doctrine of the Faith.

they became lifelong friends. Along with Hans Urs von Balthasar, Henri de Lubac,[32] Louis Bouyer,[33] and Jorge Medina[34] he helped to set up the journal *Communio*.[35] This publication challenged the "progressive" journal *Concilium,* which Hans Küng supported by his contributions. Within *Communio* there was a clear emphasis on the importance of the authority of the Pope. In this way we see a clear consonance with the ecclesial disposition of Ignatius.

Ratzinger became Archbishop of Munich and Freising following the death of Cardinal Döpfner[36] in 1976. One month later he was named a Cardinal. Cardinal Ratzinger had a clear vision of the Church's role in the world. He felt it was important to rediscover the true spirit of Vatican II, a spirit marked by unity in the Church rather than dissension. He saw the crisis within the Church as being primarily a crisis of ecclesiology marked by different understandings of the very nature of the Church. To take one example, with regard to the model of the Church as the "Body of Christ," which draws its authority from Chapter 12 of the first letter of St. Paul to the Corinthians[37] where the theme of the Body of Christ is explored, Cardinal Ratzinger asserts that the Body of Christ is not only a sociological reality that describes those gathered together for the Sunday Eucharist but also a supernatural reality that is rooted in the very life of God.

The Church is not a democratic reality but a sacramental one and thus a hierarchical one. "The Church does not exhaust herself in the 'collective' of the believers: being the 'Body of Christ' she is much more than the simple sum of her members."[38] The Church is not a club, nor a party, nor a religious state, nor a human construction. The Church is the Body of Christ. There is a divine reality present that is operative at the most profound level of each human member of the Church. Together, by the grace of God, we form with Christ, his body. Here, there is a clear consonance with the ecclesial disposition of Ignatius which emphasizes that the Church is conjoined to Christ. This is its supernatural reality alongside its visible presence within numerous local Churches throughout the world. The

---

[32] See Chapter 7.

[33] Louis Bouyer, 1913–2004. He was born in Paris into a Lutheran family and became a Lutheran minister. In 1939 he converted to Roman Catholicism and became a priest of the Oratory. He was a renowned theologian particularly in the areas of liturgy and spirituality. He was a *peritus* at Vatican II and a confirmed ecumenical theologian. He served two terms on the International Theological Commission.

[34] Jorge Medina 1926, Cardinal Jorge Arturo Medina Estévez. Also a *peritus* at Vatican II, a member of the International Theological Commission and from 1998–2002 Prefect of the Congregation for Divine Worship and Discipline of the Sacraments.

[35] *Communio*: International Catholic Review.

[36] Cardinal Julius August Döpfner 1913–76, Archbishop of Munich and Freising 1961–76.

[37] 1 Cor. 12.12–30

[38] Cardinal Joseph Ratzinger, *The Ratzinger Report*, 47.

Church came into being through the will of Christ and is thus inviolable. It is a mystery, composed of human persons, but yet it is more than human. It is a body in communion with the communion of saints. Ratzinger was concerned to emphasize that the Church does not belong to humanity but to God—it is not ours but His.[39]

The unity of the Church was of real importance for Cardinal Ratzinger and this was focused in the primacy of the Pope.[40] He saw true freedom as only possible within the certitude in morals and doctrine as established by the Magisterium. The hierarchical Church guards, within the teaching authority of the Magisterium, the treasures of the faith in terms of doctrine and moral teaching. Cardinal Ratzinger was extremely wary of both secularism and relativism and, indeed, these have been concerns also within the pontificates of Pope John Paul II, Pope Benedict XVI and Pope Francis. Pope Benedict asserted that defending the Church in our contemporary age involved defending the work of Vatican II as in continuity with the tradition of the Church. Those who asserted a break with the tradition from extremes of the left or the right only encouraged the growth of factionalism.[41] "We must always bear in mind that the Church is not ours but

---

[39] "*Communio sanctorum* means to have 'holy things' in common, that is to say, the grace of the sacraments that pours forth from the dead and resurrected Christ. It is precisely this mysterious yet real bond, this union in Life, that is also the reason why the Church is not *our* Church, which we could dispose of as we please. She is, rather, *his* Church. All that which is only *our* Church is not Church in the deep sense; it belongs to her human—hence secondary, transitory—aspect." Cardinal Joseph Ratzinger, *The Ratzinger Report*, 48. Cf. *Spiritual Exercises* 353.

[40] The Primacy of Peter as the leader of the Apostles and the "rock"; upon which Jesus said he would build his Church. "Of the Petrine Office [Ratzinger] has written that its powers are circumscribed by the tradition itself. The unity of the Church, he argues, is rooted in the unity of the Episcopate, and the unity of the Episcopate requires the existence of a Bishop who is Head of the Body or College of Bishops. He sees this head as the Roman pontiff, who as the successor of Peter is a perpetual and visible source and foundation of unity. He believes that there can be no number of bishops large enough to counterbalance the decisive weight of the See of St. Peter: 'anything else would mean substituting some sort of profane arithmetic for the holy bond of tradition.' [*The Episcopate and the Primacy* (New York: Herder & Herder 1962), 61] ... The primacy of the Bishop of Rome and the Episcopal College are proper elements of the universal Church that are 'not derived from the particularity of the Churches,' but are nevertheless interior to each one particular Church from 'outside' as it were, but as belonging already to the essence of each particular Church from 'within.' [Letter to the Bishops of the Catholic Church on Some Aspects of the Church Understood as Communion, Document of the Congregation for the Doctrine of the Faith, May 28, 1992, art. 13]." Tracey Rowland, *Ratzinger's Faith: The Theology of Pope Benedict XVI* (Oxford: Oxford University Press, 2008), 93.

[41] This theme of continuity is one which reappeared in the transition between the papacy of Benedict XVI and that of Pope Francis. Despite many media attempts to emphasize discontinuity and fragmentation, Pope Francis continued to underline continuity in doctrine and moral teaching with a freshness of style and a rich use of symbolic gestures. Cf. "Pope Francis delivered another gesture this week destined to burnish his legend for both humility and reform, deciding that an annual Mass in which newly appointed archbishops from around the world

his. Hence the 'reform,' the 'renewals'—necessary as they may be—cannot exhaust themselves in a zealous activity on our part to erect new, sophisticated structures. ... true 'reform' does not mean to take great pains to erect new facades (contrary to what certain ecclesiologies think). Real 'reform' is to strive to let what is ours disappear as much as possible so what belongs to Christ may become more visible."[42]

The Church is always in need of reform—*Ecclesia semper reformanda*—at least in her human structures, but the way of reform is in the growth in

---

receive their symbol of office will no longer be held in Rome, but in their home archdiocese. That event, called the Pallium Mass, traditionally was a highlight of the Roman summer. Francis has now taken himself out of the equation, stipulating that the pallium, a woolen cloth symbolizing service, will be presented to each archbishop individually by the papal ambassador in his country. Most people likely will see it as another way in which Francis is breaking with tradition, playing down the trappings of a royal court in the Vatican and emphasizing the importance of the local church. Those who paid careful attention during the Benedict XVI years probably would agree, except for the 'breaking with tradition' part. In truth, Francis' latest reform is not a departure from Benedict, but yet another instance in which the two pontiffs seem to be singing from the same songbook. One of Benedict's own first decisions after he took office in 2005 was that he would no longer preside personally at beatification Masses, and that those services would no longer be held in Rome. (Beatification is the last step before sainthood, allowing someone to be called 'Blessed.') That choice, too, was about the importance of the local Church, since beatification authorizes veneration of a figure for a local community, while canonization is for the entire Church. Benedict XVI was also sending a signal that the pope doesn't have to be the center of attention—the same point Francis is making about the pallium. Climate change/the environment: As the world awaits Francis' forthcoming encyclical letter on ecology, it's worth remembering that Benedict XVI devoted so much attention to the environment that he was dubbed the 'Green Pope.' Among other measures on his watch, the Vatican signed an agreement to become Europe's first carbon-neutral state (albeit a tiny one) by replanting a stretch of Hungarian forest to offset its carbon use, and installing solar panels atop the Paul VI Audience Hall. Financial clean-ups: Francis has made avoiding future financial scandals a linchpin of his Vatican reform. The clean-up began under Benedict, the first pope to open the Vatican to outside secular inspection through the Council of Europe's anti-money laundering agency Moneyval. It was also Benedict who launched a new financial watchdog agency under the leadership of Swiss anti-money laundering expert René Bruelhart, and who triggered a review of accounts at the Vatican Bank. Child sexual abuse: Francis has committed to "zero tolerance" for sexual abuse and has created a new Commission for the Protection of Minors to lead the charge. Here, too, he's building on Benedict's lead, who defended "zero tolerance" while he was a Vatican official and made it the Church's official policy as pope. Benedict was the first pope to meet with victims and the first to apologize for the crisis in his own name. He also moved aggressively to weed abusers out of the priesthood, laicizing some four hundred priests facing abuse charges in his last two years in office alone. Outreach to non-believers: Francis is celebrated for sitting down with anybody, including a left-wing atheist journalist in Italy for a couple of blockbuster conversations. That follows Benedict's example, who brought Italian Cardinal Gianfranco Ravasi to Rome to launch the "Courtyard of the Gentiles" project to foster conversations with non-believers. One of the few times Benedict has broken his post-resignation silence was to write atheist mathematician Piergiorgio Odifreddi in late 2013, thanking him for writing a book about him and raising some points for conversation." John Allen, "Meet Frankie and Benny the Everly Brothers of Popes," *Crux*, February 2, 2015.

[42] Cardinal Joseph Ratzinger, *The Ratzinger Report*, 53.

personal holiness of its members.[43] This is the way that the saints reformed the Church. "Saints, in fact, reformed the Church in depth, not by working up plans for new structures, but by reforming themselves. What the Church needs in order to respond to the needs of man in every age is holiness, not management."[44] In this manner we can learn from the saints of the past, not to think we have surpassed them.[45]

Another notable feature of Cardinal Ratzinger's ecclesiology was his Trinitarian view of the Church and the world. Within the complex web of relationships in which the Church is embodied, relations with the Trinity are of foremost importance. "Ecclesial communion is at the same time both visible and invisible. As an invisible reality, it is the communion of each human being with the Father through Christ in the Holy Spirit, and with the others who are fellow sharers in the divine nature, in the passion of Christ, in the same faith and in the same spirit."[46] Clearly such a Trinitarian view is a keynote of the ecclesial disposition of Ignatius also.

The Vatican II document *Gaudium et Spes* called for openness and dialogue with the world, but Cardinal Ratzinger placed this within the Trinitarian mystery, where the Trinity has opened itself up to the world in Christ. "Instead of the legalistic view that sees Revelation largely as the issuing of divine decrees, we have a sacramental view, which sees law and grace, word and deed, message and sign, the person and his utterance within the one comprehensive unity of the mystery."[47] God's revelation in Christ does not leave the world as it is. In the Incarnation, God does not just become a companion to the world but rather transforms it through the depth of God's love for the world as revealed in Christ's life, passion, death and resurrection. This has consequences for human action which is called to flow outwards from being drawn into the life of the Trinity. "Ratzinger links the theological virtues to Christian practices and Christian practices to participation in the life of the Trinity."[48]

The Church then has been made part of this gracious openness of God and has a service of mission and a service of charity. Through the Church, Christ saves many as His redemptive work is made operative within her. The Church proclaims Jesus' message of the Kingdom to all peoples. As an entity, the Church is never static but is always a body in progress, a "being on the way"—*Unterwegssein*. Because of this constant pilgrim

---

[43] This is something we have seen asserted in the Vatican Documents, and throughout the pontificates of John Paul II, Benedict XVI and Pope Francis.

[44] Cardinal Joseph Ratzinger, *The Ratzinger Report*, 53.

[45] Cf. Twelfth Rule, *Spiritual Exercises* 364.

[46] Letter to the Bishops of the Catholic Church on Some Aspects of the Church Understood as Communion, Document of the Congregation for the Doctrine of the Faith, May 28, 1992, art.4

[47] Joseph Ratzinger, "Revelation Itself," in H. Vorgrimler (ed.), *Commentary on the Documents of Vatican II* (New York: Herder & Herder, 1969), 171.

[48] Rowland, *Ratzinger's Faith: The Theology of Pope Benedict XVI*, 58.

nature of the Church it is important to ensure a genuine *catholic* climate that can only be facilitated by recalling the meaning of the Church as the Church of Christ. This understanding of the conjoining of Christ and the Church, as we have seen, lies at the heart of the ecclesial disposition of Ignatius. The Church, as the Church of Christ, is the locus of the real presence of God in the world. This mystery of the Church is referred to in the Vatican II document *Lumen Gentium,* "the Church or, in other words, *the Kingdom of Christ now present in mystery.*"[49] It is a truth central to all Catholic tradition and enduring across generations, linking the sixteenth century of Ignatius with our own experience in the twenty-first century.

Finally, it is important to note Cardinal Ratzinger's contribution following the death of Pope John Paul II on April 2, 2005. As Dean of the College of Cardinals, Cardinal Ratzinger presided at the funeral rites of the Pope. He delivered the powerful and poignant funeral homily in St Peter's Square, basing it upon the words of Christ to Peter the first Pope. "'Follow me.' The Risen Lord says these words to Peter. They are his last words to this disciple, chosen to shepherd his flock. 'Follow me'—this lapidary saying of Christ can be taken as the key to understanding the message which comes to us from the life of our late beloved Pope John Paul II."[50] Days later in the mass before the Conclave Cardinal Ratzinger assessed the many different challenges facing the Church. "How many winds of doctrine we have known in these last decades, how many ideological currents, how many fashions of thought? The small boat of thought of many Christians has often remained agitated by the waves, tossed from one extreme to the other: from Marxism to liberalism, to libertinism; from collectivism to radical individualism; from atheism to a vague religious mysticism; from agnosticism to syncretism, etc."[51]

He decried the "dictatorship of relativism" that had arisen which "recognizes nothing as absolute and which only leaves the 'I' and its whims as the ultimate measure."[52] By contrast he emphasized: "We have another measure: the Son of God, true man. He is the measure of true humanism. 'Adult' is not a faith that follows the waves in fashion and the latest novelty. Adult and mature is a faith profoundly rooted in friendship with Christ. This friendship opens us to all that is good and gives us the measure to discern between what is true and what is false, between deceit and truth."[53] He was insistent that the Church should mature in this adult

---

[49] Vatican II, *Lumen Gentium,* 3.
[50] Cardinal Joseph Ratzinger, homily at the funeral mass of John Paul II, St Peter's Square, April 8, 2005.
[51] Cardinal Joseph Ratzinger, homily for the election of a Pope, St Peter's Basilica, before the Conclave, April 18, 2005.
[52] Ibid.
[53] Ibid.

faith and lead others toward the same faith. Following this mass with the other Cardinals he entered the Sistine Chapel for the election of Pope John Paul II's successor. On April 19, 2005 Cardinal Ratzinger was elected as the 265th Pontiff choosing the name Benedict XVI.

The Witness of the Pontificate of Benedict XVI

To understand Pope Benedict's pontificate it is important to have some understanding of his theology. This is consistent with his theology as Cardinal Ratzinger. So it starts with an appreciation of the Church as a manifestation of Christ in the world;[54] and it continues by asserting that Christ reveals the reality of the Trinity. As Cardinal Ratzinger, he had already stated in his work *Salt of the Earth*: "Study the theme of the Church with the intention of opening a vista onto God."[55] For Pope Benedict truth and reality were intrinsically linked. He saw himself as a 'co-worker' for the truth with God, in communion with other workers for that truth. Throughout his writings there is a consistent theme that the Church is: "a divine/human reality that constitutes a *communion* – that is, mankind in the process of becoming one."[56] This communion is of all members within the Church in communion with God, encompassing unity, plurality and diversification. "The universality of the Church involves, on the one hand, a most solid unity, and on the other hand, a plurality and a diversification, which do not obstruct unity, but rather confer upon it the character of 'communion'. This plurality refers both to the diversity of ministries, charisms and forms of life and apostolate within each particular Church and to the diversity of traditions in liturgy and culture among the various particular Churches."[57]

The source of this unity is the Eucharist, which is the sacrament of the Paschal Mystery. During the course of his pontificate, Pope Benedict

---

[54] Ratzinger considered that 'while an undue emphasis on the hierarchical nature of the Church is unhealthy, one cannot consider it an accident. If it is divinely willed, then it is not caused by a primitive human craving for power. It is willed by Jesus Christ to give his body permanence amid the vicissitudes in history in order to allow every human being and every age to behold him. Ratzinger cautioned against the concept 'democracy'. It would be 'absurd' to entrust such a process to majority rule, giving the majority the task of determining what the content and nature of revelation is, and what religious truth is, and what structures Christ has willed. Human reason has not discovered revelation. Otherwise, the divinity of Christ and God's sovereignty would be jeopardized to their cores." Emery De Gaál, *The Theology of Pope Benedict XVI: The Christocentric Shift* (New York: Palgrave MacMillan, 2010), 179.

[55] Ratzinger, *Salt of the Earth*, 66

[56] D. Vincent Twomey, S.V.D., *Pope Benedict XVI The Conscience of Our Age: A Theological Portrait* (San Francisco: Ignatius Press, 2007), 58.

[57] Joseph Ratzinger, "Letter to the Bishops of the Catholic Church," art. 15. Cited in De Gaál, *The Theology of Pope Benedict XVI*, 179.

endeavored to recall the dimension of sacred mystery in the Eucharist. To this end the liturgical changes that were effected through the General Instruction on the Roman Missal aimed to focus the attention of the congregation on the profound nature of the Eucharist and draw forth a more reverent participation in the action of the mass. Those who receive Christ's body and blood in the Sacrament are transformed spiritually into the Body of Christ—the Church. This is not merely a spiritual reality but also a visible entity present within the world. The many different local communities of the Church are brought into communion with the universal Church through the ministry of the Pope. He is the focus for Church unity and the guardian of the Church's mission. The very mission of the Church across all generations is to bring human beings into relationship with Christ and through Christ with the Trinity.[58]

When Pope Benedict considered that he was no longer able to spearhead the mission of the Church due to his age and declining energies, he made the remarkable decision to resign from his ministry and spend the rest of his years in quiet contemplation for the needs of the Church and the world. At a Consistory of Cardinals on February 11, 2013, he stated: "After having repeatedly examined my conscience before God, I have come to the certainty that my strengths, due to an advanced age, are no longer suited to an adequate exercise of the Petrine ministry. I am well aware that this ministry, due to its essential spiritual nature, must be carried out not only with words and deeds, but no less with prayer and suffering."[59] He continued by outlining the many pressures that pertained to the exercise of the office of Pope and the qualities necessary for fulfilling the task which he felt that he no longer possessed in the necessary capacity. "However, in today's world, subject to so many rapid changes and shaken by questions of deep relevance for the life of faith, in order to govern the bark of Saint Peter and proclaim the Gospel, both strength of mind and body are necessary, strength which in the last few months, has deteriorated in me to the extent that I have had to recognize my incapacity to adequately fulfill the ministry entrusted to me."[60]

The poignant moments of his departure from the Apostolic Palace and the Vatican captured the hearts and minds of the world. The humility and courage evinced by Pope Benedict in taking this historic step was acclaimed both within the Church and throughout the world media.

---

[58] "[Some] Catholics tended to think of themselves, like a club or college to which they were affiliated. The fact that individual Catholics are a part of the mystical body of Christ was often overlooked. In Ratzinger's words, 'the Church grows from within and moves outwards, not vice versa' ('The Ecclesiology of Vatican II', Aversa Congress, September 15, 2001). ... [Thus] the Church exists in Eucharistic communities and that she is a service for the transformation of the human person and the entire world." Rowland, *Ratzinger's Faith*, 84.

[59] Pope Benedict XVI, Address to the Consistory of Cardinals, February 11, 2013.

[60] Ibid.

The Pope's final words were his promise as a "pilgrim" to continue to accompany the Church in prayer. "I am simply a pilgrim beginning the last leg of his pilgrimage on this earth. But I would still with my heart, with my prayers, with my reflection and with all my inner strength, like to work for the common good and the good of the Church and of humanity ... Let us go forward with the Lord for the good of the Church and the world."[61]

The Witness of the First Jesuit Pope

On March 13, 2013, around 8.30 p.m., on a wet Rome evening, Pope Francis appeared on the balcony of St Peter's Basilica dressed all in white. He stood silently for a significant period of time looking out over the vast crowd assembled below him. He smiled and the silence became eloquent. Cardinal Tauran[62] had announced the traditional phrase *Annuntio vobis gaudium magnum Habemus Papam*[63] and then the new pope's name: *Eminentissimum ac reverendissimum dominum, dominum* Giorgium Marium *Santae Romanae Ecclesiae Cardinalem* Bergoglio.[64] And then Cardinal Tauran announced the name that the new pope had chosen to be called: *Qui sibi nomen imposuit Franciscum.*[65] A Jesuit pope who took the name of Francis in honor of the great saint from Assisi, a man who embraced the fullness of poverty and who began his pontificate with the simple words: "Brothers and sisters, good evening."

Already from his own experience as Archbishop of Buenos Aires, Cardinal Bergoglio had learned a good deal about being with the poor, although it would seem that this was a gradual development through his life. He was noted as being conservative while Provincial of the Argentinian Jesuits.[66] Yet as Archbishop, he sent a generation of *curas villeros*—slum priests—to live and work among the poor: "what they, and Bergoglio, discovered was that learning was a two-way process. The slum priests were changed by the simple devotion of those they had

---

[61] Pope Benedict XVI, Final address, Castel Gandolfo, February 28, 2013.
[62] Cardinal Jean-Louis Tauran, a French man who was the proto-deacon of the College of Cardinals whose task it was to announce the name of the new pope.
[63] I announce to you a great joy, we have a pope!
[64] The most eminent and most reverend lord, Lord Jorge Mario, of Holy Roman Church Cardinal Bergoglio.
[65] Who upon himself has imposed the name Francis.
[66] "He was pretty conservative," said Fr. Michael Campbell-Johnston, who in 1977 was sent by Jesuit headquarters in Rome to pull Bergoglio into line with the social justice agenda of the order throughout the rest of Latin America. He added: "he has clearly grown in his witness for the poor." Paul Valley, *Pope Francis: Untying the Knots* (London: Bloomsbury, 2013), 59.

arrived to help."[67] There appeared to be clearly a change in Bergoglio over the years as he learned through his own experiences. Factors that assisted such a change in the man included the external events of regular contact with the poor in the slums of Buenos Aires, but alongside this there grew an understanding of liberation theology which he had found very disturbing as a younger man.[68] Bergoglio's visits to the slums brought him into contact with a huge number of ordinary people in their everyday situations.

Over his eighteen years as bishop and archbishop of Buenos Aires, one *villa* priest estimated Bergoglio must have personally talked to at least half of the people in the slum in visits where he would just "turn up, wander the alleyways, and chat to the locals and drink *mate* tea with them."[69] At the same time he took some strong stands as when he supported the *caroneros*—"some of the poorest people in Buenos Aires who make a living sorting through the city's garbage each night to find and sell recyclable materials." Bergoglio helped them to form a union and to turn this work into something from which they can make a decent living. He wanted to help them to 'protect their rights.' ... It was only one of many similar schemes Bergoglio introduced, working with government, city authorities and a variety of community organisations."[70]

The Cardinal came to denounce a clericalism which puts the clergy at the center of the Church in a way which encourages infantilism of the ordinary people, rather than the empowerment that they need. Indeed he saw clericalism as a distortion of religion, a distortion that unfortunately lay people too often collaborated with. "The priest clericalizes the layperson and the layperson kindly asks to be clericalized because deep down it is easier." Pope Francis believed that "the phenomenon of clericalism explains, in great part, the lack of maturity and Christian freedom in a good part of the Latin American laity."[71] He also saw that a form of this way of proceeding appeared to be operative with regard to bishops dealing with the Roman

---

[67] Ibid, 62.

[68] "His opposition to liberation theology was very much rooted in the mindset of the Cold War and the fear that atheistic Soviet-style communism would supplant both capitalism and Catholicism in Latin America, with Cuba as its toehold. But then the Berlin Wall came down. The Soviet Union and its empire collapsed. A new international *realpolitik* was ushered in. ... the globalisation of the world's economy prompted Bergoglio to think differently about extreme poverty. To recognise the exploitation of the poor, or their wilful marginalisation, was no longer to risk being seen to side with the forces of an anti-religious Marxism. Rather it began to sound like a form of solidarity which was part of bringing the good news to the poor." Ibid, 69.

[69] Ibid, 71.

[70] Ibid, 73.

[71] Pope Francis address to the episcopal conference of CELAM during World Youth Day in Rio, July 28, 2013.

Curia.[72] This underlined for him the importance of collegiality and he employed this principle in his dealings with the other Argentinean bishops during the six years that he was President of the Bishops Conference.[73] On June 29, 2013 during the ceremony of the blessing and imposition of the pallium on thirty-four archbishops, Pope Francis spoke about "the path of collegiality" as the road that can lead the church to "grow in harmony with the service of primacy."[74]

He later developed the theme of those who longed for a false sense of security.

> If the Christian ... wants everything clear and safe, then he will find nothing. Tradition and memory of the past must help us to have the courage to open up new areas to God. Those who today always look for disciplinarian solutions, those who long for an exaggerated doctrinal 'security', those who stubbornly try to recover a past that no longer exists – they have a static and inward-directed view of things. In this way, faith becomes an ideology among other ideologies. I have a dogmatic certainty: God is in every person's life. God is in everyone's life. Even if the life of a person has been a disaster, even if it is destroyed by vices, drugs or anything else – God is in this person's life. You can, you must try to seek God in every human life. Although the life of a person is a land full of thorns and weeds, there is always a space in which the good seed can grow. You have to trust God.[75]

The Church is composed of saints and sinners and thus is both holy and sinful. This theme is one that Pope Francis repeatedly emphasized within his Pontificate. He was concerned that all should know that the Pope recognized himself as a sinner amidst other sinners and thus open to the grace and mercy of God.

The holiness of the Church was the theme chosen by Francis for his catechesis at a general audience in October 2013.[76] He asked:

---

[72] "He resented the Curia's repeated refusal to accept his nominations for new Argentinean bishops." Valley, *Pope Francis*. He stressed that "The dicasteries of the Roman Curia are at the service of the pope and the bishops. They must help both the particular churches and the bishops' conferences. They are instruments of help. In some cases, however, when they are not functioning well, they run the risk of becoming institutions of censorship." Pope Francis, interview with Antonio Spadaro, S.J., editor, *La Civiltà Cattolica*, 2013.

[73] "Even when their decisions were not ones he agreed with, as over civil unions for same-sex couples." Ibid.

[74] Pope Francis, mass and the imposition of the pallium on thirty-four archbishops, St Peter's Square, Feast of St. Peter and St. Paul, June 29, 2013.

[75] Pope Francis, interview with Antonio Spadaro, S.J., editor, *La Civiltà Cattolica*, 2013.

[76] In the Creed, after professing that the Church is "one," the Pope said, "we also confess that she is 'holy'; we thus affirm the holiness of the Church, and this is a characteristic that has been present ever since the beginning in the conscience of the first Christians, who called themselves

How can we say that the Church is holy, if we see that the Church throughout history, during her long journey through the centuries, has experienced many moments of darkness? How can a Church be holy if she is made up of human beings, of sinners? Of men who are sinners, women who are sinners, priests who are sinners, nuns who are sinners, bishops who are sinners, cardinals who are sinners, popes who are sinners? Everyone. How can a Church like this be holy?" The Church is holy because "she comes from God who is holy, who is faithful to her and never abandons her to the power of death and evil. She is holy because Jesus Christ, Son of God, is indissolubly united to her; she is holy because she is guided by the Holy Spirit which purifies, transforms, and renews. She is not holy by our merits, but because God makes her holy" ... . The Church is holy, she does not refuse sinners; on the contrary, she welcomes them, she is open even to those who are most distant, she calls to all to allow themselves to be surrounded by the mercy, tenderness, and forgiveness of the Father, Who offers to all the opportunity to encounter Him and to walk the path to holiness. ... Is there anyone here who brings no sin with them? No, we all carry our sins with us. The Church offers to all the possibility of embarking on the road of holiness, which is the road of the Christian."[77]

The corollary of such an emphasis on the call to holiness for Pope Francis was the emphasis he placed on the reality of God's mercy and the particular expression of this in confession. Mercy was the principal subject of his first Sunday homily as Pope. "Jesus' message is mercy. For me, I say this humbly. It is the strongest message of the Lord, mercy. ... It is not easy to entrust oneself to God's mercy, because it is an inscrutable abyss. But we must do it!"[78] This theme of the mercy of God was a leitmotif of Pope Francis' pontificate[79] and is to be found in his homilies and addresses at least once a week and in the earliest days of his pontificate a number of times each week. Indeed he declared a Year of Mercy 2015–2016. He constantly wished to emphasize the loving forgiveness of God and the desire of God to exercise that forgiveness. "Let us return to the Lord. The Lord never wearies of forgiving: never! We are the ones who grow weary of asking forgiveness. And let us ask for the grace to never weary of asking forgiveness because he never wearies of forgiving. Let us ask for this grace."[80] He was concerned to emphasize that Jesus never condemns if we ask for forgiveness. It is the same message of the mercy and compassion of

---

simply 'the holy,' as they were certain of the action of God, of the Holy Spirit who sanctifies the Church." Pope Francis, General Audience, St Peter's Square, Rome, October 2, 2013.

[77] Ibid.

[78] Pope Francis, homily, Sunday Mass, St Ann's parish Vatican City, March 18, 2013.

[79] He declared the Year of Mercy. Beginning December 8, 2015.

[80] Ibid.

God that he took to the peoples of the Philippines in his visit there January 15–19, 2015.

A hallmark of Pope Francis' papacy has been a gentle humble approach to all with whom he came into contact. He saw humility at the heart of what it means to be a good shepherd. In his own life it is clear that he had learned that he needed to be humble. Those who knew him best said of him that such humility was an intellectual stance but it was also more than this. It had been nurtured through prayer, and "his humility and simplicity are actually an expression of his magisterium."[81] The way in which he exercised authority was through this humility and conjoined with his service of the Church and the many individuals he encountered both there and in the wider world.

This humility was linked with a particular simplicity of lifestyle. It was a major media story when Pope Francis decided not to wear red shoes as Pope, nor to live in the papal apartments. Yet these actions were consistent with a lifestyle he had developed that eschewed anything that might be seen to evoke a sense of privilege. When he travelled to the Conclave in March 2013 he did so wearing a pair of old shoes, despite the efforts of his staff to persuade him to a new pair. Though the Vatican had sent him a first class ticket for his flight, he travelled in economy class. Again these actions are reminiscent of the emphasis that Ignatius Loyola gave to following the poor and humble Christ and to choosing this option whenever there was the freedom so to do. This three-fold leitmotif of mercy, humility and simplicity were to characterize not just the opening days of Pope Francis' pontificate but the whole of his papacy. They were the structure built from a foundation in prayer and from which he drew his energies for the work of reform and renewal that the Cardinals had requested prior to his election to the See of Peter.

---

[81] Bishop Jorge Eduardo Lozano of Gualeguaychú, who was Cardinal Bergoglio's auxiliary in Buenos Aires for six years, cited in Valley, *Pope Francis*, 93.

9

The Centrality of Christ

Pope John Paul II, *St Peter's Square*, Rome, October 17, . . .
Holy Father, Inaugural Lecture, October 22, . . .
At his election on October 16, 1978, Pope John Paul II acknowledged . . .

9

The Centrality of Christ

John Paul II

Into the unsettled contemporary context of his elevation to the see of Peter, following the sudden death of Pope John Paul I, the first words of the newly elected Pope sounded a note of hope and indeed called for transformation. "Do not be afraid," Pope John Paul II stated, "open wide the doors to Christ."[1] The Holy Father called for a deeper following of the risen Lord and urged that individuals strive for a more profound relationship with Christ and a faithful living out of this relationship within the Church. The first encyclical of Pope John Paul II focused on Christ as Redeemer of all humanity—*Redemptor Hominis*.[2] It was this encyclical, promulgated only months after his election, that indicated the focus for his pontificate and finds an echo in his later writings. Already, we can see from his initial words to the crowds immediately following his election that his focus on the centrality of Christ with whom all are called to an intimate relationship is consonant with the ecclesial disposition of Ignatius.

There are certain key areas of focus in *Redemptor Hominis* which are the threads that reappear in later documents and teaching. Foremost amongst these is the understanding of Christ as the center of life.[3] "The Redeemer of Man, Jesus Christ, is the center of the universe and of history."[4] He is our Redeemer, and we are called to witness to the hope that the good news of Christ brings. Accordingly, understanding more about the profound nature of the Incarnation is crucial. In this context an appreciation of Mary's response is also very important. Here Pope John Paul II's great devotion

---

[1]Pope John Paul II, St Peter's Square, Rome, October 16, 1978.
[2]John Paul II, Encyclical Letter, *Redemptoris Hominis* (The Redeemer of Man), March 4, 1979.
[3]At his election on October 16, 1978, Pope John Paul II had immediately turned to seek assistance from Christ. "It was to Christ the Redeemer that my feelings and my thoughts were directed ... when, after the canonical election, I was asked: 'Do you accept?' I then replied: 'With obedience in faith to Christ, my Lord, and with trust in the Mother of Christ and of the Church, in spite of the great difficulties, I accept.'" John Paul II, *Redemptoris Hominis*, para. 2.
[4]Ibid., para. 1.

to the Mother of God under the designation of Mother of the Church, is particularly significant.

> If we feel a special need in this difficult and responsible phase of the history of the Church and of mankind, to turn to Christ, who is Lord of the church and Lord of man's history on account of the mystery of the Redemption, we believe that nobody else can bring us as Mary can into the divine and human dimension of this mystery. Nobody has been brought into it by God himself as Mary has. It is in this that the exceptional character of the grace of the divine Motherhood consists. Not only is the dignity of this Motherhood unique and unrepeatable in the history of the human race, but Mary's participation, due to this Maternity, in God's plan for man's salvation through the mystery of the Redemption is also unique in profundity and range of action.[5]

In this way also, there is a resonance with Ignatius' ecclesial disposition and his particular devotion to Mary, seeing her disposition of active receptivity as exemplary for members of the Church.

The Pope reached out particularly to young people in his encyclicals. He had a great desire to go to the ends of the earth in his search for them, and this characterized his pontificate. On his many foreign travels Pope John Paul II would always desire a meeting with young people. His enthusiasm for them and their contribution to the future of the Church were matched by a deep affection that developed amongst young people for Pope John Paul II. In 2002 in the Opening Ceremony of World Youth Day a fragile elderly pope called the assembled young people to recognize in Christ the source of their joy. "Dear young people, many and enticing are the voices that call to you from all sides … they propose a joy that comes from the superficial and fleeting pleasure of the senses … the aged Pope, full of years, but still young at heart, answers your youthful desire for happiness with words that are not his own … The key word in Jesus' teaching is a proclamation of joy. 'Blessed are they' …"[6]

---

[5]The Pope continued: "We can say that the mystery of the Redemption took shape beneath the heart of the Virgin of Nazareth when she pronounced her 'fiat.' From then on, under the special influence of the Holy Spirit, this heart, the heart of both a virgin and mother, has always followed the work of her Son and has gone out to all those whom Christ has embraced and continues to embrace with inexhaustible love. For that reason her heart must also have the inexhaustibility of a mother. The special characteristic of the motherly love that the Mother of God inserts in the mystery of the Redemption and the life of the Church finds expression in it's exceptional closeness to man and all that happens to him. It is in this that the mystery of the Mother consists. The Church, which looks to her with altogether special love and hope, wishes to make this mystery her own in an ever deeper manner." Ibid., para. 22. As we shall see this devotion to Mary was shared by his two successors and is clearly resonant with the Marian appreciation of Ignatius Loyola.

[6]The Pope continued: "People are made for happiness. Rightly then, you thirst for happiness. Christ has the answer to this desire of yours. But he asks you to trust him. True joy is a victory,

Within *Redemptor Hominis,* the Pope also clearly situates himself alongside his predecessors. Already we see this in his choice of name. Pope John Paul I wished to be linked with Pope John XXIII and Pope Paul VI in their work of reforming the Church.[7] Pope John Paul I had brought these two Popes together in his name while Pope John Paul II did likewise and also paid homage to his most illustrious predecessor. An unbroken continuity with the tradition of the Church was of real importance for him.[8] This was exemplified in his choice of name, but it was also evident in his writings. Pope John Paul II had a clear sense of the importance of the Church Fathers and the profound contribution of the early theologians.[9]

At the same time Pope John Paul II identified the Church as a pilgrim people. There is a transitory nature inherent within the Church militant. We are people on a pilgrimage, on a mission, on the move[10] and detachment from what is unnecessary is important for our journey. God will provide all that is necessary and has already provided the great gift of the Eucharist— the very body of Christ himself—from which flows the strength we need for the journey.[11] This focus on the Eucharist was a thread throughout Pope John Paul II's pontificate. He stressed the importance of reception of the Blessed Sacrament and encouraged the practice of Eucharistic Adoration.[12] "The Eucharist is the ineffable Sacrament! The essential commitment

---

something which cannot be obtained without a long and difficult struggle. Christ holds the secret of this victory." John Paul II, Opening Ceremony World Youth Day, Toronto, Thursday July 25, 2002.

[7] "I chose the same names that were chosen by my beloved Predecessor John Paul I. ... Since that pontificate lasted barely thirty-three days it falls to me not only to continue it but in a certain sense to take it up again at the same starting point. This is confirmed by my choice of these two names. By following the example of my venerable Predecessor in choosing them, I wish like him to express my love for the unique inheritance left to the Church by Popes John XXIII and Paul VI and my personal readiness to develop that inheritance with God's help." John Paul II, *Redemptoris Hominis,* para. 2.

[8] "Through these two names and two pontificates I am linked with the whole tradition of the Apostolic See and with all my Predecessors in the expanse of the twentieth century and of the preceding centuries. I am connected through one after another of the various ages back to the most remote, with the line of the mission and ministry that confers on Peter's See an altogether special place in the Church. John XXIII and Paul VI are a stage to which I refer directly as a threshold from which I intend to continue, in a certain sense together with John Paul I, into the future, letting myself be guided by unlimited trust in and obedience to the Spirit that Christ promised and sent to his Church." Ibid.

[9] Cf. *Spiritual Exercises* 363.

[10] Pope Francis in his pontificate also favored the image of a journey.

[11] "The Eucharist is the center and summit of the whole of sacramental life through which each Christian receives the saving power of the Redemption, beginning with the mystery of Baptism, in which we are buried into the death of Christ, in order to become sharers in his Resurrection, as the Apostle teaches. In the light of this teaching, we see still more clearly the reason why the entire sacramental life of the Church of each Christian reaches its summit and fullness in the Eucharist." John Paul II, *Redemptoris Hominis,* para. 20.

[12] Such reverence for the Eucharist is also resonant with the practice of Ignatius Loyola as we saw in the first section of this work.

and, above all, the visible grace and source of supernatural strength for the Church as the people of God is to persevere and advance constantly in Eucharistic life and Eucharistic piety and to develop spiritually in the climate of the Eucharist."[13] He also brought to the attention of all members of the Church the life-giving nature of the sacrament of reconciliation.[14] Within the Church, he emphasized members are called to meet Christ in the word proclaimed as well as in the sacraments, and all dialogue with other Christians is to be undertaken in and through Christ.

The document *Redemptor Hominis* begins by recalling those first minutes after his election when he said: "With obedience in faith to Christ, my Lord, and with trust in the Mother of Christ and of the Church, in spite of the great difficulties, I accept."[15] For Pope John Paul II there was an intimate link between the Incarnation, the response of Mary and his own duties as the successor of Peter. It was clear that Pope John Paul II had great trust in the action of the Holy Spirit at work within the Church, that Spirit of truth and love which is Christ's Spirit. Pope John Paul II revealed within this document also his great love for the universal Church, Christ's own body.[16]

It was within the mystery of Christ that Pope John Paul II situated his ministry. He saw his place in salvation history as the successor of Peter, following the command of Christ to shepherd Christ's people. As this document looked towards the end of the second millennium it sought to bring members of the Church to a deeper engagement with God and, particularly through Christ, to an engagement with the Father and the Holy Spirit. In this way we see that important Trinitarian dimension that lies at the heart of the ecclesial disposition of Ignatius. When individuals within the Church focus their hearts upon Christ the redeemer of all, and through such a focus are drawn to the life of the Trinity, then the Church as a whole is vibrant with the life of Christ. In the Eucharist the Church relives the death of Christ on the cross, and his resurrection. It is the efficacious sign of grace and reconciliation with God and the pledge of eternal life.[17]

Redemptor Hominis also revealed Pope John Paul II's understanding of the divine and human dimensions of the mystery of redemption. In the divine dimension, Jesus Christ, Son of the living God, became our reconciliation to the Father. This reveals that God is love; that love is greater than sin and weakness and is stronger than death. God's love is most clearly revealed in forgiveness and the welcoming embrace given to those who

---

[13] Ibid.

[14] Cf. *Spiritual Exercises* 354.

[15] John Paul II, October 16, 1978.

[16] Cf. *Spiritual Exercises* 353.

[17] In this focus, Pope John Paul II echoed the second and third rules of Rules for Thinking, Judging, and Feeling with the Church. *Spiritual Exercises* 354 and 355 respectively.

acknowledge their sinfulness.[18] "By guarding the sacrament of Penance, the Church expressly affirms her faith in the mystery of the Redemption as a living and life-giving reality that fits in with man's inward truth, with human guilt and also with the desires of the human conscience."[19] In the human dimension, the Church's primary function in every age is to point the awareness of human beings towards the mystery of God. The Church is called to help all human persons to become familiar with the profound reality of the Redemption won by Christ.

The Church's mission, therefore, according to Pope John Paul II, is to proclaim the mystery of Christ. For Christ united himself with every human person. So each person is of unique concern for the Church. Indeed, she is concerned for the vocation of each person in Christ, and for their dignity and freedom. "This is why the Church of our time—a time particularly hungry for the Spirit, because it is hungry for justice, peace, love, goodness, fortitude, responsibility, and human dignity—must concentrate and gather around that Mystery, finding in it the light and the strength that are indispensable for her mission."[20] Pope John Paul II significantly emphasized throughout his pontificate—right from the very beginning—that the Western world appeared to be undergoing a crisis of truth and freedom. In this crisis he identified a climate of agnosticism and relativism as many people seemed to have lost a sense of the reality of the transcendent. In particular, Pope John Paul II was aware of the ethical relativism that seemed in the West to be considered as an essential part of democracy.

Novo Millennio Inuente—January 2001

Over twenty years later at the beginning of the new millennium, in 2001, Pope John Paul II issued *Novo Millennio Ineunte*, an Apostolic Exhortation that reiterated many themes of his pontificate and, indeed, of his first encyclical *Redemptor Hominis*. The Pope stressed that the importance of the Jubilee Year 2000 was to offer praise to the Trinity, to live a journey of reconciliation and to be a sign of hope in the world. "The Church rejoices, gives thanks and asks for forgiveness, presenting her petitions to

---

[18] Cf. *Spiritual Exercises* 354. This is a theme echoed in the writings and addresses of Pope Benedict XVI and Pope Francis.

[19] John Paul II, *Redemptoris Hominis*, para. 20.

[20] Pope John Paul II continues, "For if ... man is the way for the Church's daily life, the Church must be always aware of the dignity of the divine adoption received by man in Christ through the grace of the Holy Spirit and of his destination to grace and glory. By reflecting ever anew on all this, and by accepting it with a faith that is more and more aware and a love that is more and more firm, the Church also makes herself better fitted for the service to man to which Christ the Lord calls her." John Paul II, *Redemptoris Hominis*, para., 18.

the Lord of history and of human consciences."[21] The three years prior to the Jubilee were focused on the understanding of different persons of the Trinity in preparation for the new Millennium.[22] Clearly such a Trinitarian foundation resonated with the ecclesial disposition of Ignatius.

Pope John Paul II called all the faithful at the beginning of the new millennium to be rooted in contemplation and anchored in the Scriptures. He asserted that this was the essential prerequisite for any ministry. "It is important that what we propose, with the help of God, should be profoundly rooted in contemplation and prayer. Ours is a time of continual movement, which often leads to restlessness, with the risk of 'doing for the sake of doing.' We must resist this temptation by trying 'to be' before trying 'to do.'"[23] Most profoundly within *Novo Millenio Ineunte* he enters into a contemplation of the face of Christ: "Is it not the Church's task to reflect the light of Christ in every historical period, to make his face shine also before the generations of the new millennium?"[24]

He cites the Incarnation as truly a self-emptying (*kenosis*) on the part of God for the sake of the redemption of human persons.[25] It is because Christ

---

[21] Pope John Paul II in the Apostolic Letter, *Tertio Millennio Adveniente,* Rome, November 10, 1994, para. 16. In addition the Pope stated: "In view of this, the two thousand years which have passed since the Birth of Christ (prescinding from the question of its precise chronology) represent an extraordinarily great Jubilee, not only for Christians but indirectly for the whole of humanity, given the prominent role played by Christianity during these two millennia. It is significant that the calculation of the passing years begins almost everywhere with the year of Christ's coming into the world, which is thus *the center* of the calendar most widely used today. Is this not another sign of the unparalleled effect of the Birth of Jesus of Nazareth on the history of mankind?" Ibid.

[22] November 10, 1994, Pope John Paul II, *Tertio Millennio Adveniente,* invited all the faithful to three years of preparation for the Jubilee. The focus of 1997 was on the person of Jesus; 1998 focused on the person of the Holy Spirit and in 1999 the person of God the Father was explored. Each year there was also a special prayer of entrustment to Our Lady. Pope John Paul considered the Jubilee to be a time of repentance and proclamation of the Kingdom of God. The jubilee had an ecumenical character reaching out to all Christians and indeed to the whole world.

[23] Pope John Paul II, Apostolic Letter, *Novo Millenio Ineunte,* Rome, January 6, 2001, para. 15. This call to prayer was reiterated by his two successors.

[24] Ibid., para. 16.

[25] "'The Word became flesh' (Jn 1.14). This striking formulation by John of the mystery of Christ is confirmed by the entire New Testament. The Apostle Paul takes this same approach when he affirms that the Son of God was born 'of the race of David, according to the flesh' (cf. Rom. 1.3; cf. 9.5). If today, because of the rationalism found in so much of contemporary culture, it is above all faith in the divinity of Christ that has become problematic, in other historical and cultural contexts there was a tendency to diminish and do away with the historical concreteness of Jesus' humanity. But for the Church's faith it is essential and indispensable to affirm that the Word truly 'became flesh' and took on *every aspect of humanity,* except sin (cf. Heb. 4.15). From this perspective, the incarnation is truly a *kenosis*—a 'self-emptying'—on the part of the Son of God of that glory which is his from all eternity (Phil. 2.6–8; cf. 1 Pet. 3.18). On the other hand, this abasement of the Son of God is not an end in itself; it tends rather towards the full glorification of Christ, even in his humanity: 'Therefore

was both God and man that we are able to draw near to the mystery of God. "Like the Apostle Thomas, the Church is constantly invited by Christ to touch his wounds, to recognize, that is, the fullness of his humanity taken from Mary, given up to death, transfigured by the Resurrection. ... Like Thomas, the Church bows down in adoration before the Risen One, clothed in the fullness of his divine splendor, and never ceases to exclaim: 'My Lord and my God.' (Jn 20.28)"[26] It is the risen Christ to whom the Church looks and by whom the ministry of the Church is nourished and made fruitful.

This contemplation of Christ[27] he asserted gives fresh impetus to Christian living. The primary work of the Church is pastoral revitalization, a work involving all members of the Church. This is not a question of just new programs. "The program already exists: it is the plan found in the Gospel and in the living Tradition, it is the same as ever. Ultimately, it has its center in Christ himself, who is to be known, loved and imitated, so that in him we may live the life of the Trinity, and with him transform history."[28] Each of the pastoral initiatives adapted to the circumstances of the diverse communities is to be set in relation to the foundational work of assisting growth in holiness. Indeed, Pope John Paul II called for a rediscovery of the universal call to holiness.[29] "Once the Jubilee is over, we resume our normal path, but knowing that stressing holiness remains more than ever an urgent pastoral task."[30] Here, his robust assertion of the importance of the Mass and prayer for Christian growth; the joyful living

---

God has highly exalted him and bestowed on him the name which is above every name, that at the name of Jesus every knee should bow, in heaven and on earth and under the earth, and every tongue confess that Jesus Christ is Lord, to the glory of God the Father' (Phil. 2.9–11)." Ibid., 22.

[26] In addition the Pope states: "The Word and the flesh, the divine glory and his dwelling among us! It is *in the intimate and inseparable union of these two aspects* that Christ's identity is to be found, in accordance with the classic formula of the Council of Chalcedon (451): 'one person in two natures.' The person is that, and that alone, of the Eternal Word, the Son of the Father. The two natures, without any confusion whatsoever, but also without any possible separation, are the divine and the human." Ibid., 21.

[27] It is important to bear in mind that: "we cannot come to the fullness of contemplation of the Lord's face by our own efforts alone, but by allowing grace to take us by the hand. Only *the experience of silence and prayer* offers the proper setting for the growth and development of a true, faithful and consistent knowledge of that mystery." Ibid., 20.

[28] Ibid., 29.

[29] Within this call we can find echoes of the third, fourth, fifth, sixth, and seventh rules for thinking with the Church: *frequent attendance at Mass* is mentioned (Third Rule, *Spiritual Exercises* 355); *the Divine Office and prayers of every kind* are also encouraged (Ibid); *religious institutes, virginity and continence and marriage* are clearly praised (Fourth Rule, *Spiritual Exercises* 356); *the vows of religion, obedience, poverty, and chastity* are extolled (Fifth Rule, *Spiritual Exercises* 357); *penances not only interior but exterior* are deemed important; and the *communion of saints* is re-appropriated for the faithful (Sixth Rule, *Spiritual Exercises* 358).

[30] Apostolic Letter, Novo Millennio Ineunte of His Holiness Pope John Paul II, January 6, 2001, para. 30.

of religious vows and penance by those in consecrated life and a renewed sense of the communion of saints[31] were key elements.

Pope John Paul II stressed that human persons need training in holiness[32] and especially in the art of prayer. For this to occur, Christian communities need to become genuine "schools of prayer" "where the meeting with Christ is expressed not just in imploring help but also in thanksgiving, praise, adoration, contemplation, listening and ardent devotion"[33] in order for each person to experience the reality of falling in love with the risen Lord. Prayer cannot be taken for granted the Pope emphasized, "Prayer develops that conversation with Christ which makes us his intimate friends.[34] This reciprocity is the very substance and soul of the Christian life, and the condition of all true pastoral life. Wrought in us by the Holy Spirit, this reciprocity opens us, through Christ and in Christ, to contemplation of the Father's face. Learning this Trinitarian shape of Christian prayer and living it fully, above all in the liturgy, the summit and source of the Church's life but also in personal experience, is the secret of a truly vital Christianity, which has no reason to fear the future, because it returns continually to the sources and finds in them new life."[35]

Prayer roots us in the truth that without Christ we can do nothing. It constantly reminds us of the primacy of Christ and, in union with him, the primacy of the interior life and of growth in holiness. This primacy of holiness and prayer is inconceivable without a renewed listening to the

---

[31] "In particular," we are greatly helped not only by theological investigation but also by that great heritage which is *the 'lived theology' of the saints*. The saints offer us precious insights which enable us to understand more easily the intuition of faith, thanks to the special enlightenment which some of them have received from the Holy Spirit [27]." With regard to prayer and the importance of mass all this is seen under the universal call to holiness. "This training in holiness calls for a Christian life distinguished above all in *the art of prayer*. The Jubilee Year has been a year of more intense prayer, both personal and communal. But we well know that prayer cannot be taken for granted. We have to learn to pray: as it were learning this art ever anew ... Prayer develops that conversation with Christ which makes us his intimate friends ... This reciprocity is the very substance and soul of the Christian life, and the condition of all true pastoral life. Wrought in us by the Holy Spirit, this reciprocity opens us, through Christ and in Christ, to contemplation of the Father's face. Learning this Trinitarian shape of Christian prayer and living it fully, above all in the liturgy, the summit and source of the Church's life, but also in personal experience, is the secret of a truly vital Christianity, which has no reason to fear the future, because it returns continually to the sources and finds in them new life [32]."Pope John Paul II, *Novo Millennio Ineunte*.

[32] "This training must integrate the resources offered to everyone with both the traditional forms of individual and group assistance, as well as the more recent forms of support offered in associations and movements recognized by the Church." Ibid., 31.

[33] "... until the heart truly 'falls in love.'" Intense prayer, yes, but it does not distract us from our commitment to history: by opening our heart to the love of God it also opens it to the love of our brothers and sisters, and makes us capable of shaping history according to God's plan." Ibid., 33.

[34] Cf. "Abide in me and I in you" (Jn 15.4).

[35] Pope John Paul II, *Novo Millennio Ineunte*, para. 32.

Word of God in order that we might become servants of that Word in the work of evangelization both of ourselves and of others. Here we see a resonance with the whole thrust of the *Spiritual Exercises* of St. Ignatius Loyola which are a period of intense prayer focused towards the discovery of the way in which the individual is loved by Christ and is to be drawn into the Church's sharing in the redemptive work of Christ for the salvation of the world. The entire mystical tradition of the Church gives eloquent witness to the same priority for prayer.[36]

Before making any practical plans, the Pope explains the importance of promoting a spirituality of communion. He then proceeds to explain what this spirituality entails. To foster such a spirituality of communion will be the most important challenge to the faithfulness of the Church. "To make the Church *the home and the school of communion*: that is the great challenge facing us in the millennium which is now beginning, if we wish to be faithful to God's plan and respond to the world's deepest yearnings."[37] This understanding of communion[38] embodies and reveals the very essence of the mystery of the Church. It implies a deep contemplation of the mystery of the Trinity dwelling within us as well as a deep love for our brothers and sisters in faith in the unity of the mystical body of Christ.[39]

There is a clear consonance here with the ecclesial disposition of Ignatius. In a sense this is a more profound elaboration of Ignatius' stress

---

[36] The great mystical tradition of the Church of both East and West has much to say in this regard. It shows how prayer can progress, as a genuine dialogue of love, to the point of rendering the person wholly possessed by the divine Beloved, vibrating at the Spirit's touch, resting filially within the Father's heart. This is the lived experience of Christ's promise: "He who loves me will be loved by my Father, and I will love him and manifest myself to him." (Jn 14.21). It is a journey totally sustained by grace, which nonetheless demands an intense spiritual commitment and is no stranger to painful purifications (the "dark night"). But it leads, in various possible ways, to the ineffable joy experienced by the mystics as "nuptial union." Ibid., 33.

[37] Pope John Paul II, *Novo Millennio Ineunte*, para. 43.

[38] Or *koinonia*.

[39] "A spirituality of communion indicates above all the heart's contemplation of the mystery of the Trinity dwelling in us, and whose light we must also be able to see shining on the face of the brothers and sisters around us. A spirituality of communion also means an ability to think of our brothers and sisters in faith within the profound unity of the Mystical Body, and therefore as 'those who are a part of me.' This makes us able to share their joys and sufferings, to sense their desires and attend to their needs, to offer them deep and genuine friendship. A spirituality of communion implies also the ability to see what is positive in others, to welcome it and prize it as a gift from God: not only as a gift for the brother or sister who has received it directly, but also as a 'gift for me.' A spirituality of communion means, finally, to know how to 'make room' for our brothers and sisters, bearing 'each other's burdens' (Gal. 6.2) and resisting the selfish temptations which constantly beset us and provoke competition, careerism, distrust and jealousy. Let us have no illusions: unless we follow this spiritual path, external structures of communion will serve very little purpose. They would become mechanisms without a soul, 'masks' of communion rather than its means of expression and growth." Pope John Paul II, *Novo Millennio Ineunte*, para. 43.

on the Church as *Spouse of Christ and Mother.*[40] Also it is clear for Ignatius that this basic understanding of the relationship between Christ and the Church is the foundation from which all practical initiatives flow. Pope John Paul II maintained that it is this primary communion that all structures within the Church are designed to serve. Much had also been done since the Second Vatican Council for the reform of the Roman Curia, the organization of Synods and the functioning of Episcopal Conferences. "But there is certainly much more to be done, in order to realize all the potential of these instruments of communion, which are especially appropriate today in view of the need to respond promptly and effectively to the issues which the Church must face in these rapidly changing times. Communion must be cultivated and extended day by day and at every level in the structures of each Church's life."[41]

From this rooted communion there will be fresh energy for the practical and concrete care for every human person—particularly the poorest. The Pope reiterated that there is a special presence of Christ in the poor, and this requires the Church to make a preferential option for them.[42] At all levels of society the Pope noted the hunger of the human heart,[43] and stressed that the only true freedom is that given by God. The Pope called for a new

---

[40] First Rule, *Spiritual Exercises* 353.

[41] The Pope continued: "There, relations between Bishops, priests and deacons, between Pastors and the entire People of God, between clergy and Religious, between associations and ecclesial movements must all be clearly characterized by communion. To this end, the structures of participation envisaged by Canon Law, such as *the Council of Priests and the Pastoral Council,* must be ever more highly valued. These of course are not governed by the rules of parliamentary democracy, because they are consultative rather than deliberative; yet this does not mean that they are less meaningful and relevant. The theology and spirituality of communion encourage a fruitful dialogue between Pastors and faithful: on the one hand uniting them *a priori* in all that is essential, and on the other leading them to pondered agreement in matters open to discussion." Pope John Paul II. Novo Millennio Ineunte, 45.

[42] "In our own time, there are so many needs which demand a compassionate response from Christians. Our world is entering the new millennium burdened by the contradictions of an economic, cultural and technological progress which offers immense possibilities to a fortunate few, while leaving millions of others not only on the margins of progress but in living conditions far below the minimum demanded by human dignity. How can it be that even today there are still people dying of hunger? Condemned to illiteracy? Lacking the most basic medical care? Without a roof over their heads?" Ibid., 50. The resonance with the homilies and addresses of Pope Francis are very clear.

[43] "The scenario of poverty can extend indefinitely, if in addition to its traditional forms we think of its newer patterns. These latter often affect financially affluent sectors and groups which are nevertheless threatened by despair at the lack of meaning in their lives, by drug addiction, by fear of abandonment in old age or sickness, by marginalization or social discrimination. In this context Christians must learn to make their act of faith in Christ by discerning his voice in the cry for help that rises from this world of poverty. This means carrying on the tradition of charity which has expressed itself in so many different ways in the past two millennia, but which today calls for even greater resourcefulness. Now is the time for a new "creativity" in charity, not only by ensuring that help is effective but also by "getting close" to those who suffer, so that the hand that helps is seen not as a humiliating handout but as a

birth of freedom encompassing truth and responsibility. For Pope John Paul II freedom was always seen in terms of truth and not in terms of power and advantage. Truth can only be found in Christ, and this is why the Pope stressed the integrity of doctrine and discipline.[44]

The relationship between faith and reason had also been an important theme for the Pope.[45] This is based on the belief that the mind can grasp truth that is permanent and universal and reason can transcend empirical data to become rooted in the concept of personal dignity. It is in this spirit of truth, faith and reason that Pope John Paul II saw the importance of dialogue in the contemporary world that includes also the challenge of ecumenism and inter-religious dialogue. In the pursuit of this latter dialogue Pope John Paul II visited the most holy accessible shrine of the Jewish faith—the "wailing wall" in Jerusalem. He also became the first Pope to set foot in a mosque. This focus on the spirit of truth, faith and reason at work by God's grace within the world is resonant with the Seventeenth Rule of the Rules for Thinking with the Church that also stresses the need for dialogue.[46]

In the conclusion of *Novo Millennio Inuente*, Pope John Paul II focused on Christ as in himself a message of hope for the world. Through the story of the life of Christ we can come to understand our own story and in his humanity we discover what it means to be a human person. We can—as it were—relive his life through the Incarnation, his ministry and the Paschal Mystery. Pope John Paul II emphasized the need to continue to be formed through the graces that Christ constantly bestows upon the Church in and through her Sacraments. The Jubilee year was a time to remember and celebrate the life, ministry, death and resurrection of Christ and to contemplate how his reality is most essentially our reality. This focus on Christ conjoined to his Church, clearly at the heart of the ecclesial disposition of Ignatius, also found a place in many of Pope John Paul's other writings. Though space does not permit further elaboration, it is important to note that his "catechesis on the Church," in a set of his Wednesday audience talks on the Creed, is another place where we might see similar evidence.

---

sharing between brothers and sisters." Ibid. Again we may trace a resonance with the words of Pope Francis in many of his homilies and addresses in 2013, the first year of his papacy.

[44] Cf. *Spiritual Exercises* 365.

[45] In particular note the Encyclical *Fides et Ratio*, September 14, 1998, where he "wished to defend the capacity of human reason to know the truth. This confidence in reason is an integral part of the Catholic intellectual tradition, but it needs reaffirming today in the face of widespread and doctrinaire doubt about our ability to answer the fundamental questions: Who am I? Where have I come from ? Where am I going? Why is there evil? And, What is there after this life?" Pope John Paul II, *Ad Limina*, Address to US Bishops, Rome, October 24, 1998.

[46] "One may speak about faith and grace as much as possible, with God's help, for the greater praise of the Divine Majesty." Seventeenth Rule, *Spiritual Exercises* 369.

In *Manus Tuas, Domine*—Into your Hands, Lord

Pope John Paul II's *Last Testament* was published in April 2005. It comprised a journal entry written on March 6, 1979 with successive additions from some of the following years. It focuses initially on the Pope's death and a number of spiritual reflections surrounding this. For our purposes what is singularly striking is the consistent disposition of openness to the Lord's will. The Pope places all things into the hands of God and also into the hands of "the Mother of my Master: *Totus Tuus*[47] ... In these hands I leave, above all, the Church."[48] Clearly the Pope continued to see the inextricable union between Christ and the Church. At the same time, his devotion to Our Lady inclined him to unite her with his petition as his most intimate intercessor. His apostolic motto "*Totus Tuus*" was not merely an expression of piety but a profound theological assertion of faith.[49]

In 1980 there is an additional note in which Pope John Paul II again entrusted himself totally to the Lord's grace. In speaking of his death he said: "I hope that He [the Lord] makes [that death] useful for this more important cause that I seek to serve: the salvation of men and women, the safeguarding of the human family ... and useful for the people with whom He particularly entrusted me, for the question of the Church, for the glory of God Himself."[50] Within this note from the Pope we can catch an echo of Ignatius' own dedication to the work of God, to the greater glory of God and the service of his Church.

Finally there is an additional series of notes made on March 17, 2000, the Jubilee year. These notations are full of thanksgiving to God for the way in which He sustained Pope John Paul II, the Church and the world over the intervening years. In particular there is great gratitude for the work of Vatican II and the great ongoing gift this is for the Church. "I am convinced that for a long time to come the new generations will draw upon the riches that this Council of the twentieth century gave us."[51]

---

[47] *Totus Tuus*,—literally "all yours." The Pope entrusted himself constantly to Mary the Mother of God and Mother of the Church.

[48] Pope John Paul II's *Last Testament* published April 8, 2005.

[49] "*Totus Tuus*. This phrase is not only an expression of piety, or simply an expression of devotion. It is more. During World War Two, while I was employed as a factory worker, I came to be attracted to Marian devotion. At first, it had seemed to me that I should distance myself a bit from the Marian devotion of my childhood, in order to focus more on Christ. Thanks to Saint Louis of Montfort, I came to understand that true devotion to the Mother of God is actually Christocentric, indeed, it is very profoundly rooted in the Mystery of the Blessed Trinity, and the mysteries of the Incarnation and Redemption." Ibid.

[50] Ibid.

[51] Ibid.

The last reference is a reflection over the years of Pope John Paul II's pontificate and it is full of gratitude to God for the kindness of those whom he has met over this time. There is an echo here of the "Contemplation to Attain the Love of God" at the end of the *Spiritual Exercises* of St. Ignatius Loyola. In this contemplation Ignatius asks the retreatant to envisage all the blessings and benefits of God that have come throughout life in and through others. In this light we might read the following: "During the more than twenty years that I am fulfilling the Petrine service *in medio Ecclesiae*[52] I have experienced the benevolence and even more the fecund collaboration of so many cardinals, archbishops and bishops, so many priests, so many consecrated persons – brothers and sisters – and, lastly, so very, very many lay persons, within the Curia, in the vicariate of the diocese of Rome, as well as outside these milieu. ... To all I want to say just one thing: 'May God reward you.' *In manus tuas, Domine, commendo spiritum meum.*"[53]

Benedict XVI—The Encounter with Christ

To encounter Christ, to have a personal relationship with Jesus is the way in which Pope Benedict emphasized the centrality of Christ. This was evident throughout his papacy. In a meeting with university students in April 2006 he exhorted them: "Never forget dear young people, that your—our—happiness depends, in the end, on the encounter and friendship with Jesus."[54] In his message for Lent 2011 he stressed the importance of the "personal encounter with our Redeemer" and focused this particularly through the sacrament of baptism. "Baptism is the encounter with Christ which informs the entire existence of the baptized imparting divine life and calling for sincere conversion."[55]

Within the opening homily for the Synod of Bishops on the New Evangelization for the Transmission of the Christian Faith in October 2012 Pope Benedict stated that evangelization always has its starting and indeed finishing points in Jesus Christ the Son of God. The whole work of the Synodal Assembly he emphasized was "dedicated to help people encounter the Lord, who alone fills existence with deep meaning and peace."[56] The final message from the Synod of Bishops reiterated this same focus on the need for encounter with Christ. Indeed during the course of the Synod it became clear that everyone has a right to an encounter with Christ. The Church was seen to be instrumental in facilitating this encounter. "The

---

[52] I.e. as Pope at the center of the Church.
[53] Into your hand Lord, I commend my spirit, Pope John Paul II, *Last Testament*.
[54] Pope Benedict XVI meeting with university students Rome April 10, 2006.
[55] Pope Benedict XVI, Message for Lent 2011.
[56] Pope Benedict XVI, homily, Opening Mass of the Synod of Bishops on the New Evangelization for the Transmission of the Christian Faith, October 7, 2012.

Church wants to render the Lord present in the lives of today's men and women so that they could encounter him."[57]

This task has universal significance: "Leading the men and women of our time to Jesus to the encounter with him is a necessity that touches all regions of the world."[58] At the same time the final message made clear that the initiative for this encounter always comes from Christ. Jesus is the one who desires the encounter with human persons.

> Before saying anything about the forms that this new evangelization must assume, we feel the need to tell you with profound conviction that the faith determines everything in the relationship that we build with the person of Jesus who takes the initiative to encounter us. The work of the new evangelization consists in presenting once more the beauty and perennial newness of the encounter with Christ to the often distracted and confused heart and mind of the men and women of our time, above all to ourselves.[59]

The place of this encounter is the Church. "The Church is the space offered by Christ in history where we can encounter him."[60] This expression of faith is the conviction which marked Pope Benedict's whole pontificate.

Christ made manifest in the Church— Consistent Theology

To understand Pope Benedict's pontificate it continues to be important to understand his theology. Throughout his writings there is a consistent theme that the Church is a *communion*. This communion is of all members sharing in the redemptive work of Christ. "Christians ... one in their calling by Jesus ... are one in grace, they will also be one in their mission, which itself is grace."[61] The source of this unity—the common bond—is the Eucharist, "which is *communio* and enables *mission*."[62] It is the sacrament of the Paschal Mystery. It is "Christ the Truth ... [who] changes us from ignorant servants into friends inasmuch as he permits us to become sharers in his own divine self-knowledge."[63] This leads to a dynamic relationship

---

[57] Final Message for the People of God of the Synod of Bishops on the New Evangelization for the Transmission of the Christian Faith, Rome October 26, 2012.
[58] Ibid.
[59] Ibid.
[60] Pope Benedict XVI, homily, Feast of the Assumption, Castel Gandolfo August 15, 2012.
[61] Cardinal Joseph Ratzinger, *Christian Brotherhood* (London: Burns & Oates, 2005), 84.
[62] De Gaál, *The Theology of Pope Benedict XVI*, 171.
[63] Joseph Ratzinger, *Jesus Christ: Today, Yesterday and Forever* (Washington, DC: John Paul Institute, 1990), 13.

both within the Church and with the world where the Church is sent on mission.[64]

Pope Benedict stated, as we have seen, that his theological perspective begins with the Church and that the problem of the Church is tied to the theological issues of our contemporary world. Indeed, he contends: "Today the problem with the Church is very closely tied to that of theology."[65] From the time of the Vatican Council, as Cardinal Ratzinger, he was concerned about the way in which theological debate had been displaced from the university to the glare of publicity in the media.

Pope Benedict thoroughly endorsed the importance of theologians sharing the results of their research and reflection, but he was concerned to emphasize that the rightful place of theological debate is the university seminar, not the pages of tabloid newspapers. "The presence of theology in the university is, in my opinion, a precious patrimony which it is incumbent upon us to defend."[66] He felt it was very unhelpful for half-formed theological ideas, which had not yet matured or been tested in academic debate, to be disseminated across the media. This could easily lead to confusion amongst the faithful.[67]

As Cardinal Ratzinger he had already made clear that "The highest ranking good, for which the Church bears responsibility, is the faith of the simple. Reverence for this faith must also be the inner criterion of all theological teaching as well."[68] Pope Benedict was aware of such confusion in many areas in the years immediately following the Council. For theology to be of true service to the Church it is important that there is theological debate. "Eventually what is of value in theological debate is incorporated into Church teaching by the authentic Magisterium [Church's teaching authority]."[69] The theologian has a privileged place

---

[64] "Thus, Christian brotherhood is neither merely a one-on-one friendship with Jesus Christ nor is it static. It is dynamic both in regard to that relationship and as a conscious participation in the grand drama of salvation history. It is the earnestness of partaking in the mystical body of Christ that is the Church." De Gaál, *The Theology of Pope Benedict XVI*, 171.

[65] Salt of the Earth, 81.

[66] He continues: "That theology be at home in the 'house of learning' and be a partner in its discourse is crucially important both for theology and for the other sciences. That theology be able to research and speak with the seriousness and liberty which pertain to scientific endeavor is a value which everyone must have at heart." Joseph Ratzinger, *The Nature and Mission of Theology: Approaches to Understanding Its Role in the Light of Present Controversy* (San Francisco: Ignatius Press, 1995), 114.

[67] There is an "extremely dubious tendency to play off the state against the Church, its alleged menace. This tendency, which in the light of recent history must be labeled as truly absurd, is usually connected with the more subtle argument that the essence of the university cannot be harmonized with the pretensions of the Church's Magisterium; the traditional place of theology in the 'house of learning' is endangered by the extension of magisterial claims." Ibid.

[68] Ibid., 68.

[69] D. Vincent Twomey, S.V.D, *Pope Benedict XVI*, 62.

within the Church but that privilege is also a responsibility and requires accountability.[70]

Pope Benedict was clear, from his own experience as a theologian, that the practice of theology should inspire and bring hope to people, not throw them into confusion and despair.[71] His homily at the requiem for Pope John Paul II in 2005 was an example of a theological homily that could inspire. Two other particular areas where Pope Benedict had concerns regarding theology were in the areas of the growth in secularism and certain developments in liturgical practice. In the first case, he believed the growth of secularism had undermined confidence in key Christian values. In regard to the reform of the liturgy there seemed to him to have developed a certain arbitrary way of dealing with Catholic ritual that had diminished a sense of reverence for the Eucharistic celebration.

There is a certain sense of resonance with the Rules for Thinking with the Church here. As Ignatius in the Sixth to the Ninth Rules praises certain devotions that have been denigrated by the Reformers, in a somewhat similar manner, Pope Benedict sought to re-appropriate certain devotions that were pushed aside after Vatican II. The Pope gave added emphasis to the importance of the Mass and to the reception of Holy Communion with the appropriate conditions and not mindlessly, or as a matter of habit. He praised the veneration of saints. [72] He stressed the importance of interior and exterior penance.[73] He praised the reverent celebration of the Eucharist in appropriate buildings with statues and paintings and all that could assist

---

[70] "Whoever does not pursue purely private research, but teaches in the name of the Church, must be cognizant of this. Accepting this commission and speaking, not in one's own name, but in the name of the common subject, the Church, includes an obligation whereby the individual imposes limits upon himself. This is so because, along with the commission, he is also entrusted with an authority which, as a private scholar and without the confidence men place in the Church's word, he would not enjoy. Together with authority he is invested with a power which is simultaneously a responsibility, inasmuch as it does not derive from him but rests upon his mission—upon the Church's name, in which he is now permitted to speak. Those who talk nowadays of the abuse of power connected with doctrinal discipline in the Church generally have in mind only the misuse of authority on the part of the Church's ministerial office, which doubtless can occur. But it is entirely forgotten that there is also a misemployment of the authority conferred by one's mission: the exploitation of the readiness to listen and to trust, which even today men still manifest towards the pronouncements of the Church, for a purely private utterance. Ecclesiastical authority actively serves this misappropriation of power when, by giving it free reign, it makes its own prestige available where it has absolutely no right to do so. The solicitude for the faith of the little ones must be more important in its eyes than the opposition of the great." Ratzinger, *The Nature and Mission of Theology*, 69.

[71] His sermons from his period as Cardinal Archbishop of Munich show a theologian capable of touching the hearts and minds of the faithful.

[72] As does the Sixth Rule of Rules for Thinking, Judging, and Feeling with the Church.

[73] In consonance with the seventh rule.

the congregation to raise their hearts and minds in wonder and praise of God.[74]

Another major area of concern for Pope Benedict, as had been the case for his predecessor, was the developments in society with respect to health care and bio-technology. "To fabricate man and make him a product of our chemical arts or any other technology is a fundamental attack on the dignity of man, who is no longer considered, as an immediate creature of God and his immortal vocation."[75] Here new social and moral dilemmas had arisen connected with the whole understanding of the value of life from its very conception until its natural end and indeed the fundamental meaning of what it means to be a human person created either male or female. These new developments have called for a further refining of Catholic moral theology.[76] In particular Pope Benedict had been concerned to protect a traditional understanding of Christian marriage. While always being careful to distinguish between the immorality of homosexual acts and the unjust discrimination against homosexual persons, he stated that: "The call for homosexual partnerships to receive a legal form that is more

---

[74] Clearly we find here an echo of the eighth rule, "We ought to praise church buildings and their decorations; also statues and paintings, and their veneration according to what they represent." *Spiritual Exercises* 360.

[75] He continued: "It is essential to respect the unique dignity of man, who is wanted and created immediately by God, through a new miracle of creation, [Through cloning] the human person becomes our product, a product of our art: thus his dignity as a human person is violated from the start." Vatican Radio, March 7, 1997, quot. M. Bardozzi, *In the Vineyard of the Lord: The Life, Faith and Teachings of Joseph Ratzinger/Benedict XVI* (New York: Rizzoli, 2005), 111–12. Cited in Rowland, *Ratzinger's Faith*, 77.

[76] "The initial attempts at reform produced two schools of thought. Morality was effectively reduced to one principle, that of calculating the consequences of an action and opting for the greater proportion of good in any human action. All actions were understood to be essentially determined by their circumstances or particular situation and were assumed to be by nature ambiguous; none was seen to be intrinsically good or bad. What mattered was that the proportion of foreseeable good effects should outweigh the evil effects. The other school recognized a multiplicity of principles governing any action, while maintaining that some actions [adultery, perjury, murder] were always to be avoided as they were intrinsically wrong, irrespective of the circumstances. Both of these schools, it is now more and more recognized, were still operating from a legalist mental framework, one tending to laxity, the other to rigorism, one dissenting from traditional Catholic teaching, the other defending it. Both have, under the influence of the contemporary revival of Aristotelian ethics and the moral theology of Thomas Aquinas, given way to a recovery of *virtue* as the context for moral discourse. Virtue is ultimately concerned with happiness and holiness as the goal of human life. It reintegrates both the human passions and divine grace into morality. The *Catechism of the Catholic Church* [1994–7] for which Ratzinger was finally responsible, has given official sanction, as it were, to the return to Thomist virtue ethics, while the encyclical *Veritatis Splendor* of Pope John Paul II [1993] into which it is presumed Ratzinger had a significant input, has brought to the earlier debate between these two earlier schools a kind of closure. It defends among other things, the affirmation that certain actions *are* intrinsically wrong and shows the significance of objective morality for stable political life." D. Vincent Twomey, S.V.D., *Pope Benedict XVI*, 64–5.

or less the equivalent of marriage ... departs from the entire moral history of mankind."[77]

The encyclicals that were published[78] during Pope Benedict's pontificate reflect a quiet but confident teacher who communicated the faith in a clear fashion. Pope Benedict's own "spiritual father" was St. Augustine, who—inspired his vocation as Bishop of Rome and Shepherd of the Universal Church. Speaking of the role of the bishop in *Spe Salvi*, he cited one of St. Augustine's sermons:[79]

> The turbulent have to be corrected, the faint-hearted cheered up, the weak supported; the Gospel's opponents need to be refuted, its insidious enemies guarded against; the unlearned need to be taught, the indolent stirred up, the argumentative checked; the proud must be put in their place, the desperate set on their feet, those engaged in quarrels reconciled; the needy have to be helped, the oppressed to be liberated, the good to be encouraged, the bad to be tolerated; all must be loved.

In his encyclicals and his other papal communications, Pope Benedict continued to articulate an ecclesiological perspective that was rooted in a supernatural perspective. He was the Vicar of Christ as well as the Servant of the Servants of God—both papal titles. As such, he reminded members of the Church—the body of Christ—that to be Church is to be in relationship with God and with one another. To be a member of the Church obliges people to look beyond themselves and act in charity towards each other.

The Pope spoke of the Church in *Spe Salvi* as a pilgrim Church, emphasizing that Christians "belong to a new society which is the goal of their common pilgrimage and which is anticipated in the course of their pilgrimage."[80] It is also significant that the Pope ended all of his encyclicals with prayers to Our Lady. Mary was seen both as Mother of the Church and as the exemplary disciple, the one closest to the Lord and thus most ready to help humanity on its pilgrimage to a deeper faith in her Son. "May the Virgin Mary—proclaimed *Mater Ecclesiae* by Paul VI and honored by Christians as *Speculum Iustitiae* and *Regina Pacis*—protect us and obtain for us, through her heavenly intercession, the strength, hope and joy necessary to continue to dedicate ourselves with generosity to

---

[77] He continued: "If this relationship [marriage] becomes increasingly detached from legal forms, while at the same time homosexual partnerships are increasingly viewed as equal in rank to marriage, we are on the verge of a dissolution of our concept of man, and the consequences can only be extremely grave." Pope Benedict XVI, "Values in a Time of Upheaval," in *What it Means to be a Christian* (San Francisco: Ignatius Press, 2006), 148.

[78] *Deus Caritas Est* in the first year of his pontificate, issued December 25, 2005, and *Spe Salvi*, in the third year of his pontificate, issued November 30, 2007. *Caritas in Veritate*, in the fifth year of his pontificate, June 29, 2009.

[79] Augustine Sermo 340, cited in Pope Benedict XVI, *Spe Salvi*, 29.

[80] *Spe Salvi*, 4.

the task of bringing about the development of the whole man and of all men."[81]

Deus Caritas Est—God is Love

The central focus of this encyclical is on the primacy of love. In a world stalked by fear of one form or another, Pope Benedict sounded a clarion call of the love of God operative within the world. The Pope explored the very word "love" which has been so debased in our contemporary context. He elucidated the nature of divine and human love.[82] Pope Benedict used the human experience of falling in love that is focused towards marriage, as a starting point.[83] His central point here was that the real promise at the heart of human love needs divine love to be fully realized. Indeed, in and through the redemptive work of Christ, human love is brought into the sphere of divine love and there made perfect. "By contemplating the pierced side of Christ,[84] we can understand the starting point of this Encyclical Letter: 'God is Love.'[85] It is there that this truth can be contemplated. It is from there that our definition of love must begin. In this contemplation the Christian discovers the path along which his life and love must move."[86]

The second part of this encyclical focuses on some of the practical implications of believing in this love of God and responding to God in love for God and for others. In particular, Pope Benedict noted the importance that the Church attaches to those who suffer. The Church is particularly called in charity to help all who suffer. Here the concept of Justice is not enough. He asserted that those who are suffering need love before anything else. In and through this encyclical, Pope Benedict enjoined on the Church the importance of charitable and social work as integral to the Church's mission.

The love of God sets the standard "for all moral and political activity: namely respect for the dignity of the other [whoever that 'other' may be, not just those that we might find more acceptable] that leads to active love,

---

[81] Spe Salvi, 79.

[82] His words were very resonant with the eighteenth rule of Ignatius' Rules for Thinking with the Church that highlights the value of pure love in the service of God.

[83] "From the standpoint of creation, eros directs man towards marriage, towards a bond which is unique and definitive; thus, and only thus, does it fulfill its deeper purpose. Corresponding to the image of a monotheistic God is monogamous marriage. Marriage based on exclusive and definitive love becomes the icon of the relationship between God and his people and vice versa. God's way of loving becomes the measure of human love. This close connection between eros and marriage in the Bible has practically no equivalent in extra-biblical literature." Pope Benedict XVI, Deus Caritas Est, para. 11.

[84] Cf. Jn 19.37.

[85] 1 Jn 4.8.

[86] Pope Benedict XVI, Deus Caritas Est, 12.

especially for those most in need."[87] It is clear that the Pope recognizes that even the most just society does not, of itself, meet the deepest need of human persons for love and the warmth and the affection of Christian charity. It is this that brings joy to the life of another. A theological way of phrasing this might be that the inner disposition of the theological virtue of charity is the necessary condition for the cardinal virtue of justice. In order to live justly, people must love one another. This reverence for "the other," even the one who may consider themselves to be our enemy, lies at the heart of the presupposition to the *Spiritual Exercises*[88] of Ignatius, as we have noted in earlier chapters, and is crucial to a practice of the ecclesial disposition.

Spe Salvi—Saved in Hope

Christian Hope is the focus of this encyclical, the good news of the redemptive love of God made known in Christ. The Pope speaks about the difficulties human persons experience concerning hope and clarifies for them the proper place of hope in Christian life. The virtue of hope is of special relevance to Christianity, and humanity needs to be reminded of its value. It is a life-giving dynamic for living a full Christian life and a vital resource for the life of the Church. It is not just that hope is a good virtue for which to strive; it is a necessity for human salvation.

There are clear references in this encyclical to features of Pope Benedict's thought that we have referenced before. He quoted often from St. Augustine whom we recall was his "spiritual father." The Pope made reference to the kingdom of God and the kingdom of man, and here we can see an allusion to Augustine's "City of God and the city of man."[89] The city of man, or the human city, does not respond to the human person's need for hope and for God. But as in *Deus Caritas Est*, Pope Benedict XVI emphasized that human beings experience God's love and salvation not in isolation but as members of a community.[90]

Throughout the whole of the encyclical the question arises always new and always current: Why do we hope? The image of the journey of hope towards our goal of Trinitarian life synthesizes and crystallizes the integral vision of Christian hope that Pope Benedict XVI offers us, because hope and salvation are inseparable. He presents hope as a dynamic reality, in a personalized, comprehensible form, and in open and current dialogue with each person and our contemporary world. Aware of our finitude and the

---

[87] D. Vincent Twomey, S.V.D., *Pope Benedict XVI*, 78 (the bracketed words are mine).
[88] *Spiritual Exercises* 15.
[89] St. Augustine, *The City of God*.
[90] For this he refered to Henri de Lubac's *Catholicisme*, which we explored in Chapter 7.

power of evil and sin in the world which we are unable to overcome hope is centered on the God who is able to vanquish sin because he personally entered into history in the person of Jesus Christ whose redemptive love takes away the sin of the world. "Through faith in the existence of this power, hope for the world's healing has emerged in history. It is, however, hope—not yet fulfillment; hope that gives us the courage to place ourselves on the side of the good even in seemingly hopeless situations, aware that, as far as the external course of history is concerned the power of sin will continue to be a terrible presence."[91]

Perhaps the most original aspect of this encyclical is the fact that it demonstrates hope in its integrity, embracing all spheres. First, it addresses time, including the past, the present and the future, looking toward eternal life. Then, it talks of the various ways in which one can come to hope: through prayer and particularly contemplative prayer. Through action, because all serious and right action of humanity is hope being enacted. Through suffering, and this is in no way to glorify suffering in a narcissistic form, but to emphasize that suffering forms part of every human existence. "We can try to limit suffering, to fight against it."[92] What we do with suffering can, by God's grace, transform our experience and lead to creative interior growth both for ourselves and for others.

In addition we come to realize more profoundly that God is very near to us when we are in pain. Christianity teaches that God—truth and love in person—is very close to those who suffer through the experience of Christ's suffering. So human beings may join their suffering to that of Christ, and in the mystery of God's loving designs, such human suffering may become part of God's redemptive work for the life of the world. "It is not by sidestepping or fleeing from suffering that we are healed, but rather by our capacity for accepting it, maturing through it and finding meaning through union with Christ, who suffered with infinite love."[93] God's compassion overflows in and through human compassion. We have already seen that suffering is a characteristic of the ecclesial disposition.

What Pope Benedict had shown already in *Deus Caritas Est*, and again in this encyclical, was that we can hope for both a better world and for eternal life, but that we are not to confuse one with the other. There is within this document a reformulation of the doctrine of Purgatory, which in the past had been a stumbling block to many Protestants. Pope Benedict is familiar, from his time as an academic theologian, with currents in German

---

[91] *Spe Salvi*, 36.
[92] He continues: "It is when we attempt to avoid suffering by withdrawing from anything that might involve hurt, when we try to spare ourselves the effort and pain of pursuing truth, love, and goodness, that we drift into a life of emptiness, in which there may be almost no pain, but the dark sensation of meaninglessness and abandonment is all the greater." Ibid., 37
[93] Ibid.

Protestant thinking. He cites the reality of Purgatory[94] in and through Christ. "Some recent theologians are of the opinion that the fire which both burns and saves is Christ himself, the Judge and Savior. The encounter with him is the decisive act of judgment. Before his gaze all falsehood melts away. This encounter with him, as it burns us, transforms and frees us, allowing us to become truly ourselves.[95]

Nevertheless, in whatever way the idea of Purgatory is to be understood, the Pope is not abandoning the concept of praying for the dead. In defending prayers for the dead, he emphasized the communal nature of our human existence. Our lives are involved with one another. "No one lives alone. No one sins alone. No one is saved alone. The loves of others continually spill over into mine: in what I think, say, do and achieve. And conversely, my life spills over into that of others ... So my prayer for another is not something extraneous to that person, something external, not even after death."[96]

Hope also teaches us to bear patiently the suffering of daily conversion to Christ in the sure hope that eternal salvation will be ours. Christ abides with us in the Church, accompanying us along the pilgrimage of our life on earth. Resonance with the ecclesial disposition is present here that awareness of Christ conjoined to his Church. He patiently waits for our move from this life to the life that is to come. His Final Coming and judgment at the end of time will purify and restore us, body and soul, and

---

[94] "For the majority of people – we may suppose – there remains in the depths of their being an ultimate interior openness to truth, to love, to God. In the concrete choices of life, however, it is covered over by ever new compromises with evil – much filth covers purity, but the thirst for purity remains, and it still constantly re-emerges from all that is base and remains present in the soul. What happens to such individuals when they appear before the Judge? ... In [Pauline] texts, it is evident that our salvation can take different forms, that some of what is built may be burned down, that in order to be saved we have to pass through 'fire' so as to become fully open to receiving God and able to take our place at the table of the eternal marriage-feast." Ibid., 46.

[95] He continued: "His gaze, the touch of his heart heals us through an undeniably painful transformation "as through fire." But it is a blessed pain, in which the holy power of his love sears through us like a flame, enabling us to become totally ourselves and thus totally of God. In this way the interrelation between justice and grace becomes clear: the way we live our lives is not immaterial, but our defilement does not stain us forever if we have at least continued to reach out towards Christ, towards truth and towards love. Indeed it has already been burned away through Christ's Passion." Ibid., 47.

[96] He continued: "In the interconnectedness of Being, my gratitude to the other – my prayer for him – can play a small part in his purification. And for that there is no need to convert earthly time into God's time: in the communion of souls simple terrestrial time is superseded. It is never too late to touch the heart of another, nor is it ever in vain. In this way we further clarify an important element of the Christian concept of hope. Our hope is always essentially also hope for others; only thus is it truly hope for me too." Ibid., 48. Clearly such prayers for the dead along with belief in Purgatory are entirely consonant with the ecclesial disposition of Ignatius and resonant with the sixth and ninth rules of the Rules for Thinking, Judging, and Feeling with the Church.

all creation to the perfection with which and for which God created the world and has called us into being as His beloved sons and daughters.

Caritas in Veritate—Charity in Truth

This encyclical focuses on the Church's social doctrine but stresses that such teaching rests on the foundation of a love expressed in truth. It stresses the importance of the human family and the importance of the gospel in building a society where freedom and justice are clearly present. "The development of peoples depends, above all on recognition that the human race is a single family working together in true communion, not simply a group of subjects who happen to live side by side."[97] The encyclical explores the theme of human economic and cultural development. Pope Benedict was unequivocal in his insistence that life issues [here echoing Pope John Paul II]—specifically abortion and euthanasia—are at the heart of justice questions. To ignore these specific issues is to be complicit in the enormous damage that is done to human culture. There are also repeated references throughout *Caritas et Veritate* to Pope Paul VI's encyclical *Humanae Vitae*. Pope Benedict clearly asserted that justice is a perennial Christian concern but that love and truth are even more central to the Christian faith. Without love and truth the pursuit of justice inevitably degenerates into utopian agendas. Indeed he emphasized[98] that ultimate justice only comes at the end of life when we meet the God who made us.

Pope Francis—Christ is the Center

On September 7, 2013 the day when he had called for prayer and fasting for peace particularly in Syria, Pope Francis spoke about the importance of the definitive encounter with Christ. "Jesus," he said, "is the centre. Jesus is the Lord. And yet, he maintained, this 'is not easily understood.' Jesus is not a lord of this or that, but is 'the Lord, the only Lord.' He is the centre

---

[97] He continued: "Pope Paul VI noted that 'the world is in trouble because of the lack of thinking.' He was making an observation, but also expressing a wish: a new trajectory of thinking is needed in order to arrive at a better understanding of the implications of our being one family; interaction among the peoples of the world calls us to embark upon this new trajectory, so that integration can signify solidarity rather than marginalization. Thinking of this kind requires a *deeper critical evaluation of the category of relation*. This is a task that cannot be undertaken by the social sciences alone, insofar as the contribution of disciplines such as metaphysics and theology is needed if man's transcendent dignity is to be properly understood." Pope Benedict XVI, *Caritas in Veritate*, para. 53.

[98] *Caritas in Veritate* [14] and [53].

that 'regenerates us, grounds us': this is the Lord, 'the centre.'"[99] This centrality of Christ in his life had been cemented by his own experience as a young man. Going to confession one day he had a profound experience of conversion and the grace that flowed from this encounter with Christ. This experience of God's compassion for him marked his life both in his relationship to God and in the call he experienced to have compassion for others. "That is the way he wants me always to look upon others: with much compassion and as if I were choosing them for Him; not excluding anyone, because everyone is chosen by the love of God."[100] So deep was the imprint of this experience that when he came to choose a motto for his episcopal consecration, it was to this experience that he looked for inspiration. "'By having compassion and by choosing' was the motto of my consecration as a bishop, and it is one of the centerpieces of my religious experience, service is the name of compassion."[101]

In Pope Francis' first address at the welcoming ceremony of World Youth Day in Rio 2013 he clearly stated that he brought neither silver nor gold to the young people but only Jesus. He emphasized that the young people should put on Christ who always accompanies his people. This call to a deep companionship with Christ was particularly focused through the experience of the Passion and here the challenge to prayer, sacrifice and service was most clearly evident. In his first homily as the new pontiff, Pope Francis spoke of the necessity to bear witness to the glory of Christ and his cross, "always Christ with his cross."[102]

"Jesus has called us to be part of a new family, his Church, [he has called] this family to walk together the paths of the Gospel."[103] This bearing witness as a member of Christ's body—the Church—is crucial in Pope Francis' programmatic pastoral activity. But for such witness to be given it is necessary for there to be a profound and mature relationship with Christ. In a homily on Ash Wednesday of 2008, the then Cardinal Bergoglio posed the question "Do I seek an encounter with Jesus that is going to fulfill me, that gives me the only happiness that cannot be lost?"[104] Without such an encounter he maintained life becomes inconsistent and loses its meaning.

In earlier years Archbishop Bergoglio had explained what such an encounter involves: "To encounter Jesus is an extraordinary thing, something that changes the path of our lives, that purifies our hearts,

---

[99] Pope Francis, homily, Casa Sancta Martae, September 7, 2013 http://en.radiovaticana. va/news/2013/09/07/pope_francis:_overcome_temptation_to_be_christians_without_jesus/ en1-726498 (accessed October 8, 2013).

[100] Paul Valley, *Pope Francis: Untying the Knots*, op. cit. 40.

[101] Ibid.

[102] Pope Francis, homily, mass for the inauguration of the new pontificate, St Peter's Square, March 19, 2013.

[103] Ibid.

[104] Cardinal Bergoglio, homily, Buenos Aires, Ash Wednesday, February 6, 2008.

makes us extraordinary, magnanimous, with wide horizons that allow for the provision for all."[105] This encounter is fundamental to our Christian identity which is not dependent upon an identity card but rather on the relationship of belonging to Christ and his Church. Indeed Pope Francis has asserted "it is not possible to find Jesus outside the Church," and he cited Paul VI who stated: "Wanting to live with Jesus without the Church, following Jesus outside of the Church, loving Jesus without the Church is an absurd dichotomy." For Pope Francis the Church as Mother[106] is of profound significance here, a Mother "who gives us our faith, a Mother who gives us our identity. ... And the Mother Church that gives us Jesus gives us our identity that is not only a seal, it is a belonging. Identity means belonging. This belonging to the Church is beautiful."[107]

Lumen Fidei—The Encyclical from Four Hands

Pope Benedict had already written a draft text of this encyclical before he resigned and the draft text was left for his successor when his pontificate came to an end on February 28, 2013. Pope Francis reviewed this text and then made his own contributions before the publication of the encyclical. In paragraph 7 he clearly states:

> These considerations on faith – in continuity with all that the Church's magisterium has pronounced on this theological virtue – are meant to supplement what Benedict XVI had written in his encyclical letters on charity and hope. He himself had almost completed a first draft of an encyclical on faith. For this I am deeply grateful to him, and as his brother in Christ I have taken up his fine work and added a few contributions of my own. The Successor of Peter, yesterday, today and tomorrow, is always called to strengthen his brothers and sisters in the priceless treasure of that faith which God has given as a light for humanity's path.[108]

This encyclical builds upon and completes the triad of encyclicals on the cardinal virtues, love, hope and faith which Pope Benedict had begun

---

[105] Archbishop Jorge Bergoglio, homily for the beginning of the academic year, April 22, 1999.
[106] Cf. also "The Church is not just another organization: 'she is Mother' he said. The Pope commented on the number of mothers present at the Mass. 'How would you feel,' he asked, 'if someone said: "She's a domestic administrator?" "No, I am the mother!" And the Church is Mother. And we are in the middle of a love story that continues thanks to the power of the Holy Spirit. All of us together are a family in the Church, who is our Mother.'" Pope Francis, homily, mass at chapel, Casa Santa Marta, April 24, 2013.
[107] Pope Francis, homily for mass with the Cardinals in the Pauline Chapel, April 23, 2013.
[108] Pope Francis, Encyclical, *Lumen Fidei*, Rome, June 29, 2013, para. 7

during his pontificate. The co-inherence of these three virtues and the focus of their correlation in the person of Christ is the conviction which sustained both the early Church, and the Church across all generations. "The conviction born of a faith which brings grandeur and fulfillment to life, a faith centered on Christ and on the power of his grace, inspired the mission of the first Christians."[109] The centrality of Christ to the life of faith is expounded through a profound reflection on the gift and meaning of faith which encompasses the whole of salvation history, illuminating the Old Testament and culminating in the person and mission of Jesus.

The magnitude of faith is unpacked through considerations of faith and truth: "Today more than ever we need to be reminded of this bond between faith and truth, given the crisis of truth in our age."[110] The dialogue between faith and reason builds upon Pope John Paul II's encyclical *Fides et Ratio* where he showed how faith and reason are mutually strengthening: "Once we discover the full light of Christ's love, we realize that each of the loves in our own lives had always contained a ray of that light, and we understand its ultimate destination;"[111] and faith and theology, too. "Clearly, theology is impossible without faith; it is part of the very process of faith, which seeks an ever deeper understanding of God's self-disclosure culminating in Christ."[112] Indeed, the encyclical underlines the inestimable privilege for theologians who participate in "God's own knowledge of himself ... for he is an eternal dialogue of communion, and he allows us to enter into this dialogue."[113] Such a calling inevitably demands the humility necessary to accepting human limitations while being open to the inexhaustible depths of divine mystery. The encyclical also reiterates previous papal teaching concerning the relationship between theologians and the magisterium of the

---

[109] He continued: "In the acts of the martyrs, we read the following dialogue between the Roman prefect Rusticus and a Christian named Hierax: 'Where are your parents?', the judge asked the martyr. He replied: 'Our true father is Christ, and our mother is faith in him?'(*Acta Sanctorum*, Junii, I, 21.) For those early Christians, faith, as an encounter with the living God revealed in Christ, was indeed a 'mother,' for it had brought them to the light and given birth within them to divine life, a new experience and a luminous vision of existence for which they were prepared to bear public witness to the end." Ibid., para. 5.

[110] He continued: "In contemporary culture, we often tend to consider the only real truth to be that of technology: truth is what we succeed in building and measuring by our scientific know-how, truth is what works and what makes life easier and more comfortable. ... The question of truth [however] is really a question of memory, deep memory, for it deals with something prior to ourselves and can succeed in uniting us in a way that transcends our petty and limited individual consciousness. It is a question about the origin of all that is, in whose light we can glimpse the goal and thus the meaning of our common path."Ibid., para. 25.

[111] He continued: "That fact that our human loves contain that ray of light also helps us to see how all love is meant to share in the complete self-gift of the Son of God for our sake. In this circular movement, the light of faith illumines all our human relationships, which can then be lived in union with the gentle love of Christ." Ibid., para. 32.

[112] Ibid., para 36.

[113] Ibid.

Pope and the bishops. In a manner fully resonant with the Ignatian ecclesial disposition it states:

> Theology also shares in the ecclesial form of faith; its light is the light of the believing subject which is the Church. This implies, on the one hand, that theology must be at the service of the faith of Christians that it must work humbly to protect and deepen the faith of everyone, especially ordinary believers. On the other hand, because it draws its life from faith, theology cannot consider the magisterium of the Pope and the bishops in communion with him as something extrinsic, a limitation of its freedom, but rather as one of its internal, constitutive dimensions, for the magisterium ensures our contact with the primordial source and thus provides the certainty of attaining to the word of Christ in all its integrity.[114]

It is made quite clear that the place where faith is truly experienced and lived is within the Church. "Faith is necessarily ecclesial; it is professed from within the body of Christ as a concrete communion of believers. It is against this ecclesial backdrop that faith opens the individual Christian towards all others. Christ's word once heard, by virtue of its inner power at work in the heart of the Christian, becomes a response, a spoken word, a profession of faith."[115] Within the rich sacramental life of the Church the Christian finds the source of the necessary grace which empowers a dynamic living of faith. The motif of the Church as mother that we have seen so redolent with the Ignatian ecclesial disposition and recurring through the previous pontificates, is once more evident in this encyclical. "The Church is a Mother who teaches us to speak the language of faith."[116]

To believe in Jesus Christ is to understand the Church as the home of faith. From this home members of the Church live out this faith in the family "the first setting in which faith enlightens the human city"[117] and the

---

[114] Ibid.

[115] Ibid., para. 22.

[116] Ibid., para. 38.

[117] Ibid., para. 52. In this paragraph dedicated to the family Pope Francis also reiterates the importance of "the stable union of man and woman in marriage. This union is born of their love, as a sign and presence of God's own love, and of the acknowledgment and acceptance of the goodness of sexual differentiation, whereby spouses can become one flesh and are enabled to give birth to a new life, a manifestation of the Creator's goodness, wisdom and loving plan. Grounded in this love, a man and a woman can promise each other mutual love in a gesture which engages their entire lives and mirrors many features of faith. Promising love for ever is possible when we perceive a plan bigger than our own ideas and undertakings, a plan which sustains us and enables us to surrender our future entirely to the one we love. Faith also helps us to grasp in all its depth and richness the begetting of children, as a sign of the love of the Creator who entrusts us with the mystery of a new person." Ibid. This concern for the family, marriage and family life was particularly evident in the Extraordinary Synod of Bishops on the Family October 2014 and the Ordinary Synod of Bishops October 2015.

wider society. In the family faith is the contextual background for the development of young people significantly in the years as they grow towards adulthood. "Young people want to live life to the fullest. Encountering Christ letting themselves be caught up in and guided by his love, enlarges the horizon of existence, gives it a firm hope which will not disappoint."[118] The call of God is to a universal brotherhood, a sharing as brothers and sisters in the love of God. "The boundless love of our Father also comes to us, in Jesus, through our brothers and sisters. Faith teaches us to see that every man and woman represents a blessing for me, that the light of God's face shines on me through the faces of my brothers and sisters."[119]

This focus on faith does not deny the reality of suffering in the world and here again the central place of Christ is crucial. God does not provide arguments to explain suffering, but rather himself in the person of his son. "In Christ, God himself wishes to share this path with us and to offer us his gaze so that we might see the light within it."[120] Again we see an acknowledgment of the reality of suffering as integral to human life as we have noted throughout this exploration both of the contemporary papacy and also as marking the lives of the exemplars of the Ignatian ecclesial disposition of previous chapters.

---

[118] He continued: "Faith is no refuge for the fainthearted, but something which enhances our lives. It makes us aware of a magnificent calling, the vocation of love. It assures that this love is trustworthy and worth embracing, for it is based on God's faithfulness which is stronger than our every weakness." Ibid., 53.

[119] Ibid., 54. Also, "As salvation history progresses, it becomes evident that God wants to make everyone share as brothers and sisters in that one blessing which attains its fullness in Jesus, so that all may be one."

[120] Ibid., 57. Cf. "If laying down one's life for one's friends is the greatest proof of love (cf. Jn 15.13), Jesus offered his own life for all, even for his enemies, to transform their hearts. This explains why the evangelists could see the hour of Christ's crucifixion as the culmination of the gaze of faith; in that hour the depth and breadth of God's love shone forth." Ibid., 16.

10

The Ecclesial Disposition and the New Evangelization

It was Pope Paul VI who initially focused the attention of the Church on the New Evangelization. In this he continued the apostolic thrust of the conciliar fathers at Vatican II. In 1967, he renamed the Congregation for the Propagation of the Faith as the Congregation for the Evangelization of Peoples. He was the first pope to make apostolic visits to other continents.[1] For the theme of the Synod of Bishops of 1974 he chose "the evangelization of the modern world," and from this Synod principally came the encyclical *Evangelii Nuntiandi*,[2] in which he stated the church "exists in order to evangelize."[3] He asserted that the most authentic expression of the Church was evangelization. Although such evangelization was to be inclusive of all it was vital that there should be explicit proclamation of Christ.

This focus on the centrality of Christ and the impulse for mission that flows from encounter with Christ is, as we have seen, a primary keynote of the Ignatian ecclesial disposition. "There is no true evangelization if the name, the teaching, the life, the promises, the kingdom and the mystery of Jesus of Nazareth, the Son of God are not proclaimed."[4] Evangelization Pope Paul emphasized could not be reduced to any ideological or socio-political developmental platform of liberation. "The Church links human liberation and salvation in Jesus Christ, but she never identifies them, because she knows through revelation, historical experience and the reflection of faith that not every notion of liberation is necessarily consistent and compatible with an evangelical vision of man, of things and of events; she knows too

---

[1] To the Holy Land and India in 1964; to New York in 1965; to Portugal, Istanbul and Ephesus in 1967; to Colombia in 1968; to Geneva and Uganda in 1969; and in 1970 to Teheran, East Pakistan, the Philippines, West Samoa, Australia, Indonesia, Hong Kong and Sri Lanka.
[2] Pope Paul VI, Encyclical *Evangelii Nuntiandi*—on the evangelization of the modern world, December 8, 1975.
[3] Ibid., para. 14.
[4] Ibid., para. 22.

that in order that God's kingdom should come it is not enough to establish liberation and to create well-being and development."[5]

With the succession of John Paul II there was a further development of this missionary impulse. He repeatedly urged the church to proclaim the gospel to all and this call to a new evangelization resounded throughout his papacy. It was not the message that was new, for the gospel retains its authenticity across all generations; what was to be new was the manner of its proclamation. It was to be "new in its ardor, its methods and its expression."[6] His many trips to countries all over the world[7] exemplified in his own person the summons he made to the Church. On a visit to Mexico in 1990 he stated: "The Lord and master of history and of our destinies has wished my pontificate to be that of a pilgrim pope of evangelization, walking down the roads of the world, bringing to all peoples the message of salvation."[8]

In the encyclical *Redemptoris Missio* he stated: "The moment has come to commit all of the Church's energies to a new evangelization and to the mission *ad gentes*. No believer in Christ, no institution of the Church can avoid this supreme duty: to proclaim Christ to all peoples."[9] In the first twenty years of his pontificate Pope John Paul II linked the new evangelization to the coming of the third millennium, and he saw the decade of the 1990s as a particular time of preparation for the great Jubilee of 2000. In *Novo Millenio Ineunte*, the Apostolic Exhortation released in January 2001 he indicated that with the new century there needed to be a renewed "apostolic outreach ... lived as the everyday commitment of Christian communities and groups."[10]

For Pope John Paul II, key characteristics of the new evangelization were: that it involved all Christians, not just clergy and religious; that it was different from the work of the foreign missions; and that it was particularly directed to cultures. For him, as for Pope Paul VI, the proclamation of Christ was central: "The new evangelization begins with the clear and emphatic proclamation of the gospel, which is directed to every person.

---

[5]He continued: "And what is more, the Church has the firm conviction that all temporal liberation, all political liberation—even if it endeavors to find its justification in such or such a page of the Old or New Testament, even if it claims for its ideological postulates and its norms of action theological data and conclusions, even if it pretends to be today's theology carries within itself the germ of its own negation and fails to reach the ideal that it proposes for itself whenever its profound motives are not those of justice in charity, whenever its zeal lacks a truly spiritual dimension and whenever its final goal is not salvation and happiness in God." Ibid., 35.

[6]Pope John Paul II, "The Task of the Latin American Bishop," Address to CELAM, March 9, 1983.

[7]During his pontificate he made 105 visits to countries throughout the world.

[8]Pope John Paul II, Mexico City, May 6, 1990.

[9]Pope John Paul II, Encyclical, *Redemptoris Missio*, December 7, 1990, para. 3.

[10]Pope John Paul II, *Novo Millenio Ineunte*, para. 31.

Therefore it is necessary to awaken again in believers a full relationship with Christ, mankind's only Savior. Only from a personal relationship with Jesus can an effective evangelization develop."[11]

In the Jubilee year of 2000, Cardinal Joseph Ratzinger gave an address to catechists and religion teachers on the Jubilee of Catechists,[12] entitled: "The New Evangelization: Building a Civilization of Love." Within this address he indicated both a consonance with the thought of Pope John Paul II on the new evangelization and his own particular leitmotif of prayer, conversion and mission. At the beginning of his address he contextualized the need for a new evangelization. Human life provides an open question as individuals search for the path for happiness. He said: "to evangelize means to show this path—to teach the art of living."[13] Jesus says he is that path. Cardinal Ratzinger asserted that the deepest form of poverty is the inability to experience joy, and "the tediousness of life considered absurd and contradictory." Such poverty he saw as widespread in contemporary society "in very different forms in the materially rich as well as the poor countries." Such an inability to experience joy "presupposes and produces the inability to love, produces jealousy, avarice—all defects that devastate the life of individuals and of the world. This is why we need a New Evangelization—if the art of living remains an unknown, nothing else works." This art can only be learned from Christ himself. It "is not the object of a science—this art can only be communicated by one who has life—he who is the Gospel personified."[14] So again we return to the centrality of Christ.

In 2007 a doctrinal note from the Congregation for the Doctrine of the Faith, of which Pope Benedict had been prefect until his election to the papacy in 2005, re-emphasized the crucial importance of Christ. "It is the same Lord Jesus Christ who, present in his Church, goes before the work of evangelizers, accompanies it, follows it, and makes their labors bear fruit."[15] Within this document there is a reiteration that the word evangelization sums up the Church's mission. It is a proclamation of the good news of Jesus Christ to all humanity and this is not undertaken by a handing on of doctrine; rather it is "to proclaim Jesus Christ by one's words and actions, that is, to make oneself an instrument of his presence and action in the world."[16] The doctrinal note echoes the words of Pope

---

[11] Pope John Paul II, *Ad Limina*, Visit of Bishops of Southern Germany, December 4, 1992. As referenced in Cardinal Avery Dulles, S.J., "John Paul II and the New Evangelization: What does it Mean?" in Ralph Martin and Peter Williamson (eds), *John Paul II and the New Evangelization* (Cincinnati, OH: Servant Books, 2006), 1–16, [13].
[12] Cardinal Ratzinger, Address to Catechists and Teachers of Religion, Jubilee of Catechists, Rome, December 12, 2000.
[13] Ibid.
[14] Ibid.
[15] Congregation for the Doctrine of the Faith, *Doctrinal Note on Some Aspects of Evangelization* (Rome, December 3, 2007), para. 1
[16] Ibid., 2.

John Paul II above that every person has the right to hear the good news of God in Christ, "so that each one can live out in its fullness his or her proper calling."[17] The document also underlines that every activity of the Church has an essential evangelizing dimension.

One activity specifically brought to attention in 2012 was the relationship between migration and the New Evangelization. Pope Benedict emphasized the urgency necessary to give fresh stimulus and impetus to evangelization in the contemporary context of a world with ever more porous frontiers, where the development of social communications had brought individuals and peoples into closer proximity. It is precisely in this new situation that there needs to be a reawakening in each baptized person of the enthusiasm and courage of the first Christians to be true heralds of the gospel. "The message of Christ is urgent in our time marked by endeavors to efface God and the Church's teaching from the horizon of life, while doubt scepticism and indifference are creeping in, seeking to eliminate all the social and symbolic visibility of the Christian faith."[18]

Pope Benedict inaugurated a new Pontifical Council for the Promotion of the New Evangelization on September 21, 2010 and in a homily at the mass he celebrated with the participants on October 16, 2011 he again reiterated the congruent mission of the Church with that of Christ himself. "The mission of the Church, like that of Christ, is essentially to speak of God, to remember his sovereignty, to remind all, especially Christians who have lost their own identity, of the right of God to what belongs to him, that is, our life."[19] The Pope also emphasized later in his homily the importance of the Holy Spirit in the inspiration of those called to evangelize. Such an assertion recalls also the Trinitarian horizon of the Ignatian ecclesial disposition. "Evangelization, to be effective, needs the power of the Spirit, who gives life to proclamation and imbues those who convey it with the 'full conviction' of which the Apostle speaks."[20]

With the impetus given by the Holy Spirit and the work of the Congregation for the promotion of the New Evangelization, Pope Benedict called a Synod of Bishops in October 2012, which was to consider The New Evangelization for the Transmission of the Christian Faith. The work of the Congregation in the two years prior to the Synod was focused towards this event with the *Lineamenta* document sent throughout the universal church for consultation and comment and then the working document the *Instrumentum Laboris* collated for the work of the Synod Fathers, the theological experts and the observers.

---

[17] Pope John Paul II, Encyclical *Redemptoris Missio*, December 7, 1990, para. 46.
[18] Pope Benedict XVI, Message of His Holiness Pope Benedict for the World Day of Migrants and Refugees: Migrants and the New Evangelization (2012) September 21, 2011.
[19] Pope Benedict XVI, homily, Mass for the New Evangelization, St Peter's Basilica, Rome, October 16, 2011.
[20] Ibid.

The Synod on the New Evangelization for the Transmission of the Christian Faith

"The gathering of bishops in Synod for the good of all Christ's people is one of those disciplines that sustains the health of Christ's Church."[21] This declaration by Archbishop Rowan Williams then Archbishop of Canterbury, at the beginning of his presentation to the Synod in October 2012, makes a significant claim, namely that the coming together of the Synod participants working for the good of the Church is in and of itself a source of health and benefit for all Christian Churches. The ecumenical implications of this were substantial, affirming as it did the work of the Synod but also underlining the more widespread influence of that work for all Christian churches. At this point we might do well to pause to consider what is a synod of bishops?[22]

The term comes from a Greek word formed by combining roots meaning "together" and "going" or "way"—so literally, the idea is going forward together. It has been used over the centuries to refer to assemblies of bishops, as in Orthodoxy, where the synod is the all-important body of bishops that elects the patriarch and establishes church law. In previous centuries, there were synods, but the term largely fell into disuse until the Second Vatican Council (1962–5). In 1965, Pope Paul VI created the Synod of Bishops to give the world's bishops a voice in crafting policy, though it's more like a sounding board than a legislature—it only advises the Pope, and it's up to him to decide what to do. With the accession of Pope Francis it became clear that the structure of the Synod would be explored and significant changes would be made to ensure a more efficient functioning of the Synod in the interests of the Church.

In terms of who is involved, a synod generally includes about twenty bishops representing the Eastern churches and 170 or so chosen by the bishops' conferences of the world. The twenty-five prelates who head Vatican offices are also voting members, as are thirty-five bishops or so named by direct papal appointment. There are generally ten religious, chosen by the Union of Superiors General. All in, that is approximately 260 voting members. In addition, there are also usually around forty-five "experts" and fifty-five "auditors." They don't vote, but the latter have a chance to speak and all have the opportunity to take part in small group discussions. There are also usually around fifteen "fraternal delegates," meaning representatives of the various Christian confessions, such as the

---

[21] Archbishop Rowan Williams, presentation to the Synod of Bishops on the Transmission of the Christian Faith, Rome, October 10, 2012.
[22] Such consideration is particularly important in the light of the Extraordinary Synod of Bishops on the Family October 2014 and the Ordinary Synod of Bishops on the Family October 2015.

Orthodox and the Baptists. They do not have a voting privilege, but they can make an intervention in the plenary session and they take part in the small group discussions. In 2012 one of those fraternal delegates was a female bishop, representing the World Methodist Council.

The New Evangelization as Understood by the 2012 Synod

Firstly, it was clear it was not to be confused with proselytism, meaning aggressive or coercive missionary campaigns. In 2007 a note from the Congregation for the Doctrine of the Faith defined proselytism this way: "The promotion of a religion by using means, and for motives, contrary to the spirit of the Gospel; that is, which do not safeguard the freedom and dignity of the human person."[23] What is important as John Paul II stated is that the faith must always be proposed, but never imposed. Secondly, the New Evangelization was not a simple and/or cynical attempt to boost Mass attendance. It included engaging broad social and cultural challenges through a distinctively Christian lens. Among those challenges, as the synod documents indicated were secularism and relativism, a "hedonistic and consumer-oriented mentality," fundamentalism and "the sects," migration and globalization, the economy, social communications, scientific and technical research, and civic and political life. But even these terms were not always clearly negative. In some countries secularism was seen as a good possibility for Christians since in a secular state it meant they were enabled to practice their faith rather than to have an official state religion imposed.

Thirdly, the new evangelization was not designed just to find more attractive and creative public relations strategies. It also meant an examination of conscience about problems inside the church. "Another fruit of transmitting the faith is the courage to speak out against infidelity and scandal which arise in Christian communities,"[24] the *Institutum Laboris* stated. Failures in evangelization could reflect the church's own incapacity to become "a real community, a true fraternity and a living body, and not a mechanical thing or enterprise."[25]

So what was it? Croatian Archbishop Nikola Eterović, the secretary of the Synod of Bishops, defined the new evangelization by distinguishing three different kinds of missionary effort: evangelization as a regular

---

[23] Congregation for the Doctrine of the Faith, *Doctrinal Note on Some Aspects of Evangelization*.
[24] *Instrumentum Laboris*, working document of the Synod on the New Evangelization and the Transmission of the Christian Faith.
[25] Ibid.

activity of the church, directed at practicing Catholics; the mission *ad gentes*, meaning the first proclamation of Christ to non-Christian persons and peoples; and the "new evangelization," meaning outreach to baptized Catholics who have become distant from the faith. Defined in those terms, the new evangelization aimed to reach out to alienated Catholics who in many cases had become effectively secularized. Europe and North America were a special preoccupation, because that's where a disproportionate share of these "distant Christians" were found. Given those realities, the document declared: "Now is the time for a new evangelization in the West."[26] At the same time it aimed to give added impetus to evangelization as a regular activity of the church and the mission *ad gentes*. "Obviously, such a special focus must not diminish either missionary efforts in the strict sense or the ordinary activity of evangelization in our Christian communities, as these are three aspects of the one reality of evangelization which complement and enrich each other."[27]

The constant assertion of the Synod was that the Church exists to evangelize and this process of evangelization is grounded in an encounter with Christ who reveals the Trinity.[28] Pope Benedict at the opening mass of the Synod stated that, "The New Evangelization reflects a programmatic direction for the life of the Church, its members, families, its communities and institutions. And this outline is reinforced by the fact that it coincides with the beginning of the Year of Faith ... on the 50th anniversary of the opening of the Second Vatican Council." He later reiterated the importance of attentiveness to Christ: "At the beginning of this Synodal Assembly, we ought to welcome the invitation to fix our gaze upon the Lord Jesus ... The word of God places us before the glorious One who was crucified, so that our whole lives, and in particular this Synodal session, will take place in the sight of him and in the light of his mystery."[29] Throughout all generations in every place "evangelization always has its starting and finishing points in Jesus Christ, the Son of God (cf. Mk 1.1); and the Crucifix is the supremely distinctive sign of him who announces the Gospel: a sign of love and peace, a call to conversion and reconciliation. My dear Brother Bishops, starting with ourselves, let us fix our gaze upon him and let us be purified by his grace."[30]

---

[26] Ibid.

[27] Ibid.

[28] Related to this is one of the most important principles of Hans Urs von Balthasar's "Christology," which is the continuity between the inner Trinitarian relations and the mission of Christ in the economy in and through the Church. Hans Urs von Balthasar was a Swiss twentieth century theologian whose work significantly influenced Pope John Paul II, Pope Benedict and Pope Francis.

[29] Pope Benedict XVI, homily, opening mass of the Synod on the New Evangelization and the Transmission of the Christian Faith, October 7, 2012.

[30] Pope Benedict continued: "At various times in history, divine providence has given birth

Encounter with Christ

The title of the Synod, easily shortened to the New Evangelization, was important to recall in understanding the purpose of the Synod: it was not focused on an abstract New Evangelization but with a clear purpose for the transmission of Christian faith. One emphatic statement that recalled the words of Pope John Paul II was that everyone has a right to the encounter with Christ. This indicated something of what became a key trajectory within the Synod: the movement from encounter with Christ through conversion to mission. This movement recalls the dynamic of the Ignatian *Spiritual Exercises*. Archbishop Timothy Costelloe[31] asserted, "The New Evangelization is an invitation to an encounter with Jesus Christ and his bride, the Catholic Church. This encounter with Christ takes place in and through the Church so as not to foster a false dichotomy between spirituality and religion."[32]

The "Message" that came from the Synod stated: "The work of the new evangelization consists in presenting once more the beauty and perennial newness of the encounter with Christ to the often distracted and confused heart and mind of the men and women of our time, above all to ourselves. We invite you all to contemplate the face of the Lord Jesus Christ, to enter the mystery of his life given for us on the cross, reconfirmed in his resurrection from the dead as the Father's gift and imparted to us through the Spirit. In the person of Jesus, the mystery of God the Father's love for the entire human family is revealed."[33] The call to contemplation here

---

to a renewed dynamism in the Church's evangelizing activity. We need only think of the evangelization of the Anglo-Saxon peoples or the Slavs, or the transmission of the faith on the continent of America, or the missionary undertakings among the peoples of Africa, Asia and Oceania. ... Even in our own times, the Holy Spirit has nurtured in the Church a new effort to announce the Good News, a pastoral and spiritual dynamism which found a more universal expression and its most authoritative impulse in the Second Vatican Ecumenical Council. Such renewed evangelical dynamism produces a beneficent influence on the two specific "branches" developed by it, that is, on the one hand the *Missio ad Gentes* or announcement of the Gospel to those who do not yet know Jesus Christ and his message of salvation, and on the other the *New Evangelization*, directed principally at those who, though baptized, have drifted away from the Church and live without reference to the Christian life. The Synodal Assembly which opens today is dedicated to this new evangelization, to help these people encounter the Lord, who alone fills our existence with deep meaning and peace; and to favor the rediscovery of the faith, that source of grace which brings joy and hope to personal, family and social life." Ibid.

[31] Archbishop Timothy Costelloe, Archbishop of Perth, Australia.

[32] Archbishop Costelloe, interview, October 2012.

[33] It continues: "The Church is the space offered by Christ in history where we can encounter him, because he entrusted to her his Word, the Baptism that makes us God's children, his Body and his Blood, the grace of forgiveness of sins above all in the sacrament of Reconciliation, the experience of communion that reflects the very mystery of the Holy Trinity and the strength of the Spirit that generates charity towards all. We must form welcoming communities in

was extended to all Christian communities with the assertion that every disciple of the Lord had an irreplaceable testimony and a responsibility to give witness, in order that the gospel might be brought to all. The indispensable prerequisite for such Christian witness and proclamation, it was emphasized, is holiness of life.

From this perspective contemplation[34] is not just one kind of activity that Christians do: it is the key to prayer, liturgy, ethics, the key to the essence of a renewed humanity that is capable of seeing the world and other subjects in the world with freedom—freedom from self-oriented, acquisitive habits and the distorted understanding that comes from them. Archbishop Rowan Williams robustly asserted in his presentation to the Synod: "To put it boldly, contemplation is the only ultimate answer to the unreal and insane world that our financial systems and our advertising culture and our chaotic and unexamined emotions encourage us to inhabit. To learn contemplative practice is to learn what we need so as to live truthfully and honestly and lovingly. It is a deeply revolutionary matter."[35] Evidently the practice of contemplation for Archbishop Rowan Williams was no light matter but a profound call to conversion and holiness of life. It became increasingly clear within the work of the Synod that the universal call to holiness is constitutive of the New Evangelization and that the saints may be seen as exemplary and effective models of the variety and forms in which this vocation can be realized. Mary was recognized as the model of a holiness that is manifest in acts of love for her. This included the supreme gift of herself to bear the incarnate word.

Conversion and Holiness

This emphasis on holiness of life echoing *Lumen Gentium's* call to universal holiness[36] was seen as a significant part of every evangelizing commitment

---

which all outcasts find a home, concrete experience of communion which attract the disenchanted glance of contemporary humanity with the ardent force of love—'See how they love one another!' ... It is up to us today to render experiences of the Church concretely accessible, to multiply the wells where thirsting men and women are invited to encounter Jesus, to offer oases in the deserts of life." XIII Ordinary General Assembly of the Synod of Bishops, The New Evangelization for the Transmission of the Christian Faith, Message, Vatican City, October 2012, 3.

[34] This focus on contemplation was a key feature also in Pope Francis' many homilies, and his Angelus address. He arranged for pocket editions of the gospel to be given to the crowds in St Peter's Square who came for the Angelus. On many occasions he spoke of the importance of contemplation e.g. "Contemplative prayer is important and can only be done with the Gospel in hand," homily, February 3, 2015, Casa Santa Marta, Vatican.

[35] Archbishop Rowan Williams, presentation to the Synod of Bishops on the The New Evangelization for the Transmission of the Christian Faith, Rome, October 10, 2012.

[36] "The Church, whose mystery is being set forth by this Sacred Synod, is believed to be

for the one who evangelizes and for the good of those so evangelized. Central to growth in holiness is the willingness to engage in ongoing conversion and this theme was re-echoed throughout the Synod significantly focusing on the conversion of those in leadership within the Church. Many bishops spoke with honesty and humility of the need for conversion and renewal in holiness in their own lives, if they were to be true and effective agents of the New Evangelization. "In these days voices among the Bishops were raised to recall that the Church must first of all heed the Word before she can evangelize the world. The invitation to evangelize becomes a call to conversion. We firmly believe that we must convert ourselves first to the power of Christ who alone can make all things new, above all our poor existence."[37]

A climate of humility prevailed in these discussions as the synod fathers stated: "With humility we must recognize that the poverty and weaknesses of Jesus' disciples, especially of his ministers weigh on the credibility of the mission. We are certainly aware—we Bishops first of all that we could never really be equal to the Lord's calling and mandate to proclaim his Gospel to all the nations."[38] Their analysis of the situation was full and frank. "We know that we must humbly recognize our vulnerability to the wounds of history and we do not hesitate to recognize our personal sins. We are, however, also convinced that the Lord's Spirit is capable of renewing his Church ... if we let him mould us."[39] The bishops recognized the call to trust in God's providential care for the work of the New Evangelization. "If this renewal were up to us, there would be serious reasons to doubt. But conversion in the Church, just like evangelization, does not come about primarily through us poor mortals, but rather through the Spirit of the Lord. Here we find our strength and our certainty that evil will not have the last word. ... The work of the new evangelization rests on this serene certainty."[40]

---

indefectibly holy. Indeed Christ, the Son of God, who with the Father and the Spirit is praised as 'uniquely holy,' loved the Church as His bride, delivering Himself up for her. He did this that He might sanctify her. He united her to Himself as His own body and brought it to perfection by the gift of the Holy Spirit for God's glory. Therefore in the Church, everyone whether belonging to the hierarchy, or being cared for by it, is called to holiness. ... However, this holiness of the Church is unceasingly manifested, and must be manifested, in the fruits of grace which the Spirit produces in the faithful; it is expressed in many ways in individuals, who in their walk of life, tend toward the perfection of charity, thus causing the edification of others; in a very special way this (holiness) appears in the practice of the counsels, customarily called 'evangelical.'" *Lumen Gentium*, Dogmatic Constitution on the Church, November 21, 1964, Chapter V, 39.

[37] XIII Ordinary General Assembly of the Synod of Bishops, The New Evangelization for the Transmission of the Christian Faith, Message, Vatican City, October 2012, 5.

[38] Ibid.

[39] Ibid.

[40] XIII Ordinary General Assembly of the Synod of Bishops, The New Evangelization for the Transmission of the Christian Faith, Message, Vatican City, October 2012, 5. The paragraph

Contemplation was seen to be an intrinsic element in this transforming process. It was seen to involve learning to wait upon the Lord without any regard to instant satisfaction; learning to examine and to relativize interior cravings and fantasies; and coming to realize where inordinate attachments exist so that these might be addressed. In short contemplation was seen as a prayerful patient practice of bringing the whole of a human life into the light and love of God's presence. The effect of such contemplative practice is a powerful revising of priorities. "Only as this begins to happen will I be delivered from treating the gifts of God as yet another set of things I may acquire to make me happy, or to dominate other people. And as this process unfolds, I become more free to love human beings in a human way, to love them not for what they may promise me, to love them not as if they were there to provide me with lasting safety and comfort, but as fragile fellow-creatures held in the love of God. I discover how to see other persons and things for what they are in relation to God, not to me. And it is here that true justice as well as true love has its roots."[41]

There was a unanimous recognition among the Synod Fathers that the New Evangelization required personal and communal conversion, new methods of evangelization and renewal of the pastoral structures, to be able to move from a pastoral strategy of maintenance to a pastoral position that is truly one grounded in mission. The New Evangelization was seen to require an authentic pastoral conversion. Such a conversion would see a change in attitudes and an embracing of new initiatives. Ultimately, there would be change in the dynamics of pastoral structures and a weeding out of those which no longer responded to the evangelical demands of the current time.

Within this exploration of conversion, the Synod fathers desired to re-appropriate the life-giving nature of the sacrament of reconciliation. They emphasized that this sacrament is the privileged place to receive God's mercy and forgiveness. It is a place for both personal and communal healing. There was a re-appropriation of teaching concerning the communal dimension of healing by the grace of the sacrament, such that a good confession contributed by grace not just to the life and health of the individual penitent but also to the life and health of the Church as a whole. The Synod Fathers asked that this sacrament be put again at the center of the pastoral activity of the Church with a renewed creativity in helping all to understand the life-giving potential of the sacrament for the individual and the Church as a whole.[42] The bishops also saw themselves

---

continues: "We are confident in the inspiration of the Spirit, who will teach us what we are to say and what we are to do even in the most difficult moments. It is our duty therefore, to conquer fear through faith, discouragement through hope, indifference through love."

[41] Address of Archbishop Rowan Williams, to the Synod of Bishops on the New Evangelization for the Transmission of the Christian Faith, October 10, 2013.

[42] In small group and individual discussions it became apparent that participants at the Synod

as personally challenged regarding their participation in this sacrament as both penitents and ministers. Many conversations outside the Synod hall focused on a renewed appreciation of this sacrament.

Mission

The Church by its very nature is missionary and the solid ground of contemplation and ongoing conversion is the spring-board for the promulgation of the mission of evangelization. The human face that Christians want to show to the world is a face marked by justice and love, and therefore formed by contemplation, by the discipline of silence and the detaching of the self from the objects that enslave it and the unexamined instincts that can deceive it.[43] Contemplation and conversion were conjoined in the mind of the synod participants. This was not to argue that internal transformation was more important than action for justice. Rather, it was to insist that the clarity and energy necessary for doing justice required prior prayer. Otherwise it would be too easy for a search for justice or for peace to become another exercise of the human will, undermined by human self-deception and the desire to control. Contemplation and action were seen to be inseparable. True prayer of its nature purifies human motivation, and it grounds and authenticates the work of the New Evangelization, while "true justice is the necessary work of sharing and liberating in others the humanity we have discovered in our contemplative encounter."[44]

Here the Synod Fathers were concerned to emphasize the vital necessity of the evangelizers being properly prepared to take their part in this mission by a good spiritual and intellectual formation. This led to consideration of formation in families, schools, parishes, and higher education establishments and the need for a renewed understanding of life-long catechesis. Alongside the proclamation of the Gospel in this way there was a renewed commitment to the dimension of justice. It was seen that greater attention needed to be given to the Church's social doctrine, understanding that it is a proclamation and witness of faith, an irreplaceable means of education in the faith.[45] This embrace of the Church's social doctrine should in turn permeate the content of catechesis, Christian education, formation of seminarians and religious, the continuing formation of bishops and priests and most especially the formation of the laity. The *Compendium of the*

---

were well aware that the lack of numbers approaching the sacrament, also meant that this source of grace for the Church as well as for the individual was not being appropriated and indeed that the Church was diminished by such non-participation.

[43] Cf. XIII Ordinary General Assembly of the Synod of Bishops, The New Evangelization for the Transmission of the Christian Faith, Message, Vatican City, October 2012, 12.

[44] Ibid. 3.

[45] Cf. *Caritas in Veritate*, 15.

Social Doctrine of the Church was recovered as a precious resource in accomplishing this continuing formation.

It was brought to the attention of Synod participants that in our contemporary reality there are new poor and new faces of poverty: the hungry, the homeless, the sick and abandoned, drug addicts, migrants and the marginalized, political and environmental refugees, the indigenous peoples. The ongoing economic difficulties seriously affect the poor. Among the poorest in contemporary society were cited the victims of loss of respect for the inviolable dignity of innocent human life. The preferential option for the poor leads the Church to seek out the poor and to work on their behalf so that they may feel at home in the Church. They are both recipients and actors in the New Evangelization, a reality that Pope Francis was quick to reiterate from the inception of his pontificate. Placing ourselves side by side with those who are wounded by life is not only a social exercise, but above all a spiritual act because it is Christ's face that shines in the face of the poor. "The presence of the poor[46] in our communities is mysteriously powerful: it changes persons more than a discourse does, it teaches fidelity, it makes us understand the fragility of life, it asks for prayer: in short it brings us to Christ."[47] Pope Francis, from the beginning of his pontificate, reiterated the same conjunction of contemplation and action—prayer and outreach to the poor.

Pope Francis and the New Evangelization

On October 14, 2013 Pope Francis met with the participants in the Plenary Assembly of the Pontifical Council for Promoting the New Evangelization. Here he emphasized a three-fold imperative: the primacy of witness; the urgency of going out to encounter others; and a pastoral program centered on the essential. The attitude of indifference to faith which is no longer seen as relevant to people's lives needs to be countered by an energetic response. He stated: "New Evangelization means to reawaken the life of faith in the heart and mind of our contemporaries."[48] Here the gift of faith received from God needs to be seen in the lives of Christians in a concrete

---

[46] During the time of the Synod various faces of the poor were brought to the immediate attention of synod participants, not just through the interventions of Bishops from the Middle East particularly and Africa, but also through the three priests who were kidnapped in E. Congo; through the death of seventeen civilians in another part of Africa; and through the decision of the Pope to send a delegation of Synod Fathers to Syria and then to experience the frustration of that plan by events and timing and security concerns. (Eventually Cardinal Robert Sarah was sent to Lebanon to the Syrian refugees there.)

[47] XIII Ordinary General Assembly of the Synod of Bishops, The New Evangelization for the Transmission of the Christian Faith, Message, Vatican City, October 2012, 12.

[48] Pope Francis, address to the Plenary Assembly of the Pontifical Council for Promoting the New Evangelization, Clementine Hall of the Apostolic Palace, October 14, 2013.

way, through "love joy and suffering, because this elicits questions,"[49] the kind of questions that were raised by the witness of the early Church to faith and charity. So, he stated that what we need especially in our contemporary times are "credible witnesses who with their life and also with the word render the Gospel visible, reawaken attraction for Jesus Christ, for God's beauty."[50] Within this form of witness Pope Francis stressed the need to employ the "language of mercy, made up of gestures and attitudes even before words."[51] Here he linked the witness of Christians to the example of Christ, asserting that all baptized persons are "*Christofor*", bearers of Christ. Therefore it is for all of us to ask ourselves if one who meets us perceives in our life the warmth of faith, sees in our face the joy of having encountered Christ. Such an assertion clearly echoes the robust presentation of the Synod on the New Evangelization when it stated that everyone has the right to an encounter with Christ.

It is from this foundation of encounter with Christ that Christians are called to encounter others. So Pope Francis declared that, "the New Evangelization is a movement towards him who has lost the faith and the profound meaning of life. This dynamism is part of the great mission of Christ to bring life to the world, the Father's love to humanity."[52] Accordingly, since the Church is part of this movement and every Christian is invited to share in the redemptive work of Christ, all Christians are called to go out to encounter others, to dialogue with them, without fear. Specifically Christians are called to reawaken[53] hope "where it is suffocated by difficult existential conditions, at times inhuman ... There is need of the oxygen of the Gospel, of the breath of the Spirit of the Risen Christ, to rekindle it in hearts."[54] All of this leads to the necessity of a common commitment to a pastoral plan

---

[49] Ibid.

[50] Pope Francis continued: "So many people have fallen away from the Church. It's a mistake to put the blame on one side or the other, in fact, it's not about talking about fault. There are responsibilities in the history of the Church and of her men, in certain ideologies, and also in individual persons. As children of the Church we must continue on the path of Vatican II, stripping ourselves of useless and harmful things, of false worldly securities which weigh down the Church and damage her true face." Ibid.

[51] Ibid.

[52] Ibid.

[53] Late in 2014 as the Year for Consecrated Life began, Pope Francis called on all those men and women in religious life and any form of consecrated life to "wake the world" with their witness to the joy of the gospel and the gracious mercy of God. He called members to "live the present with passion"; to examine their fidelity to the mission entrusted to them; to embrace the future with hope; to question what God and people were asking of them." Pope Francis, Apostolic Letter of His Holiness to All Consecrated People on the occasion of the year of Consecrated Life, November 21, 2014.

[54] Pope Francis continued: "the Church is the house whose doors are always open not only so that everyone can find welcome and breathe love and hope, but also because we can go out and bring this love and this hope. The Holy Spirit drives us to go out of our enclosure and guides us to the fringes of humanity." Ibid.

that is focused on the essential the encounter with Jesus Christ "with his mercy, with his love, and to love brothers as He loved us."[55]

The New Evangelization Imperative

It is clear from the above that Pope Francis desired a missionary Church reaching out to others from the basis of one's own encounter with Christ. In order to promote this mission of the Church he developed the three-fold leitmotif of the Synod on the New Evangelization. The focus on contemplation at the Synod he widened to prayer as a whole while not diminishing the importance of contemplation as a point to which prayer may mature. The Synod's emphasis on conversion Pope Francis both underlined and then added a robust focus on the mercy of God. Finally the Synod's reminder that the Church exists for mission a share in the redemptive work of Christ, he has directed to an outreach to all others particularly the disillusioned, the apathetic, the indifferent and especially the poor and most vulnerable.[56]

Contemplation—Prayer

In a series of interviews given to the Jesuit editor of *Civiltà Cattolica* 2013, Pope Francis indicated the importance of prayer for him, personally. "Prayer for me is always a prayer full of memory, of recollection, even the memory of my own history, or what the Lord has done in his Church." He linked this point with his own experience of making the *Spiritual Exercises* of St. Ignatius Loyola. "The memory of which St. Ignatius speaks in the first week of the *Exercises* in the encounter with the merciful Christ crucified."[57] Also it is the memory that is necessarily operative in the contemplation for experiencing divine love[58] "when [Ignatius] asks us to recall the gifts we have received. But above all, I also know that the Lord remembers me. I can

---

[55] "A project animated by the creativity and imagination of the Holy Spirit, who drives us also to follow new ways, with courage and without becoming fossilized." Ibid.

[56] In 2014 a new Commission was instituted at the Vatican, the Commission for the Protection of Minors and Vulnerable Adults. It involved survivors of sexual abuse by clergy but the parameters of its work stretched beyond the work of clerical sexual abuse to look at policies and procedures to protect minors (children and adolescents) from all forms of abuse and also to analyse the care and protection of vulnerable adults.

[57] See Chapter 2 in this work. Pope Francis added "And I ask myself: What have I done for Christ? What am I doing for Christ? What should I do for Christ?" Pope Francis, interview with Antonio Spadaro, S.J., editor, *La Civiltà Cattolica*, 2013.

[58] The last of the *Exercises*, again see Chapter 2.

forget about him, but I know that he never, ever forgets me. Memory has a fundamental role ... memory of grace."[59]

Pope Francis often asserted the importance of prayer in his homilies given at the daily mass he celebrated at Casa Santa Marta where he lived. On October 8, 2013 he said: "The first task in life is prayer. But not the prayer of words, like parrots; but prayer of the heart: to look at the Lord to listen to the Lord, to ask the Lord. We know that prayer can work miracles."[60] He emphasized also the importance of courage in prayer. "A prayer that is not courageous is not a real prayer." Christians need to have: "The courage to trust that the Lord listens to us, the courage to knock on the door."[61] On October 10, 2013 Pope Francis reiterated that it is important that Christians do not pray out of habit but with fervor of belief that the Lord himself is present with us in prayer, he said: "the Lord gives us grace and himself. He is this grace. He himself is the one who brings us the grace."[62] One way of attending to this presence of Christ Pope Francis indicated was in contemplation of Christ's suffering humanity and also in attending to his Blessed Mother. Living the message of the Gospel is demanding he said and it requires "strong things" from a Christian: "the ability to forgive, magnanimity, love for enemies." There is only one way to be able to put it into practice: "to contemplate the Passion, the humanity of Jesus and to imitate the behavior of His Mother."[63]

Apart from an emphatic assertion of the importance of personal prayer for the New Evangelization Pope Francis also indicated the necessity of communal prayer both in the liturgy and in other intercessory ways. In September 2013 he called for a global prayer vigil for peace, particularly in Syria and over 100,000 people joined him in St Peter's Square. In addition local prayer vigils were arranged in Cathedrals and churches throughout the world to pray with the Pope and to join in this global intercessory initiative. The Pope's belief that prayer can work miracles and his commendation of personal and communal prayer in, and beyond, the Eucharistic liturgy are key resonances with the Ignatian ecclesial disposition.

Conversion

"Conversion is not something that we can promise to do; it must actually be accomplished."[64]

---

[59] Pope Francis, interview with Antonio Spadaro, S.J., editor, *La Civiltà Cattolica*, 2013.

[60] Pope Francis, homily, Casa Santa Marta, October 8, 2013.

[61] Ibid.

[62] Pope Francis, homily, Casa Santa Marta, October 10, 2013.

[63] Pope Francis, homily, Casa Santa Marta, September 12, 2013.

[64] Hans Urs von Balthasar, *Epilogue*, trans. Edward T. Oakes, S.J. (San Francisco: Ignatius Press, 2004), 118.

This succinct observation from the last pages of *Epilogue* is uncompromising in the challenge it presents. For Hans Urs von Balthasar conversion has nothing to do with vain promises, procrastination, or even prodigious activity. It is something that has actually to be accomplished and the accomplishment involves always the divine initiative of love calling forth a human response. Echoing throughout Balthasar's theology is the pre-eminent divine call to conversion which is both a mysterious gift of grace given and an ongoing condition or dynamic disposition of dialogue with God. This work of prevenient grace is also intrinsically personal, as the core action of all conversion is that dawning awareness of one's own reality through an encounter with Christ. It involves both a divesting of the disguises and subterfuges that have become accretions to the ego and a renunciation of self-seeking which ultimately brings peace to the soul.

Conversion is brought about by a call from Jesus, it is not a monologue but a dialogue between the individual and Christ. As Balthasar himself stated: "*Lumen Gentium cum sit Christus*. The great light of the world, for which people are searching today, is Christ."[65] Following from this, in *Lumen Gentium*, we encounter the *telos* of such conversion with the assertion that all Christians are called to the perfection of love and holiness. Conversion is of necessity an individual process and yet it is also situated within the larger drama of redemption. It is focused in a dialogue between God and human persons where the entire Trinity is involved, where infinite and finite freedom are engaged, and where the role of the Church is made manifest.

Pope Francis—Conversion and God's Mercy

When Pope Francis was asked in an interview how he would identify himself his reply startled many. He said: "I am a sinner. This is the most accurate definition. It is not a figure of speech or a literary genre. I am a sinner. ... The best summary, the one that comes more from the inside and I feel most true is this: I am a sinner whom the Lord has looked upon."[66] When Archbishop of Buenos Aires, he had taken as his motto, *Miserando atque Eligendo*—by having mercy and by choosing him, and he felt that this was fundamentally true for his own life as noted in the experience of his early life referenced in chapter eight. From the earliest days of his pontificate Pope Francis asserted the importance of God's mercy and the desire of God to grant forgiveness. At the same time he recognized the diffidence

---

[65] Hans Urs von Balthasar, *Test Everything: Hold Fast To What is Good*, trans. Maria Shrady (San Francisco: Ignatius Press, 1989), 17.
[66] Pope Francis, interview with Antonio Spadaro, S.J., editor, *La Civiltà Cattolica*, 2013.

of many in believing in the mercy of God. The first Sunday homily that he gave he said: "It is not easy to entrust oneself to God's mercy, because it is an abyss beyond our comprehension, but we must!" He embellished his remarks by saying. "The Lord never tires of forgiving, never! It is we who tire of asking for his forgiveness. Let us ask for the grace not to tire of asking for forgiveness."[67]

For Pope Francis God's mercy is a foundation stone for his vision of the Church and central to this vision is the reality of confession as experienced in the sacrament of reconciliation. He continued to assert the difference between the Church and any other organization. He said: "The Church is not a club for those who consider themselves perfect. The Church is a hospital for sinners."[68] Accordingly central to the mission of mercy in the Church is the sacrament of reconciliation in which we experience in a personal and direct way the mercy and forgiveness of God and are healed by grace. Teaching about this sacrament formed the basis for many of Pope Francis' homilies in Autumn 2013.

In a homily in October he focused entirely on the Sacrament of Reconciliation. He asserted that to go to confession was to encounter the love of Christ and this needed the transparency and sincerity of heart of a child not running away from but welcoming "the grace of shame"[69] that makes human persons perceive the reality of God's forgiveness. The Pope elaborated his thoughts by indicating how he understood that many adults who truly believed found it excruciating to confess to a priest and this is often what led them to avoid the sacrament altogether. Yet he emphasized that it is our human experience that we do not do the good we wish to do but that "when I want to do good, evil is close to me."[70] He continued, "This is the struggle of Christians. It is our struggle every day. And we do not always have the courage to speak … about this struggle. We always seek a way of justification … it is our struggle."[71]

The Pope reiterated how important it is to recognize our struggle. "And if we don't recognize this, we will never be able to have God's forgiveness. If being a sinner is a word, a way of speaking, a manner of speaking, we have no need of God's forgiveness. But if it is a reality that makes us slaves, we need the interior liberation of the Lord."[72] Pope Francis clearly reinforced church teaching on the necessity of individual confession. "Confession of sins done with humility is something the Church requires of all of us." He

---

[67] Pope Francis, homily, St Ann's Parish, Vatican City, Rome, March 17, 2013.

[68] Pope Francis, interview with Antonio Spadaro, S.J. editor, *La Civiltà Cattolica*, 2013.

[69] This is in accord with Ignatius Loyola's suggested grace for the first week of the *Spiritual Exercises*, see Chapter 2.

[70] Pope Francis, homily, Casa Santa Marta, Rome, October 25, 2013. Translation provided by Fr. Thomas Rosica, CSB.

[71] Ibid.

[72] Ibid.

stated, "To recognize that it is God who saves me." This practice is not like going to a psychiatrist, "it is saying to the Lord, 'Lord I am a sinner because of this, that and the other thing." It requires concreteness and honesty and a sincere ability to be ashamed of one's mistakes. Here is where we can imitate little children. "Little children have that wisdom: when a child comes to confess, he never says anything general. ... They have that simplicity of truth. And we always have the tendency to hide the reality of our failings. But there is something beautiful when we confess our sins as they are in the presence of God, we always feel that grace of shame. Being ashamed in the sight of God is a grace."[73]

The heart of conversion Pope Francis maintained is a coming forth from self-sufficiency to recognize and accept our true indigence. We are dependent beings and conversion is the humility to entrust ourselves to the love of the Other (who is God), a love that becomes the measure and criteria of our lives. Conversion does not imply moralism; reducing Christianity to morality loses sight of the essence of Christ's message: the gift of our new friendship, the gift of communion with Jesus and thereby with God. Whoever converts to Christ does not mean to create his own moral autonomy for himself, and does not intend to build his own goodness through his own strengths. Rather the one who is converted to Christ knows himself/herself as a sinful person truly dependent upon God's mercy and care and linked to a great community of brothers and sisters in the church. As Pope Francis said in his homily November 5, 2013: "The Church is not the Church only for good people. Do we want to describe who belongs to the Church ... The sinners."[74]

Mission—Outreach

At the Synod of Bishops of October 2012, Fr. Robert Prevost, the then Prior General of the Order of St. Augustine, gave a powerful intervention on the context of contemporary mission indicating the influence of the mass media in "fostering within the general public enormous sympathy for beliefs and practices that are at odds with the gospel, for example abortion, homosexual lifestyle and euthanasia." He continued by emphasizing that religion is at best tolerated and deemed quaint "when it does not actively oppose ethical issues that the media have embraced as their own." When religious voices do steadfastly stand in opposition then mass media can target religion, castigating it as ideological, intolerant, and insensitive to "the so-called vital needs of people in the contemporary world." The mass media is very accomplished in its programmatic espousal of anti-Christian

---

[73] Ibid.
[74] Pope Francis, homily, Casa Santa Marta, November 5, 2013.

views. "The sympathy for anti-Christian lifestyle choices, that mass media fosters is so brilliantly and artfully engrained in the viewing public that when people hear the Christian message it often inevitably seems ideologically and emotionally cruel by contrast to the ostensible humaneness of the anti-Christian perspective."[75]

In the month of September 2013 Pope Francis focused on a similar theme when he addressed the participants in the Plenary Assembly of the Pontifical Council for Social Communications. He stated that the goal of the Church for its communication efforts was "to understand how to enter into dialogue with the men and women of today in order to appreciate their desires, their doubts and their hopes."[76] He then indicated that it was important to examine if the Church's communications were indeed enabling people to encounter Christ. "The challenge is to rediscover, through the means of social communication as well as by personal contact, the beauty that is at the heart of our existence and our journey, the beauty of faith and of the encounter with Christ."[77] In a globalized world there exists paradoxically "a growing sense of disorientation and isolation; we see, increasingly a loss of meaning to life, an inability to connect with a 'home,' and a struggle to build meaningful relationships."[78] Within this environment Pope Francis raised a fundamental question. "Are we capable of communicating the face of a Church which can be a 'home' to everyone?"[79] To meet this challenge, he indicated, it would be necessary to build the Church as we continue to walk to build home together with others.[80]

Pope Francis had already indicated that we needed to proclaim the gospel on every street corner. When it comes to social issues, he stated it is one thing to have a meeting to study the problem of drugs in a slum neighborhood and quite another to go there, live there and understand

---

[75] Fr. Robert Prevost, Prior General of the Order of St. Augustine, intervention Synod of Bishops on the New Evangelization for the Transmission of the Christian Faith, October 2012. He continued: "If the New Evangelization is going to counter these mass media produced distortions of religious and ethical reality successfully, pastors, preachers, teachers and catechists are going to have to become far more informed about the context of evangelizing in a world dominated by mass media."

[76] Pope Francis address to the participants in the Plenary Assembly of the Pontifical Council for Social Communications, September 21, 2013.

[77] Ibid.

[78] He continued: "It is therefore important to know how to dialogue, and how to enter with discernment, into the environments created by new technologies, into social networks, in such a way as to reveal a presence that listens, converses, and encourages. Do not be afraid to be this presence, expressing your Christian identity as you become citizens of this environment. A Church that follows this path learns how to walk with everybody!" Ibid.

[79] Ibid.

[80] He stated: "The great digital continent does not only involve technology, but is made up of real men and women who bring with them what they carry inside, their hopes, their suffering, their concerns, their pursuit of truth, beauty and the good." Ibid.

the problem from the inside and study it. "I see clearly that the thing the church needs most today is the ability to heal wounds and to warm the hearts of the faithful; it needs nearness, proximity. I see the Church as a field hospital[81] after a battle. It is useless to ask a seriously injured person if he has high cholesterol and about the level of his blood sugars! You have to heal the wounds. Then we can talk about everything else. Heal the wounds … heal the wounds."[82] Later in the same interview he emphasized the importance once more of the Church moving out to encounter others. "Instead of being just a church that welcomes and receives by keeping the doors open, let us try also to be a church that finds new roads, that is able to step outside itself and go to those who do not attend mass, to those who have quit or are indifferent."[83]

During the course of a pilgrimage that he made to Assisi on October 4, 2013, Pope Francis Assisi visited sick and disabled children and young people at the Seraphic Institute. He approached each of the residents and held their hands, caressed their faces, signed the Cross on their foreheads and often kissed them on the cheek. He put aside his prepared text and spoke simply comparing the scars of Christ to the suffering carried by the young people before him. "These scars (in the sick) need to be recognized and listened to," he said. Referring to the Eucharist in the tabernacle, he said: "Jesus chooses to be present there in the simplicity and meekness of the bread. And Jesus is hidden in these children, these young people."[84] In another focus on vulnerable people, following his Vigil for Peace, in a message to the Food and Agriculture Organization Pope Francis commented "Hunger and malnutrition can never be considered a fact of life, to which we accustom ourselves, almost as if it were 'part of the system.' Something must change in us, in ourselves, in our mentality, in our societies."[85]

Pope Francis had already given some indications of what he considered his own important emphases for mission and outreach. In his General Audience June 12, 2013, he prayed "May the church be the place of God's mercy and love, where everyone can feel themselves welcomed, loved, forgiven, and encouraged to live according to the good life of the

---

[81] This was an image of the Church dear to the heart of Pope Francis and one he returned to many times. For example, in his homily of February 5, 2015, Casa Santa Marta, Vatican.

[82] Pope Francis, interview with Antonio Spadaro, S.J., editor, *La Civiltà Cattolica*, 2013.

[83] Ibid. He continued: "The ones who quit sometimes do it for reasons that if properly understood and assessed, can lead to a return. But that takes audacity and courage."

[84] Pope Francis, at the Seraphic Institute Assisi, October 4, 2013. He continued: "A Christian adores Jesus, seeks Jesus, knows how to recognize the scars of Jesus. When Jesus rose he was beautiful. He didn't have his wounds on his body, but he wanted to keep the scars, and he brought them with him to heaven. The scars of Jesus are here, and they are in heaven before the Father. We care for the scars of Jesus here, and he from heaven shows us his scars and tells all of us: I am waiting for you."

[85] Pope Francis, message to the Food and Agriculture Organization, October 2013.

Gospel. And in order to make others feel welcomed, loved, forgiven, and encouraged, the church must have open doors so that all might enter. And we must go out of those doors and proclaim the Gospel."[86]

The Importance of the Family in the New Evangelization and the Life of the Church

In October 2013 Pope Francis took part in a very large family celebration in St Peter's Square, Rome. Officials estimated that there were over 200,000 people present even before the rally began. The celebration had been organized by the Pontifical Council for the Family, for the year of faith and the theme was "Families live the joy of the faith." It followed directly after the annual meeting of the Pontifical Council. From his election onwards Pope Francis took the family as one of the central themes of his pontificate, and in October 2013 he announced that an extraordinary Synod of Bishops for 2014 and the Ordinary Synod of Bishops in 2015 would both be devoted to the Family. The former was entitled "Pastoral Challenges to the Family in the Context of the New Evangelization." The Relator General for the Synod, Cardinal Péter Erdő made the important point that this Extraordinary Synod would act as a bridge between the 2012 Synod on the New Evangelization and the 2015 Ordinary Synod on the Family.

Unusually, no Apostolic Exhortation was written after the New Evangelization Synod October 2012. Pope Benedict resigned before writing it and Pope Francis stated he would not write it. Nevertheless from the Synod itself, came a message to the universal Church and this message gave evidence of the real concern of the Synod participants to encourage and support the family, acknowledging its unique role in the transmission of the faith. "Ever since the first evangelization, the transmission of the faith from one generation to the next found a natural home in the family."[87] Within

---

[86] Pope Francis, General Audience, St Peter's Square, Rome, June 12, 2013. Cf. Also, "And from a more systematic point of view, it is harmonious with the Pope's emphases to say that the mission of the Church must be mediating what we can call social grace, that is, grace whose effects heal the effects of social sin in human situations. The Pope has called attention in particular to the social sins structured into the global economic system and the machines of war. A theology that would mediate the significance and role of the gospel in our respective cultural matrices in a way that would contribute to the emergence of a grace that heals the effects of social sin must collaborate with committed experts in other disciplines to construct viable alternatives to the destructive paths down which the growing disparity between rich and poor, the exploits of warring nations, and religious hostilities are taking us." Robert Doran, S.J., Convocation Address, University of St. Michael's College, November 2, 2013.

[87] XIII Ordinary General Assembly of the Synod of Bishops, The New Evangelization for the Transmission of the Christian Faith, Message, Vatican City, October 2012, 7. The section

this same section of the "Message" the Synod members acknowledged the many challenges and crises that beset contemporary marriage and family life. "It is surrounded by models of life that penalize it and neglected by the politics of society to which it is a fundamental cell."[88]

The very severity of the pressures on the family impelled the synod fathers to say that they needed to develop "specific paths of accompaniment before and after matrimony."[89] They then took up a theme prevalent in the discussions at the Synod, the concern for those living in irregular situations. The painful nature of these situations was something shared by the bishops in their discussions and the message reflected this reality when it stated: "To all of them we want to say that God's love does not abandon anyone, that the Church loves them, too, that the Church is a house that welcomes all, that they remain members of the Church even if they cannot receive sacramental absolution and the Eucharist. May our Catholic communities welcome all who live in such situations and support those who are on the path of conversion and reconciliation."[90]

Finally the message underlined the supernatural horizon of human existence as witnessed in the gift of marriage and family life. Family life is the first place where members may see how the gospel transforms "the fundamental conditions of existence in the horizon of love." Alongside this witness, however, is another profound one namely, how temporal existence has "a fulfillment that goes beyond human history and attains to eternal communion with God."[91] It was these insights that were brought to bear on the preparations for the extraordinary and the ordinary Synods of 2014 and 2015.

Archbishop Bruno Forte, who served as Special Secretary for the 2014 Extraordinary Synod, in his introduction of the preparatory document highlighted the *pastoral* nature of the theme: the Family. This was clearly evidenced in the preparatory document, which offered a series of pertinent reflection questions for the local churches around the world, that were significantly pastoral and practical in nature. For example, in the section entitled "The Pastoral Care of the Family in Evangelization," one challenging question reads: "What specific contribution can couples and families make to spreading a credible and holistic idea of the couple and

---

continued: "In the context of the care that every family provides for its little ones, infants and children are introduced to the signs of faith, the communication of first truths, education in prayer, and the witness of the fruits of love. Despite the diversity of their geographical, cultural and social situations, all the Bishops of the Synod reconfirmed this essential role of the family in the transmission of the faith. A new evangelization is unthinkable without acknowledging a specific responsibility to proclaim the Gospel to families and to sustain them in their task of education." Ibid.

[88] Ibid.
[89] Ibid.
[90] Ibid.
[91] Ibid.

the Christian family today?" While another question investigates: "What pastoral care has the Church provided in supporting couples in formation and couples in crisis situations?" Such concrete questions sought specific information, challenged ongoing reflection, and sought to ensure that the Synod would engage with the lives and experiences of real people on the ground. They also gave an indication that practical pastoral policy would be forthcoming from the Synod deliberations.

In an address to the President of the Republic of Italy, Giorgio Napoletano, November 14, 2013, Pope Francis again reiterated the importance of support for the family seeing it as the 'fulcrum of hope and social problems. He emphasized that, "the Church continues to promote the efforts of all, individuals and institutions, in support of the family, which is the primary location in which the human being is formed and grows, and where values are transmitted along with the examples that make them credible. The family needs the stability and recognition of mutual bonds in order to carry out fully its unique role and to achieve its mission. While the family makes its energies available to society, it asks in return to be appreciated, valued and protected."[92]

Contemplative compassionate pastoral practicalities we have seen were key elements for Pope Francis in discerning the way in which the Church moved forward in the three-fold trajectory of prayer, conversion and mission. These same elements he expressed as being vital also for those who would be catechists. In an address to participants in the International Conference on Catechesis, for the year of faith, in September 2013, he underlined the importance of the witness given by catechists through their lives, even before they articulated anything about the faith. The first priority was a deep ongoing proximate relationship with Christ which needs the discipline of regular prayer. Here he emphasized the importance of contemplation, letting oneself be gazed upon by the Lord. "This warms the heart, igniting the fire of friendship with the Lord, making you feel that he truly sees you, that he is close to you and loves you."[93] Praying in this way the Pope stressed leads the individual to put Christ at the center of life rather than oneself, and from this flows a willingness to go out to others, to engage in Christ's redemptive work. "This is the true dynamism of love, this is the movement of God himself! God is the centre, but he is always self-gift, relationship, love that gives itself away … and this is what we will become if we remain united to Christ. He will draw us into this dynamism of love."[94]

This is the very heart of a catechist's work, to go lovingly to others,

---

[92] Pope Francis, Address to the President of the Republic of Italy Giorgio Napoletano, Quirinal Palace, Rome, November 14, 2013.
[93] Pope Francis, Address to the Catechist Participants in the International Conference on Catechesis, September 28, 2013.
[94] Ibid.

bearing witness to Christ and talking about him. It is this systolic and diastolic movement of union with Christ and then engaging with others. Always the gift of faith generates mission. Finally there is the risky commitment to go to the outskirts to move beyond an individual's comfort zone, to creatively engage with people who can be disturbingly different, but always with the knowledge of being close to God in such an enterprise. The Pope described himself as a catechist also. As a man called to spearhead the New Evangelization, Pope Francis exemplified within his own person the importance of prayer, conversion and outreach that had been the continuous and developing leitmotif of his two predecessors and gave his own creative contribution through symbol, gesture and simplicity of word.

In Summary the Three Popes and the Ecclesial Disposition

Pope John Paul II

We have seen that the ecclesial disposition of Ignatius can be traced not only in Jesuits and those like Mary Ward of the Ignatian family but also within the highest leadership of the Church. In particular, during the pontificate of Pope John Paul II we can observe that disposition made manifest. We see that same prominence of a deep relationship with Christ and the awareness that Christ and the Church are conjoined. There is a clear sense of the importance of the Trinitarian foundation of faith and an awareness of the Trinity at work within the world. A deep love and loyalty to the Church is accompanied by an abiding awareness of the importance of the papacy as a focus for union at the center of the Church. There is the recognition that human persons, graced by God, are able to respond to God with magnanimity, with courage, and with generosity. Prayer is a deep source of interior nourishment for each Pope and is a practice consistently recommened for members of the Church. Finally, there is that same willingness to embrace the cross of suffering that for Pope John Paul II was clearly part of his later years. The extraordinary dignity, humility, and serenity with which he bore his increasing frailty was a remarkable sign of hope and inspiration for many throughout the world.

Pope Benedict XVI

Pope Benedict as the "Sovereign Pontiff" was the guarantor of Jesuit mission and vows. He objectively guided the Church. The "General Examen" of the Jesuit *Constitutions* states that the Society of Jesus is for the "salvation and perfection for the members' own souls and also for those of others."[95] On occasion this had been interpreted in a very individualistic manner. Such a perspective was, however, contrary to the mindset of St. Ignatius. Pope Benedict clarified the communal relationship of salvation in the Church in Spe Salvi:

> This real life, towards which we try to reach out again and again, is linked to a lived union with a 'people', and for each individual it can only be attained within this 'we'. It presupposes that we escape from the prison of our 'I', because only in the openness of this universal subject does our gaze open out to the source of joy, to love itself – to God.[96]

From the beginning of his pontificate, Pope Benedict affirmed: "my decided will is to pursue the commitment to enact Vatican Council II, in the wake of my predecessors and in faithful continuity with the millennia-old tradition of the Church."[97] He had clearly valued the tradition of the Church throughout his life. As we have seen both the positive doctors and the scholastic doctors may be found amongst those from whom he drew the inspiration for both his books and his encyclicals, in resonant accord with the ecclesial disposition of Ignatius. His clear pronouncements and his concern for the liturgical celebration of the Mass were also consonant with the ecclesial disposition we have been exploring.

Pope Benedict saw the Eucharist as the heart of all Christian life and the source from which the Church finds strength for her mission of evangelization. The Eucharist is of such importance because it makes Christ visibly present within His Church. "Christ who continues to give Himself to us, calling us to participate in the banquet of His body and His blood. From this full communion with Him comes every other element of the life of the Church."[98] These other elements would include the communion of members of the Church with one another. Also there is the commitment to take the good news of Christ to others outside the Church in an embracing of the New Evangelization. Finally, there is the fire of love that the Eucharist inspires, a loving charity towards all but particularly towards the poorest and most marginal members of society.

Pope Benedict also emphasized the real importance of prayer in a life that is characterized by hope. Here he brought before us the vital nature of contemplative prayer. This is not opposed to any proper understanding

---

[95] General Examen, Constitutions 3.
[96] Spe Salvi, 14.
[97] Pope Benedict XVI, from the first message which he delivered in Latin at the end of the morning Mass with the members of the College of Cardinals in the Sistine Chapel, April 20, 2005.
[98] Ibid.

of those who are not contemplative religious but living the temporal life of the world. Rather, it was to emphasize that there can be a form of contemplation while involved in all the different activities of ordinary family life and work. It is also noteworthy that it was to the life of contemplative prayer for the Church and the world that Pope Benedict turned when he felt it was incumbent upon him to resign from the papacy due to age and infirmity. The humility and courage with which he submitted his resignation and entered this contemplative phase of his life was an extraordinary witness of Christian discipleship.

Pope Francis

For Pope Francis it was impossible to overstate the vital importance of prayer as foundational for his whole life. As Cardinal Bergoglio he had stated, "Prayer should be an experience of giving way of surrendering, where our entire being enters into the presence of God."[99] This place of prayer is the bedrock from which true listening, dialogue and transformation occur. It is a place of "looking at God, but above all sensing that we are being watched by Him. This happens in my case, when I recite the rosary or the psalms or when I joyfully celebrate the Eucharist. But the moment when I most savor the religious experience is when I am before the tabernacle. Sometimes I allow myself to fall asleep while sitting there and just let Him look at me. I have the sense of being in someone else's hands, as though God were taking me by the hand."[100] The final reality is that he puts himself into the presence of God "and, aided by His Word, go forward in what he desires."[101]

Pope Francis eloquently made the connection between prayer and action: the fruit of contemplation should be seen in action particularly on behalf of the most vulnerable. Indeed he asserted that it is vital that we put into practice the Christian words that we preach. "Anyone who utters Christian words without putting them into practice hurts oneself and others, because they are based on pride and cause division in the Church."[102] Fundamental to such action—reaching out to the poorest—is a spirit of hope and a spirit of joy. Pope Francis frequently reiterated the importance of these two theological virtues as gifts of the Holy Spirit given to individuals for the building up of the Church in her mission to the world. Hope for the Christian, he maintained, is much more than simple optimism: "it is constant expectation, it's a gift from the Holy Spirit, it's a miracle of

---

[99] Pope Francis, interview with Antonio Spadaro, S.J. editor, *La Civiltà Cattolica*, 2013.
[100] Ibid.
[101] Ibid.
[102] Pope Francis, homily, Casa Santa Marta, Vatican City, December 5, 2013.

renewal that never lets you down."[103] He continued to say that "Hope has a name, Hope is Christ."[104] Elaborating on the meaning of hope the Pope said that it creates a tension directed towards the revelation of Jesus Christ, towards true joy that is eternal life.[105] The Pope asserted, "Jesus, the hope, renews everything. So hope is a constant miracle. The miracle of what He's doing in the Church. The miracle of making everything new: of what He does in my life, in your life, in our life. He builds and he rebuilds. And that is precisely the reason for our hope."[106]

Alongside the virtue of hope there is that profound call to joy that was evident both in Pope Francis' public appearances and in his first Apostolic Exhortation, *Evangelii Gaudium*, where he stated clearly: "The joy of the gospel fills the hearts and lives of all who encounter Jesus. Those who accept his offer of salvation are set free from sin, sorrow, inner emptiness and loneliness. With Christ joy is constantly born anew."[107] He identified a great danger to this spirit of joy, namely, "the desolation and anguish born of a complacent yet covetous heart, the feverish pursuit of frivolous pleasures, and a blunted conscience."[108] And he warned that the effect of this was to neglect the Church's mission to the poor and the most vulnerable. "Whenever our interior life becomes caught up in its own interests and concerns there is no longer room for others, no place for the poor. God's voice is no longer heard, the quiet joy of his love is no longer felt and the desire to do good fades."[109]

Such a cluttered interiority then has no means of perceiving the reality of God in all things which lies at the heart of the Ignatian expression "to seek and find God in all things." When the Pope was specifically asked how it might be possible to see God everywhere as the Pope had proclaimed in Rio de Janeiro at World Youth Day 2013, he stated: "God manifests himself in historical revelation, in history. Time initiates processes and space crystallizes them. God is in history, in the processes."[110] With this understanding it becomes clear that it is important to begin "long-run historical processes ... God manifests himself in time and is present in the processes of history. This gives priority to actions that give birth to new historical dynamics. And it requires patience, waiting."[111]

---

[103] Pope Francis, homily, Casa Santa Marta, Vatican City, October 29, 2013.

[104] Ibid.

[105] Ibid.

[106] Pope Francis continued: "Christ is the one who renews every wonderful thing of the Creation; He's the reason for our hope. And this hope does not delude because He is faithful. He can't renounce Himself. This is the virtue of hope." Ibid.

[107] Pope Francis, Apostolic Exhortation, *Evangelii Gaudium*, November 24, 2013, 1.

[108] Ibid., 2.

[109] Ibid.

[110] Pope Francis, interview with Antonio Spadaro, S.J., editor, *La Civiltà Cattolica*, March 2013.

[111] Ibid. He continued: "Finding God in all things is not an empirical *eureka*. When we desire

In concluding this section we might just recall that in the lives and pontificates of Pope John Paul II and Pope Benedict XVI and Pope Francis we have clear resonances with the ecclesial disposition of Ignatius. There is that same Trinitarian rooting of their lives and their thought. This profound depth of appreciation of the Trinity is appreciably the result of a deep intimate relationship with Christ. There is a consistent assertion of the worth and dignity of the graced human person who always stands in the possibility of conversion. There are significant areas of suffering in the lives of these three men, not least within undertaking the task of shepherding the universal Church.

to encounter God, we would like to verify him immediately by an empirical method. But you cannot meet God this way. God is found in the gentle breeze perceived by Elijah. The senses that find God are the ones St. Ignatius called spiritual senses. Ignatius asks us to open our spiritual sensitivity to encounter God beyond a purely empirical approach. A contemplative attitude is necessary: it is the feeling that you are moving along the good path of understanding and affection toward things and situations. Profound peace, spiritual consolation, love of God and love of all things in God – this is the sign that you are on this right path." Ibid.

Conclusion

The relationship between Jesus and the Father is "the 'matrix' of the link between us as Christians: if we are intimately inserted in this 'matrix', in this ardent fire of love, then we can truly become one heart and one soul, because God's love burns away all our selfishness, our prejudices, our divisions, both internal and external. If we are thus rooted at the source of Love, which is God, we encounter a reciprocal movement: from brothers and sisters to God. The experience of fraternal communion leads me to communion with God. God's love burns away our sins.[1]

Pope Francis clarifies in this citation the centrality of divine rootedness for Christian action and outreach. The Church is ontologically grounded in communion with Jesus Christ. This is a fundamental insight in understanding the Ignatian ecclesial disposition. In and through Christ, Christians are drawn gratuitously into Trinitarian life, with the necessary purification that such a process involves, and then impelled to move out to encounter others and particularly those most in need. There is a constant dynamic movement from encountering Christ, being drawn deeper into relationship with the Father and being empowered by the Spirit to share that divine love and life with the human persons to whom we are sent. This is the missionary imperative of the Church pulsing with the vigorous life of Christ her head and glowing with the fervor of the joy of the gospel, a joy which is to be shared.[2]

Our exploration of the ecclesial disposition of Ignatius has taken us on a journey across many centuries. We have considered the witness of the lives and writings of a variety of exemplars: one of the early companions; a woman; and two twentieth century theologians. We have also traced a sense of resonance with this disposition in the contemporary papacy and the lives and writings of three Pontiffs. For each person, the graced gift of this disposition involved an intimate relationship with Christ and the blessing of a glimpse of something of the reality of the Trinity at work within the world, drawing human persons towards union.

It is this relationship with Christ and this Trinitarian horizon which rooted their love for the Church. The dimension of suffering has marked each of the persons under consideration and indeed is a key characteristic

[1]Pope Francis, General Audience October 30, 2013.
[2]Cf. Pope Francis, *Evangelii Gaudium*.

in lives revealing courage and generosity. A growing contemplative spirit sustained their activities, and faithfulness to the Church formed a dominant motif in the rhythm of their lives. In each figure whose life and work we have reviewed, we have also seen some echoes of the Rules for Thinking, Judging, and Feeling with the Church that are one practical application of Ignatius' ecclesial disposition. Ignatius wrote these rules for the *Spiritual Exercises* particularly having in mind the members of the Society of Jesus, and it is to the Society that we return for our penultimate considerations before looking at the significance of the ecclesial disposition for all members of the Church.

The General Congregation of the Society of Jesus is the governing body of the Society under the Pope. It is the General Congregation that elects the General Superior and his assistants. Successive General Congregations[3] in the twentieth century had spoken of the importance of not pushing aside the Rules for Thinking, Judging, and Feeling with the Church. Rather they had asked for a more vigorous application of the rules in a spirit of fervor, and with a real fidelity to the Pope. "Fidelity to the Vicar of Christ conditions our fervor," Father Peter-Hans Kolvenbach stated in 2003.[4] For Ignatius this faithfulness was inspired by love.[5] It is a bond of love and service stretching across the generations that unites the Society of Jesus to the Pope.

This bond was further strengthened through the work of the 35th General Congregation in 2008. At the opening liturgy of the Congregation, Cardinal Rodé, the then Prefect of the Congregation for Institutes of Consecrated Life and Societies of Apostolic Life, spoke particularly about the role of Jesuits in restoring a feeling for the Church within other religious communities as well as their own: "Consecration to service to Christ cannot be separated from consecration to service to the Church."[6] He continued by indicating that love for Christ includes a love for the Church, a love "based on faith, a gift of the Lord which, precisely because he loves us, he gives us faith in him and in his Spouse, which is the Church."[7]

---

[3]General Congregation 32 (St. Louis: Institute of Jesuit Sources, 1977), 233; General Congregation 33 (St. Louis: Institute of Jesuit Sources, 1984), 7.

[4]Father General Peter-Hans Kolvenbach, Final Allocution to the Congregation of Procurators, Rome, September 23, 2003.

[5]Ibid. "Out of love for her whom the Lord wished to be His spouse – in Ignatius' language of love – we cannot remain silent. We should associate ourselves with the work of the Spirit in our human history by continuing the work of the mission of Christ in building up the body of Christ – which is His Church, the people of God on route toward the Kingdom to come." Ibid.

[6]"Love for the Church in every sense of the word ... is not a human sentiment which comes and goes according to the people who make it up or according to our conformity with the dispositions emanating from those whom the Lord has placed to direct the Church." Cardinal Franc Rodé, Opening Liturgy, 35th General Congregation of the Society of Jesus, January 7, 2008.

[7]Ibid. "Without the gift of faith in the Church there can be no love for the Church."

Pope Benedict, in a letter to Father General Peter-Hans Kolvenbach, S.J., reiterated the vital importance of Jesuits living ever more fully the charism of the Society of Jesus "in full fidelity to the Magisterium of the Church."[8] Indeed, the Pope indicated that: "the Church has even more need today of this fidelity of yours, which constitutes a distinctive sign of your Order."[9] If the work of Jesuits was to manifest ever more fruitfulness in the many diverse areas of their work, it was crucial, Pope Benedict stated, that "the life of the members of the Society of Jesus, as also their doctrinal research, [to] be always animated by a true spirit of faith and communion in 'humble fidelity to the teachings of the Magisterium'."[10] The Pope concluded the letter by emphasizing the way successive Pontiffs have esteemed the Society of Jesus and valued Jesuit contributions to the life of the Church.[11]

The warmth of Pope Benedict's own esteem for the Society was palpably present to delegates when he met with them towards the end of their work in the General Congregation. "The Church needs you, counts on you, and continues to turn to you with confidence,"[12] he stated. Once more the Pope encouraged the delegates, that while they were seeking the presence of God in many places even beyond the confines of the Church, in order to build bridges of understanding and dialogue: "you must at the same time loyally fulfill the fundamental duty to the Church, of fully adhering to the word of God, and of the authority of the Magisterium to preserve the truth and the unity of the Catholic doctrine in its totality."[13]

These signs of affection and confidence from the Holy Father to the delegates of the General Congregation elicited a response that appeared in the first decree of 35th General Congregation, entitled "'With Renewed Vigor and Zeal,' The Society of Jesus Responds to the Invitation of the Holy Father." This document is more a prayerful reflection than a legal statement. The delegates of the Congregation were obviously deeply moved by Pope Benedict's words "that touched our hearts, stirring and inspiring

---

[8]Letter of His Holiness Pope Benedict XVI to the Reverend Father Peter-Hans Kolvenbach, S.J., Superior General of the Society of Jesus, Rome, January 10, 2008. He continued: "such as described in the following formula which is well familiar to you: 'To serve as a soldier of God beneath the banner of the Cross and to serve the Lord alone and the Church, his spouse, under the Roman Pontiff, the Vicar of Christ on earth' [Apostolic Letter *Exposcit Debitum* July 21, 1550]. One treats here of a 'peculiar' fidelity confirmed also, by not a few among you, in a vow of immediate obedience to the Successor of Peter."

[9]Ibid.

[10]Ibid.

[11]Ibid. "The continuity of the teachings of the Successors of Peter stands to demonstrate the great attention and care which they show towards the Jesuits, their esteem for you, and the desire to be able to count always on the precious contribution of the Society to the life of the Church and to the evangelization of the world."

[12]Address of His Holiness Benedict XVI to delegates of 35th General Congregation, February 21, 2008.

[13]Cf. *Spiritual Exercises* 367.

our desire to serve the Church."[14] This affective response sets the tone for the entire document. We find within the paragraphs that follow clear references that characterize the ecclesial disposition of Ignatius. There is a focus on the relationship of intimate union with Christ which is stated as "first in importance"[15] for all Jesuits. There is a recalling of the *Spiritual Exercises*,[16] with delegates humbly admitting the reality of weakness and sinfulness but desiring to serve the Lord and His Church faithfully.[17] Full adherence is given by the General Congregation "to the faith and teaching of the Church, as they are presented to us in the intimate relationship that unites Scripture, Tradition and the Magisterium."[18]

The 35th General Congregation called all Jesuits to a greater generosity in the living out of their vocation, especially in prayer, community life and apostolate.[19] The depth of prayer springs from that intimacy with Christ which enables Jesuits to glimpse the working of the Trinity within the world. The final paragraphs of this decree renew the commitment of the Society of Jesus to its founding mission and the love and service of the Church that this involved. "Conscious of our responsibility, in, with and for the Church, we desire to love it more and help others love it more, for it leads the world to Christ humble and poor and announces to every person that *Deus Caritas Est*.[20] We cannot separate the love of Christ from this 'sense of the Church,'[21] which leads 'the entire Society to seek to integrate itself more and more vigorously and creatively in the life of the Church so that we may experience and live its mystery within ourselves.'"[22]

Pope Francis echoed these sentiments in his homily at the Gésu on the Feast of the Holy Name of Jesus, January 3, 2014. He reminded his brother Jesuits that Ignatius had desired that the Society be designated by the name of Jesus and that Jesuits were called to come together under the standard of the cross which means: "to have the same sentiments of Christ. It means to think like Him, love like Him, see like Him, walk like Him. It means to do what He did

---

[14] "With Renewed Vigor and Zeal," The Society of Jesus Responds To The Invitation of the Holy Father, 35th General Congregation, Decree 1.

[15] Ibid., para. 2.

[16] Ibid., paras 3 and 4.

[17] Ibid. "This means recognizing, with honesty to ourselves and before God, that some of our reactions and our attitudes have not always been expressed as our Institute demands of us: to be 'men humble and prudent in Christ.'" [Formula of the Institute, *Exposcit debitum* [July 15, 1550], para 14.

[18] Ibid., para 8. Cf. *Spiritual Exercises* 361.

[19] Paras 9 and 10, ibid.

[20] Benedict XVI, encyclical, *Deus Caritas Est*.

[21] *Spiritual Exercises* 352–70.

[22] General Congregation 33, D. 1 n.8. Cited in "With Renewed Vigor and Zeal," para. 16. I recognize that Jesuits differ in their response here. Some Jesuits would have been far more impressed if the Congregation had expressed its fidelity with respect to the concrete issues the Holy Father mentioned, by including very specific statements. Jesuits can and do interpret fidelity in contradictory ways.

and with his same sentiments, with the sentiments of his Heart." The heart of Christ, he emphasized, referencing Paul's letter to the Philippians,[23] is the heart of a God willing to empty himself out of love and this is the example for every Jesuit. "We are called to this abasement. ... To be men who do not live centered on themselves because the center of the Society is Christ and his Church. And God is the *Deus Semper Maior,* the God who always surprises us."[24]

The Pope asserted that it is vital that this God who surprises be at the center of the Society and all the apostolate otherwise the Society of Jesus would become disorientated. The consequences of such a centering he emphasized is a certain incompleteness, a certain restlessness always open to seeking the leading of God. "Because of this, to be a Jesuit means to be a person of incomplete thought, of open thought: because one always thinks looking at the horizon which is the ever greater glory of God, who cease-lessly surprises us. And this is the restlessness of our void, this holy and beautiful restlessness!"[25]

This restless search for God inevitably involves a tension and we have seen that such a healthy tension is a key living dynamic of the Ignatian ecclesial disposition, something to be embraced rather than to attempt to resolve, "if our heart is always in tension: a heart that does not settle down, a heart that does not shut itself in on itself, but which beats the rhythm of a journey to undertake together with all the faithful people of God."[26] It is this divinely inspired restlessness that will both give peace of heart and fresh energy for the apostolate. "Only this restlessness gives peace to the heart of a Jesuit, a restlessness that is also apostolic, which must not make us grow tired of proclaiming the *Kerygma,* of evangelizing with courage. It is the restlessness that prepares us to receive the gift of apostolic fruitfulness. Without restlessness we are sterile."[27]

The documents of the General Congregation 35 clearly set a renewed direction for the interaction of the Society with the Holy Father. In terms of mutual esteem and affection the General Congregation pledged once more the allegiance of all the Society of Jesus to the Church and to love and serve more faithfully the Roman Pontiff. This renewal of the relationship between the Society of Jesus and the Holy Father had clear implications for the Church in general. It did mean, for example, that within Jesuit Institutions such as Jesuit universities, there would be a real sense of that adherence to the Church and a love and loyalty for the Pope.[28] It would imply that Jesuit

---

[23] Phil. 2.4–11

[24] Pope Francis, homily, Gésu, January 3, 2014.

[25] Pope Francis, homily, Gésu, Feast of the Holy Name of Jesus, January 3, 2014.

[26] He continued "It is necessary to seek God to find Him, and to find him in order to seek Him again and forever." Ibid.

[27] Ibid.

[28] I recognize that some would see the climate at certain Jesuit universities, as far removed from what the Pope is asking for.

theologians would manifest within their work that sense of being firmly rooted in the Church and living the necessary tension that is particular to the ecclesial disposition of Ignatius.

The Work of Contemporary Jesuit Theologians and the Church

Fr. Kolvenbach had emphasized in 2003 that a special faithfulness was necessary in teaching and theological research.[29] Pope Benedict in a letter to him had indicated that a key concern for the Holy Father was the theological activity of members of the Society of Jesus. Jesuit theologians have significant responsibilities in forming the minds of others in the areas of theology and spirituality. Pope Benedict suggested that it would be helpful for the 35th General Congregation to "reaffirm in the spirit of Saint Ignatius, its own total adhesion to Catholic doctrine, in particular on those neuralgic points which today are strongly attacked by secular culture."[30]

As a theologian himself, Pope Benedict recognized the particular problems associated with theological research, and the need to remain in harmony with the Magisterium in order not to create confusion for others in the Church. For this very reason the Holy Father invited Jesuit theologians: "to further reflect so as to find again the fullest sense of your characteristic 'fourth vow' of obedience to the Successor of Peter, which not only implies readiness to being sent in mission to foreign lands, but also—in the most genuine Ignatian sense of 'feeling with the Church and in the Church'—'to love and serve' the Vicar of Christ on earth with that 'effective and affective' devotion that must make of you his precious and irreplaceable collaborators in his service of the universal Church."[31] This appeal to the loving service that Jesuits offer the Church in and through their loving loyalty

---

[29] "The Church is buffeted by contradictory currents and polarizations that obscure the true face of ecclesial authority. Precisely because this situation is confused and tense, the elaboration and expression of our theological views, and the choices of our pastoral options and liturgical practices ought always to seek primarily and actively to grasp the faith and thought of the Church. Our goal here is the goal of the Society: 'to aid souls.' All men and women who attend our schools, our catechetical centers and our parochial and social classes have the right to know first the teaching of the Church as it touches all the reaches of human life [General Congregation 34, 317]. This mission will not change the teacher of theology into a mere drill master, because animated by the spirit of faith and by love of the Church, by creative competence and by a constructive critical sense, he will try to communicate in depth and to explain in a positive way, what God continues to say to the Church through Scripture, Tradition and the Magisterium—all at the same time." Fr. Kolvenbach S.J., Letter to the Society of Jesus 2003.
[30] Ibid., "as for example the relationship between Christ and religions; some aspects of the theology of liberation; and various points of sexual morality, especially as regards the indissolubility of marriage and the pastoral care of homosexual persons."
[31] Pope Benedict, February 21, 2008.

to the Pope also reinforces the first rule of the Rules for Thinking with the Church. The intimacy of that obedience offered to the Church as *true Spouse of Christ*[32] arises from a deep love for Christ and therefore for His Church. It is this love, common to both the Pontiff and members of the Society, which enables a "spirit of obedience to the will of God, to Jesus Christ, that becomes humble obedience to the Church."[33]

In like manner, the documents of the 35th General Congregation emphasized, particularly with respect to theologians, "What the Church expects from us is sincere collaboration in the search for the full truth to which the Spirit leads us, in full adherence to the faith and the teaching of the Church."[34] It is acknowledged that there are particular difficulties associated with this task, and for this reason it required that Jesuit theologians be "rooted at the very heart of the Church."[35] This stance of being rooted in the Church while at the same time walking the "new frontiers" of contemporary theological debate leads again to a real tension. Crucially this tension is a creative possibility not a negative reality. "This tension, specific to the Ignatian charism, opens the way to true creative fidelity."[36] Such tension I reiterate lies at the heart of the ecclesial disposition. As Pope Francis stated in his homily during mass with his Jesuit brethren at the Gésu, January 3, 2014, "We are men in tension; we are also contradictory and inconsistent men, sinners, all. But men who want to walk under the gaze of Jesus. We are little, we are sinners, but we want to militate under the standard of the Cross of the Society conferred with the name of Jesus. We who are egoistic want, however, to live an agitated life of great desires."[37]

It is noteworthy that Pope Francis, in his address to the International Theological Commission December 2013, made similar points when he stated that he saw one of the tasks of theologians was: "To hear, distinguish, and interpret the many voices of our age, and to judge them in the light of the divine word, so that revealed truth can always be more deeply penetrated, better understood, and set forth to greater advantage."[38] He spoke of his understanding of the vocation of theologians whom he saw as being called to be "'pioneers' in the Church's dialogue with cultures; a dialogue that is both critical and benevolent, which must encourage the welcome of the Word of God on the part of persons 'from every nation, race, people, and tongue.'" This reflected the issues that the Commission had dealt with in their assembly, with its theme of "The Relationship between Monotheism and Violence." "Your reflection," the Pope stated, "bears witness that

---

[32] First Rule, *Spiritual Exercises* 353.
[33] Pope Benedict, February 21, 2008.
[34] "With Renewed Vigor and Zeal," para. 7.
[35] Ibid., para. 13.
[36] Ibid.
[37] Pope Francis, homily, Church of the Gésu, Feast of the Holy Name of Jesus, January 3, 2014.
[38] Pope Francis, Address to the International Theological Commission, December 6, 2013.

God's revelation truly constitutes Good News for all humanity. God is not a threat for humankind. Faith in the one and thrice holy God is not and can never be a source of violence or intolerance. On the contrary, its highly rational character confers a universal dimension upon it, capable of uniting persons of good will." Conversely Pope Francis emphasized "the definitive Revelation of God in Jesus Christ now renders every recourse to violence 'in the name of God', impossible. It is precisely by His refusal of violence, by His having conquered evil with good with the blood of His Cross, that Jesus has reconciled humans with God and with themselves."[39]

The Pope reasserted the importance of peace: "It is this very concept of peace that has been the focus of your reflection on the Church's social doctrine, which has the goal of translating God's love for the human person, made manifest in Christ Jesus, into a concrete reality of societal life." This peace is first made manifest in the Church's own witness and the social message that she brings to the world. "Fraternal relations between believers, authority as service, sharing with the poor: all of these traits, which have characterized ecclesial life from its origin, can and must constitute a living and attractive model for the diverse human communities, from the family to civil society."[40]

This significant witness of the people of God is prophetic, the Bishop of Rome emphasized: "By the gift of the Holy Spirit, the members of the Church possess a 'sense of faith.' This is a kind of 'spiritual instinct' that makes us think with the Church sentire cum Ecclesia[41] and discern that which is in conformity with the apostolic faith and is in the spirit of the Gospel. Of course, the sensus fidelium[42] cannot be confused with the sociological reality of a majority opinion." Therefore it is one of the tasks of theologians to develop appropriate criteria that "allow the authentic expressions of the sensus fidelium to be discerned. ... This attention is of greatest importance for theologians."[43]

Pope Benedict XVI often pointed out that the theologian must remain attentive to the faith lived by the humble and the small, to whom it pleased the Father to reveal that which He had hidden from the learned and the wise.[44] "Your mission, therefore, is both fascinating and risky. It is fascinating because research in and teaching of theology can become a true path to holiness, as attested by many Fathers and Doctors of the Church. But it is also risky because it bears temptations with it: hardness of heart, pride, even ambition," the Pope observed, recalling a letter from St. Francis of

---

[39] Ibid.
[40] Ibid.
[41] Think with the mind of the church.
[42] The sense of the faithful.
[43] Pope Francis, Address to International Theological Commission, December 6, 2013.
[44] In this way Pope Francis also reiterated his call for a certain humility and simplicity to be the keynotes of theological endeavor.

Assisi to St. Anthony of Padua regarding this danger. It warns: "I am glad that you are teaching the brothers sacred Theology provided that, in the study, you do not extinguish the spirit of holy prayer and devotion."[45] At the conclusion of the audience the Holy Father entrusted the theologians to the Immaculate Virgin so that they might "grow in this spirit of prayer and devotion and thus, with a profound sense of humility, be true servants of the Church."[46] The following year with a substantially new Commission Pope Francis emphasized the integration of theology and spirituality in the life of the theologian. "Your mission is to serve the Church, which presupposes not only intellectual competence, but also spiritual dispositions."[47] In particular Pope Francis highlighted the importance of women theologians in the life of the Commission and the service of the Church. The participation of women is "a presence that becomes an invitation to reflect on the role that women can and must have in the field of theology". In fact, "the Church recognizes the indispensable contribution of woman in society, with a sensibility, an intuition and certain peculiar capacities that are generally more proper of women than of men ... I am pleased to see how many women ... offer new contributions to theological reflection" (Apostolic Exhortation, *Evangelii Gaudium*, 103). Thus, in virtue of their feminine genius, women theologians can highlight for the benefit of all, certain unexplored aspects of the unfathomable mystery of Christ."[48]

The Ecclesial Disposition for All—A Church of Passion and Hope

And what of those who are not members of the Society of Jesus? The ecclesial disposition of Ignatius, I would argue, is also of positive assistance to all members of the Church. Every member who authentically lives this disposition contributes to the life of the Church. The rarely referenced Rules for Thinking, Judging, and Feeling with the Church are one practical application of this disposition and have been re-appropriated by the Jesuits, but they can also be helpful in the lives of others. They are once more being seen as an integral part of the *Spiritual Exercises* of Ignatius. They are acknowledged to be not rules that oppress but a series of clear guidelines that may lead to freedom. They free individuals and communities from becoming enmeshed in negativity; they free for the resolution of issues regarding the exercise of authority and they free the person[s] to grow in love for the Church in union with Christ and to take their part in

---

45 Pope Francis, Address to the International Theological Commission, December 6, 2013.
46 Ibid.
47 Pope Francis, Address to the International Theological Commission, December 6, 2014.
48 Ibid.

his redemptive mission. This involves the exercise of the service of charity which is a constitutive element of the Church's mission, indeed a vital expression of her very being. "By her nature the Church is missionary, she abounds in effective charity and a compassion which understands, assists and provides."[49]

Union with Christ in an intimacy of knowledge is vital here for each one of us. It is a knowledge that is not merely knowledge of the intellect, acquired through study—epistemological—though it is this as well. Neither is it merely an understanding arrived at through our experience—an existential knowledge—though it includes this too. Rather, it is fundamentally an apprehension at the level of our very being—an ontological knowledge—of God's passionate loving commitment to each one of us. This is the primordial reality that Ignatius is concerned that we should understand and is fundamental to the ecclesial disposition. This is the intimate knowledge of Christ that the retreatant prays for in the second week of the *Spiritual Exercises*. It is this most profound apprehension, this intimacy with Christ that fuelled Ignatius' passionate commitment to the Church. Our growing intimacy with Christ will deepen our love for the Church.

The struggle of Christ, as Ignatius understands it, *is* the struggle of the Church. It is revealed most clearly in the Paschal Mystery. In this redemptive act of Christ's passion, death and resurrection, the love of the Triune God is made known, a love that reaches into the depths of death for the salvation of human beings. The Paschal Mystery stands at the very center of Christian faith and is the primordial revelation of who God is in God's very self and in relation to humanity.[50]

Ignatius came to interpret and to symbolize the profound contradiction that lies central to all human history primarily as an enormous and continual struggle not between human beings but about human beings and the very destiny of human life. The definitive victory of redemption has been won by Christ. At the same time, Christ's redemptive work continues in our world in and through the Church. Therefore it is also present in and through our own lives and work as members of the Church. We are part of the mission of the Church and this is something integral to our very selves, "it is not an 'extra' or just another moment in life. Instead, it is something I cannot uproot from my being without destroying my very self. *I am on a mission* on this earth; that is the reason why I am here in this world. We have to regard ourselves as sealed, even branded,

---

49 Pope Francis, *Evangelii Gaudium*, 179.
50 Accordingly, as Aidan Nichols indicates, "in the event of reconciliation on the Cross the true character of God—and so the divine immanence—God's 'in-God-self-ness'—is seen." Aidan Nichols, O.P., *Divine Fruitfulness: A Guide Through Balthasar's Theology Beyond the Trilogy* (Washington, DC: Catholic University of America Press, 2007), 166.

by this mission of bringing light, blessing, enlivening, raising up, healing and freeing."[51]

But how is the Church to be a true reflection of Christ in this struggle? What about when the Church appears to be divided, polarized, and at enmity within its own members? In our contemporary scenario, when the Church has been humiliated by public scandal, many seem paralyzed by grief and cynicism. When mourning abounds and when the grievous sins of a minority seem to obliterate the memory of the compassionate, faithful service of the dedicated majority, how is the face of Christ to be seen within the Church? Pope Francis insisted that this is not the time to yield to discouragement and complaint. He suggested that what is vital here is that we become more ardently aware of the dignity of every human person made in the image of God and therefore everyone as worthy of our service, "because they are God's handiwork, his creation. God created that person in his image, and he or she reflects something of God's glory. Every human being is the object of God's infinite tenderness, and he himself is present in their lives. Jesus offered his precious blood on the cross for that person. Appearances notwithstanding, every person *is immensely holy and deserves our love.*"[52]

It is this faith in the love of God for each human being that distinguished Pope Francis' attitude to mission. "Everyone needs to be touched by the comfort and attraction of God's saving love" he insisted, a love "which is mysteriously at work in each person, above and beyond their faults and failings."[53] If the Church really takes up this mission orientation then members will be sent out to everyone and above all to the poor and sick, the ones who are usually despised or overlooked. In this endeavor there may be difficulties and mistakes but Pope Francis continued to reiterate: "I prefer a Church which is bruised, hurting and dirty because it has been out on the streets, rather than a Church which is unhealthy from being confined and from clinging to its own security."[54] Indeed he emphasized that the Church is called to realize that "as the Aparecida document nicely put it: ours is not an age of change, but a change of age. So today we urgently need to keep putting the question: what is it that God is asking of us?"[55]

Here, I suggest the ecclesial disposition may assist us. Within the *Spiritual Exercises*, as we have seen, Ignatius suggests a prayer for the ongoing purification of our own spirit. This is vital if the ecclesial disposition is to

---

[51] Pope Francis, *Evangelii Gaudium*, 273.

[52] Ibid., 274.

[53] Ibid., 45

[54] He continued: "I do not want a Church concerned with being at the center and then ends by being caught up in a web of obsessions and procedures. If something should rightly disturb us and trouble our consciences, it is the fact that so many of our brothers and sisters are living without the strength, light and consolation born of friendship with Jesus Christ, without a community of faith to support them, without meaning and a goal in life." Ibid., 49.

[55] Pope Francis, Address to Brazilian Bishops in Rio de Janeiro, July 27, 2013.

be integral to our lives enabling us to contribute to the life of the Church. Against the subtext of a Church in struggle Ignatius proposes this crucial prayer for enlightenment, asking for the grace of a knowledge of the deceptions of the enemy of our human nature in order to reject them and knowledge of the way Christ is calling us individually in order to follow him more closely. This prayer of the Triple Colloquy is, indeed, the cutting edge for ongoing conversion to the call of Christ.[56]

The Triple Colloquy is a prayer in which one asks to be drawn at an ever-deeper level into the experience of Christ which is often when we become fearful. For we know the experience of Christ includes the Passion. It is the way of the humble, poor and loving Christ. Indeed, all Christians at some time in their lives must face the full, dramatic horror of the Cross when they confront the suffering of Christ for their sinfulness, their alienation from themselves and God through sin, and the continuing suffering of Christ in the contemporary human realities of poverty, violence and oppression. This way of Christ inevitably means being open and willing to embrace the reality of the Cross in our lives both as individuals and as communities. It means living a life of ongoing conversion and through that way of the Cross being drawn deeply into the life of the Trinity. It inexorably means coming into confrontation with our own very human temptations to independence and self-aggrandizement. When we pray in this way we are actually praying to enter into Christ's work and his way, and to accept the consequences that may flow from this. Always the final hermeneutic is the Cross, without which there can be no Resurrection.

It is important to recognize the tension that exists at the heart of our Christian endeavors, where the Spirit of God speaks through the experience of individual discernment but where this always needs to be ratified in relation to the body, namely the Church. As we have seen, Ignatius saw no definitive conflict but a creative tension between the freedom of the Spirit operating both in the individual and in the authoritative voice of the Church. For Ignatius, this tension could not be understood as conflict. He saw all human beings as individuals in relation to the Church. This understanding was reaffirmed by Vatican II in the document on the Church *Lumen Gentium*.[57] Our difficulty is that we desire to resolve that tension. It is part of our unwillingness to live with our own limitations and the fragmentary nature of human existence, the place where the Cross truly touches our lives. When we begin to see that this place of tension is also a place of freedom and creativity, and a place that deepens our human integrity, then this is reason for hope.

Hope is closely related to joy. Real joy is something that can co-exist

---

[56] *Spiritual Exercises* 155. See Chapter 2.

[57] *Lumen Gentium* 10. All people are in relationship to the Church by the very fact of a common human creation, whether they are members of a Christian denomination, members of other religious faiths, agnostics or even atheists. Thus all have a relationship with the body of Christ.

with suffering. It has nothing to do with mindless optimism. In the fourth week of the *Spiritual Exercises* the grace for which the retreatant prays is to joy in Christ's joy at being fully alive. The source of our joy then is not in ourselves, but in the reality of God's definitive victory in Christ and the continuation of the redemptive mission of Christ. This is the foundation of the reality of our being and gives our hope a sense of the future as well as of the present. Hope thus becomes the certainty of the irrevocability of God's love operative in individual lives and corporately in the life of the Church.

We have seen that for Ignatius, the Church is more than merely a context within which the human person comes to experience God. Primarily the Church for Ignatius was the visible embodiment of Christ himself. And it was to Christ, our Creator and Lord, and to his greater glory that he offered his service and that of the members of his order which is why the spirituality underpinning the Society of Jesus is ecclesial.

The call of Christ to the Church today is a call to a passionate loving commitment to Christ himself, the one who is her Lord and Head. It is a call of commitment also to the body, the Church, of which we are all members. This finds a practical form in the ecclesial disposition of Ignatius. In and through this commitment the passionate love of God flows into the Church's mission, which is the redemptive work of Christ for the life of the world. This divine passionate love continues to awake in the Church a new sense of mission, a realization that mission is the responsibility of all the members of the People of God. Those who have encountered Christ cannot keep him for themselves, they must proclaim him by the witness of their lives.

Pope Francis emphasized that a new apostolic outreach is needed, one which is lived as the everyday commitment of every member of the Church and all Christian communities. Such action will not be without difficulty particularly when directed to alleviating the suffering of the poor and most vulnerable. The reality of the Cross, which is a share in the Passion of Christ, is an inevitable part of life within the Church, which is—as we are— both sinful and holy. Yet, this intimate loving union with Christ, which leads into the heart of the Trinity, is the source of our hope as individuals and communally as the Church. It is the heart of the gospel. In a Church of passion and hope, the ecclesial disposition of Ignatius is a beacon of light and life to illuminate a darkened world.

Let us refuse to be robbed of hope, or to allow our hope to be dimmed by facile answers and solutions which block our progress, "fragmenting" time and changing it into space. Time is always much greater than space. Space hardens processes, whereas time propels towards the future and encourages us to go forward in hope.[58]

---

[58] Pope Francis, *Lumen Fidei*, Encyclical on The Light of Faith, June 29, 2013, para. 57.

SELECTED BIBLIOGRAPHY

Books

Baldovin, S.J., John F. *The Urban Character of Christian Worship: The Origins, Development, and Meaning of Stational Liturgy*, Orientalia Christiana Analecta, ed. Robert Taft, S.J., no. 228. Rome: Pont. Institutum Studiorum Orientalium, 1987.

Bangert, William V. *To The Other Towns: A Life of Blessed Peter Favre First Companion of St. Ignatius*. Westminster, MD: Newman Press, 1959.

Blazynski, George. *Pope John Paul II: A Man from Kraków*. London: Sphere Books, 1979.

Beguiriztain, S.J., P. Justo. *The Eucharistic Apostolate of St. Ignatius Loyola*, trans. John H. Collins, S.J., 1955.

Bergoglio, Jorge Mario. *In Him Alone is Our Hope: Spiritual Exercises Given to His Brother Bishops in the Manner of Saint Ignatius of Loyola*, trans. Fr. Vincent Capuano, S.J. and Andrew Matt. Canada: Pierre-Marie Dumont, 2013.

Calvin, John. *Institutes of The Christian Religion*, Vol. XXI, ed. John T. McNeill, trans. Ford Lewis Battle. Philadelphia: Westminster Press, MCMLX.

Caraman, S.J., Philip. *A Study in Friendship: St. Robert Southwell and Henry Garnet*. India: Gujarat Sahitya Prakash, 1991.

Carey, Patrick W. *Avery Cardinal Dulles SJ: A Model Theologian, 1918–2008*. New York and Mahwah, NJ: Paulist Press, 2010.

Chambers, M. C. E. *The Life of Mary Ward [1585–1645]*, Vol. 1. London: Burns & Oates, 1882.

Christianson, Gerald, Izbicki, Thomas M., and Bellito, Christopher M. *The Church, The Councils and Reform: The Legacy of the Fifteenth Century*. Washington DC: Catholic University of America Press, 2008.

Clancy, S.J., Thomas H. *The Conversational Word of God: A Commentary on the Doctrine of St. Ignatius of Loyola concerning Spiritual Conversation, with Four Early Jesuit Texts*. St Louis: Institute of Jesuit Sources, 1978.

Clark, Francis. *Eucharistic Sacrifice and the Reformation*. Westminster, MD: The Newman Press, 1960.

Collins, Michael. *Pope Benedict XVI Successor to Peter*. Dublin: Columba Press, 2005.

Corella, S.J., Jesus. *Sentir La Iglesia: Commentario a las reglas Ignacianas para el sentido verdadero de Iglesia*. Bilbao: Ediciones Mensajero. Sal Terrae, 1996.

Cover IBVM, Jeanne. *Love The Driving Force: Mary Ward's Spirituality: Its Significance for Moral Theology*. Milwaukee: Marquette University Press, 1997.

Cross, Claire. *Church and People 1450–1660: The Triumph of the Laity in the English Church*. London: Fontana Collins, 1987.

Decrees of the 35th General Congregation of the Society of Jesus. Oxford: Way Books, 2008.

De Gaál, Emery. *The Theology of Pope Benedict XVI: The Christocentric Shift*. New York: Palgrave MacMillan, 2010.

Guibert, S.J., Joseph de. *The Jesuits Their Spiritual Doctrine and Practice: A Historical Study*, trans. William J. Young, S.J. St. Louis: Institute of Jesuit Sources, 1972.

Devlin, Christopher. *The Life of Robert Southwell: Poet and Martyr*. London: Longmans, 1956.

Drummond, Robert Blackley. *Erasmus His Life and Character As Shown in His Correspondence and Works*, Vol. 2. London: Smith, Elder & Co., 1873.

Dulles, S.J., Avery. *The Resilient Church: The Necessity and Limits of Adaptation*. Garden City, NY: Doubleday, 1977.

Dulles, S.J., Avery. *A Church to Believe In: Discipleship and the Dynamics of Freedom*. New York: Crossroad, 1982.

Dulles, S.J., Avery. *Models of Revelation*. Garden City: Doubleday, 1983.

Dulles, S.J., Avery. *The Catholicity of the Church*. Oxford: Clarendon, 1985.

Dulles, S.J., Avery. *The Reshaping of Catholicism: Current Challenges in the Theology of Church*. San Francisco: Harper & Row, 1988.

Dulles, S.J., Avery. *The Craft of Theology: From Symbol to System*. New York: Crossroad, 1992.

Dulles, S.J., Avery. *A Testimonial to Grace and Reflections on a Theological Journey*. Kansas City: Sheed & Ward, 1996.

Dulles, S.J., Avery. *The Priestly Office: A Theological Reflection*. New York: Paulist Press, 1997.

Dulles, S.J., Avery. *Magisterium: Teacher and Guardian of the Faith*. Naples Florida: Ave Maria University, 2007.

Dulles, S.J., Avery. *Church and Society: The Laurence J. McGinley Lectures 1988–2007*. New York: Fordham University Press, 2008.

Egan, S.J., Harvey. *The Spiritual Exercises and the Ignatian Mystical Horizon*. St. Louis: Institute of Jesuit Sources, 1976.

Farge, James K. *Orthodoxy and Reform in Early Reformation France: The Faculty of Theology of Paris, 1500–1543*. Leiden: Brill, 1985.

Fischer, Heinz Joachim. *Pope Benedict XVI: A Personal Portrait,* trans. Brian McNeil. New York: Crossroad, 2005.

Austin Flannery, O.P. (ed.). *Vatican Council II: The Conciliar and Post Conciliar Documents*. Dublin: Dominican Publications, 1992.

Fritz, Ronald, H. *New Worlds: The Great Voyages of Discovery, 1400–1600*. Stroud: Sutton, 2002.

Futrell, S.J., John Carroll. *Making an Apostolic Community of Love: The Role of the Superior According to St. Ignatius Loyola*. St Louis: Institute of Jesuit Sources, 1970.

Ganss, S.J., George E. *The Spiritual Exercises of Saint Ignatius: A Translation and Commentary*. Chicago: Loyola University Press, 1992.

Gribble, C.S.C., Richard. *Renewing Apostolic Religious Life in America: A Solution to the Crisis*. Washington, DC: Catholic University of America, 2012.

Haigh, Christopher. *The English Reformation Revised*. Cambridge: Cambridge University Press, 1987.

Idigoras, J. Ignacio Tellechea. *Ignatius of Loyola The Pilgrim Saint,* trans. and ed. [with a preface] Cornelius Michael Buckley, S.J. Chicago: Loyola University Press, 1994.

Janelle, Pierre. *Robert Southwell: The Writer: A Study in Religious Inspiration*. London: Sheed and Ward, 1935.

Jeffrey, David Lyle (ed.). *A Dictionary of Biblical Tradition in English Literature*. Grand Rapids, MI: Wm B. Eerdmans, 1992.

Jones, Kenneth C. *Index of Leading Catholic Indicators: The Church Since Vatican II*. Fort Collins, CO: Oriens, 2003.

Kenworthy-Browne, Christina (ed.). *Mary Ward 1585–1645: 'A Briefe Relation' with Autobiographical Fragments and a Selection of Letters*. London: Catholic Record Society, Boydel Press, 2008.

Kirmse, Anne-Marie O.P. and Canaris, Michael M. (eds). *The Legacy of Avery Cardinal Dulles SJ: His Words and Witness*. New York: Fordham University Press, 2011.

Lubac, Henri de. *Paradoxes*. Paris: Livre Francais, 1946.

Lubac, Henri de. *The Splendour of the Church*, trans. Michael Mason. London: Sheed and Ward, 1956.

Lubac, Henri de. *L'Église Dans La Crise Actuelle*. Paris: Cerf, 1969.

Lubac, Henri de. *Les Églises Particuliéres dans L'Église Universelle*. Paris: Cerf, 1971.

Lubac, Henri de. *The Motherhood of the Church*, trans. Sr. Sergia Englund, OCD. San Francisco: Ignatius Press, 1982.

Lubac, Henri de. *Entretien autour de Vatican II: Souvenirs et Réflexions*. Paris: Catholique-Cerf, 1985.

Lubac, Henri de. *The Christian Faith: An Essay on the Structure of the Apostles' Creed*, trans. Richard Arnandez. San Francisco: Ignatius Press, 1986.

Lubac, Henri de. *Theological Fragments,* trans. Rebecca Howell Balinski. San Francisco: Ignatius Press, 1989.

Lubac, Henri de. *At the Service of The Church: Henri de Lubac Reflects on the Circumstances that Occasioned His Writings,* trans. Anne Elizabeth Englund. San Francisco: Ignatius Press, 1993.

Lubac, Henri de. *Corpus Mysticum: The Eucharist and the Church in the Middle Ages,* trans. Gemma Simmonds, C.J., with Richard Price and Christopher Stephens, eds Laurence Paul Hemming and Susan Frank Parsons. Notre Dame, IN: University of Notre Dame Press, 2007.

Martin, Dennis D. *Fifteenth Century Carthusian Reform: The World of Nicholas Kempf*. Leiden: Brill, 1992.

McCoog, S.J., Thomas (ed.). *The Reckoned Expense: Edmund Campion and the Early English Jesuits*. Woodbridge: Boydell Press, 1996.

McDonald, James H. and Pollard Brown, Nancy (eds). *The Poems of Robert Southwell SJ*. Oxford: Clarendon Press, 1967.

McLaughlin, Megan. *Sex, Gender and Episcopal Authority in an Age of Reform 1000–1122*. Cambridge: Cambridge University Press, 2010.

McNeill, John T. (ed.). *Calvin: Institutes of The Christian Religion*, Vol. XXI, trans. Ford Lewis Battle. Philadelphia: The Westminster Press, 1960.

McPartlan, Paul. *The Eucharist Makes the Church: Henri de Lubac and John Zizioulas in Dialogue*. Edinburgh: T&T Clark, 1993.

Milbank, John. *The Suspended Middle: Henri de Lubac and the Debate concerning the Supernatural*. Grand Rapids, MI and Cambridge: Wm B. Eerdmans, 2005.

Munitiz, S.J., Joseph and Endean, S.J., Philip. *Saint Ignatius of Loyola: Personal Writings*, trans. with intro. and notes. London: Penguin Classics, 1996.

Murphy, S.J., Edmond C. and Padberg, S.J., John W. (eds). *The Spiritual Writings of Pierre Favre*. St. Louis: Institute of Jesuit Sources, 1996.

Nichols, Aiden. *Divine Fruitfulness: A Guide Through Balthasar's Theology Beyond the Trilogy*. Washington, DC: Catholic University of America Press, 2007.

Nichols, Aidan. *The Realm: An Unfashionable Essay on the Conversion of England*. Oxford: Family Publications, 2008.

O'Donnell, S.J., John. *Hans Urs von Balthasar*. London: Geoffrey Chapman, 1992.

O'Leary, S.J., Brian. *Pierre Favre and Discernment*. Oxford: Way Books, 2006.

O'Malley, S.J., John. *The First Jesuits*. Cambridge, MA: Harvard University Press, 1993.

O'Malley, S.J., John. *Trent and All That: Renaming Catholicism in the Early Modern Era*. Cambridge, MA: Harvard University Press, 2000.

O'Rourke Boyle, Marjorie. "Angels Black and White: Loyola's Spiritual Discernment in Historical Perspective," *Theological Studies* 44 (1983): 241–57.

Olsen, Glen W. (ed.). *Christian Marriage: A Historical Study*. New York: Crossroad, 2004.

Orchard, Gillian, (ed.). *Till God Will: Mary Ward Through Her Writings*. London: Darton Longman & Todd, 1985.

Padberg, John W. (ed.). *The Constitutions of The Society of Jesus And Their Complementary Norms: A Complete English Translation of the Official Latin Texts*. St. Louis: Institute of Jesuit Sources, 1996.

Palmer, S.J., Martin E. (ed.). *On Giving the Spiritual Exercises: The Early Jesuit Manuscript Directories and the Official Directory of 1599*. St. Louis: Institute of Jesuit Sources, 1996.

Palmer, S.J., Martin E., Padberg, S.J., John W., and McCarthy, S.J., John L. (eds). *Ignatius of Loyola Letters and Instructions*. Saint Louis: Institute of Jesuit Sources, 2006.

Peters, Henrietta. *Mary Ward: A World in Contemplation*, trans. Helen Butterworth. Leominster: Gracewing, 1994.

Phipps, William E. *Clerical Celibacy: The Heritage*. New York: Continuum, 2004.

Pilarz, S.J., Scott R. *Robert Southwell and the Mission of Literature 1561–1595*. Aldershot: Ashgate, 2004.

Purcell, Mary. *The Quiet Companion*. Chicago: Loyola University Press, 1970.

Rahner, S.J., Hugo. *Saint Ignatius Loyola: Letters to Women*. Edinburgh and London: Nelson, 1960.

Rahner, S.J., Hugo. *Ignatius the Theologian*. New York: Herder & Herder, 1968.

Rahner, S.J., Hugo. *The Vision of St. Ignatius In The Chapel of La Storta*. Rome: Centrum Ignatium, 1975.

Rahner, S.J., Hugo. *Saint Ignatius Loyola: Letters to Women*. New York: Crossroad, 2007.

Rait, Jill (ed.). *Christian Spirituality II*. New York: Crossroad, 1987.

Ratzinger, Joseph. *Introduction to Christianity*. London: Burns & Oates, 1969.

Ratzinger, Cardinal Joseph. *The Ratzinger Report, An Exclusive Interview on the State of the Church with Vitterio Messori*. San Francisco: Ignatius Press, 1985.

Ratzinger, Cardinal Joseph. *The Nature and Mission of Theology: Approaches to Understanding Its Role in the Light of Present Controversy*. San Francisco: Ignatius Press, 1995.

Ratzinger, Cardinal Joseph. *Salt of the Earth: Christianity and The Catholic Church at the end of the Millennium: An Interview with Peter Seewald*. San Francisco: Ignatius Press, 1997.

Ratzinger, Cardinal Joseph. *Milestones: Memoirs 1927–1977*. San Francisco: Ignatius Press, 1998.

Ratzinger, Cardinal Joseph. *God's Word: Scripture, Tradition, Office*, trans. Henry Taylor. San Francisco: Ignatius Press, 2008.

Ravier, S.J., André. *Ignatius of Loyola and The Founding of the Society of Jesus*, trans. Maura Daly, Joan Daly, and Carson Daly. San Francisco: Ignatius Press, 1987.

Rowland, Tracey. *Ratzinger's Faith: The Theology of Pope Benedict XVI*. Oxford: Oxford University Press, 2008.

St. Augustine. *The City of God*.

St. Thérèse of Lisieux. *Autobiography of A Soul*. New York: Doubleday, 2001.

Saward, John. *The Mysteries of March: Hans Urs von Balthasar on the Incarnation and Easter*. London: Collins 1990.

Schindler, David L. (ed.). *Love Alone is Credible: Hans Urs von Balthasar as Interpreter of the Catholic Tradition*, Vol. 1. Grand Rapids, MI: Wm B. Eerdmans, 2008.

Schussler Fiorenza, Elizabeth. *Discipleship of Equals: A Critical Feminist Ekklesia-logy of Liberation*. New York: Crossroad, 1993.

Strothmann, F. W. and Locke, Frederick W. (eds). *The History of Ideas*. New York: Frederick Ungar Publishing Co., 1961.

Southwell, Robert. *Two Short letters and Short Rules of a Good Life*, ed. Nancy Pollard Brown. Charlottesville: University Press of Virginia, 1973.

Speyr, Adrienne von. *The Book of All Saints*. San Francisco: Ignatius Press, 2008.

Stourton, Edward. *John Paul II: Man of History*. London and New York: Hodder & Stoughton, 2006.

The Constitutions of The Society of Jesus And Their Complimentary Norms: A Complete English Translation of the Official Latin Texts, ed. John W. Padberg. St. Louis: Institute of Jesuit Sources, 1996.

The Society of Jesus. *Decrees and Documents of the 35th General Congregation*. Oxford: The Way Publications, 2008.

Taft, Robert. *The Liturgy of the Hours in East and West: The Origins of the Divine Office and its Meaning for Today*, 2nd edn. Collegeville, MN: Liturgical Press, 1983.

Toner, Jules. *Discerning God's Will: Ignatius of Loyola's Teaching on Christian Decision Making*. St. Louis: Institute of Jesuit Sources, 1991.

Valley, Paul. *Pope Francis: Untying The Knots*. London; Bloomsbury, 2013.

Veale, Joseph. *Manifold Gifts,* Oxford: Way Books, 2006.

Vincent Twomey S.V.D., D. *Pope Benedict XVI The Conscience of Our Age: A Theological Portrait*. San Francisco: Ignatius Press, 2007.

Voderholzer, Rudolf. *Meet Henri de Lubac: His Life and Work*, trans. Michael J. Miller. San Francisco: Ignatius Press, 2008.

Von Balthasar, Hans Urs. *Prayer*, trans. A. V. Littledale. New York: Sheed & Ward, 1961.

Von Balthasar, Hans Urs. *A Theology of History,* trans. from the German *Theologie Der Geschichte*, 2nd edn. Einsiedeln, 1959. New York: Sheed & Ward, 1963.

Von Balthasar, Hans Urs. *The Christian State of Life*, trans. Mary Frances McCarthy. San Francisco: Ignatius Press, 1983.

Von Balthasar, Hans Urs. *The Theology of Henri de Lubac*. San Francisco: Ignatius Press, 1983.

Von Balthasar, Hans Urs. *Truth is Symphonic: Aspects of Christian Pluralism,* trans. Graham Harrison. San Francisco: Ignatius Press, 1987.

Von Balthasar, Hans Urs. *Explorations in Theology I: The Word made Flesh*. San Francisco: Ignatius Press, 1989.

Von Balthasar, Hans Urs. *Test Everything: Hold Fast To What is Good*, trans. Maria Shrady. San Francisco: Ignatius Press, 1989.

Von Balthasar, Hans Urs. *Mysterium Paschale; The Mystery of Easter*, trans. Aidan Nichols, O.P. Edinburgh: T&T Clark, 1990.

Von Balthasar, Hans Urs. Hans. *My Work: In Retrospect*. San Francisco: Ignatius Press, 1993.

Von Balthasar, Hans Urs. *Theo-Drama Theological Dramatic Theory II: Dramatis Personae: Man in God*, trans. Graham Harrison. San Francisco: Ignatius Press, 1988.

Von Balthasar, Hans Urs. *Theo-Drama Theological Dramatic Theory V: The Last Act*, trans. Graham Harrison. San Francisco: Ignatius Press, 1998.

Von Balthasar, Hans Urs. *Epilogue*, trans. Edward T. Oakes, S.J. San Francisco: Ignatius Press, 2004.

Von Balthasar, Hans Urs. *Love Alone is Credible,* trans. D. C. Schindler. San Francisco: Ignatius Press, 2004.

Weigel, George. *Witness to Hope: The Biography of John Paul II*. New York: Harper Collins, 1999.

Woods, Susan K. *Spiritual Exegesis and the Church in the Theology of Henri de Lubac*. Grand Rapids, MI: Wm B. Eerdmans and Edinburgh: T&T Clark, 1998.

Wojtyla, Karol. *Sources of Renewal: The Implementation of Vatican II*. San Francisco: Harper and Row, 1980.

Wright, Mary. *Mary Ward's Institute: The Struggle for Identity*. Sydney: Crossing Press, 1997.

Wulf, S.J., Friedrich (ed.). *Ignatius Loyola His Personality and Spiritual Heritage 1556–1956*. St. Louis: Institute of Jesuit Sources, 1977.

Young, William J. (trans. and selector). *Letters of Ignatius Loyola*. Chicago: Loyola University Press, 1959.

Articles

Alexander, Neil. "Luther's Reform of the Daily Office," *Worship,* 57 (1983).

Arrupe, S.J., Pedro. "The Trinitarian Inspiration of the Ignatian Charism," *Studies in the Spirituality of the Jesuits* 33/3 (May 2001): 1–49.

Baldovin, S.J., John. "The Urban Character of Christian Worship: The Origins, Development and Meaning of Stational Liturgy," in *Orientalia Christiana Analecta,* ed. Robert Taft, S.J., no. 228. Rome: Pont Institutum Studiorum Orientalium, 1987.

Bouwsma, William James. "The Spirituality of Renaissance Humanism," in *Christian Spirituality II,* ed. Jill Rait. New York: Crossroad, 1987.

Buckley, S.J., Michael. "Ecclesial Mysticism in the *Spiritual Exercises* of Ignatius," *Theological Studies* 56 (1995): 441–63.

Congar, Yves. "L'ecclésiologie de S. Bernard," in *Etudes d'ecclésiologie médiévale* 7: 136–7.

Daniélou, Jean. "The Ignatian Vision of the Universe and of Man," in *Revue D'Ascetique et Mystique.* Toulouse, 1950, 5–17.

Dulles, S.J., Avery "The Papacy for a Global Church," *America,* July 15, 2000.

Dulles, S.J., Avery "The Future of the Papacy," *First Things,* March 2001.

Healy, Nicholas and Schindler, David. "For the Life of the World: Hans Urs von Balthasar on the Church as Eucharist," in *The Cambridge Companion to Hans Urs von Balthasar.* Cambridge: Cambridge University Press, 2004, 51–63.

Henrici, S.J., Peter. "Hans Urs von Balthasar: A Sketch of His Life," in *Hans Urs von Balthasar: His Life and Work,* ed. David L. Schindler. San Francisco: Ignatius Press, 1991, 7–43.

Hill, Geoffrey. "The Absolute Reasonableness of Robert Southwell," in *The Lords of Limit: Essays on Literature and Ideas.* New York: Oxford University Press, 1984, 19–37.

Kolvenbach, S.J., Peter Hans. "The Rules for Thinking, Judging, Feeling in The Post-Conciliar Church," *Review of Ignatian Spirituality* 105, XXXV (I/2004): 19–27.

Kereszty, Roch. "Bride and 'Mother' in the Super Cantica: An Ecclesiology for Our Time?", *Communio* 20 (1993) :415–36.

Mitchell, Nathan D. "Reforms, Protestant and Catholic," in *The Oxford History of Christian Worship,* eds Geoffrey Wainwright and Karen B. Westerfield Tucker. Oxford: Oxford University Press, 2006, 307–50.

O'Malley, S.J., John W. "Renaissance Humanism and the Religious Culture of the First Jesuits," *Heythrop Journal* XXXI (1990): 471–87.

O'Rourke Boyle, Majorie. "Angels Black and White: Loyola's Spiritual Discernment in Historical Perspective," *Theological Studies* 44 (1983): 241–57.

Padberg, S.J., John. "Ignatius, the Popes and Realistic Reverence." *Studies in the Spirituality of the Jesuits* 25 (May 1993): 1–38.

Quash, Ben. "Ignatian Dramatics," *The Way* 38 (January 1998): 77–86.

Schreiner, Susan E. *The Oxford Encyclopedia of the Reformation,* Vol. II, article on 'faith.' Oxford: Oxford University Press, 1996.

Servais, Jacques. "Balthasar as Interpreter of the Catholic Tradition," in *Love Alone is Credible, Volume 1: Hans Urs von Balthasar as Interpreter of the Catholic Tradition*, ed. David L. Schindler. Grand Rapids, MI: Wm B. Eerdmans, 2008, 191–208.

Veale, S.J., Joseph. "St. Ignatius Asks, 'Are you sure you know who I am?'" *Studies in the Spirituality of the Jesuits* 33/4 (September 2001): 1–38.

Winter, Ernst. F. "Introduction to Discourse on Free Will, by Erasmus and Martin Luther: Milestones of Thought" in *The History of Ideas,* eds F. W. Strothmann and Frederick W. Locke. New York: Frederick Ungar Publishing Co., 1961.

Young, R. V. "The Reformations of the Sixteenth and Seventeenth Centuries," in *Christian Marriage: A Historical Study*, ed. Glenn W. Olsen. New York: Crossroad, 2004.

Ecclesial Documents

Apostolic Letter. *Regimini Militantis Ecclesiae*, September 27, 1540, Paul III.

Apostolic Letter. *Exposcit Debitum*, July 21, 1550, Julius III.

Apostolic Letter, *Pastoralis Romani Pontificis*, January 13, 1631, Urban VIII

Congregation for the Doctrine of the Faith, *Instruction on the Ecclesial Vocation of the Theologian,* 1990.

Congregation for the Doctrine of the Faith. *Dominus Iesus* (On the Unicity and Salvific Universality of Jesus Christ and the Church). August 2000.

Pope Benedict XVI. Encyclical Letter, *Deus Caritas Est* (God is Love), December 25, 2005.

Pope Benedict XVI. Encyclical Letter, *Spe Salvi* (Saved in Hope), November 30, 2007.

Pope Benedict XVI. *Sacramentum Caritatis*, (The Eucharist as the Source and Summit of the Church's Life and Mission), Post-Synodal Exhortation on the Eucharist, February 22, 2007.

Pope Benedict XVI. Letter of His Holiness to the Reverend Father Peter-Hans Kolvenbach, S.J. Superior General of the Society of Jesus, Rome, January 10, 2008.

Pope Benedict XVI. Address of His Holiness to members of the 35th General Congregation of the Society of Jesus, February 21, 2008.

Pope Benedict XVI. Encyclical Letter, *Caritas in Veritate* (Charity in Truth), June 29, 2009.

Pope Benedict XVI. Message for Lent, 2009.

Pope Benedict XVI. *Verbum Domini,* The Post-Synodal Apostolic Exhortation on the Word of God in the Life and Mission of the Church, September 30, 2010.

Pope Benedict XVI. Message of His Holiness Pope Benedict for the World Day of Migrants and Refugees: Migrants and the New Evangelization (2012), September 21, 2011.

Pope Francis. Encyclical, *Lumen Fidei*, Rome, June 29, 2013.

Pope Francis. Apostolic Exhortation, *Evangelii Gaudium*, November 24, 2013.

Pope John Paul II. Apostolic Constitution, *Pastor Bonus*, On the Pastoral Character of the Activity of the Roman Curia, June 28, 1988.

Pope John Paul II. Apostolic Letter Novo Millenio Ineunte (at the close of the great jubilee of the year 2000).

Pope John Paul II. Encyclical *Christifideles Laici,* On the Vocation and Mission of the Lay Faithful in the Church and the World, December 30, 1988.

Pope John Paul II. Encyclical Letter, *Redemptoris Hominis* (The Redeemer of Man), March 4, 1979.

Pope John Paul II. Encyclical *Redemptoris Missio,* December 7, 1990.

Pope John Paul II in the Apostolic Letter, *Tertio Millennio Adveniente,* Rome, November 10, 1994.

Pope John Paul II. Encyclical, *Fides et Ratio* (On the Relationship between Faith and Reason), September 15, 1998.

Pope Paul VI. *Perfectae Caritatis* (On the Adaptation and Renewal of Religious Life), October 28, 1965.

Pope Paul VI. *Humanae Vitae,* Encyclical Letter of His Holiness Pope Paul VI on the Regulation of Birth, 25, July 1968.

Pope Paul VI. Encyclical *Evangelii Nuntiandi* (On the Evangelization of the Modern World), December 8, 1975.

XIII Ordinary General Assembly of the Synod of Bishops. "The New Evangelization for the Transmission of the Christian Faith, Message," Vatican City, October 2012.

INDEX